Latino Children and Families
in the United States

Latino Children and Families in the United States

Current Research and Future Directions

Edited by
Josefina M. Contreras
Kathryn A. Kerns
Angela M. Neal-Barnett

Praeger Series in Applied Psychology
Stevan E. Hobfoll, Series Adviser

Westport, Connecticut
London

Library of Congress Cataloging-in-Publication Data

Kent Psychology Forum (12th : 2000)
  Latino children and families in the United States : current research and future directions /
edited by Josefina M. Contreras, Kathryn A. Kerns, and Angela M. Neal-Barnett.
    p. cm.—(Praeger series in applied psychology)
  Papers originally presented at the 2000 Kent Psychology Forum.
  Includes bibliographical references and index.
  ISBN 0-275-97053-1 (alk. paper)
    1. Hispanic American children—Social conditions—Congresses.   2. Hispanic American
families—Social conditions—Congresses.   3. Hispanic American children—Psychology—
Congresses.   4. Hispanic American parents—Psychology—Congresses.   5. Parenting—
United States—Congresses.   6. Child development—United States—Congresses.
  I. Contreras, Josefina M., 1960–   II. Kerns, Kathryn A., 1961–   III. Neal-Barnett,
Angela M., 1960–   IV. Title.   V. Series.
  E184.S75 K46   2002
  305.23—dc21   2002021570

British Library Cataloguing in Publication Data is available.

Library of Congress Catalog Card Number: 2002021570
ISBN: 0-275-97053-1

First published in 2002

Praeger Publishers, 88 Post Road West, Westport, CT 06881
An imprint of Greenwood Publishing Group, Inc.
www.praeger.com

Printed in the United States of America

The paper used in this book complies with the
Permanent Paper Standard issued by the National
Information Standards Organization (Z39.48-1984).

P

Contents

Illustrations

Acknowledgments

The 2000 Kent Psychology Forum and this book could not have happened without the contributions of many. Community representatives provided knowledge and invaluable insights gained through their direct work with Latino families in the Cleveland, Ohio, area. Their contributions helped broaden our perspective and are reflected in many of the chapters in this book. Community representatives included Megan Ahern, social worker, Hispanic Senior Center; Darilyn Cardona-Mendez, M.S.S.A., L.S.W., MetroHealth Medical Center; Norma Cofresi, Ph.D., clinical psychologist, Cleveland State University; Kim Cuthbertsen, M.S.S.A., L.I.S.W., Center for Families and Children; Maureen Dee, L.I.S.W., C.C.D.C. III, director, Cuyahoga County Chemical Dependency Services, Catholic Charities Services; Teo Feliciano, M.S.S.A., director, Hispanic Senior Center; Nidia Perez, M.S.S.A., L.I.S.W., Hispanic program coordinator, Center for Families and Children; and Mary Rothstein, M.A., Catholic Social Services. In addition, the Applied Psychology Center, sponsor and organizer of the Kent Forum series, provided the resources that made the conference possible. The center's support is gratefully acknowledged. Special thanks to Kathleen Floody: her careful attention to all of the preparations for the conference and the book was invaluable. Finally, I would like to thank my son, Vicente Contreras, for his patience while I was away and for his understanding of my work.

Josefina M. Contreras

Introduction

Josefina M. Contreras

As we begin the 21st century, the Latino population in the United States continues to increase and now represents 12% of the total U.S. population (U.S. Census Bureau, 2000). Just a few years into this century, Latinos will become officially the largest minority group in the United States. Yet, remarkably, little attention has been paid to understanding parenting and child development processes among Latino families. Although research on the cultural and contextual factors influencing parenting processes and child developmental outcomes among Latino families is beginning to emerge, the field is in need of further structure and direction. To this end, I embarked on the planning and organization of the 2000 Kent Psychology Forum, a three-day conference focusing on the conceptual, methodological, and theoretical issues involved in the study of Latino children and families. The forum was part of an annual series of conferences sponsored by the Applied Psychology Center of the Department of Psychology at Kent State University, Kent, Ohio. The goal of the Kent Forum series is to advance the research and understanding of applied areas of psychology. The conference brought together leading scholars working in the field; community representatives engaged in research, clinical, or community work with Latino families; and graduate students to dialogue, share methods and findings, and chart the future direction of the field. This volume is the result of this conference.

The goal of both the conference and this volume was not only to present state-of-the-art research on Latino children and families but also to develop frameworks that can guide and enhance future research in this field. Thus, in addition to discussion of the research and findings presented by each of the

scholars, discussions throughout the conference centered around the development of theoretical, conceptual, and methodological approaches that would
enhance the research and understanding of Latino children and families and
provide directions for the future of the field. These discussions have been in-
corporated into the individual chapters in the book, as well as in the final concluding chapters.

The volume is organized into four sections. In the first section, "Cultural
Context of Latino Families," contributors provide a description of the context
in which Latino children and families are embedded. In Chapter 1, Ana Mari
Cauce and Melanie Domenech-Rodríguez provide an integration of different
literatures to present a rich picture of both the values that can be considered
"Latino" and the social, demographic, and health context of Latino families in
the United States. In Chapter 2, Mark Roosa, Antonio Morgan-Lopez, Willa
Cree, and Michele Specter examine the parenting and socialization beliefs and
practices of different Latino subgroups and provide a framework for identifying the origins of these beliefs and practices. Finally, in Chapter 3, Nancy
Gonzales, George Knight, Antonio Morgan-Lopez, Delia Saenz, and Amalia
Sirolli provide a thorough review and discussion of the literature examining
the relations between acculturation and the adjustment of Latino youth across
different domains of functioning.

In the second section, "Parenting Processes in Latino Families," contributors present innovative research examining the parenting beliefs and practices
of Latino families from different socioeconomic and cultural backgrounds. In
Chapter 4, Margarita Azmitia and Jane Brown used in-depth interviews with
parents of Mexican descent to uncover parents' beliefs and expectations regarding their children's passage through adolescence and the strategies they
use to help their children stay on the "good path of life." Using focus group
methodology, Yvonne Caldera, Jacki Fitzpatrick, and Karen Wampler describe coparenting processes among Mexican-American families and demonstrate the many ways in which Mexican American mothers and fathers work
together and coordinate their parenting efforts. In Chapter 6, Robin Harwood, Amy Miller, Vivian Carlson, and Birgit Leyendecker examine the child-
rearing beliefs and practices of middle-class Puerto Rican (island residents)
and Anglo mothers. They report both within and between group differences
in beliefs and practices, as well as correspondence between the mothers' child-
rearing beliefs and their parenting behaviors. In Chapter 7, the final chapter
of this section, Josefina Contreras, David Narang, Madinah Ikhlas, and Jennifer Teichman propose a conceptual model of the determinants of parenting
among Latina adolescent mothers and provide empirical evidence supporting
aspects of the model.

In the first chapter (Chapter 8) of the third section of the volume, "Research Methods and Interventions with Latino Families," George Knight,
Jenn-Yun Tein, Justin Prost, and Nancy Gonzales highlight the importance of
measurement equivalence in the study of Latino children and families and

provide a perspective on how to evaluate the equivalence of measures and use relevant theory to make sense of the statistical findings. The last two chapters in this section discuss issues related to parenting interventions for Latino families. In Chapter 9, Larry Dumka, Vera Lopez, and Sara Jacobs Carter present a comprehensive review and analysis of parenting interventions that have been adapted for Latino parents and provide extensive recommendations for enhancing the cultural competence of these interventions. In Chapter 10, Luis Zayas and Lisseth Rojas-Flores discuss strategies that combine emic and etic approaches to improve services to Latino families and provide illustrations of culturally sensitive interventions that integrate these two approaches.

"Conclusions and Recommendations for the Future of the Field" is the fourth and last section of the book . First, in Chapter 11, Angel Lugo Steidel, Madinah Ikhlas, Irene Lopez, Reece Rahman, and Jennifer Teichman—clinical psychology graduate students who participated in the conference—present their views on the challenges and rewards of conducting ethnic minority research and provide recommendations for others who are embarking on careers in ethnic minority research. In Chapter 12, the final chapter, Josefina Contreras presents conclusions and recommendations for future research on Latino children and families derived from the presentations and discussions throughout the conference. Specifically, she presents recommendations regarding the content areas that future research needs to address, the characteristics of research programs that are most likely to help advance our understanding of parenting and developmental processes, and the methodological approaches that are likely to be most fruitful.

REFERENCES

U.S. Census Bureau. (2000). *The Hispanic population in the United States: Population characteristics, March 2001.* Washington, D.C.: U.S. Government Printing Office.

Part I

Cultural Context of Latino Families

1

Latino Families:
Myths and Realities

*Ana Mari Cauce and
Melanie Domenech-Rodríguez*

As we leap into the 21st century, we carry forward the legacy of a century that saw this nation struggle with creating a consciousness surrounding issues of race and ethnicity. In this past century, a process that began with an awareness of the differences, similarities, and nuances of being an ethnic minority and an ethnic majority member in this country progressed to the development of programs to address disparities.

The beginning of this new millennium bids us to look toward the future. This future is one in which the U.S. citizenry will literally look different than anything we have heretofore thought of when we think "American." This new look was captured in a compelling fashion by a *Time* magazine cover (December 2, 1993) showing a series of faces of different ethnicities morphed together, resulting in the coffee-with-milk–colored face of the American future.

Fears about this future look are enough to result in some vague millennial racial and ethnic unease, but this unease also comes from the actual events that ended the 1990s and began the 2000s. The 1990s brought us the confirmation hearings for Supreme Court Justice Clarence Thomas in 1991, the Rodney King/Los Angeles police incident and ensuing riots in 1992, Proposition 187, the anti-immigration act of California in 1994, the O.J. Simpson trial in 1997,[1] and the anti-affirmative action initiatives in the states of California and Washington at the close of the decade. And, in 2001, was the most shocking incident of all: the collapse of the World Trade Towers on September 11 at the hands of terrorists from the Middle East, all of whom were brown-skinned. Thus, every few years some major public event has brought to the forefront the question of ethnicity and its powerful impact in shaping public opinion and action.

The events surrounding the turn of the century sometimes featured issues of race in its purest forms. For example, the O.J. Simpson/Rodney King trials brought into the public consciousness the very different orientations that Black and White Americans have toward law enforcement and the legal establishment. But there was also a more subtle and elusive consciousness emerging, a nascent understanding that the next century would be less about Black and White and more about what lay in between, that brownish morphed image of *Time* magazine, a face that most resembles that of the Latino.[2]

It should not be surprising that this face of mixed ethnicity should look Latino. Latinos are a mixed-race people, who have typically referred to their mix as either "mestizo" or "mulatto," referring to the mixing of Spanish with indigenous Native Americans or African slaves, respectively. Much has been made about the challenge to traditional U.S. Census categories, coming from those who now define themselves as biracial or multiracial (Root, 1996), but Latinos have been more quietly defying these same categories for decades. Latinos started being counted in the census in the 1930s, when 1.3 million "Mexicans" were reported. Two decades later the U.S. Census reported the presence of 2.3 million persons with "Spanish surnames," and two decades after that, in 1970, the U.S. Census reported 9.1 million persons of "Spanish origin." It was not until 1990 that "Hispanics" were counted—at 22.4 million (U.S. Census Bureau, 1993)—and the decision was made to separate ethnicity (or national origin) and race, such that Hispanics were asked to answer questions about both ethnicity and race. However, even this multilayered system has not worked well: 40% of Latinos checked the "other race" category in the 1990 Census (U.S. Census Bureau, 1999a). In the 2000 Census, over 42% of Latinos marked the "other race" category and over 6% indicated that they belonged to multiple racial groups (U.S. Census Bureau, 2001d).

Indeed, the term "Hispanic," which is what Latinos are officially referred to by Census trackers and in other official documents, is a label of convenience that has been used to refer to people with family origins in Mexico, Central or South America, the Spanish-speaking Caribbean, and Spain. The term "Latino," which is preferred by many who are called "Hispanics" and was introduced into government nomenclature in the 2000 Census, refers to the same group minus those of exclusively Spanish–European ancestry. This distinction means little in terms of actual numbers, but it makes an important historical and psychological differentiation between those whose origins can be exclusively traced to the country that produced the colonizers of Latin America and those who are descended from the lands that were a product of this colonization (that is, a mixture of the colonizers, the colonized, and select others).

Their shared history in Spanish colonization has everything to do with the racial diversity of Latinos. Unlike English migration to the United States, which was enacted by northern Europeans as part of families, the Spanish came to the Americas not as settlers, but as *conquistadores* (conquerors) male-only groupings. Not surprisingly, these men interbred with the indigenous

women often through rape, but also as part of new interracial family groupings. The fact that these new people of the Americas, a mixture of the old and
new worlds, are lumped together with Spaniards by the U.S. Census is yet one
more indicator of just how misunderstood Latinos are by and in this country,
whose people typically exclude them from the "American" descriptor that
seems to be reserved for only one portion of the Americas.

Another anachronistic feature of Census counting is the exclusion of Puerto
Ricans residing on the island, even though they are U.S. citizens. Latinos will
not officially become the largest ethnic minority group in the United States
until a few years into this new century. If mainland Puerto Ricans were combined with even a conservative estimate of the undocumented, and as such un-
counted, Latinos in the country, we would find that they already are the
largest ethnic minority group in the United States.[3] Moreover, their growth
throughout the 20th century—escalating from both immigration and higher-
than-average birth rates—was unprecedented and unmatched. Between 1995
and 2000 alone, the Latino population was projected to contribute 35% of the
national population growth (U.S. Department of Commerce, 1997). They
will contribute 44% of the nation's population growth between 2000 and
2020, and 62% from 2020 to 2050 (U.S. Department of Commerce, 1997).
Indeed, in every year between now and the end of the century, Latinos are
projected to add more people to the United States than any other single
race/ethnic group including non-Hispanic Whites (U.S. Department of Commerce, 1996a). By mid-century, one in every four "Americans" will be able to
trace their heritage to a Latin American country.

Latinos, like other ethnic/racial groups, are not equally distributed across
the country. In the year 2000, there were 32.8 million Latinos in the United
States (U.S. Census Bureau, 2001b). That same year, almost 77% of all Latinos lived in just seven states: California, Texas, New York, Florida, Illinois,
Arizona, and New Jersey (U.S. Census Bureau, 2001a). And while New Mexico is not included because its population is relatively small, over 42% of residents there are Hispanic (U.S. Census Bureau, 2001a). Before the midway
point of the 21st century, Latinos will be the largest ethnic group in most, and
perhaps all, of these states. It was projected that by 2025 Latinos would be the
largest ethnic group in our most populous state, California, comprising 43%
of the population (U.S. Department of Commerce, 1996b). The 2000 census
shows that this projection is well on its way to becoming fact; 32.4% of California residents were Latino (U.S. Census Bureau, 2001e).

Who are these ethnic people, this *raza*,[4] that U.S. officials have such a hard
time counting and classifying? Thus far, even this brief description clearly
suggests just how much the Latino racial/ethnic group has been a social construction, one "made in the U.S.A." As race/ethnicity is increasingly viewed as
a social construction, not only for Latinos, but for all our American racial/eth-
nic groupings, the family acquires a central role as the primary socializing
agent for those core values that make up this constructed culture and race.

This chapter will focus on the available knowledge regarding Latino families at the very beginning of the 21st century. It will begin with a brief demographic profile, highlighting some of the distinctive features of each ethnic group. This will be followed by a section on Latino family socialization strategies and goals, with an emphasis on values that have been considered a Latino signature. Our goal is to examine the degree to which these values represent myths about Latinos or actual features of their family life. We conclude by suggesting how immigration and acculturation may affect these values and by providing some directions for future research on Latinos and their families.

LATINOS AND THEIR FAMILIES: WHO ARE THEY?

Latinos in the United States are typically treated as if they are one large, relatively homogeneous group. However, the typical Latino remains as elusive as the typical American. Latinos have come into the United States from various countries, each with their unique historical and cultural traditions. Moreover, even when they are from the same country, different waves of immigration have pulled from different economic or regional sectors resulting in different demographic and adaptive profiles.

Mexican Americans

Mexican Americans, or Chicanos, are by far the largest Latino group, accounting for about 66% of the American Latino population (U.S. Census Bureau, 2001b). A substantial portion of this group did not actually immigrate to the United States. Prior to 1848, Mexico included much of what is now the U.S. Southwest. Thus, there is truth in the cliché that Mexicans did not immigrate to the United States, rather California and Texas migrated to them. However, while the U.S. takeover of this territory following the Guadalupe Hidalgo treaty turned Mexicans living in this region into U.S. citizens, it also gradually displaced them from their lands and made them part of a colonial labor force (Barrera, 1979).

These laborers were the original Mexican Americans, but at present, about a third of Mexican Americans in this country arrived as a result of actual immigration. In a somewhat ironic twist, the new wave of immigration from Mexico, primarily into the U.S. Southwest, is referred to as the *Reconquista* (reconquest). Between 1960 and 1990, the numbers of U.S. residents that were born in Mexico significantly increased: from 575,902 in 1960 to almost 4.3 million in 1990 (Gibson & Lennon, 1999). Mexico has been the number one source of legal immigrants to the United States, and the proportion has been steadily climbing. In 1998 almost 20% of all immigrants came from Mexico (Immigration and Naturalization Service, 1998). Roughly 95% of those immigrating to the United States were immediate relatives of U.S. citizens or were sponsored by a family member (Immigration and Naturalization Service, 1998).

Puerto Ricans

Puerto Ricans comprise 9% and almost 3 million of the Latinos in the United States (U.S. Census Bureau, 2001b), and there are an additional 3.8 million Puerto Ricans at home on the island (U.S. Census Bureau, 2001a). Puerto Ricans are the poorest of the Latino groups, with almost 26% living in poverty in 1996 (U.S. Census Bureau, 2001b).

Puerto Rico became a territory of the United States following a successful invasion by U.S. soldiers into Puerto Rico during the Spanish-American War of 1898. The Paris Treaty signed in 1899 ceded to the United States the islands of Puerto Rico and Cuba. While Cuba later became an independent nation, Puerto Rico continues to be a U.S. territory. Puerto Ricans were given U.S. citizenship in 1917. However, it was not until 1945 that a Puerto Rican native filled the governors' seat. In 1948 the people of Puerto Rico cast the first electoral vote to elect a governor. Prior to this, governors were appointed to the island by the president of the United States. In 1952, Puerto Rico became a commonwealth.

Puerto Ricans are unique in that they are all U.S. citizens, whether they were born on the island or on the mainland United States. As such, Puerto Ricans have had more freedom to travel between their home country and the U.S. mainland. Nonetheless, there is a great deal of diversity in how connected Puerto Ricans are to the island. For example, some refer to themselves as "Nuyoricans," reflecting an identity that simultaneously fuses the island culture with that of the mainland and highlights the marginal status of second- and third-generation Puerto Ricans living on the mainland who may not speak Spanish or do so very poorly (Maldonado-Denis, 1980; Seda Bonilla, 1974).

Cubans

Cubans comprise 4% of the Latino-origin population in the United States (U.S. Census Bureau, 2001b). The over 1.3 million Cuban Americans in the United States are older, more educated, and more economically advantaged than any of the other Latino subgroups owing to different migration reasons and patterns.

Bernal and Shapiro (1996) identify four phases of migration among Cuban Americans: the first is related to Fidel Castro's revolution and lasts from 1959 to 1965; the second spans from 1965 to 1973 and resulted in the "Freedom Flights"; the third wave occurred in 1980 and the refugees are known as *Marielitos*; and the last phase, between 1991 and 1994, resulted from economic hardship following the disintegration of the Soviet Union, which had sustained the Cuban economy. Each wave brought to the United States a different portion of the Cuban population. The initial phase brought White, educated, middle- to upper-class professionals. The second phase brought middle- to lower-middle-class professionals. The third phase was comprised of more Afro-Cuban immigrants that were either working class or unemployed. The fourth phase brought a myriad of people suffering from the economic hardship that continues to envelop the vast majority of the Cuban populace following the withdrawal of economic and political support of the Soviet Union. Thus, even within this relatively small group, there is greater diversity than is typically acknowledged.

Although Mexican Americans, Puerto Ricans, and Cubans represent the largest groups of Latinos from specific countries, Latino groups from other countries are rapidly growing and together represent close to 30% of all Latinos in the United States. This is a very heterogeneous group that includes Central American refugees from El Salvador and Nicaragua; white-collar and professional workers from Argentina, Chile, and Uruguay; and those leaving severely harsh economic conditions in countries such as the Dominican Republic. Some of these immigrants most closely resemble the profile of first-wave Cuban immigrants; others look more like the more economically disadvantaged recent immigrants from Puerto Rico (Ginorio, Guttierrez, Cauce, & Acosta, 1995; Portes & Truelove, 1987).

CHANGE AND CHALLENGE FOR LATINO FAMILIES

As our examination of Latino subgroups illustrates, the large heterogeneity within and between each Latino group belies the uniformity with which they are typically treated, both in the popular press and by academic researchers. But, there are some characteristics that give some meaning to this classification of convenience. Their shared history of Spanish colonization and shared regional origin in Latin America has resulted in a common language and gives the Catholic Church a central role in shaping values (Moore & Pachon, 1985; Tienda & Ortiz, 1986). Moreover, most share a history of relatively recent immigration, and within the United States they are subject to the similar stereotypes and discrimination, providing for some sense of common identity, if only for political reasons.

As we examine the changes and challenges facing Latinos and describe their familial values, we will refer to them as a group, while pointing out subgroup differences when they are large and/or there is research that addresses them. However, it is important to keep in mind that overall figures or general descriptions typically best fit Mexican Americans, the largest Latino group.

Family Structure and Composition

Over the last several decades, some of the most dramatic changes in family structure and composition have been for Latinas. Compared to their White counterparts, they are less likely to be married, more likely to be heads of households, and more likely to have younger children at younger ages, outside of marriage.

The U.S. Department of Commerce (1996a) reports that Latino families have 3.71 members on average compared to 2.97 for White and 3.31 for Black families. Puerto Rican women tend to have their first child before marriage, while Mexican Americans and Cuban Americans tend to do so within marriage. Cuban American women have the lowest fertility rates and are older at the time of their first marriage. These fertility figures reflect trends in their countries of origin (Darabi, Dryfoos, & Schwartz, 1986; Darabi & Ortiz, 1987). In UNICEF's *The State of the World's Children* (2000), the fertility rate for Cuban women in 1998 was 1.6, compared to 2.7 for Mexican women.

Compared to White families, Latino families are more apt to be headed by a single parent. Among non-Hispanic Whites, 82.2% of all families were headed by a married couple, compared to 68% for Latinos (U.S. Census Bureau, 2000). Female-headed households accounted for 13% of White families and almost 28% of Latino families (U.S. Census Bureau, 2000).

But, there is considerable variation among Latino subgroups, with female-headed households almost twice as common among Puerto Ricans, as compared to Mexicans or Cubans (U.S. Census Bureau, 1993). This large percentage of single-parent families translates into an even larger percentage of children growing up in such families, since Latinos tend to have relatively large families.

Education, Employment, and Income

The typical Latino child lives with a parent or parents who are less educated and poorer than her White counterpart. Forty-three percent of Latinos have not completed high school, compared to 11.6% of non-Hispanic Whites (U.S. Census Bureau, 2001b). Almost two thirds of Puerto Ricans in the United States have not completed a high school education. Almost 50% of Mexicans and slightly over 25% of Cubans did not complete a high school education (U.S. Census Bureau, 2001b). However, it is worth noting that while these education completion numbers are low, even when compared to those of African Americans, they have been climbing steadily since the 1970s (U.S. Census Bureau, 1993, 2001b).

Ethnic disparities are even greater when education is examined in terms of college graduation. Among Whites, 28.1% of those over 25 graduated from college, compared to 10.6% of Latinos (ranging between roughly 7% for Mexican Americans to 23% for Cuban Americans) (U.S. Census Bureau, 2001b). Thus, it is not surprising that the median income level of Latino households ($28,330 in 1998) was considerably lower than that of non-Hispanic Whites ($42,439; U.S. Census Bureau, 1999d). In a similar vein, poverty is especially great for Latino families: about 23% of Latino families were living in poverty in 1999, almost three times that of non-Latino Whites (U.S. Census Bureau, 2001b). The numbers are similarly dismal for children: 30.3% of Latinos under the age of 18 are living in poverty, well over three times the rate of non-Hispanic Whites (U.S. Census Bureau, 2001a). The poverty rates were highest among Puerto Rican families (almost 26% of families), closely followed by Mexican Americans (24.1%) and lowest among Central and South Americans (16.7%) (U.S. Census Bureau, 2001b). Poverty rates are particularly high for Latino families headed by females. Here the poverty rate was 47.3% compared with 20.7% for non-Hispanic White female-headed households (U.S. Census Bureau, 1999c).

The wage and poverty disparities between Latino families and their white counterparts reflect the different position of Latinos in the labor force. For example, in 2000 over 28% of Latino men worked as operators, transportation workers, or handlers, compared with about 17% of non-Hispanic males (U.S. Census Bureau, 2001c). Conversely, only 11% of Latino men held managerial or professional positions compared to 32% for non-Hispanic White males (U.S. Census Bureau, 2001c). In a similar vein, Latinas were twice as likely as non-Latinas to be employed as machine operators, transportation workers, and handlers, and more apt to be in sales and service occupations (64%) than their non-Latina counterparts (57%; U.S. Census Bureau, 2001c).

Thus, whether one examines poverty rates, family income, or occupational status, indicators suggest that Latinos have fewer economic resources available to support their child-rearing efforts. All of these indicators suggest that Latinos occupy an especially vulnerable ecological niche in our society. But, such static and simple demographics probably underestimate their vulnerability. For example, differences in income distribution are magnified when one examines accumulated assets instead of simple yearly earnings. An examination of the assets of householders in 1993 indicated that households with White householders had a median net worth of $45,740, compared to $4,656 for those with Latino householders—a tenfold difference, and a figure not statistically different from that of African Americans (Eller & Wallace, 1995). Perhaps more shocking is a recent report from the Federal Reserve that shows that during the economic expansion between 1995 and 1998 Latinos were the only ethnic group to lose ground, falling by 24%, while the incomes of African Americans, Asian Americans, and Whites were improving (Kennickell, Star-McCluer, & Surette, 2000).

Health Care and Health Risks

The portrait of Latinos at risk continues when one examines health factors. In comparison to other American children, Latino children, with the exception of Cubans, are less likely to have received prenatal care (Carter-Pokras & Zambrana, 2001). Among Mexican American farmworking women, the miscarriage and stillbirth rates range from 24% to 31%, and their children are also less likely to receive important vaccines such as flu and pneumonia (Carter-Pokras & Zambrana, 2001). Other serious problems faced by Latino infants include higher rates of infectious disease, asthma, TB, and ear infection and a higher rate of mortality due to AIDS (Dusenbury, Diaz, Epstein, Botvin, & Caton, 1994; Marks, Garcia, & Solis, 1990; Mendoza, 1994). This pattern of lesser health care and greater health risk continues for Latinos throughout the preschool and school years. Compared to their White counterparts, they were much less apt to receive routine health care or to be covered by health insurance (Carter-Pokras & Zambrana, 2001; Federal Interagency Forum on Child and Family Statistics, 2001; Treviño & Moss, 1984).

By the time they reach puberty, the differential pattern of health risks is further magnified and aggravated by issues of poverty, low educational levels, and limited access to health information and services (Mendoza, 1994). Latino youth are at greater risk for substance use and for sexually related risks, such as STDs, HIV/AIDS, and teenage and unwanted pregnancy (U.S. Department of Health and Human Services [USDHHS], 1997; Marks, García, & Solis, 1990). These health risks endanger not only their own lives but also those of their future children, creating a cycle of risk. In addition, young Latino males, whether Mexican American, Puerto Rican, or Cuban American, were more likely to die young as a result of homicide than White adolescents (Anderson, 2001; Council on Scientific Affairs, 1991).

Latino youth also appear to be at greater risk for mental health–related problems. In a study of several thousand 10–17 year olds from diverse ethnic backgrounds, including African Americans, Asian Americans, Native Americans, and Whites, only Mexican Americans were found to have elevated rates of major depression, even when socioeconomic status was controlled (Joiner, Dineen Wagner, Berenson, & Marquina, 1998). Ironically, surveys that have contrasted U.S.–born Latinos with immigrants suggest that those that are U.S.–born tend to have the highest mental health risks (USDHHS, 2001; Vega & Amaro, 1994).

With these health concerns, it is striking that 35.3% of the Latino population are uninsured, compared to 11.9% of non-Hispanic Whites (U.S. Census Bureau, 1999b). Among the poor, 44% of Latinos are uninsured, representing the highest rates reported among the poor (U.S. Census Bureau, 1999b).

In sum, the demographic portrait that emerges of Latinos in the United States is less than a pretty one. As we start the new century, Latino families face greater adversity and challenge than their White counterparts. So do their children. Latino children are much more apt to be born into a poor or low-income, single-parent household and less likely to have received prenatal care and ongoing, regular medical care after they are born. Not surprisingly, they are also less likely to survive into adulthood, owing to both their poorer health care and greater exposure to violence, including homicide. These facts set the stage upon which Latino family values play out, serving as a source of support and strength within an ecological niche characterized by much vulnerability and risk.

LATINO SOCIALIZATION STRATEGIES AND VALUES

The goal of socialization within the family is to develop individuals who will be capable of functioning as competent adult members of a social group. It is through the socialization process that children acquire the attitudes, beliefs, roles, and competencies that are a prerequisite to successful participation in their society.

For Latinos, as is the case for Whites, the family has been considered the major socialization agent (García Coll, Meyer, & Brillion, 1995). The processes by which socialization takes place include observational learning, conditioning, and internalization, which are considered universal. However, it has been posited that socialization goals for American children of color, including Latinos, may be different from those of their White counterparts for two main reasons: (a) cultural norms and values are different than those of majority White Americans who share a common Western European heritage, and (b) the different ecological niches they grow up in, which includes their different socioeconomic status, family structures, and risk environments, as just discussed. These two sources of difference are not mutually exclusive. In fact, they may interact with each other in important ways. For example, culture, in large part, develops as an adaptation to a specific ecological niche (García Coll et al., 1996).

A growing number of social scientists have noted that the differences between the socialization goals of ethnic minority parents and those of majority White parents are rooted in their distinct cultural norms. Parents, in large part, socialize their children to develop those instrumental competencies that are most valued within their culture (García Coll, 1990; Ogbu, 1994, 1995). Values that have been considered distinctly Latino include *familismo, personalismo, marianismo,* and *machismo.* While various observations and case studies find support for these values as organizing frameworks within diverse Latino communities, it is less clear how much empirical evidence there is to support their existence or distinctiveness.

Personalismo and Familismo

Personalismo and *familismo* are related values that have been defined in a variety of ways. *Personalismo* refers to the importance that Latinos place on personal goodness and getting along with others, values considered more important than individual ability and material success. *Familismo* refers more specifically to the importance of family closeness and getting along with and contributing to the well-being of the family, often viewed as an extended one. Together, these values anchor a Latino culture that has been described as one that values a collective rather than an individualistic orientation, with an emphasis placed on family solidarity, obligation, and parental authority (Ramírez, 1990).

When one takes into account that many of these descriptions were based on observation, often coming out of clinical work, the amount of empirical support that has backed up these claims is quite impressive. Baca Zinn (1994) writes about the concept of "familism" specifically for Mexican origin families. She outlines four distinct components of familism: demographic, normative, structural, and behavioral. According to her, demographic familism refers to demographic characteristics such as family size. Normative familism looks at the value people place on family unity and solidarity. Structural familism addresses multigenerational households or extended family systems. Finally, behavioral familism refers to the degree to which families and kin networks interact. A look at Latino family structural characteristics already provided evidence for demographic families: Latino families tend to be larger than those of non-Hispanic Whites (U.S Census Bureau, 2001b). We will next look at the evidence for the other three types of familism.

Support for normative familism is provided by a study described in more detail by Zayas and Rojas-Flores (Chapter 10, this volume). Research using a focus group methodology with Puerto Rican mothers found that they put a much higher premium on family closeness and respect for authority compared to independence and assertiveness (Gonzales Ramos, Zayas, & Cohen, 1998). These findings receive further corroboration in a study of Mexican immigrant parents who found that they placed greater value on conformity to authority than on autonomy, opposite the pattern found for White Americans (Okagaki and Sternberg, 1993). Whether definitions of familism focus on cultural values or specific behaviors, they always have family closeness at the center, with "family" defined to include the nuclear and extended family (Bernal & Shapiro, 1996; Falicov, 1996; Keefe, 1984; Zea, García, Belgrave & Quezada, 1997).

Support for structural familism lies in the fact that Mexican Americans have more tightly integrated local extended families than their White counterparts (Keefe, 1984). Keefe also found that Mexican Americans were less geographically mobile than Whites even when socioeconomic status is controlled. While there is no evidence that Mexican Americans value kin more than White Americans, they do place greater importance on regular face-to-face contact, physical touch, and sharing of "minor joys and sorrows" with nuclear as well as extended family members (Keefe, 1984). A study by Burr and Mutchler (1999) underscores this finding. The authors state that older Latinos and African Americans are more likely than Whites to report that each generation should provide "co-residence assistance" when needed.

There is also support for behavioral familism, in that Latinos place a great deal of value on living in proximity to family, including kin (Farr and Wilson-Figueroa, 1997; Hurtado, 1995; Keefe & Padilla, 1987). Compared to a matched sample of Anglos in the Los Angeles area, Mexican immigrants were more likely to have kin in town and to be related to people in more households. In addition, they had more households that they visited weekly than did

Anglos. Reinforcing the power of *compadrazgo*,[5] 88% reported having compadres[6] with 80% of them living in town. However, in some recognition of change, only about half said their compadres were really like relatives, with 46% saying they were more like friends (Keefe, 1984).

In Puerto Rico, where *compadrazgo* is also practiced, compadres report that they were selected to help maintain family values, norms, and traditions. Most also say they would be willing to provide a home for the child if the parents died. Over 85% believed that their role included providing food, clothing, money, and emotional support to the child if the parents could not. Over 95% visited their child and gave them presents, at least occasionally (Hurtado, 1995).

Nonetheless, the distinction between family and friends is not trivial. In recognition of the unique role of family, Mexican immigrants in this study reported that when they were having an emotional problem they were more likely than Anglos to speak with a relative. In contrast, Anglos were more likely to speak with a friend. In general, for Anglos, the distinction between family and friends was not there, proximity seemed to be the main determinant of which they would use for help. For Latinos, however, the very clear preference was for familial support; friends were seldom used for support. As one study participant noted, "Mexicans are a proud people, we stay in a little circle within the family."

Marianismo and Machismo

Marianismo, based on the Catholic ideal of the Virgin Mary, emphasizes the woman's role as mother and celebrates the mother's self-sacrifice and suffering for her children (Ramírez, 1990; Ginorio et al., 1995). *Machismo*, on the other hand, stresses the man's role not as father but as head of household. Taken together and exaggerated to the point of caricature, these Latino values have been used to paint a portrait of the "ideal" Latino family type as that of the self-sacrificing mother and the dominant, tyrannical man. Taken one step further, the Latino family has been viewed as one in which patriarchy and pathology run rampant (Baca Zinn, 1979).

The construct of *machismo* has been viewed in various ways, depending on both the time and the perspective of the observer. From a feminist perspective, *machismo* has been defined as "exaggerated masculinity, physical prowess, and male chauvinism" (Baca Zinn, 1994, p. 74). But others have noted that historically *machismo* "represented an appropriate mechanism to insure the continuation of Mexican family pride and respect" (Sánchez, 1999, p. 129). The fact that *machismo* led to the oppression of women is viewed as simply a necessary by-product in service of the larger goal of maintaining family stability and tradition (Alvirez & Bean, 1976; Mirande, 1977). To what degree is there truth in these stereotypes? And, to what degree are Latino families rigidly gendered?

Early ethnographic work, mainly conducted in rural Mexico in the 1960s (Mummert, 1993) suggests that gender relations were quite patriarchal. In this rural environment, there was a clear-cut division of labor, with men and women having different spheres for activities. Men, with their eldest sons, economically supported the family, and women cared for the home and children and largely stayed within the domestic sphere. Men had a great deal of autonomy, but women's movements were curtailed and restricted. Early marriage was the norm, and a woman often resided in the home of her husband's parents and was accountable to her mother-in-law (resembling the classic patriarchy in some Asian and Muslim societies). And, as *marianismo* suggests, the mother–child bond was often seen as stronger than the husband–wife bond.

Many of the most salient and important contributions to our understanding of Latino families come from feminist reinterpretations and critiques in the last decade. These feminist examinations of *machismo* and its functions reinterpret earlier observations. They note that a woman's role within the family has traditionally been a strong one and they also note the positive aspects of *machismo*, men acting as providers, protectors, and representatives of their families to the outside world (Bach-y-Rita, 1982; Panitz, McConchie, Sauber, & Fonseca, 1983; Ramírez, 1967).

Feminist interpretations also note that to the degree that rigid gender roles may have characterized rural Mexico in the past, urbanization, migration, and industrialization have transformed these more patriarchal arrangements in Mexico. In fact, as early as 1982 there was even a serious female presidential candidate in Mexico.

Often what has propelled women into these roles has been their increasing participation in the workforce. While this has not always decreased women's domestic responsibilities, it has expanded their spatial mobility. For example, in present-day Mexico there are all-female *cervezerías* (beer halls) and working in a factory has become almost a rite of passage for young Mexican women who, unlike previous generations, do not turn all of their earnings over to families. Even after marriage, women's work outside the home translates into greater decision-making power within the home (Arias and Mummert, 1987).

In the United States, Latinas, who typically work outside the home, likewise report less rigid gender roles than may have traditionally been the case. Baca Zinn's (1982) ethnographic work suggests that while employed Latinas often espoused the ideology of patriarchy and *machismo*, their employment challenged their husband's dominance. Indeed, while *machismo* and *marianismo*, like *familismo* and *personalismo*, are values that inform behavior, they are not behavior patterns themselves. There is a difference between legacies and realities.

Whether lower-status Mexican American farmworking women, or high-achieving, highly educated Latinas, gender roles in Latino families are becoming less rigid and more egalitarian. For example, many married farmworker women work in the fields with their husbands. In a study of working-class Chicano families in Texas (Williams, 1988), women continued to play a key role in the transmission of values and culture, but while "traditional" values, including the importance of religion and church attendance, were often espoused, they played a less central role in the workplace or school and seemed less clear-cut guides to decision making. A survey of Latino heads of households in California found that Latinos and Latinas agreed, at roughly similar rates, that men should do housework, that it is all right for the wife to earn more than the husband, that women have the right to use birth control, and that women have the right to decide if they want an abortion (Hurtado, Hayes-Bautista, Burciaga Valdez, & Hernández, 1992).

Nonetheless, these moves toward more egalitarian gender roles within the family are not coming without a struggle (Baca Zinn, 1994). For example, Latinas have had a difficult time with culturally prescribed manners to express emotions. Rivera-Arzola and Ramos-Grenier (1997) examined the incidence of *ataques de nervios*[7] (literally meaning "nerve attacks") in Puerto Rican women from a feminist perspective. They concluded: "Puerto Rican society discourages assertive expressions of emotion among women" (Rivera-Arzola & Ramos-Grenier, 1997, p. 135). It is through the physical manifestation of the emotions that arise during stressful times—and the authors would argue that stress and anger are intimately associated—that Puerto Rican women can express their inability to manage the stress, and receive social support to overcome a particular situation.

Latinas have also struggled to gain access to higher education. In qualitative studies of high-achieving Latinas, most reported that their mothers had been equally or more influential than their fathers in fostering their education (Gandara, 1982; Hernández, Vargas-Lew, & Martínez, 1994). Latino parents are more reluctant to allow daughters to attend a university, and Latino boys get more parental support for higher education than do girls (Cohen, Chacón, Camarena, González, & Stover, 1983; López, 1995).

When investigating the behaviors of young adults, the substance use literature has particularly poignant examples of gender differences. When studies have examined substance use by both ethnicity and gender, it has been found that Mexican American males consume more than White males, who in turn consume more than White females. All surpass Mexican American females in their use (Chavez & Swaim, 1992; Vega, Alderete, Kolody, & Aguilar-Gaxiola, 1998). While the meanings of these differences have not been well investigated, higher use among Mexican American males may reflect the *machismo* role that often entails greater risk taking and bravado. Conversely, Mexican American women are expected to stay closer to home and family values, which may serve to discourage substance use. Further support for the fact that as adolescents Latinas are expected to stay close to home and support the family, girls in the 9th and 10th grade have been found to serve as language brokers[8] for their parents more often than their male counterparts (Buriel, Perez, DeMent, Chavez, & Moran, 1998).

In sum, evidence supporting the degree to which the values of *marianismo* and *machismo* inform gender roles within Latino families is mixed. Whether or not the rigid distinctions implied by these roles ever existed is unclear, but even if they did at some point, they do not at present. Latinas are attaining increasingly egalitarian relationships within the families, but this change in role is not accompanied by a change in ideology. Latinas show some reluctance to let go of the notion that males should have the prominent role as breadwinners and as family representatives to the outside world. Gender differences in various spheres, including family support for higher education and adolescent substance use also remain. These are not unlike those found among European American Whites, but they are more exaggerated.

CONCLUSIONS AND FUTURE DIRECTIONS

In this chapter we began by providing a demographic portrait of Latinos in the United States. This portrait was one of diversity. Yet, in painting a composite group portrait, generalizations were necessary. When a specific Latino subgroup markedly diverged from the overall profile, we pointed it out to avoid oversimplifications, but that was inevitable as well. Thus, before concluding, it is important to highlight that Latino families encompass a great deal of structural, socioeconomic, regional, and cultural diversity. Although they have most often been written about and studied in contrast to European American White families, there is as much diversity within each Latino group as there is between Latino groups or between Latinos and White Americans. In other words, while most Latinos are poorer than White Americans, some are quite wealthy. Likewise, while many Latinos drop out of school in high school, others go on for doctoral degrees. And there are many Latinos growing up in two-parent families in which both parents work. Still, the group-level disparities between Latino and White families and children are so large that it is important to keep them in mind in any discussion of the different (from White) socialization and childrearing strategies used by Latino parents. Precisely because these differences are often large and in many areas, we should be very careful about attributing differences between Latinos and Whites to ethnicity or culture (Cauce, Coronado, & Watson, 1998).

In speaking about what is uniquely Latino about Latino families, we have stressed the importance of two sets of values: *familismo* and *personalismo* and *marianismo* and *machismo*. The anthropologist John Ogbu (1995) has referred to these types of values and their corresponding socialization practices and behaviors as primary cultural differences. We would expect these differences to be more marked the closer one's cultural proximity to the country of origin. First-generation Latinos, in general, would be expected to demonstrate behaviors more concordant with Latino values than second-generation Latinos.

Differences based on primary cultural values and norms are much more striking and obvious. The cultural quandary of a first-generation Salvadoran woman who has just entered the United States and speaks only Spanish is more vivid than that of the English-speaking second-generation Chicano mother wearing a San Antonio Spurs T-shirt. However, Ogbu's (1985, 1994, 1995) studies of African Americans in school have described in compelling fashion how it is secondary cultural norms, which are developed in the United States, that often have the most persistent and extensive negative effects. This is, in part, because while voluntary minorities are motivated to break down cultural barriers, the motivation for involuntary minorities is to maintain these boundaries. Similar work has not been conducted with Latinos, but the fact that delinquency and other externalizing behaviors are higher in later generations would suggest that some similar processes might hold for Latino families. (A more complete review of the acculturation process is provided by Gonzales, Knight, Morgan-Lopez, Saenz, & Sirolli in Chapter 3 of this volume).

The tensions between the positive roles Ogbu (1994, 1995) tends to ascribe to primary cultural values and his more negative portrayals of secondary cultural values is reminiscent of the two dominant theories of migration and settlement: one emphasizing social continuity and its positive features, the other social breakdown and its negative features. As a portrayal of the realities of people of color coming to this country (whether as voluntary or involuntary minorities), neither really hits the mark. Immigrants draw on the traditional social norms and frameworks they bring from their homelands, but in keeping with ecological models, these are modified by their new social environments. They bring their cultural and ideological baggage to their new setting, but as they unpack it, it gets rearranged. For example, women may take on new activities such as driving and working for wages, which may lead to new decision-making roles within the family. Similarly, youths may take on new roles as cultural brokers or students, which may lead to new careers and possibilities.

Family formation and family roles are key to this settlement and resettlement, to the unpacking and rearrangement. It is the family that creates a tie with the new community. For example, immigrant children may become tied to their peers and new surroundings and do not want to return to their country of origin, even if the original move was viewed as temporary. The work of Szapocznik and Kurtines (1980, 1993) has illustrated how the different speeds at which children, mothers, and fathers acculturate can result in tension and conflict. But, as Gonzales et al. (Chapter 3, this volume) note, the work in this area is still in the early stages.

We know even less about how acculturation and/or immigration change core Latino values, such as *familismo* or *machismo*. Holding onto core values may help families maintain continuity and tradition in a new setting, yet when held on to too tightly, they can interfere with optimal adjustment. Indeed, while the risks associated with being an immigrant are stressed, immigration also represents opportunities for growth and positive change.

Portes and Rumbaut (1995) have drawn on the common entomology of travel and travail to suggest how both risk and resilience characterize the immigration process. For example, one source of challenge and opportunity for minority children who are immigrants, or whose parents are immigrants, is that they may come to serve as "cultural brokers" (Buriel et al., 1998). If they can deal with it effectively, it may serve as a source of pride and provide them with a valued role within their family. However, it may also represent a source of extreme stress when age-inappropriate demands are placed on a young child. For example, a preschool child may find himself helping to negotiate a loan for his family.

As we stand poised on the cusp of a new era, we would do well to create research agendas that allow us to examine both the challenges and opportunities facing Latino families. There is no simple answer to questions such as: Is acculturation good for Latinos? or Does *familismo* represent a source of strength for Latino families? One can as readily answer yes or no, depending on the perspective one takes, the situation involved, and the rest of the socioecological picture. It is time to move beyond this stage of simplicity.

In addition to examining the traditional questions about Latinos and their families in a more complex manner, there are some areas of investigation that remain almost unexplored. Below we list three that we find especially intriguing.

1. How does phenotypic variation in skin color affect within-family relationships or intergroup relationships? Because of the mixed race origin of Latinos, they vary widely in skin color, both within and between families, yet extremely little work has addressed the implications of this whether in terms of Latino self-identity or their interpersonal relationships. A cursory look at political figures, television personalities, and other prominent personalities in Latin American countries invariably yields a light-skinned majority.

2. How does language(s) proficiency, which varies with acculturation, affect child–parent relationships? With some immigrant children losing their Spanish more quickly than their parents and becoming proficient in English, language can become a barrier to parent–child communication. We know little about how this phenomenon above what we know about acculturation more generally.

3. How and when do children maintain their Latino identification in the face of increased intermarriage with White Americans? Projections that suggest that Latinos will be the largest minority group in the near future are based on the premise that Latinos will maintain their identification as such, even while other data suggests that by the second generation out-marriage rates, mostly to White Americans, are extremely high. Under what conditions does this assumption hold, and are there any conditions in which it does not?

These questions represent but a few examples of areas in which we know very little. They illustrate how the study of Latinos can help us learn more about this group of people, a worthy endeavor in its own right. They also illustrate how the study of Latinos can help us understand more fundamental questions about culture and human development. For example, an understanding of how phenotype affects within- and between-group relationships, as well as personal identity, has implications for members of all ethnic groups; and an understanding of how language affects parent–child relationships could inform our work with any immigrant. An understanding of these issues can also help us understand interpersonal relationships more generally. The paradoxical nature of studying seemingly unique aspects of families and children in context is that it is precisely this type of study that inevitably leads to more generalizable truths about human nature.

NOTES

1. The murders actually occurred in 1994.

2. The terms "Latino" or "Latinos" will be used to refer to people of Latin American origin or descent, including Mexican Americans, Puerto Ricans, Cubans, and Central and South Americans. The terms "Latina" or "Latinas" is used when referring specifically to women of Latin American origin or descent. For other ethnic groups the terms "White" or "Anglo," "African American," and "Asian American" will be used preferentially. Other terms, such as "Hispanic," "European American," and "black," are also used, specifically when citing other authors' work that uses those labels.

3. There were over 3.8 million Puerto Ricans living on the island in 1990 (U.S. Census Bureau, 2001b).

4. *Raza* is the Spanish word for race; however, it suggests more a "people" than a race in the English sense.

5. *Compadrazgo* refers to the relationship between compadres. The two people involved in a compadre relationship are a godparent or baptismal parent and the parent of the child who was baptized.

6. Compadres have been categorized under the rubric of fictive kin by some authors (e.g., Keefe, 1984).

7. *Ataque de nervios* is a culture-bound syndrome according to the fourth edition of the *Diagnostic and Statistical Manual of Mental Disorders* (American Psychiatric Association, 1994). An *ataque* usually follows a stressful family event. Common symptoms include uncontrollable shouting, verbal or physical aggression, crying spells, and trembling, among others.

8. Language brokers are the children that interpret for their immigrant parents.

REFERENCES

Alvirez, D., & Bean, F. D. (1976). The Mexican American family. In C. H. Mindel & R. W. Haberstein (Eds.), *Ethnic families in America* (pp. 72–103). New York: Elsevier.

American Psychiatric Association. (1994). *Diagnostic and Statistical Manual of Mental Disorders* (4th ed.). Washington, D.C.: Author.

Anderson, R. N. (2001). Deaths: Leading causes for 1999. *National Vital Statistics Reports, 49*, 11. Hyattsville, Maryland: National Center for Health Statistics.

Arias, P., & Mummert, G. (1987). *Familia, mercados de trabajo y migración en el centro-occidente de México* [Family, labor markets, and migration in central-western Mexico]. *Nueva Antropología, 9*, 105–127.

Baca Zinn, M. (1979). Chicano family research: Conceptual distortions and alternative directions. *Journal of Ethnic Studies, 7,* 59–71.

Baca Zinn, M. (1982). Qualitative methods in family research: A look inside Chicano families. *California Sociologist,* Summer, 58–79.

Baca Zinn, M. (1994). Adaptation and continuity in Mexican-origin families. In R. L. Taylor (Ed.). *Minority families in the United States: A multicultural perspective* (pp. 64–94). Englewood Cliffs, NJ: Prentice Hall.

Bach-y-Rita, G. (1982). The Mexican American: Religious and cultural influences. In R. M. Becerra, M. Karno, & J. I. Escobar (Eds.), *Mental health and Hispanic Americans: Clinical perspectives* (pp. 29–40). New York: Grune & Stratton.

Barrera, M. (1979). *Race and class in the southwest.* Notre Dame, IN: University of Notre Dame Press.

Bernal, G., & Shapiro, E. (1996). Cuban families. In M. McGoldrick, J. Giordano, and J. K. Pearce (Eds.), *Ethnicity and family therapy* (2nd ed., pp. 155–168). New York: Guilford.

Buriel, R., Perez, W., DeMent, T. L., Chavez, D. V., & Moran, V. R. (1998). The relationship of language brokering to academic performance, biculturalism, and self-efficacy among Latino adolescents. *Hispanic Journal of Behavioral Sciences, 20,* 283–297.

Burr, J. A., & Mutchler, J. E. (1999). Race and ethnic variation in norms of filial responsibility among older persons. *Journal of Marriage and the Family, 61,* 674–687.

Carter-Pokras, O., & Zambrana, R. E. (2001). Latino health status. In M. Aguirre-Molina, C. W. Molina, & R. E. Zambrana (Eds.), *Health issues in the Latino community* (pp. 333–351). San Francisco: Jossey-Bass.

Cauce, A. M., Coronado, N., & Watson, J. (1998). Conceptual, methodological, and statistical issues in culturally competent research. In M. Hernandez & M. Isaacs (Eds.), *Promoting cultural competence in children's mental health services* (pp. 305–329). Baltimore: Paul H. Brookes.

Chavez, E. L., & Swaim, R. C. (1992). An epidemiological comparison of Mexican American and White non-Hispanic 8th- and 12th-grade students' substance use. *American Journal of Public Health, 82,* 445–447.

Cohen, E. G., Chacón, M. A., Camarena, M. M., González, J. T., & Stover, S. (1983). Chicanas in California postsecondary education. *La Red/The Net, 65,* 73–79.

Council on Scientific Affairs (American Medical Association). (1991). Hispanic health in the United States. *Journal of the American Medical Association, 265,* 248–254.

Darabi, K., Dryfoos, J., & Schwartz, D. (1986). Hispanic adolescent fertility. *Hispanic Journal of the Behavioral Sciences, 8,* 157–171.

Darabi, K., & Ortiz, V. (1987). Childbearing among young Latino women in the United States. *American Journal of Public Health, 77,* 25–28.

Dusenbury. L., Diaz, T., Epstein, J. A., Botvin, G. J., & Caton. M. (1994). Attitudes toward AIDS and AIDS education among multi-ethnic parents of school-aged children in New York City. *AIDS Educations and Prevention, 6,* 237-248.

Eller, T. J., & Wallace, F. (1995). *Asset ownership of households: 1993.* U.S. Bureau of the Census, Current Population Reports, P-70-47. Washington, DC: U.S. Government Printing Office.

Falicov, C. J. (1996). Mexican families. In M. McGoldrick, J. Giordano, & J. K. Pearce (Eds.), *Ethnicity and Family Therapy* (2nd edition, pp. 169–182). New York: Guilford.

Farr, K. A., & Wilson-Figueroa, M. (1997). Talking about health and health care: Experiences and perspectives of Latina women in a farmworking community. *Women and Health, 25,* 23–40.

Federal Interagency Forum on Child and Family Statistics. (2001). *America's children: Key national indicators of well–being, 2001.* Washington, DC: U.S. Government Printing Office.

Gandara, P. (1982). Passing through the eye of the needle: High-achieving Chicanas. *Hispanic Journal of Behavioral Sciences, 4,* 167–179.

García Coll, C. T. (1990). Developmental outcome of minority infants: A process-oriented look into our beginnings. *Child Development, 61,* 270–289.

García Coll, C. T., Lambert, G., Jenkins, R., McAdoo, H. P., Crnic, K., Wasik, B. H., & Garcia, H. V. (1996). An integrative model for the study of developmental competencies in minority children. *Child Development, 67,* 1891–1914.

García Coll, C. T., Meyer, E. C., & Brillon, L. (1995). Ethnic and minority parenting. In M. Bornstein (Ed.), *Handbook of parenting: Vol. 2. Biology and ecology of parenting* (pp. 189–209). Hillsdale, NJ: Erlbaum.

Gibson, C. J., & Lennon, E. (1999). *Historical Census statistics on the foreign-born population in the United States: 1850–1990.* Population Division Working Paper No. 29. Washington, DC: Population Division, U.S. Census Bureau.

Ginorio, A., Guttierrez, L., Cauce, A. M., & Acosta, M. (1995). The psychology of Latinas. In C. Travis (Ed.), *Feminist perspectives on the psychology of women* (pp. 89–108). Washington, D.C.: American Psychological Association.

Gonzalez Ramos, G., Zayas, L. H., & Cohen, E. V. (1998). Child-rearing values of low-income, urban Puerto Rican mothers of preschool children. *Professional Psychology: Research and Practice, 29,* 377–382.

Hernández, A., Vargas-Lew, L., & Martínez, C. (1994). Intergenerational academic aspirations of Mexican-American females." An examination of mother, daughter, and grandmother triads. *Hispanic Journal of Behavioral Sciences, 16,* 195–204.

Hurtado, A. (1995). Variations, combination, and evolutions: Latino families in the United States. In R. E. Zambrana (Ed.), *Understanding Latino families: Scholarship, policy, and practice,* (pp. 40–61). Thousand Oaks, CA: Sage.

Hurtado, A., Hayes-Bautista, D. E., Burciaga Valdez, R., & Hernández, A. C. R. (1992). *Redefining California: Latino social engagement in a multicultural society.* Los Angeles: Chicano Studies Research Center, University of California–Los Angeles.

Immigration and Naturalization Service. (1998). *Immigrants, fiscal year 1998.* Retrieved October 4, 2001, from <http://www.ins.usdoj.gov/graphics/aboutins/statistics/imm98.pdf>.

Joiner, T. E., Dineen Wagner, K., Berenson, A., & Marquina, G. S. (1998). *On fatalism, pessimism, and depressive symptoms among Mexican American and other adolescents attending an obstetrics-gynecology clinic.* Unpublished manuscript.

Keefe, S. E. (1984). Real and ideal familism among Mexican Americans and Anglo Americans: On the meaning of "close" family ties. *Human Organization, 43*(1), 65–70.

Keefe, S. E., & Padilla, A. M. (1987). *Chicano Ethnicity.* Albuquerque: University of New Mexico Press.

Kennickell, A. B., Starr-McCluer, M., & Surette, B. J. (2000). *Recent changes in U.S. family finances: Results from the 1998 Survey of Consumer Finances.* Retrieved October 5, 2001, from <http://www.federalreserve.gov/pubs/oss/oss2/98/bull0100.pdf>.

López, E. M. (1995). Challenges and resources of Mexican American students within the family, peer group, and university: Age and gender patterns. *Hispanic Journal of Behavioral Sciences, 17*, 499–508.

Maldonado-Denis, M. (1980). *The emigration dialectic: Puerto Rico and the US.* New York: International Publishers.

Marks, G., García, M., & Solis, J. M. (1990). Health risk behaviors of Hispanics in the United States: Findings from HHANES, 1982–84. *American Journal of Public Health*, (Supplement), 20–26.

Mendoza, F. S. (1994). The health of Latino children in the United States. *The Future of Children, 4*(3), 43–72.

Mirande, A. (1977). The Chicano family: A reanalysis of conflicting views. *Journal of Marraige and the Family, 39*, 750–751.

Moore, J., & Pachon, H. (1985). *Hispanics in the United States.* Englewood Cliffs, NJ: Prentice Hall.

Mummert, G. (1993). Changes in the formation of western rural families: Profound modifications [*Cambios en la formación de las familias rurales del Occidente: Modificaciones profundas*]. *Demographic Studies, 6*, 23–24.

Ogbu, J. U. (1985). A cultural ecology of competence among inner-city Blacks. In M. B. Spencer & G. K. Brookins, (Eds.), *Beginnings: The social and affective development of Black children* (pp. 45–66). Hillsdale, NJ: Erlbaum.

Ogbu, J. U. (1994). From cultural differences to differences in cultural frame of reference. In P. M. Greenfield & R. R. Cocking (Eds.), *Cross-cultural roots of minority child development* (pp. 365–391). Hillsdale, NJ: Erlbaum.

Ogbu, J. U. (1995). Origins of human competence: A cultural-ecological perspective. In N. R. Goldberger & J. B. Veroff (Eds.), *The culture and psychology reader* (pp. 245–275). New York: New York University Press.

Okagaki, L., & Sternberg, R. J. (1993). Putting the distance into students' hands: Practical intelligence for school. In R. R. Cocking & K. A. Renninger (Eds.), *The development and meaning of psychological distance* (pp. 237–254). Hillsdale, NJ: Erlbaum.

Panitz, D. R., McConchie, R. D., Sauber, S. R., & Fonseca, J. A. (1983). The role of machismo and the Hispanic family in the etiology and treatment of alcoholism in Hispanic American males. *American Journal of Family Therapy, 11*, 31–44.

Portes, A., & Rumbaut, R. G. (1995). *Immigrant American: A portrait* (2nd ed.). Berkeley: University of California Press.

Portes, A., & Truelove, C. (1987). Making sense of diversity: Recent research on Hispanic minorities in the United States. *Annual Review of Sociology, 13*, 359–385.

Ramírez, M. (1967). Identification with Mexican family values and authoritarianism in Mexican Americans. *Journal of Social Psychology, 73*, 3–11.

Ramírez. O. (1990). Mexican American children and adolescents. In J.T. Gibbs & L. N. Huang (Eds.), *Children of color* (pp. 224–250). San Francisco: Jossey-Bass.

Rivera-Arzola, M., & Ramos-Grenier, J. (1997). Anger, *ataques de nervios*, and *la mujer puertorriqueña*: Sociocultural considerations and treatment implications. In J. G. García & M. C. Zea (Eds.), *Psychological interventions and research with Latino populations* (pp. 125–141). Boston: Allyn & Bacon.

Root, M. P. P. (Ed.). (1996). *The multiracial experience: Racial borders as the new frontier.* Thousand Oaks, CA: Sage.

Sánchez, G. (1999). Excepts from becoming Mexican American: Ethnicity, culture, and identity in Chicano Los Angeles, 1900–1945. In S. Coontz, M. Parson, &

G. Raley (Eds.), *American families: A multicultural reader* (pp. 128–153). New York: Routledge.

Seda Bonilla, E. (1974). *Requiem para una cultura*. Rio Piedras, PR: Ediciones Bayoan.

Szapocznik, J., & Kurtines, W. M. (1980). Acculturation, biculturalism, and adjustment among Cuban Americans. In A. M. Padilla (Ed.), *Acculturation: Theory, models, and some new findings* (pp. 140–159). Boulder, CO: Westview.

Szapocznik, J., & Kurtines, W. M. (1993). Family psychology and cultural diversity: Opportunities for theory, research, and application. *American Psychologist, 48*, 400–407.

Tienda, M., & Ortiz, V. (1986). Hispanicity and the 1980 census. *Social Science Quarterly, 67*, 3–20.

Treviño, F. M., & Moss, A. J. (1984). Health indicators for Hispanic, Black, and White Americans. *Vital and Health Statistics, 10*, 1–88.

UNICEF. (2000). *The state of the world's children*. New York: UNICEF and Oxford University Press.

U.S. Census Bureau. (1993). *We the American Hispanics*. Washington, DC: U.S. Government Printing Office.

U.S. Census Bureau. (1999a). *Findings on questions on race and Hispanic origin tested in the 1996 National Content Survey*. Retrieved June 16, 2000, from <http://www.census.gov/population/www/documentation/twps0016/report.html>.

U.S. Census Bureau. (1999b). *Health insurance coverage: Consumer income*. Washington, DC: U.S. Government Printing Office.

U.S. Census Bureau. (1999c). *Poverty in the United States: 1998*. Washington, DC: Government Printing Office.

U.S. Census Bureau. (1999d). *Money income in the United States: 1998*. Washington DC: U.S. Government Printing Office.

U.S. Census Bureau. (2000). *The Hispanic population in the United States: Population characteristics, March 1999*. Washington, DC: U.S. Government Printing Office.

U.S. Census Bureau. (2001a). *The Hispanic population*. Retrieved October 4, 2001, from <http://www.census.gov/prod/2001pubs/c2kbr01-3.pdf>.

U.S. Census Bureau. (2001b). *The Hispanic population in the United States: Population characteristics*. Retrieved October 4, 2001, from <http://www.census.gov/population/socdemo/hispanic/p20-535/p20-535.pdf>.

U.S. Census Bureau. (2001c). *The Hispanic population in the United States: Population characteristics, March 2000: Data tables*. Retrieved October 4, 2001, from <http://www.census.gov/population/www/socdemo/hispanic/ho00dtabs.html>.

U.S. Census Bureau. (2001d). Overview of race and Hispanic origin. Retrieved October 18, 2001, from <http://www.census.gov/prod/2001pubs/c2kbr01-1.pdf>.

U.S. Census Bureau. (2001e). *Profiles of general demographic characteristics: 2001 census of population and housing*. Retrieved October 4, 2001, from http://www.census.gov/Press-Release/www/2001/2khus.pdf

U.S. Department of Commerce. (1996a). *United States Department of Commerce news*. Washington, DC: U.S. Government Printing Office. Retrieved March 5, 2001, from <http://www.census.gov/Press-Release/cb96-36.html>.

U.S. Department of Commerce. (1996b). *United States Department of Commerce news*. Washington, DC: U.S. Government Printing Office.

U.S. Department of Commerce. (1997). *Census facts for Hispanic Heritage Month*. Press Release No. CB-97FS.10. Washington, DC: U.S. Government Printing Office.

U.S. Department of Health and Human Services, Public Health Service. (1997). *Healthy people 2000: Progress review on Hispanic Americans*. Retrieved June 16, 2000, from <http://odphp.osophs.dhhs.gov/pubs/hp2000/PROGRVW/Hispanics/HispanicAm.htm>.

U.S. Department of Health and Human Services. (2001). Mental health: Culture, race, and ethnicity—A supplement to *Mental Health: A Report of the Surgeon General*. Rockville, MD: Author.

Vega, W.A., & Amaro, H. (1994). Latino outlook: Good health, uncertain prognosis. *Annual Review of Public Health, 15*, 39–67.

Vega, W.A., Alderete, E., Kolody, B., & Aguilar-Gaxiola, S. (1998). Illicit drug use among Mexicans and Mexican Americans in California: The effects of gender and acculturation. *Addiction, 93*, 1839–1850.

Williams, N. (1988). Role making among married Mexican American women: Issues of class and ethnicity. *Journal of Applied Behavioral Sciences, 24*, 203–217.

Zea, M. C., García, J. G., Belgrave, F. Z., & Quezada, T. (1997). Socioeconomic and cultural factors in rehabilitation of Latinos with disabilities. In J. G. García & M. C. Zea (Eds.), *Psychological interventions and research with Latino populations* (pp. 217–234). Boston: Allyn & Bacon.

2

Ethnic Culture, Poverty, and Context: Sources of Influence on Latino Families and Children

Mark W. Roosa, Antonio A. Morgan-Lopez, Willa K. Cree, and Michele M. Specter

Although Latinos are a large and rapidly growing group, until relatively recently little research had been done on Latinos in the United States. Despite a growing number of studies, we have an incomplete picture of Latinos, their values, and their child-rearing beliefs and practices. In part, this knowledge gap is due to a common practice in research on Latinos: comparing small, convenient samples of low-income Latinos with middle-class non-Latino Whites that confounds culture and social class, thus produces results that are difficult or impossible to interpret. Another primary contributor to this knowledge gap is the tremendous diversity within Latinos that is often overlooked or ignored by researchers. Latino families differ on a number of important dimensions, including (a) their place of origin, the ecological niches to which generations of their families have adapted, (b) their reasons for being in the United States, (c) their social class or economic circumstances, (d) their degree of socialization in the values and traditions of their ethnic culture (i.e., enculturation), and (e) their acculturation level, the time they have been in the United States and the degree to which they have adopted aspects of the mainstream culture. Because Latinos are such a diverse group, we should expect diversity in values and child-rearing beliefs and practices among Latinos. Any description of Latinos in general will not be very useful.

In this chapter, we review literature on the values and parenting beliefs and practices of the three most commonly studied Latino groups in the United States: Mexican Americans, Puerto Ricans, and Cuban Americans. These groups differ significantly from one another on a number of demographic characteristics (see Cauce & Rodríguez, Chapter 1, this volume). In addition, these Latino subgroups differ from one another because of their unique historical blend of indigenous and imported cultures and both long-term and recent political histories. Differences in country of origin, reason for immigration, and education and economic status before immigration also play significant roles in defining these groups today. Thus, these groups of Latinos come from differing ecological niches and cultural traditions and are scattered across a variety of ecological niches and conditions within the United States.[1] Both cultural background and current circumstances provide opportunities and make demands on these Latino subgroups, thereby influencing their values and parenting beliefs and practices.

Previous reviews of the research on Latinos have recognized the diversity between (e.g., Mexicans and Cubans) and within subgroups (e.g., Marin & Marin, 1991), pointed out that much of the research has confounded social class and ethnicity (García Coll, Meyer, & Brillon, 1995), and acknowledged that there is considerable overlap between characteristics of Latinos and both other minority groups and Anglos (García Coll et al., 1995; Harrison, Wilson, Pine, Chan, & Buriel, 1990). However, having made such acknowledgments, reviewers often begin cataloging characteristics of Latinos as if they were a homogeneous group. In addition, most reviews emphasize characteristics of Latinos that are thought to be different from the characteristics of the mainstream culture, or other minority groups, while similarities are deemphasized or completely overlooked. Furthermore, culture is claimed as the explanatory factor for any differences, usually without accounting for contextual factors such as social class, living environment, social isolation, minority status or discrimination, other resources or stressors, or combinations of these factors that might influence values and parenting beliefs and practices (Bronfenbrenner, 1979; Harrison et al., 1990; LeVine, 1977; Malpass & Symonda, 1974; McLoyd, 1990; Ogbu, 1981). Finally, these attributions often are made without any specific references to the culture of origin or evidence that practices seen in the studied group are reflective of practices in their native culture. Thus, with the best of intentions, we may have created, and become familiar and comfortable with, an empirical picture of Latino families that may be seriously biased or at least misleading. In much the same way that earlier researchers often misused social class (Bronfenbrenner, 1986), we may have created a "black box" called ethnicity or culture and conveniently used it as an explanation for any between-group differences. Whenever researchers use a discrete dimension, such as ethnicity, to guide research, there is always a danger of developing stereotypes that ignore variations within groups and exaggerate differences between groups (Hoff-Ginsberg & Tardiff, 1995).

A growing concern of applied scientists in recent years has been how to provide services, interventions, and therapies that are culturally attractive, sensitive, and effective—that is, culturally competent—to minority groups (Castro, 1998). In order to develop culturally competent services and interventions, or to modify existing interventions and services in ways that make them culturally competent, scientists and practitioners need accurate information about the targeted groups. Our concern is whether the current research base provides the knowledge needed to guide the development of culturally competent services and interventions for the various Latino subgroups.

The purpose of this chapter is to examine some of what is known about the values and parenting practices of Latino subgroups in the United States. In our review, we attempt to determine whether characteristics commonly attributed to Latinos are, in fact, related to cultural heritage, to other factors, or, perhaps most likely, to some combination of culture and other factors. Most important, we introduce theoretical models of the origins of value systems and socialization beliefs and practices to provide a framework for identifying the sources of influence on Latino families' current values and parenting practices. Our goal is to contribute to the efforts begun by others of going beyond the black-box approach and identifying processes and contexts that may have major influences on the values and parenting beliefs and practices of the most common Latino subgroups in the United States. Based on an improved understanding of these values, behaviors, and parenting practices, we can begin to understand how services and interventions may need to be adapted to serve these subgroups better and outline a research agenda for strengthening the foundation for culturally informed services and interventions with Latino subgroups. We begin our review by examining links between culture, values, and parenting because it is primarily through values that ethnic culture influences family behavior and child-rearing practices.

CULTURE, VALUES, AND PARENTING

Ethnicity and culture are part of our self-concept, our intuitive definition of ourselves (Dilworth-Anderson, Burton, & Boulin Johnson, 1993). Ethnicity refers to members of a group who have shared a geographic region and a period of time and, thereby, have developed a shared identity. In the case of Latinos in the United States, when considered as a single group, ethnicity is defined by a common original language and geographic origin in Mexico, Central and South America, and the Caribbean. Culture refers to the common language, history, symbols, beliefs, unquestioned assumptions, and institutions that are part of the heritage of members of an ethnic group (Schweder & LeVine, 1984). The terms "ethnicity" and "culture" often are used interchangeably.

Values are our perceptions of what is desirable or undesirable, good or bad, that guide much of our decision making and behavior (Williams & Albert, 1990). Groups of people who share ecological niches and historical experiences (i.e., ethnic/cultural groups) hold similar values, called "cultural values." These value systems grow out of repeated successful experiences in meeting the challenges posed by the ecological niche and taking advantage of opportunities the ecological niche offered. Over generations, parents choose or learn socialization strategies that are guided, at least in part, by these cultural values and a desire to instill these values in their children (Arnett, 1995; LeVine, 1977; Ogbu, 1981). Parents want their children to develop competencies consistent with these values. Although Latinos come from a variety of ecological niches in the Americas and the Caribbean, their shared language and historical connections to Spain and the Catholic Church provide the foundation for expecting *some* similarities in values and parenting beliefs and practices.

However, ethnic groups are not the only groups that share value systems. Other "social-address" variables, in particular social class, define groups who currently share ecological niches, including environmental challenges and opportunities. Because of the need to adapt to similar ecological niches, people of different ethnic backgrounds who share other social addresses may share a variety of values and make similar choices of parenting goals and strategies (Harrison et al., 1990; McLoyd, 1990; Ogbu, 1981; Super & Harkness, 1986). For instance, research has shown that value systems and socialization practices are strongly influenced by parents' occupations, job demands, and working conditions (Hoff-Ginsberg & Tardiff, 1995). Parents are socialized on the job about what society values; what types of skills, attitudes, and behaviors are rewarded; and what types of contextual demands, including biases and prejudices, adults need to cope with to be successful. In turn, parents adopt these values and try to instill them in their children to assure their success in similar circumstances. Thus, values and parenting behavior are influenced by other sociodemographic factors and related processes in addition to ethnicity or culture of origin.

In addition, the parenting of any individual family or group can vary widely from culturally prescribed practices as parents adapt to short- or long-term pressures or unusual circumstances (Harrison et al., 1990; LeVine, 1977; McLoyd, 1990; Ogbu, 1981). Such variations generally occur with little or no parental awareness of, or concern for, long-term consequences for the child, family, or group. LeVine (1977) has argued that there is a universal hierarchy of goals that guide parenting decisions and practices and, in particular, deviations from culturally prescribed practices. At the top of this hierarchy is the health and survival of the child. Next in this hierarchy is developing the child's ability for economic success in adulthood. When these basic goals are met, parents strive to develop children's abilities to express and practice other, more abstract, cultural values (e.g., manners, morals). Thus, immigrant parents living in a U.S. inner-city environment that is unfamiliar and perhaps frightening to them may adopt parenting strategies to protect their children from physical harm and dangerous influences without knowing or caring how those strategies may impact children's later social skills or ability to succeed in school. Cultural values may provide a general or initial template for guiding parental decisions and socialization practices. However, the opportunities and threats provided by immediate environmental conditions may determine how fully parents try to instill cultural values in their children or deviate from culturally prescribed norms and practices.

Super and Harkness (1986) proposed a "developmental-niche" framework for understanding influences on parenting that moves us beyond the simple social-address model. They described a child care system made up of three subsystems: the physical and social settings of child-care, culturally regulated child-rearing goals and practices, and the psychological makeup of the caretakers. The regularities and consistencies across these subsystems and across developmental stages help children learn the rules and values of their culture. Most important, when change is introduced in any subsystem, the other subsystems attempt to maintain culturally prescribed norms and practices. However, when change is large and/or persistent, homeostatic mechanisms common to all systems lead to changes in the other subsystems to maintain harmony among them. Like LeVine's hierarchy of goals (1977), this framework is dynamic and provides guidance in identifying and understanding processes that guide or influence parenting behavior.

Knight, Bernal, Cota, Garza, and Ocampo (1993) proposed another process model that identifies variables that play key roles in minority children's socialization, a model consistent with the developmental-niche framework (Super & Harkness, 1986). Knight et al.'s model looks at three sets of contextual variables: the family's social ecology, joint socialization of familial and nonfamilial agents, and the child's ethnic identity and cognitive abilities. Family social ecology includes the family's background, their generational status (since immigration), ethnic identity, acculturation, language used with family, and parents' cultural knowledge. The second set of contextual factors looks at the socialization efforts of familial and nonfamilial agents. This includes the effects of joint socialization by family and nonfamily members, interactions with the majority culture, urbanization of the community, socioeconomic status of the neighborhood and the family, the political impact of being part of a minority culture, socioeconomic status and other characteristics of the community, and characteristics of the dominant group. Knight et al. hypothesized that family background, family structure, and social ecology variables influence the socialization content that parents provide for their children, in other words, the degree to which parents socialize their children to the values and traditions of their ethnic culture (i.e., enculturation) and to the host culture (i.e., acculturation). This socialization content, in turn, influences the nature of children's ethnic identity, which also influences subsequent behavior. Thus, socialization content is the mediating link between family background variables and children's ethnic identity, which likely influences later decisions about how much to adopt ethnic versus majority culture values. Knight et al.'s model is far more complete and complex than previous models that have looked at the socialization process for minority children in that it reflects the complexity and interrelatedness of a variety of contextual factors in this process.

These three models (LeVine, 1977; Knight et al., 1993; Super & Harkness, 1986) encourage researchers to identify processes and contexts that account for deviations from culturally prescribed values, parenting beliefs, and practices.

These models help us understand why parenting may not change much or at all initially after an event such as immigration (e.g., resistance of systems to change), why families in unsafe environments may adopt parenting practices and norms that are inconsistent with their culturally prescribed parenting values (e.g., hierarchical nature of values), and why parenting changes with acculturation (e.g., adaptation of caretakers to requirements for success in the new culture, adaptation to new social settings such as U.S. schools). Perhaps most important, these models demonstrate both the fluidity of values in response to contextual demands and why knowledge of a family's ethnicity/culture alone may not always be a good predictor of their values or parenting beliefs and practices. The heterogeneity of values and parenting beliefs and practices within Latino subgroups and the fluidity of these family characteristics pose a serious challenge for anyone designing interventions or providing services to these groups.

In the review that follows, we examine literature on the values and parenting practices of Latino subgroups in the United States while attempting to identify processes or contexts that might be responsible for differences that have been identified within and across groups. However, before proceeding with the more general review, we provide an example of the type of analysis that is necessary to identify factors and processes that influence values and practices beyond ethnicity/cultural background.

CASE STUDY

The extended family (i.e., nuclear family plus some combination of grandparents, other kin, and non-kin who are treated as relatives) often has been described as a characteristic of Latino groups in general and as representing an important Latino value (García-Coll et al., 1995; Marín & Marín, 1991). Having and maintaining an extended family or kinship network has implications for children's roles in the family, child care and socialization decisions and practices, and the transmission of values to children. To what degree is this interrelated set of values and practices based on culturally derived values? Similar values and practices have been described for a variety of minority groups in the United States, including African Americans and Native Americans (Harrison et al., 1990). Similarly, research on low-income Appalachian Whites has identified similar values and practices as commonplace (Larsen, 1978; Peterson & Peters, 1985). In fact, the extended family was the normative family unit in most cultures prior to industrialization and the rural-to-urban transition.

Rather than having roots in a particular cultural tradition, the extended family is more likely an adaptive strategy (Harrison et al., 1990) used when families face high demand–low resource situations. Thus, we would expect the extended family to be more common among low-income or resource-poor groups and among marginalized, minority, or isolated groups. In these situations, the pooled resources of family members, real or "adopted," are necessary for safety, survivability, and/or economic success in a particular niche (LeVine, 1977). We also would expect the extended family to be rarer in less challenging environments in which families have the resources to meet their needs alone (e.g., middle-class families). Indeed, Vernon and Roberts found that differences in kinship support for Anglos and Mexican Americans disappeared when education and socioeconomic status were controlled. Similarly, Sabogal and Marín (1987) reported that first-generation Latinos of varied origins reported higher scores on familial obligations and family importance than second-generation Latinos who grew up in the United States. Thus, both social class and acculturation may be associated with declines in the importance of the extended family to Latinos.

For those living in extended families, we would expect a different constellation of parenting values and associated socialization practices than we would find in other families (LeVine, 1977; Super & Harkness, 1986). Some of these values and practices likely will be adapted to the same ecological niche that made the extended family necessary or adaptive. Still, other values will derive from adaptations to the conditions of life within an extended family (e.g., maintaining peace and harmony across generations, clear lines of authority, means of decision making). Undoubtedly, cultural values will influence specifically how families from a given ethnic group adapt to living in extended families. For instance, Latino extended family systems have different structures and roles than African American or Native American extended families (Harrison et al., 1990).

Taking a broader perspective on family values and parenting practices, as demonstrated in this example, gets us away from simple social-address explanations. This approach also helps us focus on the contexts to which families are adapting and the commonalties among families or ethnic groups adapting to the same context while providing some guidance for understanding the unique adaptations of various groups. This type of analysis also should help avoid simplistic "deficit" explanations of differences that often are associated with comparative research designs (Cauce et al., 1998). Finally, this type of analysis should help us avoid simplistic dependence on stereotypes, even those that are empirically derived (e.g., based on group means), to represent all members of any group.

RESEARCH ON LATINO VALUES

Several studies and reviews have described the value system of various Latino subgroups usually in contrast to middle-class Anglos. For instance, Chandler (1979) described Mexican Americans as holding values such as fatalism, past and present time orientation, close integration with extended family, and distrust of non-kin. Albert (1983, 1996) described Latinos in general as more likely than Anglos to value cooperation, collectivism (i.e., emphasizing the group rather than the individual), *respeto* (i.e., the importance of showing and maintaining respect), *simpatia* (i.e., emphasis on behaviors that lead to harmonious social relationships), and the belief that authority should not be questioned (see also Marín & Marín, 1991). Additionally, Cuban Americans have been described as relatively high on collectivism, subjugation to nature, and present orientation (Szapocznik, Scopetta, de los Angeles Aranalde, & Kurtines, 1978). Finally, Puerto Ricans have been described as being relatively fatalistic, oriented toward respecting authority without question (Wurzel, 1983) and both present and future oriented (Lorenzo-Hernandez & Ouellette, 1998). These descriptions hint that there may be several areas of cross group similarity as well as areas of variation among Latino subgroups. Very little research has examined the variation between these groups of Latinos or the immense variation within each group.

However, Rosado (1980) and Casavantes (1970) have argued that many Puerto Ricans and Mexican Americans may be more likely to value the present over the past and future as a function of economic survival and social-class status rather than as a function of culture. Similarly, Marín and Triandis (1985) report that collectivism is negatively related to per capita income and occupational mobility among Mexican Americans. Knight and Kagan (1977) and Madsen (1967) have suggested that social class is positively related to competitive behavior among Mexican Americans. Similarly, Lucas and Stone (1994) reported that Mexican American and Anglo community college students, groups relatively similar in social class, were similar in interpersonal competitiveness. Thus, there is ample evidence that social class may account for at least some reported differences in values between Latino subgroups and middle-class Anglos, while also accounting for important within-group variation (Marín & Triandis, 1985).

Degree of acculturation to the United States also has been associated with variations in values. This should not be surprising given that acculturation often involves adopting some values of the host culture. For instance, less acculturated Latinos are more likely to have a collectivist orientation than their more acculturated peers (Hofstede, 1980). Kagan and Knight (1979) found second-generation Mexican American youth more likely than third-generation Mexican American youth to value altruism and equality. Kagan and Madsen (1971) found Mexican children to be more likely to endorse a cooperative orientation than their Mexican American peers, while both groups were lower on competitive orientation than Anglo children. However, Wurzel (1983) found no difference in cooperative/competitive orientation as a function of years in the United States among Puerto Rican youth.

Research also suggests that there is a difference in the values that Mexican American and Puerto Rican families transmit to their children based on the acculturation level of the parents. Research has shown that, in less acculturated families, the values of humility and respectfulness guide parenting practices and decisions, while in highly acculturated families, the values of independence and creativity are emphasized (Zayas & Solari, 1994). Other studies have shown that teenage Latino mothers emphasize values more similar to Anglo and African

American teenage mothers than those emphasized by older Latino mothers (Vega, Khoury, Zimmerman, Gil, & Warheit, 1995). Finally, while Mexican American parents born in the United States may stress that their children should retain Mexican culture, they place less emphasis on living near relatives than parents born in Mexico (Hurtado, Rodriguez, Gurin, & Beals, 1993).

Other demographic factors also may play a role in explaining variations in values for Latinos. Reported differences in the perspectives of rural (Chandler, 1979) and urban Mexican Americans (Grebler, Moore, & Guzman, 1970) suggest that living context might be related to variations in values. However, it remains to be seen whether living context is different from, or a proxy for, differences in acculturation or the level of local support for Latino cultural values. Majority–minority status may also play a role in value orientations. Espinoza and Garza (1985) found that when their groups were in the numerical majority, Anglo and Mexican American students did not differ on within-group competitiveness but, when in the minority, Mexican Americans were significantly more competitive. That is, Mexican American students were more likely to emphasize personal success than group success, compared to Anglos, when both groups were numerical minorities. Finally, although there is not much research on the topic, we should not be surprised if some of the differences in the values systems of Latino subgroups were accounted for by differences in their political histories (Lorenzo-Hernandez & Oullette, 1998) and/or reasons for immigration to the United States (Ogbu, 1991).

This brief review has shown evidence that many factors in addition to ethnic background influence people's values and account for variations from culturally prescribed values. Given the modal research design that compared a sample of low-income Latinos with a middle-class sample of Anglos, it is likely that our empirically based beliefs about Latinos' values (a) are biased toward low social class Latinos, (b) exaggerate the extent of differences between Latinos' and others in the same social class or other social context, and (c) ignore or underestimate differences between distinct Latino subgroups (e.g., Mexican Americans, Puerto Ricans). Because parenting beliefs and practices reflect family values (LeVine, 1977), we might expect a similar situation when we examine the literature on Latino parenting.

RESEARCH ON LATINO PARENTING

In their investigation of desirable and undesirable socialization goals among Anglo and Puerto Rican mothers, Harwood, Schoelmerich, Ventura-Cook, Schulze, and Wilson (1996) found that both culture and socioeconomic status contributed independently to group differences, but that cultural effects were greater. Mothers from five sociocultural groups (middle-class Anglos, middle-class island Puerto Ricans, lower-class Anglos, lower-class immigrant Puerto Ricans, and lower-class island Puerto Ricans) described desirable characteristics of adults and children. When socioeconomic status was controlled,

Puerto Rican mothers placed the highest value on proper demeanor, whereas Anglo mothers chose self-maximization, reflecting basic differences in value orientations.

Another study of child-rearing values found that mothers ranked their child-rearing goals differently depending on both culture and acculturation. When lower-income Puerto Rican mothers with young children ranked child-rearing values in order of importance, they ranked honesty, respectfulness and obedience, and responsibility as the top three choices (Gonzalez-Ramos, Zayas, & Cohen, 1998). In comparison, Anglo mothers selected assertiveness, independence, and creativity as their top choices. However, the more acculturated the Puerto Rican mother, the higher she ranked independence and creativity.

Similarly, Okagaki and Sternberg (1993) asked American-born Anglo and Mexican American parents as well as immigrant parents from Cambodia, Mexico, the Philippines, and Vietnam about child-rearing techniques and about what characterizes a competent child. Anglo and Mexican American parents chose developing autonomy over conformity in their children, adhering to contemporary American cultural beliefs that favor intellectual and social individuality. The immigrant parents favored conformity to external standards over developing autonomy, which may be attributed either to adaptive strategies of trying to fit in to their minority status within the United States or the cultural beliefs of their country of origin. Socioeconomic status was not controlled in this study.

In a study of cultural variations in parenting, Julian, McKenry, and Mc-Kelvey (1994) examined parenting attitudes, behaviors, and involvement in Anglo, African American, Mexican American, and Asian American mothers and fathers in two-parent families in the United States. When socioeconomic status was controlled, they found that while there were some between-group differences, there were far more similarities. Focusing on just Mexican Americans and Anglos, this study found that Mexican American fathers placed greater emphasis on child compliance and harmony (getting along well with others) than did Anglo parents. Mexican American fathers wanted their children to do well in athletics more so than Anglo parents or Mexican American mothers did. In addition, Mexican American parents valued self-control and academic success more than Anglo parents. Finally, Mexican Americans used praise with their children significantly less than Anglo parents. However, Mexican American and Anglo parents were similar on several other measures, including the importance of children being independent and controlling their temper. Similarly, when socioeconomic status, maternal educational level, marital status, and age of child were matched in a sample of mothers from the United States and Mexico, no significant differences between the groups were found in terms of discipline styles, expectations, or nurturing (Solis Camara & Fox, 1995). In contrast, MacPhee, Fritz, and Miller-Heyl (1996) reported that Mexican American parents were more likely to use spanking, scolding, threats, or criticism to discipline and manage children than Anglo parents, even when socioeconomic status was controlled.

In an observational study of parent–child interactions in Mexican families and subsequent cross-cultural comparisons, Bronstein (1994) reported finding more similarities than differences in parenting styles. She found that there was a positive relationship between warm, supportive parenting behavior and positive child behaviors, that controlling and restrictive parenting was negatively related to assertive, independent child behavior and positively related to submissive, compliant child behavior. These patterns replicated Baumrind's (1967, 1971) findings with middle-class Anglo parents. Finally, Bronstein (1994) reported that punitive and hostile parenting by Mexican Americans was positively related to aggressive as well as submissive child behavior, results that reflected earlier findings with Anglo samples (Maccoby & Martin, 1983). The results of these studies are interesting and important: Despite differences in parenting values, goals, and practices outlined earlier, relationships between parenting behaviors and child outcomes were consistent for Mexican Americans and Anglo parents. Thus, the contents of parenting interventions can be similar for these groups although the method of presentation, motivators used, and other aspects of delivering the intervention might need to differ.

In this brief review, we find evidence that parenting beliefs and practices are influenced by cultural background, social class, and acculturation level. Similar to the research on values of Latino families, we need to take a broader perspective to understand the cumulative influences of multiple factors on parenting behavior. Using such a perspective, scientists and practitioners are more likely to choose, adapt, or develop appropriate services or interventions for meeting the needs of a targeted high-risk group. By looking at multiple influences on family values and parenting, practitioners and researchers are less likely to use interventions designed to fit a stereotype based on a single characteristic of the targeted group and are more likely to meet the groups' needs.

CONCLUSIONS/IMPLICATIONS

Undoubtedly, there is more than a grain of truth to the common stereotype of U.S. Latinos that includes such characteristics as being more group- than individual-oriented; being strongly committed to family, in particular the extended family; being focused on the present; emphasizing proper demeanor in socializing children; and so on. Evidence for this profile has been reported in research with multiple Latino subgroups and replicated in multiple studies. However, as with all stereotypes, the most common profile of Latinos underestimates the diversity within Latinos as a whole (e.g., differences between Mexican Americans and Puerto Ricans) as well as within Latino subgroups (e.g., differences between Mexican Americans based on acculturation or social class) and exaggerates differences between Latinos and both other minority groups and the majority culture. Furthermore, much of the current research is based on small, convenience samples of low-income Latinos from a single location so that we cannot be sure to what degree our empirically based stereotypes accurately represent even low-income Latinos. Without more research into the complexity of both within- and between-subgroup differences for Latinos, research with more representative samples, and research that goes beyond single social-address designs, in essence research that takes us beyond simple stereotypes, applied scientists and practitioners have a limited research base to guide the development of culturally competent services and interventions.

Much work remains to be done before we are ready to begin addressing the major questions about how best to serve Latinos in the United States. It seems clear, given the common findings about differences in values and parenting practices between middle-class Anglos and many low-income Latino subgroups, that services and interventions that target Latinos need to be adapted to make them more attractive and effective with these groups. However, despite some general guidelines (Castro, 1998; Marín & Marín, 1991), we do not have enough information at this time to provide definitive answers to some of the challenging questions that applied scientists and practitioners have about developing and delivering culturally competent programs for Latinos, including:

1. What are the essential elements of a culturally competent intervention for at-risk Latino families?
2. How would these elements differ for various subgroups of Latinos?
3. Would a culturally competent program for low-income, at-risk Latinos be appropriate for low-income, at-risk families in general in some settings?
4. When making programs culturally competent, do we need to focus on different sets of core values depending on whether our services or interventions have to do with job training, language or literacy training, or parent training?
5. Would a culturally competent program that proved successful with Latinos in Los Angeles be appropriate in Houston, Miami, New York City, or rural Iowa?

Throughout this chapter, we have focused on a limited portion of the research literature on Latinos and some of the questions that remain to be answered before we have a clear enough picture of Latinos and Latino families to be able to provide optimal interventions and services. However, before these and other questions can be dealt with adequately, there are some fundamental issues about definitions and basic assumptions that need to be addressed so that scholars can carry on a meaningful dialogue about the research issues. First, there is the question of what we mean by cultural values. In much of the literature on Latinos' values, relative value positions are described primarily in comparison to Anglos. Comparisons of means on a measure of values determines which group is described as high or low on a given value without much or any consideration for the absolute meaning of either mean score (i.e., both groups could have been high on that value). In contrast, some researchers have defined a "cultural response" to questions about values as the agreement of at least 50% of the representatives of a group regarding the importance of that value (Triandis, 1996). Using this approach, we get a clearer view of the level of endorsement of various value positions in a group and we can easily describe two groups as being high (or low) on a given value, such as commitment to the family, without necessarily assigning them to relative positions based on mean differences. Researchers need to be clear about how they define cultural values and the degree to which they represent a given group. Similarly, practitioners need to be careful in interpreting statements about the values of particular groups.

A second major issue has to do with the assumption that we can neatly and accurately separate out influences on values and parenting behavior into discrete categories such as ethnic culture, social class, acculturation, discrimination, and living context, to name but a few. In fact, most of these influences are so intertwined that methodologically and statistically their separate influences cannot be determined clearly. Furthermore, complete disaggregation of the influences on family values and parenting beliefs and practices into discrete sources may not be useful. Attempts to identify values and parenting practices that are due solely to ethnic origin/culture, or any other social-address variable for that matter, are likely to contribute to the solidification and perhaps elaboration of current stereotypes of members of these groups, while being of limited utility to practitioners and applied researchers. In practice, the individuals, families, and communities that we target for interventions or service delivery represent the temporary, ever-changing result of a mass of interacting influences on value systems and parenting practices.

There probably are cases in which one social-address variable is the predominant influence in a given set of circumstances. For instance, when we are dealing with the most desperate at-risk groups (e.g., those living in poverty in bad housing in unsafe neighborhoods with unfriendly and ineffective schools), we might reasonably expect more similarities than differences across ethnic groups as people struggle to meet their most fundamental needs (LeVine, 1977; McLoyd, 1990; Ogbu, 1981). However, we also should expect culturally specific or influenced adaptations to this adversity (e.g., Harrison et al., 1990). Similarly, when we are working with recently arrived immigrants from one Latino subgroup living in barrios dominated by similar families, we might expect to find evidence of very strong ethnic/cultural influences on values, beliefs, and practices because of community support. Even in these conditions we should not expect to find homogeneity. However, most often we will not find such clear-cut cases and instead must deal with the results of complex interactions among multiple sources of influence on values, beliefs, and practices.

It is time to move beyond simplistic attempts to generalize values or parenting practices to families because of their ethnicity/culture or any other single social-address category. The resulting stereotypes are not useful for providing a foundation for culturally competent service delivery or intervention. Most likely, the most important results of future research on Latino groups will come in the form of significant interactions among sources of influence. Given the dramatic diversity within Latinos on a wide variety of sociodemographic characteristics, there is little reason to expect there will be many significant and stable main effects based on ethnicity/culture. More important to the development of culturally competent services and interventions will be the many important interactions between ethnicity/culture and these sociodemographic characteristics, the culturally specific or influenced adaptations of Latino subgroups to specific social contexts. As we learn more about how family values and parenting vary from culturally prescribed norms in particular contexts, we also will learn more about the variables that need to be targeted for change in effective interventions and how best to package these interventions to be attractive to particular Latino subpopulations. However, the complexity of the influences on Latinos' values and parenting and the low likelihood of broad generalizations for any Latino subgroup lead us to the following question: Does developing culturally competent interventions or services ultimately mean anything other than adaptation to local values, needs, and circumstances, the unique interactions among cultural background, social class, and local context?

The first steps toward gaining a clearer picture of Latinos and various Latino subgroups so that culturally competent interventions or services are possible are fairly simple. Taking the most obvious lessons from the literature, we know that there is little to gain from studies of Latinos that do not assess and account for variation in country of origin, acculturation status, reason for migration, and social class. Second, research with larger and more representative samples from multiple locations or settings would increase our confidence in the generalizability of the results as well as give us a better idea of within-group variation. Third, research based on more complex conceptualizations of variations in values and socialization (Harrison et al., 1990; Knight et al., 1993; LeVine, 1977; Super & Harkness, 1986) probably would help accelerate our understanding of the complexity of influences on Latinos' value orientations and socialization practices. Use of these models invariably means paying greater attention to meaningful interactions between ethnicity/culture and other sociodemographic and contextual factors. Finally, thoughtful combinations of cross-group comparative studies and in-depth studies of single subgroups are likely to help us get the most comprehensive and sensitive perspective on Latinos in general, similarities and differences among Latino subgroups, and similarities and differences among Latino subgroups and other minority groups as well as Anglos. This final suggestion also would help us understand the degree to which we can rely on generalizations about various subgroups of Latinos in developing interventions as opposed to making adaptations solely to fit the local target population. Applied scientists and practitioners should not, and cannot, delay the delivery of interventions and services for at-risk Latinos until such an extensive and comprehensive research program is completed. However, the quality of services and interventions provided should improve as we move away from simplistic stereotypes based solely on culture of origin or any other single target-group characteristic.

AUTHORS' NOTE

Work on this chapter was supported, in part, by grants 5-P30-MH39246 to support a Preventive Intervention Research Center and 5-T32-MH18387 to support training in prevention research, and the Cowden Fellowship Program of the Department of Family and Human Development at Arizona State University. The authors gratefully thank Nancy Gonzales for thoughtful comments on drafts of this chapter and Rosanita Ratcliff for her energetic help and support.

NOTES

1. Because of the diversity among Latinos from different countries of origin, we will refer to a specific subgroup whenever possible.

REFERENCES

Albert, R. D. (1983). Mexican-American children in educational settings: Research on children's and teachers' perceptions and interpretations of behavior. In E. Garcia (Ed.), *The Mexican American child: Language, cognition, and social development* (pp. 183–194). Tempe: Arizona State University.

Albert, R. D. (1996). A framework and model for understanding Latin American and Latino/Hispanic cultural patterns. In D. Landis & R. S. Bhagat (Eds.), *Handbook of intercultural training* (2nd ed., pp. 327–348). Thousand Oaks, CA: Sage.

Arnett, J. J. (1995). Broad and narrow socialization: The family in the context of a cultural theory. *Journal of Marriage and Family, 57,* 617–628.

Baumrind, D. (1967). Child care practices anteceding three patterns of preschool behavior. *Genetic Psychology Monographs, 75,* 43–83.

Baumrind, D. (1971). Current patterns of parental authority. *Developmental Psychology Monographs, 4,* 1–103.

Bernal, G., & Enchautegui de Jesus, N. (1994). Latinos and Latinas in community psychology: A review of the literature. *American Journal of Community Psychology, 22,* 531–557.

Bronfenbrenner, U. (1979). *The ecology of human development: Experiments by nature and design.* Cambridge, MA: Harvard University Press.

Bronfenbrenner, U. (1986). Ecology of the family as a context for human development: Research perspectives. *Developmental Psychology, 22,* 723–742.

Bronstein, P. (1994). Patterns of parent–child interaction in Mexican families: A cross-cultural perspective. *International Journal of Behavioral Development, 17,* 423–466.

Casavantes, E. (1970). Pride and prejudice: A Mexican-American dilemma. *Civil Rights Digest, 3,* 22–27.

Castro, F. G. (1998). Cultural competence training in clinical psychology assessment, clinical intervention, and research. In C. D. Belar (Ed.), *Comprehensive clinical psychology: Socio-cultural and individual differences* (pp. 127–140). New York City: Pergamon.

Cauce, A., Coronado, N. & Watson, J. (1998). Conceptual, methodological, and statistical issues in culturally competent research. In M. Hernandez & M. Isaacs (Eds.), *Promoting cultural competence in children's mental health services* (pp. 305–329). Baltimore: Paul H. Brookes.

Chandler, C. R. (1979). Traditionalism in a modern setting: A comparison of Anglo and Mexican-American value orientations. *Human Organization, 38*, 153–159.

Dilworth-Anderson, P., Burton, L. M., & Boulin Johnson, L. (1993). Reframing theories for understanding race, ethnicity, and families. In P. G. Boss, W. J. Doherty, R. LaRossa, W. R. Schumm, & S. K. Steinmetz (Eds.), *Sourcebook of family theories and methods: A contextual approach* (pp. 627–649). New York: Plenum.

Espinoza, J., & Garza, R. (1985). Social group salience and interethnic cooperation. *Journal of Experimental Social Psychology, 21*, 380–392.

García Coll, C. T., Meyer, E. C., & Brillon, L. (1995). Ethnic and minority parenting. In M. H. Bornstein (Ed.), *Handbook of parenting* (Vol. 2, pp. 189–209). Hillsdale, NJ: Erlbaum.

Gonzalez-Ramos, G., Zayas, L. H., & Cohen, E. V. (1998). Child-rearing values of low-income, urban Puerto Rican mothers of preschool children. *Professional Psychology: Research and Practice, 29*, 377–382.

Grebler, L., Moore, J. W., and Guzman, R. C. (1970). *The Mexican-American people: The nation's second largest minority.* New York: Free Press.

Harrison, A. O., Wilson, M. N., Pine, C. J., Chan, S. Q., & Buriel, R. (1990). Family ecologies of ethnic minority children. *Child Development, 61*, 347–362.

Harwood, R. L., Schoelmerich, A., Ventura-Cook, E., Schulze, P. A., & Wilson, S. P. (1996). Culture and class influences on Anglo and Puerto Rican mothers' beliefs regarding long-term socialization goals and child behavior. *Child Development, 67*, 2246–2461.

Hoff-Ginsberg, E., & Tardiff, T. (1995). Socioeconomic status and parenting. In M. H. Bornstein (Ed.), *Handbook of parenting.* Vol. 2 (pp. 161–188). Hillsdale, NJ: Erlbaum.

Hofstede, G. (1980). *Culture's consequences: International differences in work-related values.* Beverly Hills, CA: Sage.

Hurtado, A., Rodriguez, J., Gurin, P., & Beals, J. L. (1993). The impact of Mexican descendants' social identity on the ethnic socialization of children. In M. E. Bernal & G. P. Knight (Eds.), *Ethnic identity* (pp. 131–162). Albany: State University of New York Press.

Julian, T. W., McKenry, P. C., & McKelvey, M. W. (1994). Cultural variations in parenting: Perceptions of Caucasian, African American, Hispanic, and Asian-American parents. *Family Relations, 43*, 30–37.

Kagan, S., & Knight, G. (1979). Cooperation-competition and self-esteem: A case of cultural relativism. *Journal of Cross-Cultural Psychology, 10*, 457–467.

Kagan, S., & Madsen, M. (1971). Cooperation and competition of Mexican, Mexican-American, and Anglo-American children of two ages under four instructional sets. *Developmental Psychology, 5*, 32–39.

Knight, B. P., Bernal, M. E., Cota, M. K., Garza, C. A., & Ocampo, K. A. (1993). Family socialization and Mexican American identity and behavior. In M. E. Bernal

& G. P. Knight (Eds.), *Ethnic identity* (pp. 105–129). Albany: State University of New York Press.

Knight, G., & Kagan, S. (1977). Acculturation of pro-social and competitive behaviors among second- and third-generation Mexican-American children. *Journal of Cross-Cultural Psychology, 8*, 273–284.

Larsen, O. F. (1978). Values and beliefs of rural people. In T. R. Ford (Ed.), *Rural U.S.A.: Persistence and change* (pp. 91–112). Ames: Iowa State University.

LeVine, R. A. (1977). Child rearing as cultural adaptation. In H. P. Leiderman, S. R. Tulkin, & A. Rosenfeld (Eds.), *Culture and infancy: Variations in the human experience* (pp. 15–27). New York: Academic Press.

Lorenzo-Hernandez, J., & Ouellette, S. (1998). Ethnic identity, self-esteem, and values in Dominicans, Puerto Ricans, and African Americans. *Journal of Applied Social Psychology, 28*, 2007–2024.

Lucas, J. R., & Stone, J. L. (1994). Acculturation and competition among Mexican-Americans: A reconceptualization. *Hispanic Journal of Behavioral Sciences, 16*, 129–142.

Maccoby, E. E., & Martin, J. A. (1983). Socialization in the context of the family: Parent–child interaction. In P. H. Mussen (Ed.), *Handbook of child psychology* (4th ed., Vol. 4, pp. 1–101). New York: Wiley.

MacPhee, D., Fritz, J., & Miller-Heyl, J. (1996). Ethnic variations in personal social networks and parenting. *Child Development, 67*, 3278–3295.

Madsen, M. C. (1967). Cooperative and competitive motivation of children in three Mexican sub-cultures. *Psychological Reports, 20*, 1307–1320.

Malpass, R. S., & Symonds, J. D. (1974). Value preferences associated with social class, sex, and race. *Journal of Cross Cultural Psychology, 5*, 282–300.

Marín, G., & Marín, B. V. (1991). *Research with Hispanic populations*. Newbury Park, CA: Sage.

Marín, G., & Triandis, H. C. (1985). Allocentrism as an important characteristic of the behavior of Latin Americans and Hispanics. In R. Diaz-Guerrero (Ed.), *Cross-cultural and national studies in social psychology* (pp. 85–104). Amsterdam: Elsevier Science.

McLoyd, V. C. (1990). The impact of economic hardship on Black families and children: Psychological distress, parenting, and socioemotional development. *Child Development, 61*, 311–346.

Ogbu, J. U. (1981). Origins of human competence: A cultural-ecological perspective. *Child Development, 52*, 413–429.

Ogbu, J. U. (1991). Minority coping responses and school experience. *Journal of Psychohistory, 18*, 433–457.

Okagaki, L., & Sternberg, R. J. (1993). Parental beliefs and children's school performance. *Child Development, 64*, 36–56.

Peterson, G. W., & Peters, D. F. (1985). The socialization values of low-income Appalachian White and rural Black mothers: A comparative study. *Journal of Comparative Family Studies, 16*, 75–91.

Rosado, J. W. (1980). Important psychocultural factors in the delivery of mental health services to lower-class Puerto Rican clients: A review of recent studies. *Journal of Community Psychology, 8*, 215–226.

Sabogal, F., & Marín, G. (1987). Hispanic familism and acculturation: What changes and what doesn't. *Hispanic Journal of Behavioral Sciences, 9*, 397–412.

Schweder, R., & LeVine, R. A. (1984). *Culture theory: Essays on mind, self, and emotion.* Cambridge, England: Cambridge University Press.

Solis Camara, P., & Fox, R. A. (1995). Parenting among mothers with young children in Mexico and the United States. *Journal of Social Psychology, 135,* 591–599.

Super, C. M., & Harkness, S. (1986). The developmental niche: A conceptualization of the interface of child and culture. *International Journal of Behavioral Development, 9,* 545–569.

Szapocznik, J., Scopetta, M. A., de los Angeles Aranalde, M., & Kurtines, W. M. (1978). Cuban value structure: Treatment implications. *Journal of Consulting and Clinical Psychology, 46,* 961–970.

Triandis, H. C. (1996). The psychological measurement of cultural syndromes. *American Psychologist, 51,* 407–415.

Vega, W. A., Khoury, E. L., Zimmerman, R. S., Gil, A. G., & Warheit, G. J. (1995). Cultural conflicts and problem behaviors of Latino adolescents in home and school environments. *Journal of Community Psychology, 23,* 167–179.

Vernon, S. W., & Roberts, R. E. (1985). A comparison of Anglos and Mexican Americans on selected measures of social support. *Hispanic Journal of Behavioral Sciences, 7,* 381–399.

Williams, R. M., & Albert, E. M. (1990). Values: The concept of values. *International Encyclopedia of the Social Sciences, 16,* 283–291.

Wurzel, J. (1983). Differences between Puerto Rican and Anglo-American secondary school students in their perception of relational modalities. *International Journal of Intercultural Relations, 7,* 181–190.

Zayas, L. H., & Solari, F. (1994). Early childhood socialization in Hispanic families: Context, culture, and practice. *Professional Psychology: Research and Practice, 25,* 200–206.

3

Acculturation and the Mental Health of Latino Youths: An Integration and Critique of the Literature

Nancy A. Gonzales, George P. Knight, Antonio A. Morgan-Lopez, Delia Saenz, and Amalia Sirolli

Together the various Latino populations are one of the largest and fastest growing minority groups, comprising approximately 12% of the total U.S. population and 15% under the age of 20 (U.S. Census Bureau, 2001a). The Latino populations include a large number of immigrants and, relative to other ethnic groups, they are young; 39% of Latinos are under 20 years of age compared to 29% of all other Americans (U.S. Bureau of Census, 2001b). Thus, in the next decade, a growing and substantial proportion of U.S. youths will face the challenge of adapting to life as a member of a political minority group and in a host culture that may have different rules, different values, and a different language from their culture of origin. Several authors (e.g., Gonzales & Kim, 1997; Phinney, 1990; Szapocznik, & Kurtines, 1980) suggest the challenges created by these experiences represent a substantial risk for Latino youths and may lead to negative mental health outcomes such as depression, low self-esteem, or conduct problems, as well as negative life outcomes such as school failure, drug and alcohol abuse, and financial instability. To the extent this is true, acculturation will play an important role in determining the mental health and social service needs of a substantial segment of the U.S. population. A better understanding of the link between acculturation and mental health is therefore critical from a public health and public policy perspective (Knight, Gonzales, Birman, & Sirolli, in press).

As one of the most important intragroup characteristics of Latinos, acculturation involves the changes that result at both the group level and the individual psychological level from sustained contact between two or more distinct cultures (Berry, Trimble, & Olmedo, 1986). At the psychological level, acculturation may result in the gradual incorporation of cultural beliefs, values, behaviors, and language of the dominant society, as well as changes in one's sense of belonging to the host culture (Rogler, Cortes, & Malgady, 1991). The acculturation process also impacts on mental health–relevant variables including exposure to stressful life events, help-seeking behavior, family functioning, and subjective feelings of distress (Marín, 1992; Szapocznik & Kurtines, 1993; Vega, Gil, Warheit, Zimmerman, & Apospori, 1993). Consequently, it is not surprising that acculturation is often viewed as an important factor to consider in research on the psychological functioning and mental health of Latinos.

Despite the importance of this issue, relatively little is known about the impact of acculturation on Latino children's mental health. While there have been at least two major attempts to synthesize the literature on the relation of acculturation and mental health outcomes for Latinos, this literature has been based primarily on adult populations. Rogler et al. (1991) reviewed 30 publications in an attempt to synthesize findings on acculturation and mental health status. Their review highlighted a number of problems with the literature, including problems in how acculturation and mental health were assessed across studies, and in the formulations linking acculturation and mental health that precluded a meaningful integration.

There are several reasons why a separate review of child and adolescent studies on the topic is now warranted. First, there have been no prior efforts to synthesize the literature specifically for Latino youths. A review of this literature would be timely now because research with younger populations has increased in recent years. Much of the work has been published since Rogler et al. (1991) and has followed important advances in the theory and measurement of acculturation, which potentially address previous problems in the literature. Second, the process by which acculturation may impact mental health outcomes and the issues involved in studying these processes are likely to be different for children and adolescents than for adults. Children and adolescents are developing cognitively, socially, and emotionally in ways that make them more susceptible to acculturation-related pressures. Moreover, children's daily activities and cultural influences are embedded to a great extent within a number of social contexts, particularly their families, schools, and peer groups (Bronfenbrenner, 1979; Oetting, Donnermeyer, Trimble, & Beauvais, 1998). Whereas it is possible for adults to choose to remain relatively less acculturated and to interact primarily with individuals who share their cultural background and values, children have much less ability to control their exposure to cultural influences as they move from one social context to another. Thus, they are more likely than their parents to acculturate more rapidly; to be exposed to a greater variety of influences across their social worlds; and to experience incompatibilities in the cultural norms, values, and expectations to which they must adapt.

This chapter is based on a review of 34 empirical publications relevant to acculturation and either mental health or substance use among general population samples of Latino youths under the age of 18. Substance use was included because it represents an active area for research on acculturation and it reflects an important psychosocial outcome with obvious implications for mental health. Studies were included if they assessed alcohol or illicit substance use but not if they focused only on tobacco use. Table 3.1 lists the studies along with the Latino subgroups studied, the dimensions of acculturation or enculturation that were assessed, and the mental health or substance use outcomes. It is important to note that some of these studies are based on overlapping samples. Our review of these studies attempts to address the following questions: Is there evidence for an association between acculturation and mental health or substance use for Latino youth? Does the relationship between acculturation and mental health or substance use vary by developmental level, type of outcome, or for different Latino subgroups? What is the status of research in this area with respect to current theory on acculturation?

THEORETICAL PERSPECTIVES ON ACCULTURATION RESEARCH

According to recent theoretical developments, acculturation processes and phenomena occur at the macro- and the micro level, and they are multifaceted, multidirectional, and encompass bicultural and multicultural processes that unfold continuously over time (Berry et al., 1986; Marín, 1992). A full understanding of acculturation processes requires research designs and research measures that can account for such complexity. For example, numerous scholars (e.g., Cuellar, Arnold, & Maldonado, 1995; Félix-Ortiz, Newcomb, & Myers, 1994) recommend acculturation measures that assess multiple domains. Available measures most typically assess behaviors such as language use (e.g., English and Spanish) and food preferences, affiliation with nonethnic peers, feelings of identity and loyalty, and endorsement of cultural values, though other dimensions also may be important (Cuellar et al., 1995; Zane & Mak, 1999).

Acculturation theory also suggests that it is important to measure aspects of two or more cultures (e.g., host culture and ethnic culture) independently along these various dimensions (e.g., Berry et al., 1986; Birman, 1998; Cuellar, Arnold, & Maldonado, 1995). Bicultural models allow for the possibility that acculturation to the majority culture does not necessarily preclude retention of one's ethnic culture. In terms of language use, for example, an acculturating individual may learn to speak English while simultaneously losing his ability to speak Spanish, may retain and use Spanish language skills along with English, or may remain monolingual in Spanish. By assessing variation in relation to two or more cultures separately, it becomes possible to examine the

Table 3.1
Studies, Latino Subgroups, Acculturation and Enculturation Measures, and Outcomes Included in Review

Authors	Latino Groups Studied	Acculturation / Enculturation Measures	Outcomes Assessed
1. Bautista de Domanico, Crawford & Wolfe(1994)	Mexican American 10th graders; N=62	Bicultural identity	Self-esteem, psychological well-being
2. Bettes, Dusenbury, Kerner, James-Ortiz & Botvin (1990)	Puerto Rican & Dominican American adolescents; N=1131	Language preference	Alcohol and cigarette use
3. Birman (1998)	Latino immigrant adolescents in junior and senior high school (60% from El Salvador); N-123	Acculturation to American and Hispanic culture; biculturalism	School competence, peer competence, family competence, self-worth
4. *Brook, Whiteman, Balka & Cohen. (1997)	Puerto Rican adolescents (grades 7-10); N=600	Importance of ethnicity, familism	Cigarette, alcohol & marijuana use; delinquency
5. *Brook, Whiteman, Balka, Win, & Gursen (1998)	Puerto Rican adolescents (ages 16-24); N=555	Ethnic affiliation, language preference, familism	Legal and illicit drug use
6. Brooks, Stuewig, & LeCroy (1998)	Mexican American early adolescents; N-413	Language use	Substance use
7. Buriel, Calzada & Vasquez (1982)	Mexican American male adolescents (ages 13-16); N=81	Generation status	Delinquency
8. Carvajal, Photiades, Evans & Nash (1997)	Mexican American early adolescents (ages 11-14); N=448	Language use, ethnic peer preference	Cigarette, alcohol and marijuana use
9. Dumka, Roosa & Jackson (1997)	Mexican American 4th graders; N=121	ARSMA (mothers)	Depression, conduct problems
10. Felix-Ortiz & Newcomb (1995)	Mexican American adolescents (grades 9 & 10); N=516	Cultural familiarity, language preference, traditional family roles	Legal and illicit substance use

11. Franco (1983)	Mexican American children (grades 1,3,6,9,12); N=92	ARSMA	Self esteem, self concept
12. Fridrich & Flannery (1995)	Mexican American early adolescents (grades 6 & 7); N=274	Generational status, language preference	Delinquent behavior
13. *Gil & Vega (1996)	Cuban American & Nicaraguan American adolescents (grades 6 & 7); N=885	Acculturative stress	Self esteem
14. *Gil, Vega, & Dimas (1994)	Mixed Latino adolescents, predominantly Cuban (grades 6 & 7); N=4296	Language preference, acculturative stress, family pride	Self-esteem
15. Gowen, Hayward, Killen, Robinson, & Taylor (1999)	Unspecified Latino 9th graders; N=132	Language preference and length of residence	Body dissatisfaction, weight concerns, partial syndrome eating disorder
16. Hovey & King (1996)	Mexican American adolescents (ages 14-20); N=70	Generational status, language preference	Depression, suicidal ideation
17. Joiner & Kashubeck (1996)	Mexican American junior and senior high school students (ages 12-18); N=120	ARSMA	Anorexic and bulimic symptoms, body image ideal and dissatisfaction
18. Katragadda & Tidwell (1998)	Mexican American adolescents (grades 9-12); N=240	ARSMA	Depression
19. Knight, Virdin & Roosa (1994)	Mexican American early adolescents (ages 9-13); N=70	ARSMA (mothers)	Global self worth, depression, conduct problems
20. Martinez & Dukes (1997)	Multiethnic junior and senior high school students (unspecified Latinos); N=992	Ethnic identity	Self esteem, purpose in life, self confidence
21. Perez & Padilla (1980)	Mexican American adolescents (ages 9-17); N=339	Language use	Alcohol, marijuana and inhalant use
22. Phinney, Chavira & Tate (1995)	Mixed Latino 9th graders, mostly Mexican American; N=109	Ethnic identity	Self-esteem

(continued)

49

Table 3.1
(Continued)

23. Phinney, Cantu & Kurtz (1997)	Mixed Latino adolescents, mostly Mexican American (ages 15-17);N=372	Ethnic identity, American identity	Self-esteem
24. Pumariega (1986)	Unspecified Latino females (ages 16-18); N=138	Acculturation questionnaire	Eating attitudes
25. Rasmussen, Negy, Carlson, & Burns (1997)	Mexican American 8th graders; N=242	ARSMA short-form	depression, suicidal ideation, self esteem
26. *Rotheram-Borus (1989)	Multiethnic adolescent sample (grades 9 & 10); Total N=330 (28% Puerto Rican American)	Ethnic identity, peer reference group	self esteem, internalizing symptoms
27. *Rotheram-Borus (1990)	Multiethnic adolescent sample (grades 9 & 10); Total N=330 (30% Latino)	Reference group label	Self esteem, social competence
28. Rumbaut (1994)	Multiethnic adolescents (ages 12-17); N=5264	Familism, American preference	self esteem, depression
29. Samaniego & Gonzales (1999)	Mexican American early adolescents (grades 7 & 8); N=214	Generational status, language use	delinquency
30. Scheier, Botvin, Diaz & Ifill-Williams (1997)	Multiethnic 7th graders, 40% Latino unspecified; N=1815/1303	Ethnic identity	alcohol & marijuana use
31. *Vega, Gil, & Zimmerman (1993)	Cuban American early adolescents (grades 6 & 7); N=1700	Language preference	alcohol and cigarette use
32. *Vega, Gil, Warheit, Zimmerman & Apospori (1993)	Cuban American early adolescents (grades 6 & 7); N=1843	Acculturative stress (language conflicts, acculturation conflicts, perceived discrimination)	disposition to deviance, delinquent behavior
33. *Vega, Khoury, Zimmerman, Gil, & Warheit (1995)	Multiethnic adolescents, 50% Cuban American (ages 10-16); N=2360	Language preference	problem behaviors
34. Wall, Power, & Arbona (1993)	Mexican American adolescents (grades 9-12); N=244	Generational status, language preference, ethnic loyalty	susceptibility to delinquent peer pressure

* sample overlaps with other study included in review

effects of acculturation as more than a linear progression from Latino oriented to American oriented. It becomes possible to examine the effects of multiple adaptational options, including biculturality in which individuals may speak the language and feel equally confident with both cultures, hold values and respect the norms of both cultures, and retain a dual cultural identity.

Implicit to a bicultural model is the notion that exposure to the ethnic culture is equally important to an understanding of how Latino youths adapt to the whole of their cultural experiences. In their work on ethnic identity development, Knight, Bernal, Cota, Garza, and Ocampo (1993) focus on the dual processes of acculturation and enculturation; whereas acculturation has typically referred to the processes of learning about and adapting to the host culture, enculturation is the process of learning about and adapting to one's ethnic culture. For developing youths, acculturation is largely the result of contact with the host culture in the form of interactions with majority members at school and in the community, including experiences with the mainstream media and television. Enculturation is largely the result of the socialization experiences of the youth within the family and ethnic community. That is, the family and ethnic community communicate beliefs, values, traditions, and language associated with the ethnic culture to the child. In general, these two processes are most often occurring simultaneously to jointly determine the youth's social identity status. A complete understanding of the impact of acculturation on mental health outcomes probably requires a full examination of the entire social system in which the youth exists. Thus, when we review findings on the effects of acculturation in the following section, we include findings relevant to both acculturation and enculturation whenever possible.

The foregoing are critical issues that are likely to have a substantial impact on whether and how acculturation predicts psychosocial outcomes for Latinos and other minority populations. In reviewing the empirical literature on the relationship between acculturation and mental health variables, we also review the extent to which these issues are addressed in the literature. Our intention is to describe the current state of the art in this evolving area of research and make recommendations for advancing the field to the next level of inquiry.

EMPIRICAL EVIDENCE LINKING ACCULTURATION, MENTAL HEALTH, AND SUBSTANCE USE

We restricted our search to empirical papers published between 1980 and 2000 to reduce variability caused by large differences over time in patterns of immigration, the demographic profile of the United States, and the political climate surrounding immigration issues. Moreover, the bulk of the literature on acculturation with Latino youths has been published in the last 10 years. Among the 34 studies we identified, 10 examined the effects of acculturation on externalizing outcomes (e.g., delinquency, conduct problems, illegal behavior), 9 on substance use (alcohol and illicit substances), 7 on depression or internalizing symptoms, and 3 on eating disorder symptoms; 13 examined the relation of acculturation-related domains and measures of general self-worth or self-esteem. All studies are based on U.S. Latino groups; we did not include studies that examined differences between Latinos and Anglos nor did we include studies comparing U.S. Latinos with youths living in Latin American countries, though such comparisons have often been used to make inferences about the effects of acculturation. Studies that sampled non-Latino ethnic groups were only included if they conducted analyses separately for Latinos in general or at least one specific Latino subgroup. The overwhelming majority of studies are based on adolescent samples, primarily junior high school and high school samples.

Though the majority of articles refer explicitly to acculturation, others examine related dimensions such as ethnic identity or generation status. Several studies also included measures of acculturative stress that assess the extent to which participants have experienced stressors, such as language barriers, cultural conflicts with nonethnic individuals, and conflicts with family members. These studies were included but not because we view acculturative stress as a dimension of acculturation/enculturation. Acculturative stress is a related phenomenon, experienced by some but not all acculturating individuals, that reveals important information about the underlying experiences and processes by which acculturation may lead to difficulties for particular individuals.

Though we searched for research relevant to all Latino subgroups, a majority of studies focused on Mexican Americans (53%), followed by Cuban Americans (15%) and Puerto Ricans (12%); however, the proportion of research on Cuban Americans is misleading because all five studies are based on the same sample of adolescents living in Dade County, Florida. Currently, these three Latino subgroups comprise approximately 64%, 5%, and 11% of the Latino population, respectively. Of those studies that included multiple Latino groups, most conducted separate analyses by group or conducted analyses on the full sample after demonstrating a lack of differences across groups. Only a few studies failed to specify the particular Latino subgroup sampled. Thus, unlike Rogler et al. (1991), we found much greater attention to intragroup variability and less of a tendency toward "ethnic gloss" or overly generalized labels when defining study samples. This is important because the various Latino subgroups differ in important ways, such as socioeconomic status and education and migration patterns, which may impact acculturation and enculturation processes. Subgroup differences in prevalence rates for problems, such as depression and substance use, also have been reported (Gonzales & Kim, 1997; Roberts & Sobhan, 1992).

With some notable exceptions, most studies were restricted to a test of the main effects of acculturation. That is, most studies provide a simple test (typically a correlation) of whether more or less acculturated youths have more problems. Though we believe this is a limitation, and we discuss this limitation in subsequent sections, the following review section is devoted primarily to a summary of these main effect findings. As will be shown, these findings vary depending on the particular mental health or substance use outcome targeted, and depending on which acculturation or enculturation dimensions are assessed.

Global Indicators of Acculturative Status: Language and Generation

The majority of studies used a measure of acculturation such as the Acculturation Rating Scale for Mexican Americans (ARSMA; Cuellar, Arnold, & Maldonado, 1995) or a measure with similar items based predominantly or exclusively on language use or language preference, often used in combination with generation status. Four of these studies examined the link between acculturation and problem behaviors for Mexican Americans and showed increased involvement in delinquent activity and greater susceptibility to antisocial peers (ethnicity of peers unspecified) among more acculturated adolescents (Buriel, Calzada, & Vasquez, 1982; Fridrich & Flannery, 1995; Samaniego & Gonzales, 1999; Wall, Power, & Arbona, 1993). This pattern was supported even when based solely on generation differences or nativity (U.S. versus foreign born). In a large, economically diverse sample of 6th- and 7th-grade Cuban males, Vega, Gil, Warheit et al. (1993) also reported a link between generation status and delinquent behavior. In another study based on this same sample, Vega and colleagues also found a positive relationship between aspects of acculturative stress and problem behavior (Vega, Khoury, Zimmerman, Gil, & Warheit, 1995); adolescent reports of acculturative stress, including language conflicts, acculturation conflicts, and perceived discrimination, predicted total number of parent- and teacher-reported problems, as well as scores in the clinical caseness range, after controlling for family education and income. Only two studies failed to support a relationship between higher levels of acculturation and higher levels of child deviance, however these studies assessed acculturation level of parents and not the children themselves (Dumka, Roosa, & Jackson, 1997; Knight, Virdin, & Roosa, 1994).

A total of four studies found higher rates of alcohol and drug use, including more frequent use, use of greater quantities, higher rates of lifetime use, and use of more serious substances among more acculturated adolescents (Brook, Whiteman, Balka, Win, & Gursen, 1998; Félix-Ortiz & Newcomb, 1995; Perez & Padilla, 1980; Vega, Gil, & Zimmerman, 1993). One study found that a combination of language used at home and school and language used by the media (radio and television) was associated with psychosocial risks leading to increased substance use, but only for males (Brooks, Stuewig, & LeCroy, 1998). The positive relation between higher acculturation and substance involvement was supported for Puerto Rican, Cuban American, and Mexican American adolescents and from early through late adolescence.

Only three studies failed to find a relation between higher acculturation level and substance use. Bettes, Dusenbury, Kerner, James-Ortiz, and Botvin (1990) found no relation between acculturation and alcohol or cigarette use in a combined sample of Dominican and Puerto Rican adolescents. However, acculturation was based solely on responses to two items about language use and ethnicity, and socioeconomic status and acculturation were highly confounded in the sample. Carvajal, Photiades, Evans, and Nash (1997) also failed to find an effect for language use, but this study used future intentions to use as the outcome criterion for a relatively young adolescent sample and was restricted on the language dimensions because it was limited primarily to second- and third-generation Latinos (predominantly Mexican American). Restriction of range on acculturation measures, produced when study participants are sampled predominantly at the higher or lower extremes of acculturation, was a problem in many of the studies we reviewed. Finally, Brook, Whiteman, Balka, & Cohen (1997) found no relation between two dimensions of enculturation—the importance of one's ethnicity and the cultural value of familism—on drug use or delinquency. However, in a subsequent study, Brook et al. (1998) showed that these variables interact with other risk factors to predict adolescent delinquency and drug use.

Two studies directly examined the relationship between acculturation level and depressive symptomatology, using standard measures of both (Hovey & King, 1996; Katragadda & Tidwell, 1998). Both studies used the ARSMA to assess acculturation levels of predominantly Mexican American adolescents and found no relation to self-reported symptoms of depression. Generation status also failed to show a relation for one of these studies. On the other hand, both of these studies showed a positive relation between dimensions of acculturative stress and depression. Moreover, Rumbaut (1995) found English-language competence was related to lower depression for Latino high school students, and Rasmussen, Negy, Carlson, and Burns (1997) showed that higher scores on the ARSMA (higher acculturation) predicted suicidal ideation among predominantly Mexican American eighth graders after controlling for depression and self-esteem. Finally, as we will discuss, two studies found an empirical link between depression and parent acculturation level. Together these studies suggest that the acculturation–depression link, if it exists, is not straightforward.

The relation of acculturation to self-esteem also has been mixed for Latino youths, showing no relation for Mexican American schoolchildren in one study (Franco, 1983), and a positive relation for Cuban but not Nicaraguan adolescents in another (Gil & Vega, 1996). Earlier studies, not included in our review, also showed a quadratic relationship between successive generations and self-esteem, with second-generation youths having higher levels than either first or third generation (Kagan & Knight, 1979; Knight & Kagan, 1977). As with depression, however, acculturative stress has been more consistent in predicting lower self-esteem for Latino youths (Gil & Vega, 1996). Also, Birman (1998) examined measures of both acculturation and enculturation on perceived competence of Latino refugee adolescents. By examining these relations across a range of life spheres and contexts, the findings showed differential effects of these two aspects of cultural adaptation that varied depending on the different life contexts in which youths were engaged. For example, whereas Hispanicism (i.e., high on enculturation) predicted positive self-perceptions of competence with Latino peers and Americanism (i.e., high on acculturation) predicted positive self-perceptions of competence with non-Latino peers, perceived family competence was predicted by Americanism and not Hispanicism. Neither Hispanicism nor Americanism predicted general self-worth, but biculturalism (being high on both) was positively related to general self-worth.

Eating disorders are widely thought to be "culture-bound" phenomenon, determined in part by the overemphasis on thinness in westernized cultures, particularly the United States. Consequently, there has been a lot of speculation about whether the various U.S. immigrant populations should evidence an increase in prevalence of eating disorders as they become more Americanized and internalize American cultural ideals regarding beauty and weight. Three studies examined the relation of acculturation to outcomes associated with eating disorders in samples of junior and senior high schools students and found mixed results for this hypothesis. Pumariega (1986) reported a positive relation between acculturation level and problematic attitudes toward eating and weight with a sample of Hispanic high school students (specific ethnic groups were not specified). In contrast, Joiner and Kashubeck (1996) found no relation between acculturation and eating attitudes using the same measures with a slightly younger sample of Mexican American adolescents. Gowen, Hayward, Killen, Robinson, and Taylor (1999) also failed to find a relation between acculturation and either weight concerns or body dissatisfaction, but found that acculturation was positively associated with structure-interview–defined partial syndrome eating disorders in ninth-grade Hispanic girls (subgroup unspecified). Studies with young adult samples have reported similarly mixed findings (Jane, Hunter, & Lozzi, 1999; Lester & Petrie, 1995). Overall the limited evidence suggests that if there is a relation between acculturation and eating disorders, it varies depending on how eating symptomatology is assessed and on other factors, such as education level, which have varied across studies.

Cultural Identity

A number of studies construed the relationship between acculturation and mental health status according to concepts such as ethnic identity, choice of reference group (e.g., ethnic, mainstream, bicultural), or one's sense of belonging or loyalty to a particular cultural group. Though there are important differences between these aspects of identity and between the scales constructed to measure them, we will use the term "cultural identity" to refer collectively to such measures. The term is consistent with Oetting et al.'s study (1998) that defines cultural identity as the extent to which a person feels involved in a culture along with their feeling that they are invested in that culture or have a stake in that culture. In line with bicultural models that account for both acculturative and enculturative processes, and consistent with the extensive work of Phinney (e.g., Phinney, 1992; Phinney, Cantu, & Kurtz, 1997), cultural identity can include those aspects of identification with one's ethnic culture (ethnic identity) and identification with the mainstream culture (mainstream identity). However, most studies focus exclusively on ethnic identity, thus providing much of the limited evidence available on the link between enculturation and psychological functioning.

Though mainstream identity is seldom included in studies on the effects of ethnic identity, it is widely believed that ethnic identity and mainstream identity should both have mental health–promoting effects and that a bicultural identity (high on both) should be most adaptive. In support, the available studies focusing on self-esteem have consistently found a positive relation between ethnic identity and self-esteem (Martinez & Dukes, 1997; Phinney et al., 1997; Phinney, Chavira, & Tate, 1995). These findings are not surprising because they converge with a recent meta-analysis that found a moderate relationship between ethnic identity and self-esteem that was robust across ethnicities, genders, and age groups (Bat-Chava & Steen, 2000). However, evidence for the effects of mainstream cultural identity or bicultural identity is not as strong. Phinney et al. (1997), for example, found that ethnic identity predicted higher self-esteem for three distinct ethnic groups, including Latinos, whereas mainstream identity was only predictive for White students.

We found only two studies that purported to assess bicultural identity and these studies provided mixed support for the positive effects of biculturalism. Bautista de Domanico, Crawford, & Wolfe (1994) asked Mexican American high school students to respond to questions about six dimensions of acculturation and used their responses to categorize them as bicultural, primarily U.S., or primarily Mexican oriented. In comparison to the other groups, the bicultural students reported greater self-esteem, ability to socialize in diverse settings, and psychological well-being. Rotheram-Borus (1990) also categorized a sample of Latino students (subgroups unspecified) based on their answers to two questions about their cultural identity and found bicultural identity was not related to self-esteem, social competence, or grades.

The few studies that examined ethnic identity in relation to other outcomes are not as consistent as those that focused on self-esteem. For example, a measure of the importance of one's ethnicity was related to lower levels of delinquency in one study (Brook et al., 1997). In contrast, Rotheram-Borus (1989) showed that ethnic identity achievement—having a clear sense of one's ethnicity and the importance of ethnicity—was related to increased problem behavior, including increased delinquency. Also, in one study that used adolescents' own reference-group choices to assess cultural identity, Rotheram-Borus (1990) found that Latinos who chose mainstream (versus bicultural or ethnically identified) reported fewer behavior problems.

Regarding the link between cultural identity and substance use, previous research, including studies with adults, has been notably inconsistent. Some have found ethnic identity to be associated with decreased drug use (e.g., Burnam, Hough, Karno, Escobar, & Telles, 1987) whereas others have found a positive relationship (e.g., Markides, Krause, & Mendes de Leon, 1988). In studies of bicultural students, some have found a positive relationship with drug use (e.g., Amaro, Whitaker, Coffman, & Hereen, 1990) and others have not (Szapocznik & Kurtines, 1980). However, a group of recent studies suggest that ethnic identity may be best conceptualized as a protective factor in relation to substance use or stage of drug use. In a study of Puerto Rican adolescents living in East Harlem, New York City, Brook et al. (1998) found U.S. birth was positively related to the stage of drug use, preferring Spanish to English was inversely related to drug use, but ethnic identity was unrelated to late adolescents' drug stage. However, when ethnic identity was examined in interaction with other risk and protective factors for drug use, it was shown to protect against the effects of drug-related personal risks, family drug tolerance and modeling, peer deviant attitudes and modeling, and drug availability in predicting stage of drug use. The protective effect of viewing drugs as harmful also interacted with and was enhanced by ethnic identity factors, including a sense of attachment to one's ethnic group and identification with Puerto Rican friends, leading to a lower stage of drug use. Similar interactive effects were found by Félix-Ortiz and Newcomb (1995) in a study predicting frequency and quantity of drug and alcohol use among predominantly Mexican American adolescents in Los Angeles, and by Scheier, Botvin, Diaz, and Ifill-Williams (1997) in a prospective study of risk factors predicting a seventh to eighth grade increase in substance use among Latino youths in New York City. According to several scholars (e.g., Oetting et al., 1998; Schinke, Moncher, Palleja, Zayas, & Schilling, 1988) these interactive patterns are indicative of the complexity of relationships that need to be considered when examining the association of ethnic identity and drug use. These findings also suggest that inconsistencies in earlier findings may be attributed to the fact that most studies have been restricted to the examination of main effects. Interactive effects also have been reported for other enculturation domains, such as familism (Brook et al., 1998) and family pride (Gil, Vega, & Dimas, 1994) and may explain the failure of previous studies to detect main effects.

Acculturation of Parent

In contrast to findings based on acculturation of children, three studies assessed the acculturation level of Mexican American mothers and showed no relation to parents' or children's self-report of externalizing (Dumka et al., 1997; Knight et al., 1994; Vega et al., 1995). On the other hand, two of these studies found evidence for a link between mother's acculturation and her child's depression. Although these studies used identical measures of both acculturation and depression, one of these studies found that high acculturation levels predicted increased depressive symptoms (Knight et al., 1994), while the other found that high acculturation was associated with fewer depressive symptoms (Dumka et al., 1997). These differences might reflect uncontrolled socioeconomic factors that varied between the two studies. Acculturation has been shown to have quite distinct and even opposite effects on psychosocial variables such as parenting behavior, depending on whether socioeconomic status is parceled out (Gonzales, Barr, & Formoso, 1997). Such contradictory findings also may have resulted from differences in acculturation levels represented in the sample; one study was limited to predominantly immigrant and unacculturated Mexican American mothers (restriction of range problem), while the other study included predominantly more acculturated mothers. Other studies suggest differential effects of acculturation for high versus low acculturation groups and for immigrant versus nonimmigrant samples (Buriel, 1988; Carvajal et al., 1997; Vega et al., 1995; Wall et al., 1993).

A few studies assessed acculturation levels of both parents and adolescents and, in so doing, revealed differential effects of parent versus adolescent acculturation levels. For example, Gil and Vega (1996) found that adolescent acculturation level was associated with increased self-esteem for Nicaraguan adolescents whereas maternal acculturation level was associated with lower self-esteem for this group. Parents' acculturation levels also have been differentially related to educational outcomes. While length of residency has been associated with decreased academic performance for Latino students (Fernandez & Nielsen, 1986; Rumbaut, 1995), length of parents' residency has been associated with higher levels of academic performance (Portes & MacLeod, 1996).

Though only a few studies assessed acculturation for more than one family member, two points are worth mentioning on this issue. First, parent and child acculturation indicators clearly reflect distinct processes and certainly cannot be combined into a single index. The meaning of each and the mechanisms by which each impact children's development are likely to be quite distinct, despite the fact that parent and child acculturation levels should correlate. For most youths, parents are the primary socializing agents responsible for the ethnic socialization or enculturation of Latino youths. Accordingly, parent acculturation should be of central concern in attempts to understand the dual processes of acculturation and enculturation and their impact on children's adjustment. Though a few studies have examined acculturation-related differences in parenting attitudes and practices, and in family processes as a function of mothers' acculturation level (Gutierrez, Sameroff, & Karrer, 1988; Rueschenberg & Buriel, 1989; Sabogal, Marín, Otero-Sabogal, Marín, & Perez-Stable, 1987), few studies have then linked these processes to children's acculturation and psychosocial adjustment. The role of fathers' acculturation level has been ignored altogether.

Second, there is great interest in the theoretical literature with the impact of discrepancies in rates of acculturation between parents and adolescents. In the widely cited treatment research of Szapocznik and his colleagues (e.g.,

Szapocznik & Kurtines, 1993; Szapocznik, Kurtines, Santisteban, & Rio, 1990), it has been suggested that intergenerational differences emerge when younger and second-generation Cubans acculturate at a faster rate and have greater participation in the host culture than older and first-generation Cuban parents, particularly unacculturated mothers, who maintain more intense participation in the ethnic culture. As they become Americanized and move away from their roots, youngsters may reject their parents and their culture of origin, giving rise to serious family conflicts, loss of the emotional bond between parents and children, and adolescents' rejection of parental authority (Szapocznik & Kurtines, 1993; Szapocznik, Scopetta, & King, 1978). These processes are expected, in turn, to predict problem behaviors such as delinquency and substance use.

As a step toward understanding these culturally based conflicts, Szapocznik's group has developed measures of acculturation, which assess cultural characteristics such as language preference and usage, customs, and preferences for Cuban or Anglo American idealized lifestyles (Szapocznik et al., 1978). Using such measures, they examined the acculturation scores of Cuban adolescent children and their parents and found that the greatest acculturation disparities occur between sons and their mothers. However, it is important to note here that while these researchers documented the presence of acculturation disparities, they have not documented that it is these disparities that lead to psychological or family problems. Moreover, while several studies have assessed the presence of intergenerational conflict and have shown that it predicts poor mental health outcomes for a variety of Latino groups, neither the conflicts nor the mental health outcomes have been linked empirically to parent–child discrepancies on acculturation- or enculturation-related dimensions. This is surprising given the strong interest in this issue in the Latino family literature.

General Summary of Findings

The most consistent picture that emerges from this literature is a pattern of increased problematic behaviors, including increased rates of delinquency and substance use among more acculturated Latino adolescents. These problems were all found to be more prevalent for Latino youths who are born in the United States relative to their immigrant peers, for those who speak English more than Spanish, and, to a lesser extent, for those who are more similar behaviorally and attitudinally to their Anglo peers. This pattern is further supported by research that shows decreased academic performance, higher dropout rates, increased use of tobacco, and greater involvement in risky sexual behavior among more acculturated Latino youths (Epstein, Botvin, & Diaz, 1998; Ford & Norris, 1993; Rumbaut, 1995). A number of hypotheses, too numerous to list in total, have been offered to account for these findings. For example, increased problems among more acculturated Latino youths have been attributed to their increased vulnerability to the pressures of discrimination and minority status, decreased adherence to cultural values and

attitudes that protect against internalization of negative stereotypes and prejudices, disruptions in traditional practices that hold Latino families and communities together, increased conflict between more acculturated Latino
youths and parents, and increased exposure and vulnerability to deviant peer
models. Incidentally, strong empirical evidence is greatly lacking about
whether these mediational processes are associated with both acculturation
and mental health or substance use and whether these processes account for
the links between acculturation and these problem outcomes.

Evidence regarding the link between acculturation and other mental health
outcomes is much less conclusive, largely due to a lack of research with Latinos that focus on outcomes other than delinquency and substance use. The
paucity of available studies on depression for Latino youths is striking, particularly given evidence that some Latino groups, especially Mexican Americans,
may have higher rates of depression relative to non-Hispanic White and other
minority groups (Knight et al., 1994; Roberts & Sobhan, 1992). The available
literature suggests little, if any, consistent effects of acculturation on depression, self-esteem, or eating disorders. On the other hand, there is evidence for
increased depressive symptoms and lower self-esteem among adolescents exposed to more acculturation-related stressors (Hovey & King, 1996; Vega et
al., 1993a). Clearly some youths experience difficulties during the acculturation process and these difficulties are related to a host of psychosocial problems. Unfortunately, the available literature does not identify why some
acculturating youths will have such problems while many others will not.

Though ethnic identity was related to increased self-esteem, it showed a
more mixed relation to mental health and substance use. The emerging evidence suggests that ethnic identity may operate as a protective factor in predicting substance use. Future research should focus on how ethnic identity
moderates the impact of risk and protective factors in other areas, such as
delinquency and depression. Greater attention to interactive effects might
help to account for inconsistencies across studies examining the effects of ethnic identity as well as other aspects of acculturation and enculturation.

Given substantial diversity across the Latino groups and the lack of a sizable
body of literature for any single group, it is not possible to draw conclusions
about differential effects of acculturation based on country of origin. The
current literature also provides little information about developmental or age-
related differences in the effects of acculturation because it is almost exclusively
limited to adolescence. On one hand, an adolescent bias makes sense because
many acculturation-intensifying developmental processes, such as identity and
autonomy development, become heightened during adolescence. Also, acculturation influences are likely to be more pronounced as youths spend more
time with peers outside the family context during adolescence; and problems
such as substance use, eating disorders, delinquency, and depression also become more salient during adolescence. On the other hand, lack of information
for younger children limits our understanding of acculturation as a develop-

mental phenomenon. Knowledge about when acculturation-based differences begin to emerge would be extremely useful in suggesting mechanisms of influence and in making decisions regarding the timing of interventions and policies related to acculturation and enculturation.

CORRESPONDENCE BETWEEN THEORY AND RESEARCH

While there have been significant advances in our thinking about the influence of acculturation and enculturation, as reflected in the relatively rich theoretical writing on this topic, our empirical understanding of these processes has been much slower. It is likely that the weaknesses in the empirical database regarding acculturation and enculturation are the results of several limitations in this research literature. Furthermore, these limitations are likely the result of the complexity of issues caught up in the study of these processes. In the following sections, we discuss how the current literature has addressed four critical issues that have emerged in the theoretical writing on acculturation. In doing so, we highlight particular problems with existing research that severely limit our understanding of the role of acculturation and enculturation as processes that impact the psychological well-being of Latino children. We then close with recommendations for advancing the literature beyond its current state.

Acculturation and Enculturation Are Multidimensional Processes

Despite widespread agreement in the theoretical literature regarding the multidimensional nature of acculturation, the majority of studies assessed a narrow range of behavioral indicators, often only focused on language skills. Furthermore, even when multiple dimensions were assessed, the scoring procedures often ignored the multidimensional nature by combining all dimensions into a single index. As frequently discussed in the theoretical literature (e.g., Cuellar, Arnold, & Gonzalez, 1995; Cuellar, Arnold, & Maldonado, 1995; Phinney, 1992), the continuing lack of a multidimensional approach is a serious limitation from a measurement perspective and because it restricts the type and complexity of effects that can be examined.

Studies that rely on language ability or language preference as a measure of acculturation do so under the assumption that language is a valid measure or at least a reliable proxy measure. Undoubtedly, language is one of the most easily measured dimensions of acculturation, particularly when scales simply ask respondents to indicate what language they use or prefer to use in various social settings. And, the use of language as a shorthand measure for evaluating acculturation is supported by results from factor analyses of multidimensional scales, in which items dealing with language preference and ability tend to account for the majority of variance in the factor. However, since the available scales have typically been dominated by language items with inadequate assessment of other domains, such findings are not surprising. Further, although language retention may well be the single most important component in acculturation, it does not wholly represent the acculturation process.

By attending primarily to language, we may be missing other important aspects of acculturation. Marín (1992) suggests that acculturation occurs at three levels of superficiality: (a) the lowest level being changes in the learning of facts about one's cultural history as well as changes in the consumption of foods and use of media; (b) the second level being changes in central behaviors that are at the core of the person's social life such as language use; and (c) the least superficial and most significant level being changes in values and norms that prescribe the person's worldviews and interaction patterns. Similarly, Gordon (1964) suggested that acculturation to a new culture occurs with respect to language first, followed by behavioral participation, and identification with the new culture occurring only later, perhaps only in the next generation. Marín (1992) posed the question of whether, by concentrating on the more superficial changes (e.g., media language use and personal language use) produced by acculturation, we are dealing with highly unreliable estimates of an important personal process.

The preponderance of language and the underrepresentation of other dimensions in the measurement scales also may result in a skewed assessment of an individual's acculturation and in an inaccurate understanding of how it relates to mental health. The various domains of culture change, such as language, values, and affiliations, do not necessarily change at the same pace nor do they impact on youths' social and emotional functioning in the same manner (Cuellar, Nyberg, Maldonado, & Roberts, 1997). For example, Félix-Ortiz and Newcomb (1995) examined multiple components of acculturation and adolescents' use of alcohol and illicit drugs. They found differential effects depending on the type of drug use, gender, and the particular aspect of acculturative status. Certain components were associated with increased drug use (e.g., defensive Latino activism), whereas others were associated with decreased drug use (e.g., traditional family role expectations). A unidimensional measure of acculturation that is distilled into a single score could not capture the complexity of these relationships and may account for conflicting results found across studies.

Even more problematic in the literature is the common practice of using generation status as the sole marker of acculturation or combining generation status with other cultural dimensions to assess acculturation level. Generation status is a demographic variable that is confounded with other processes that are related to one's nativity and immigration history. Observed differences in mental health status between generations could well signify differences such as the immigration experience, the historical period covering the life span, stage of life cycle, social mobility, and socioeconomic status. A few studies have examined generation status and language use as separate indicators, allowing for examination of unique effects. For example, Adams,

Astone, Nunez-Womack, and Smodlaka (1994) found that immigrant status and English-language proficiency uniquely predicted higher academic achievement. As this case illustrates, it would be misleading to combine English proficiency and nonimmigrant (vs. immigrant) status into a single index because they each have unique and, in this case, opposite effects. As we will discuss later, it may also be inaccurate to examine the effects of English-language proficiency on academic achievement without also examining the role of Spanish-language proficiency.

A number of studies also have shown that generation status moderates the effects of acculturation and other risk and protective factors associated with psychosocial functioning. For example, Wall et al. (1993) examined English-language use as a marker for acculturation and found that it was significant in predicting susceptibility to antisocial peer pressure for first-generation but not for second- or third-generation Mexican American adolescents. Buriel (1988) found that Spanish-language use was predictive of academic achievement for third-generation but not first- or second-generation Mexican Americans. Vega et al. (1995) found that perceived discrimination and perceptions of closed society predicted increased problems and higher rates of caseness on the Child Behavior Checklist (Achenbach & Edelbrock, 1983) for U.S.–born but not foreign-born Cuban adolescents. These authors speculate that U.S.–born youths may be more sensitive than their foreign-born counterparts to the minority group definitions of self that likely emerge from specific interactions in the school, as well as other settings outside the home. In fact, there is growing empirical evidence that the adaptation process for American-born ethnic minorities is qualitatively different from immigrants, which suggests that the former may be a great source of error variance when assessed by acculturation measures (Rumbaut, 1995; Vega et al., 1995).

Acculturation and Enculturation Are Bicultural (or Multicultural) Processes

Few studies utilized a bicultural framework by measuring one's adaptation to the ethnic culture (enculturation) separately from their adaptation to the host culture (acculturation). Instead, the majority measured acculturation along a continuum representing the culture of origin at one extreme and the host culture at the other extreme. Even among studies that specifically set out to examine the effects of biculturalism, most studies that we reviewed assume that bicultural individuals simply fall at some midway point on a scale ranging from unacculturated to highly acculturated.

As one notable exception, Félix-Ortiz and Newcomb (1995) utilized a multidimensional, bicultural framework and tested models of influence that included complex interactions among these dimensions. For alcohol and inhalant use, they found that familiarity with Latino culture and American culture interacted to predict these types of drug use distinctly from language variables.

Marginal students, those low on both dimensions of familiarity, used alcohol more and in greater amounts. Biculturals used certain drugs less often than marginals, but used them more frequently than either Latino-identified or American-identified students. To account for these patterns, these researchers speculated that the stress of negotiating two cultural systems is associated with greater drug use or perhaps the biculturals may have adopted both American-type high-frequency and Mexican-type high-quantity drinking.

Due to interest in the issue of bilingualism, examples of bicultural analyses also are available in the education literature. For example, as previously mentioned, several studies have shown achievement is higher for adolescents who retain Spanish-speaking abilities (e.g., Ainsworth-Darnell & Downey, 1998; Rumbaut, 1995). However, when both English and Spanish ability are taken into account, a more complex pattern emerges. Rumberger and Larson (1998) found that bilingual students—those who are fluent in both English and Spanish—have better grades and complete more credits than either limited English-proficiency students or English-only students. As these examples illustrate, continuing failure to examine the separate and joint impact of ethnic and mainstream adaptations has prevented the opportunity to explore the complex dynamics of biculturalism.

Acculturation and Enculturation Are Socially Embedded Processes

Today's Latino children are likely to take many different pathways toward integrating into the larger society, depending on a variety of conditions and contexts, vulnerabilities, and resources (Portes & Zhou, 1993; Rumbaut, 1995). One path may result in nearly total integration or assimilation into the mainstream middle class; an alternative type of adaptation may lead to identification with the inner-city underclass; yet another may combine upward mobility and heightened ethnic awareness and identification with ethnic communities (Rumbaut, 1994, 1995). Such divergent modes have and will continue to occur. For example, fieldwork in the 1980s with Mexican-descent students in a California high school distinguished five different ethnic identity types—including recently arrived and longer-term Mexican immigrants who did especially well in school; Mexican Americans who had become totally integrated and adapted to the dominant culture; and the more acculturated but more troubled "Cholos" (a cultural subgroup often associated with gangs)—all of whom differed profoundly in their achievement and aspirations (Matute-Bianchi, 1986).

To understand how the acculturation process and its effects can vary greatly for different people (e.g., Berry, 1988), one must understand these processes as nested within youths' primary socializing contexts (Oetting et al., 1998). This point was made salient in the research on cultural identity that shows that the effects of strongly identifying with one's ethnic culture vary as a function of factors such as whether family members and peers provide models of drug use. As explained by Oetting et al. in their discussion of the potential protective role of cultural identity, identification with a cultural group cannot protect against substance use when the person is involved in subcultures that actually encourage substance use. Thus, research on acculturation and enculturation must incorporate other risk and protective factors relevant to the mental health and substance use trajectories of Latino youths and develop models that account for the particular behaviors, attitudes, and values to which youths are exposed in their families, schools, and communities.

Despite a few examples of contextually rich studies, particularly in the area of substance use, the current literature thus far has been simplistic in its examination of context. However, research on acculturative stress represents an important exception. An acculturative stress perspective suggests that individuals will be predisposed to social and emotional difficulties to the degree that they experience stress during the acculturation process (Gonzales & Kim, 1997; Vega et al., 1995). As suggested by Phinney (1990), Latinos and other groups of minority youths must cope with two salient types of acculturative pressures. First, they must cope with the conflict generated by the pressures of adapting to two different sets of cultural norms and values simultaneously, those transmitted by the culture of origin (through enculturation), and those transmitted by the host culture (through acculturation). Furthermore, they must cope with stereotyping and prejudice directed at them and to members of their group, experiences that, under certain conditions, can lead to negative views of self. However, depending on the social contexts in which these processes unfold for acculturating youths, some individuals will experience intense acculturative conflicts while others will not. Thus, research on acculturative stress has been important in identifying specific dimensions of acculturative stress experienced by immigrants and other Latino youths; by showing that acculturative stress predicts higher rates of depression, delinquency, and substance use even when acculturation levels do not; and by showing that acculturative stress may interact with acculturation level to predict some emotional and behavioral outcomes (Hovey & King, 1996; Vega et al., 1993a; Vega et al., 1995).

The individual's immediate social context also may determine the extent to which particular acculturative options are situationally adaptive and thus more or less likely to predict positive mental health outcomes. For example, an ethnic minority person existing in an overwhelmingly ethnic community may be well served to be highly enculturated. In contrast, such a person existing in a very integrated community is much more likely to be well served by being highly bicultural. This issue is relevant to the psychological concept of distinctiveness (Ethier & Deaux, 1994) and is illustrated by recent research on cultural identity, which has shown interactive effects of group identity with social context variables, such as the composition of one's school or neighborhood. This research has shown that ethnic identity is more salient and has a stronger effect on psychological well-being when minority group members are in an incongruent social environment than when they share their environment with similar others (Bat-Chava, Allen, Seidman, Aber, & Ventura, 1995). Thus, an understanding of the interaction between person-level variables (e.g., ethnic identity) and the situational context (e.g., demographic composition of the classroom or the local community) may allow for an increased understanding of the complex interplay of factors involved in predicting mental health outcomes.

As a whole, the current empirical literature has not accounted for the various ways in which the social context shapes youths acculturation and enculturation experiences and the impact of these experiences on their mental health status. For reasons previously outlined, the literature has largely ignored context. Indeed, in several important respects, the literature provides an especially skewed picture of context for Latino youths precisely because it has been conducted within very limited settings. Virtually all of the studies we found on the link between acculturation and both problem behaviors and substance use were conducted with low-income, inner-city samples. Thus, at best, the literature provides information relevant to acculturation and enculturation within a poor, urban context. As the Latino population continues to grow, Latino youths are becoming a visible presence in a wide variety of residential settings. The dual processes of acculturation and enculturation, and the mental health relevance of these processes, may well be quite different in non-urban and nonpoor settings.

Acculturation and Enculturation Processes Unfold Over Time

Finally, one of the most difficult limitations of the empirical literature is the near complete absence of research that even approximates assessing acculturation and enculturation as "processes." That is, acculturation and enculturation are processes of change and therefore require methodologies that are appropriate for assessing change (Bernal, 1996). Unfortunately, this research literature includes almost no longitudinal investigations attempting to assess the degree of cultural change individuals experience over increased exposure to the host culture and the socialization regarding the ethnic culture. With only a single exception (Brook et al., 1998), researchers investigating acculturation settled for single-point-in-time assessments (i.e., the measurement of acculturative status and/or ethnic identity) and assumed that these indices were acceptable indices of the respective processes. Given the incredible variability in the length and degree of exposure of individuals to the ethnic and host cultures, these static assessments may provide us with little or no information regarding the degree of cultural change.

Studying change in acculturation or enculturation over time might also help to disentangle issues of causality. Is it acculturation that "causes" some problems (e.g., delinquency), or is acculturation a consequence of greater delinquent peer involvement resulting from some other dimension of psychosocial functioning, such as poor family relations? This type of study could also shed light on the variables that predict increases in acculturation and enculturation. Although we know that demographic indices of exposure to the host culture (e.g., generation status, length of U.S. residence) relate to acculturation, very little is known about the mechanisms that lead immigrants and successive generations to maintain their culture of origin, or U.S.–born children to learn and value their culture of origin.

WHERE DO WE GO FROM HERE?

Despite recent theoretical advances, our understanding of the effects of acculturation and enculturation remains at the most rudimentary level. For research in this area to advance further, the next generation of research must keep pace with available theoretical conceptualizations and with continuing changes that take place for Latinos at the national level. One necessary first step is the refinement and appropriate use of measures that assess acculturation and enculturation as complex phenomena, including measures that adequately sample the major behavioral and attitudinal domains related to these processes, along with core cultural values that were almost totally absent from the studies we reviewed. Few such measures exist (for recent exceptions see Cuellar, Arnold, & Gonzalez, 1995; Félix-Ortiz et al., 1994). It is essential for future research to utilize a multidimensional framework to assess acculturation-related dimensions and move beyond simple marker variables. As our review illustrates, the various dimensions of culture may change at differential rates and they may operate independently and interactively to impact children's psychosocial functioning. Attention to the dual processes of acculturation and enculturation, and use of appropriate methods to examine their effects, are important to advance our understanding of the variety of adaptations Latino youths make in responding to bicultural influences and conflicts. In fact, as the United States becomes increasingly more multicultural, it may become necessary to assess adaptations and changes in relation to multiple, blended cultural influences.

Secondary to the acquisition of appropriate measures, future research should formulate and test more complex process models linking acculturation and key psychological and developmental outcomes, utilizing longitudinal designs to capture the underlying change processes that are inferred. Indeed, we believe the foregoing discussion advances one particularly critical point about how the current literature has been limited in its attempt to understand whether and how acculturation processes impact the social-psychological functioning of Latino children and adolescents. To date, most of the literature, whether focused on emotional, behavioral, or academic outcomes, has looked for main effects and, in so doing, has been limited to an overly simplistic question: Who has more problems, more- or less-acculturated youths? Analyses to address this question have often been pursued in the absence of a strong theory about how acculturation levels alone should predict poor outcomes.

On the other hand, our review did reveal some consistencies across studies that addressed this question. Global indicators of acculturation level, such as language use and generation status, do seem to account for a significant and, in some cases, substantial proportion of variance in behavioral outcomes such as delinquency and substance use. As such, these findings highlight an important epidemiological phenomenon. However, as only a starting point, these findings are still limited by the nature of the question being asked because they do not go beyond the description of general trends to inform about the underlying processes that mediate the link between acculturation and problematic youth behavior. Moreover, even in the case of delinquency and substance use, the findings have been inconsistent. And, for some outcomes and for some aspects of acculturation, the findings have been utterly contradictory. Such inconsistencies suggest that, if there are general trends to be found, they doubtless do not apply to all Latinos. Indeed, we believe what is needed in the literature is the development and evaluation of more complex models of the effects of acculturation, particularly models that look at the interactions among aspects of acculturation and enculturation with each other; these dimensions with demographic variables including socioeconomic status and generation status; and with other risk and protective factors within youths' primary socialization contexts.

In conceptualizing and testing such complex models, there are several processes that warrant inclusion and more careful scrutiny than the literature has thus far provided. For example, several theorists suggest that the family undergoes transformation as individual family members acculturate and that disruption at the family level place some children at increased risk for problematic outcomes (Szapocznik et al., 1990). A better understanding of how the family changes with acculturation and enculturation—in terms of core values such as *familismo* and *respeto*, their interaction patterns, and parenting practices—is critical to strengthen our understanding of Latino child development. Changes in parents, children, and siblings and the effects of these changes at each stage of the life cycle are of interest as are discrepancies in levels of acculturation and enculturation between family members. Children's developing social identities are also an area of theoretical interest. Many Latino youths must seek out and sustain a sense of possibilities for the self within social contexts (e.g., low education, under/unemployment, negative stereotypes) that do not afford construction of plausible futures in which conventional paths, such as school success, lead to occupational success in adulthood (Day, Borkowski, Punzo, & Howsepian, 1994; Oyserman & Markus, 1990). Moreover, during early adolescence when peer acceptance and group conformity are at a peak, the process of identity construction for Mexican American youths is heavily influenced by their association with culturally salient peer reference groups (Matute-Bianchi, 1986; Rotheram-Borus, 1990).

Our review showed that the effects of these identity processes are quite complex and may play a role in life choices about such matters as substance use and academic persistence that have a long-term psychological impact. More research is needed to better understand the emerging social identities and peer group choices of Latino youths, how these are shaped in response to the particular opportunities and challenges they face as ethnic minorities in varying social contexts, and the implication of these experiences and identity choices for subsequent mental health.

Finally, along with the major changes recommended throughout this chapter, future research should attend to numerous methodological limitations that have characterized research with Latinos in general. These include a predominant bias toward inner-city, poor samples; failure to account for effects related to socioeconomic status and nativity that confound our understanding of the effects of acculturation; and examination of the effects of acculturation with samples that are overly restricted on the primary variables of interest. By attending to the issues outlined in this chapter, we believe the next generation of research will be better positioned to address more interesting questions: Under what conditions is acculturation associated with increased levels of acculturative stress and poor mental health outcomes? Under what conditions is greater enculturation protective for children? Does biculturalism produce the most adaptive mental health profile and, if so, what factors promote or hinder biculturalism? Do intergenerational conflicts occur as the result of differential acculturation between parents and children and, if so, what family factors operate to either prevent or exacerbate such problems? Answers to such questions ultimately will prove more useful as an aid to public policy decisions and development of programs for Latino youths.

AUTHORS' NOTE

The authors wish to thank Khahn Dinh, Adam McCray, and Mark Roosa for their thoughtful input regarding this chapter.

REFERENCES

Achenbach, T., & Edelbrock, C. (1983). *Manual for the Child Behavior Checklist and Revised Child Behavior Profile*, Burlington: University of Vermont.

Adams, D., Astone, B., Nunez-Womack, E., & Smodlaka, I. (1994). Predicting the academic achievement of Puerto Rican and Mexican American ninth-grade students. *Urban Review, 26*(1), 1–14.

Ainsworth-Darnell, J. A. & Downey, D. B. (1998). Assessing the oppositional culture explanation for racial/ethnic differences in school performance. *American Sociological Review, 63*, 536–553.

Amaro, H., Whitaker, R., Coffman, G., & Heeren, T. (1990). Acculturation and marijuana and cocaine use: Findings from HHANES 1982–1984. *American Journal of Public Health, 80*, 54–60.

Bat-Chava, Y., Allen, L., Seidman, E., Aber, J. L. & Ventura, A. (1995). *Ethnic identity among African-American, White, and Latino urban adolescents: Nomothetic and idiographic approaches.* Unpublished manuscript.

Bat-Chava, Y., & Steen, E. M. (2000). *Ethnic identity and self-esteem: A meta-analytic review.* Manuscript under editorial review.

Bautista de Domanico, Y., Crawford, I., & Wolfe, A. S. (1994). Ethnic identity and self-concept in Mexican-American adolescents: Is bicultural identity related to stress or better adjustment? *Child and Youth Care Forum, 23*(3), 197–206.

Bernal, M. E. (1996). How did you do it? *Counseling Psychologist, 24*(2), 269–272.

Berry, J. W. (1988). Acculturation and psychological adaptation: A conceptual overview. In J. W. Berry and R. C. Annis (Eds.), *Ethnic psychology: Research and practice with immigrants, refugees, native peoples, ethnic groups, and sojourners.* Amsterdam: Swets & Zeitlinger.

Berry, J. W., Trimble, J. E., & Olmedo, E. L. (1986). Assessment of acculturation. In W. J. Lonner, J. W. Berry (Eds.), *Field methods in cross cultural research: Vol. 8. Cross cultural research and methodology series,* (pp. 291–324). Beverly Hills, CA: Sage.

Bettes, B. A., Dusenbury, L., Kerner, J., James-Ortiz, S., & Botvin, G. J. (1990). Ethnicity and psychosoial factors in alcohol and tobacco use in adolescence. *Child Development, 61,* 557–565.

Birman, D. (1998). Biculturalism and perceived competence of Latino immigrant adolescents. American *Journal of Community Psychology, 26*(3), 335–354.

Bronfenbrenner, U. (1979). *The ecology of human development: Experiments by nature and design.* Cambridge, MA: Harvard University Press.

Brook, J. S., Whiteman, M., Balka, E. B., & Cohen, P. (1997). Drug use and delinquency: Shared and unshared risk factors in African American and Puerto Rican adolescents. *Journal of Genetic Psychology, 158*(1), 25–39.

Brook, J. S., Whiteman, M., Balka, E. B., Win, P. T., & Gursen, M. D. (1998). Drug use among Puerto Ricans: Ethnic identity as a protective factor. *Hispanic Journal of Behavioral Sciences, 20*(2), 241–254.

Brooks, A. J., Stuewig, J., & LeCroy, C. W. (1998). A family based model of Hispanic adolescent substance use. *Journal of Drug Education, 28*(1), 65–86.

Buriel, R. (1988). Sociocultural correlates of achievement among three generations of Mexican American high school seniors. *American Educational Research Journal, 25*(2), 177–192.

Buriel, R., Calzada, S., & Vasquez, R. (1982). The relationship of traditional Mexican American culture to adjustment and delinquency among three generations of Mexican American male adolescents. *Hispanic Journal of Behavioral Sciences, 4*(1), 41–55.

Burnam, M. A., Hough, R. L., Karno, M., Escobar, J. I., & Telles, C.A. (1987). Acculturation and lifetime prevalence of psychiatric disorders among Mexican-Americans in Los Angeles. *Journal of Health and Social Behavior, 28,* 89–102.

Carvajal, S. C., Photiades, J. R., Evans, R. I., & Nash, S. G. (1997). Relating a social influence model to the role of acculturation in substance use among Latino adolescents. *Journal of Applied Social Psychology, 27,* 1617–1628.

Cuellar, I., Arnold, B., & Gonzalez, G. (1995). Cognitive referents of acculturation: Assessment of cultural constructs in Mexican Americans. *Journal of Community Psychology, 23,* 339–356.

Cuellar, I., Arnold, B., & Maldonado, R. (1995). Acculturation rating scale for Mexican Americans—II: A revision of the original ARSMA scale. *Hispanic Journal of Behavioral Sciences, 17*(3), 275–304.

Cuellar, I., Nyberg, B., Maldonado, R. E., & Roberts, R. E. (1997). Ethnic identity and acculturation in a young adult Mexican origin populations. *Journal of Consulting and Clinical Psychology, 25*(6), 535–549.

Day, J. D., Borkowski, J. G., Punzo, D., & Howsepian, B. (1994). Enhancing possible selves in Mexican American students. *Motivation and Emotion, 18*, 79–103.

Dumka L. E., Roosa, M. W., & Jackson, K. M. (1997). Risk, conflict, mother's parenting, and children's adjustment in low-income, Mexican immigrant, and Mexican American families. *Journal of Marriage and the Family, 59*, 309–323.

Epstein, J. A., Botvin, G. J., & Diaz, T. (1998). Linguistic acculturation and gender effects on smoking among Hispanic youth. *Preventive Medicine, 27*, 583–589.

Ethier, K. A., & Deaux, K. (1994). Change: Maintaining identification and responding to threat. *Journal of Personality and Social Psychology, 67*, 243–251.

Félix-Ortiz, M., & Newcomb, M. D. (1995). Cultural identity and drug use among Latino and Latina Adolescents. In G. J. Botvin (Ed.), *Drug abuse prevention with multi-ethnic youth* (pp. 147–165). Newbury Park, CA: Sage.

Félix-Ortiz, M., Newcomb, M. D., & Myers, H. (1994). A multidimensional scale of cultural identity for Latino and Latina adolescents. *Hispanic Journal of Behavioral Sciences, 16*(2), 99–115.

Fernandez, R. M., & Nielsen, F. (1986). Bilingualism and Hispanic scholastic achievement: Some baseline results. *Social Science Research, 15*, 43–70.

Ford, K., & Norris, A. E. (1993). Urban Hispanic adolescents and young adults: Relationship of acculturation to sexual behavior. *Journal of Sex Research, 30*(4), 316–323.

Franco, J. N. (1983). A developmental analysis of self-concecpt in Mexican American and Anglo school children. *Hispanic Journal of Behavioral Sciences, 5*(2), 207–218.

Fridrich, A. H., & Flannery, D. J. (1995). The effects of ethnicity and acculturation on early adolescent delinquency. *Journal of Child and Family Studies, 4*(1), 69–87.

Gil, A. G., & Vega, W. A. (1996). Two different worlds: Acculturation stress and adaptation among Cuban and Nicaraguan families. *Journal of Social and Personal Relationships, 13*(3), 435–456.

Gil, A. G., Vega, W. A., & Dimas, J. M. (1994). Acculturative stress and personal adjustment among Hispanic adolescent boys. *Journal of Community Psychology, 22*, 43–54.

Gonzales, N. A., Barr, A., & Formoso, D. (1997, June). *Acculturation and family process among Mexican American families.* Keynote address presented at the 1997 NIMH Family Research Consortium Meeting, San Antonio, Texas.

Gonzales, N. A., & Kim, L. S. (1997). Stress and coping in an ethnic minority context: Children's cultural ecologies. In S. A. Wolchik & I. N. Sandler (Eds.), *Handbook of children's coping: Linking theory and intervention. Issues in clinical child psychology* (pp. 481–511). New York: Plenum.

Gordon, M. M. (1964). *Assimilation in American life: The role of race, religion, and national origins.* New York: Oxford University Press.

Gowen, L. K., Hayward, C., Killen, J. D., Robinson, T. N., & Taylor, C. B. (1999). Acculturation and eating disorder symptoms in adolescent girls. *Journal of Research on Adolescence, 9*(1), 67–83.

Guttierrez, J., Sameroff, A. J., & Karrer, B. M. (1988). Acculturation and SES effects on Mexican-American parents' concepts of development. *Child Development, 59*, 250–255.

Hovey, J. D., & King, C. A. (1996). Acculturative stress, depression, and suicidal ideation among immigrant and second-generation Latino adolescents. *Journal of the American Academy of Child and Adolescent Psychiatry, 35*(9), 1183–1192.

Jane, D. M., Hunter, G. C., & Lozzi, B. M. (1999). Do Cuban American women suffer from eating disorders? Effects of media exposure and acculturation. *Hispanic Journal of Behavioral Sciences, 21*(2), 212–218.

Joiner, G., & Kashubeck, S. (1996). Acculturation, body image, self-esteem, and eating disorder symptomatology in adolescent Mexican American women. *Psychology of Women Quarterly, 20*(3), 419–435.

Kagan, S., & Knight, G. P. (1979). Cooperation–competition and self-esteem: A case of cultural relativism. *Journal of Cross-Cultural Psychology, 10*, 457–467.

Katragadda, C. P., & Tidwell, R. (1998). Rural Hispanic adolescents at risk for depressive symptoms. *Journal of Applied Social Psychology, 28*, 1916–1930.

Knight, G. P., Bernal, M. E., Cota, M. K, Garza, C. A., & Ocampo, A. (1993). Family socialization and Mexican American identity. In M. E. Bernal and G. P. Knight (Eds.), *Ethnic identity: Formation and transmission among Hispanics and other minorities.* (pp. 105–129). Albany: State University of New York Press.

Knight, G. P., Gonzales, N. A., Birman, D. & Sirolli, A. (in press). *Acculturation and encluturation among Hispanic youths.*

Knight, G. P., & Kagan, S. (1977). Acculturation of pro-social and competitive behaviors among second- and third-generation Mexican-American children. *Journal of Cross-Cultural Psychology, 8*, 273–283.

Knight, G. P, Virdin, L., & Roosa, M. (1994). Socialization and family correlates of mental health outcomes among Hispanic and Anglo-American families. *Child Development, 65*, 212–224.

Lester, R., & Petrie, T. A. (1995). Personality and physical correlates of bulimic symptomatology among Mexican American female college students. *Journal of Counseling Psychology, 42*(2), 199–203.

Marín, G. (1992). Issues in the measurement of acculturation among Hispanics. In K. F. Geisinger (Ed.), *Psychological testing of Hispanics.* Washington, DC: American Psychological Association.

Markides, K. S., Krause, N., & Mendes de Leon, C. F. (1988). Acculturation and alcohol consumption among Mexican Americans. *American Journal of Public Health, 78*, 1178–1181.

Martinez, R. O., & Dukes, R. L. (1997). The effects of ethnic identity, ethnicity, and gender on adolescent well-being. *Journal of Youth and Adolescence, 26*, 503–516.

Matute-Bianchi, M. E. (1986). Ethnic identities and patterns of school success and failure among Mexican-descent and Japanese-American students in a California high school: An ethnographic analysis. *American Journal of Education, 95*, 233–255.

Oetting, E. R., Donnermeyer, J. F., Trimble, J. E., & Beauvais, F. (1998). Primary socialization theory: Culture, ethnicity, and cultural identification: The links between culture and substance use. *Substance Use and Misuse, 33*(10), 2075–2107.

Oyserman, D., & Markus, H. (1990). Possible selves in balance: Implications for delinquency. *Journal of Social Issues, 46*, 141–157.

Perez, R., & Padilla, A. (1980). Correlates and changes over time in drug and alcohol use within a barrion population. *American Journal of Community Psychology, 8*, 621–636.

Phinney, J. S. (1990). Ethnic identity in adolescents and adults: Review of research. *Psychological Bulletin, 108*(3), 499–514.

Phinney, J. S. (1992). The multigroup ethnic identity measure: A new scale for use with diverse groups. *Journal of Adolescent Research, 7*(2), 156–176.

Phinney, J. S., Cantu, C. L., & Kurtz, D. A. (1997). Ethnic and American identity as predictors of self-esteem among African-American, Latino, and White adolescents. *Journal of Youth and Adolescence, 26*(2), 165–185.

Phinney, J. S., Chavira, V., & Tate, (1995). Parental ethnic socialization and adolescent coping with problems related to ethnicity. *Journal of Research on Adolescence, 5*(1), 31–53.

Portes, A., & MacLeod, D. (1996). Educational progress of children of immigrants: The roles of class, ethnicity, and school context. *Sociology of Education, 69*, 255–275.

Portes, A., & Zhou, M. (1993). The new second generations: Segmented assimilation and its variants. *Annals of the American Academy of Political and Social Science, 530*, 74–96.

Pumariega, A. J. (1986). Acculturation and eating attitudes in adolescent girls: A comparative and correlational study. *Journal of the American Academy of Child Psychiatry, 25*(2), 276–279.

Rasmussen, K. M., Negy, C., Carlson, R., & Burns, J. M. (1997). Suicide ideation and acculturation among low socioeconomic status Mexican American adolescents. *Journal of Early Adolescence, 17*(4), 390–407.

Roberts, R. E., & Sobhan, M. (1992). Symptoms of depression in adolescence: A comparison of Anglo, African, and Hispanic Americans. *Journal of Youth and Adolescence, 21*, 639–651.

Rogler, L. H., Cortes, D. E., & Malgady, R. G. (1991). Acculturation and mental health status among Hispanics: Convergence and new directions for research. *American Psychologist, 46*(6), 585–597.

Rotheram-Borus, M. J. (1989). Ethnic differences in adolescents' identity status and associated behavior problems. *Journal of Adolescence, 12*, 361–374.

Rotheram-Borus, M. J. (1990). Adolescents' reference-group choices, self-esteem, and adjustment. *Journal of Personality and Social Psychology, 59*(5), 1075–1081.

Rueschenberg, E., & Buriel, R. (1989). Mexican American family functioning and acculturation: A family systems perspective. *Hispanic Journal of Behavioral Sciences, 11*, 232–244.

Rumbaut, R. G. (1995). The new Californians: Comparative research findings on the educational progress of immigrant children. In R. G. Rumbaut and W. A. Cornelius (Eds.), *California's immigrant children: Theory, research, and implications for educational policy* (pp. 17–69). San Diego, CA: Center for U.S.–Mexican Studies.

Rumbaut, R. G. (1994). The crucible within: Ethnic identity, self-esteem, and segmented assimilation among children of immigrants. *International Migration Review, 28*(4), 748–794.

Rumberger, R. W., & Larson, K. A. (1998). Toward explaining differences in educational achievement of Mexican American language-minority students. *Sociology of Education, 71*, 69–93.

Sabogal, F., Marín, G., Otero-Sabogal, R., Marín, B. V., & Perez-Stable, E. J. (1987). Hispanic familism and acculturation: What changes and what doesn't? *Hispanic Journal of Behavioral Sciences, 9*, 397–412.

Samaniego, R. Y., & Gonzales, N. A. (1999). Multiple mediators of the effects of acculturation status on delinquency for Mexican American adolescents. *American Journal of Community Psychology, 27*(2), 189–210.

Scheier, L. M., Botvin, G. J., Diaz, T., & Ifill-Williams, M. (1997). Ethnic identity as a moderator of psychosocial risk and adolescent alcohol and marijuana use: Concurrent and longitudinal analyses. *Journal of Child and Adolescent Substance Abuse, 6*(1), 21–47.

Schinke, S. P., Moncher, M. S., Palleja, J., Zayas, L. H., & Schilling, R. F. (1988). Hispanic youth, substance abuse, and stress: Implications for prevention research. *International Journal of the Addictions, 23*(8), 809–826.

Szapocznik, J., & Kurtines, W. M. (1980). Acculturation, biculturalism, and adjustment among Cuban Americans. In A. M. Padilla (Ed.), *Acculturation: Theory, models, and some new findings* (pp. 139–159). Boulder, CO: Westview.

Szapocznik, J., & Kurtines, W. M. (1993). Family psychology and cultural diversity: Opportunities for theory, research, and application. *American Psychologist, 48*, 400–407.

Szapocznik, J., Kurtines, W., Santisteban, D. A., & Rio, A. T. (1990). Interplay of advances between theory, research, and application in treatment interventions aimed at behavior problem children and adolescents. *Journal of Consulting and Clinical Psychology, 58*(6), 696–703.

Szapocznik, J., Scopetta, M. A., & King, O. E. (1978). Theory and practice in matching treatment to the special characteristics and problems of Cuban immigrants. *Journal of Community Psychology, 6*, 112–122.

U.S. Census Bureau. (2001a). *Projections of resident population by race, Hispanic origin, and nativity: Middle series, 2050–2070* [On-line]. Available: <http://census.gov/population/projections/nation/summary/np-t5-g.txt>.

U.S. Census Bureau. (2001b). *Resident population estimates of the United States by sex, race, and Hispanic Origin: April 1, 1990 to July 1, 1999, with short-term projection to November 1, 2000* [On-line]. Available: <http://census.gov/population/estimates/nation/intfile3-1.txt>.

Vega, W. A., Gil, A. G., Warheit, G. J., Zimmerman, R. S., & Apospori, E. (1993). Acculturation and delinquent behavior among Cuban American adolescents: Toward an empirical model. *American Journal of Community Psychology, 21*(1), 113–125.

Vega, W. A., Gil, A. G., & Zimmerman, R. S. (1993). Patterns of drug use among Cuban-American, African-American and White, Non-Hispanic boys. *American Journal of Public Health, 83*, 257–259.

Vega, W. A., Khoury, E. L., Zimmerman, R. S., Gil, A. G., & Warheit, G. J. (1995). Cultural conflicts and problem behaviors of Latino adolescents in home and school environments. *Journal of Community Psychology, 23*, 167–179.

Wall, J. A., Power, T. G., & Arbona, C. (1993). Susceptibility to antisocial peer pressure and its relation to acculturation in Mexican American adolescents. *Journal of Adolescent Research, 8*(4), 403–418.

Part II

Parenting Processes in Latino Families

4

Latino Immigrant Parents' Beliefs about the "Path of Life" of Their Adolescent Children

Margarita Azmitia and Jane R. Brown

Recently, school-based initiatives across the country have sought to promote the academic success of Latino children through programs that teach parents "how to work with the education system to make it effective for their child" (Mijares, quoted in Canto, 1998). Staff see the potential of their programs as stemming from the cultural sensitivity of both content and personnel. These programs can help Latino parents learn about the goals, expectations, and practices of the school system, and teachers, administrators, and staff—who are primarily of European American ancestry—can learn about the goals, expectations, values, and practices of Latino families (Cooper et al., 1994; Tharp & Gallimore, 1988). One important contribution researchers can make to these school-based initiatives is to help replace what are often limited, stereotypic, and static perceptions with greater understanding of the dynamic nature of Latino parents' beliefs, goals, and guidance. Such understanding can strengthen partnerships among diverse families, teachers, administrators, and students.

Research has shown that Latino students' cultural values are resources in their achievement (Suarez-Orozco, 1995; Valenzuela & Dornbusch, 1994). It has also been shown that immigrant Latino parents hold high aspirations for their children's educational attainment (Cooper et al., 1994; Goldenberg & Gallimore, 1995; Henderson, 1997). Latino parents' beliefs about their children's education, however, are inextricably bound to more basic beliefs about children's moral development (Delgado-Gaitán, 1992; Reese, Balzano, Gallimore, & Goldenberg, 1995; Valdés, 1996). Reese and her colleagues carried out extensive interviews with immigrant Latino parents of young elementary schoolchildren about the beliefs and goals they held for their children's future. The Latino parents they interviewed articulated a concept of *educación* that was much broader than its English translation of "education" in that moral development was the central component and academic achievement only one element. Parents frequently used the metaphor "following the good path of life" (*el buen camino*), to explain their developmental goals for their children. The path of life metaphor comprised a network of beliefs that related moral development to schooling and to positive and negative developmental outcomes more generally. Key components of this belief network include *respeto* (respect) toward elders and responsibility to the family, components that have also been included in the concept of familism, a value endorsed by Latino families (Sabogal, Marín, Otero-Sabogal, Marín, & Perez-Stable, 1987).

In Reese, Balzano, and their colleagues' (1995) study, Latino parents spontaneously offered their beliefs about the path of life when answering open-ended questions about their hopes and dreams for their children's futures. Parents mentioned both general goals for their children's futures as well as specific beliefs about challenges the children faced in staying on the good path of life and the guidance strategies parents used to help them do so. In the present study, we built on Reese, Balzano, and their colleagues' work in two ways. First, by asking parents explicitly to describe what the good and the bad path of life meant to them. Our questions addressed how parents judged their children's progress on the path of life, the challenges they saw ahead for them, and the strategies they used to support and guide their children along the good path or through crossroads or to help them get back on track if they had strayed.

Second, we focused on parents of older children and the transition to adolescence. Adolescence poses educational and personal challenges for young people. In his recent review of the literature, Arnett (1999) found evidence of variability in youths' developmental pathways and qualified empirical support for the belief that adolescence involves some degree of "storm and stress," characterized by conflict with parents, mood disruptions, and risk-taking behavior. Although it has been argued that there is less parent–child conflict among Latino than European American families (Suarez-Orozco & Suarez-Orozco, 1995), immigrant Latino parents have voiced concern that in the United States their adolescent children are less under their control than they would be in their home countries. They are particularly worried that their children are spending more time outside the family and possibly coming under the influence of *malas compañías* (bad influences, typically from peers; Kroesen, Reese, & Gallimore, 1998). In their interviews with Latino parents of preschoolers, Reese, Balzano, and their colleagues (1995) also found that many believed they would only have until adolescence to inculcate their children with the morals and values they held. These parents believed that once children reached adolescence, they would be subject to many influences outside the family and the foundation parents had laid would be tested (Reese, et al., 1995). Taken together, these findings support our proposal that adolescence is an important period in which to examine Latino parents' beliefs about their children's development.

Reese, Balzano, and their colleagues (1995) carried out their work in Los Angeles, a large urban center that poses many challenges for Latino youth. The work that we discuss in this chapter was carried out in a small city in the central valley in northern California that is surrounded by farmland and thus is relatively rural compared to Los Angeles. An additional goal of our study was to explore whether *malas compañías*, and especially peers, also played an important role in "our" parents' concerns about the challenges their children were facing or would face during their adolescent years. Before proceeding with the details of our study, we briefly review research on parents' belief systems.

PARENTS' BELIEF SYSTEMS

Two important issues have been raised by research on parents' belief systems. First, how great are individual differences in beliefs among parents who are members of the same cultural group? Second, do parents' beliefs change over time? These two questions are significant because it is often presumed that parents' beliefs about child development and the tasks of adulthood influence their views of their own children's development and the guidance strategies they employ (Goodnow, 1988; Sigel & McGillicuddy-DeLisi, 1992). In an earlier review of developmental research on parents' beliefs, Goodnow (1988) noted that evidence of cross-cultural differences in beliefs was a more robust finding than evidence of within-culture variability in beliefs. Goodnow's finding of cross-cultural differences in parents' beliefs was consistent with theories that emphasize the shared values and beliefs that organize and motivate the practices of cultural communities (e.g., Cuellar, Arnold, & Gonzalez, 1995; D'Andrade & Strauss, 1992). Others have stressed, however, that it is important not to assume homogeneity within cultural groups and note substantial differences in parenting beliefs and practices within groups of Latino parents (Harwood, Schoelmerich, Ventura-Cook, Schulze, & Wilson, 1996; Leyendecker & Lamb, 1999; Romo & Falbo, 1996).

In a recent paper, Grusec, Goodnow, and Kuczynski (2000) proposed that the emphasis on the shared values, beliefs, and practices or members of particular cultural communities may have led us to underestimate within-culture variation and impeded the development of methodologies that are sensitive to variation and change in belief systems and strategies over time. They suggested that one way to assess change may be to investigate whether and how parents actively select and adapt cultural beliefs, values, and practices in response to the changing demands of their everyday environments and their children's characteristics and actions. Experiences such as immigration, schooling, and increased knowledge about parenting can change parents' belief systems and practices (Harkness, Super, & Keever, 1992). Sabogal et al. (1987), for example, found that the process of acculturation leads to shifts in some dimensions of

Latinos' concept of familism. While there are a variety of factors that can be examined to assess continuity and change in parents' beliefs and socialization strategies, in the present study we focused on the role of children's characteristics and experiences. In particular, we asked: To what extent do parents hold the same beliefs for more than one child in the family? Can we link differences in beliefs to their children's experiences? Are these differences reflected in within-family variations in parents' socialization practices?

Recent work in family relationships and behavior genetics has questioned the assumption that siblings living in the same family experience the same social environment (Daniels & Plomin, 1985). Differences in siblings' experiences have been linked to parents' and children's characteristics and development as well as to how experiences outside the family influence parents' socialization practices (Dunn & Plomin, 1990; Grusec et al., 2000). This research consistently shows that one environment that differs for siblings is their friendship and peer network (Rowe, 1994). If siblings have different peer groups, and if peer influences or pressures are one of the greatest concerns of parents of adolescents, then we may expect that parents' beliefs about the challenges their children face and the guidance strategies they use to help them stay on the good path will also differ. Testing this hypothesis is important because it not only adds to our understanding of the nature of immigrant parents' beliefs but also challenges us to appreciate the complexity of their experiences raising children in the United States.

We examined three potential sources of differences in parents' beliefs for two of their children. First, we considered whether parents perceived different challenges for early versus middle or late adolescents; the younger siblings in our sample were early adolescents, but the older siblings were either middle or late adolescents. Arnett (1999) has suggested that early, middle, and late adolescence are each associated with unique storm-and-stress events. For example, parent–child conflict is usually highest in early adolescence, mood disruptions peak in middle adolescence, and risk-taking behaviors are more common in late adolescence. Second, we considered potential gender variations in parents' perceptions of their children's progress along the path of life and of the challenges they were currently facing or would face in the future. Adolescence is a period in which gender differences in behaviors become particularly salient (Hill & Lynch, 1983), and Latino parents often have gendered expectations for their adolescent children (Chacón & Cohen, 1982). Third, we investigated whether parents' beliefs for their two children differed as a function of whether one of their children had strayed off the good path or was at a crossroads. As Sameroff (1975) noted, parents may be more likely to seek out new information or reexamine their beliefs about children's development when problems arise. As long as life proceeds smoothly, parents need not question their assumptions.

Most studies that address the question of whether parents' ideas change as a result of their children's experiences have examined between-group differences, with number of children or length of parenting as a proxy for change over time (see Goodnow, 1988). In one longitudinal study, however, Goldenberg, Gallimore, Reese, and Garnier (1998) did find evidence that parents' expectations for their children's educational achievement changed over the grade-school period, and that these changes followed changes in the children's school performance. These findings add support to our hypothesis that parents may modify some of their beliefs as a result of their children's behavior or experiences. We now briefly summarize our analytic approach.

LEVELS OF ANALYSES OF OUR CORPUS OF DATA

Our first level of analysis was descriptive. We wished to increase our understanding of the cultural beliefs that comprised the path of life metaphor that Reese and her colleagues first described (Reese, Balzano et al. 1995; Reese, Gallimore, Goldenberg, & Balzano, 1995). We also investigated whether this metaphor continued to be meaningful to parents as their children reached adolescence and made the transition to a new school, new friends, and new experiences. In addition to discussing the more abstract and value-laden beliefs parents held about a good path of life, we investigated several specific beliefs about their own children's journey, including parents' attributions about where they saw each child on the path of life; the challenges they saw ahead for their children, and the strategies they used to guide their children during this period.

Our second level of analysis concerned the uniformity of parents' descriptions of their beliefs and strategies. Do particular themes hold meaning for the majority of parents when they talk about desirable developmental outcomes, challenges, or guidance strategies? Consistent with Grusec et al.'s (2000) position that there is more homogeneity in parents' shared abstract beliefs and practices than in their everyday application, we anticipated greater agreement across parents in their more abstract visions than in their specific attributions and ideas about individual children. To test this hypothesis, we first elicited parents' definitions of the good and the bad path of life and then asked them to describe and make attributions separately for where each child was on the path of life, the past, present, and future challenges the child faced; and the guidance strategies the parent had used or was using to guide their child. We examined variations in parents' beliefs that might be associated with three factors: age, gender, and parental concern. We compared parents' beliefs about the younger and older of the pair of siblings in each family to assess whether a child's age or life experiences influenced parents' beliefs and descriptions. We also investigated whether the pattern of parents' beliefs differed for boys and for girls. The third comparison we made was based on individual characteristics of the children. We hypothesized that parents' heightened concern about how children were progressing on the path of life would be associated with specific perceived challenges and that parents would advocate more restrictive guidance strategies for those children than for those about whom they had no concerns.

While the first and second levels of analysis allowed us to assess parents' beliefs and whether these beliefs varied as a function of their children's age, gender, and life experiences, the cross-sectional nature of these analyses did not allow us to measure change in these beliefs over time. To this end, our third and final level of analysis explored stability and change in parents' beliefs longitudinally. A subset of 13 families was interviewed at two time points one year apart, and their responses to the questions were compared. Because the number in this subset was small, our examination is qualitative and descriptive and is intended to generate ideas for future research.

METHOD

Participants

Families were drawn from a sample of Latino students participating in a larger study of the transition from elementary to middle or junior high school (Azmitia & Cooper, 1996). The 27 families selected for the study each had two adolescent siblings. In all families, the younger of the two siblings was in the first year of junior high or middle school and the older of the two siblings was still in school and at least one year ahead of the younger. The younger siblings were all 11 or 12 years old and the older siblings ranged in age from 12 to 18 years old. There were eight brother–brother pairs, three sister–sister pairs, nine younger brother–older sister pairs, and seven younger sister–older brother pairs. A subset of 13 families had also been interviewed a year prior when the younger sibling was still in elementary school. A limited comparison of the interviews from year 1 and year 2 of these parents is addressed as well.

All but three of the fathers were born in Mexico: two were born in the United States and one in Central America. All but two of the mothers were born in Mexico: one was born in the United States and one in Central America. The mean number of years of education for fathers was 7.6 (SD = 4.4) and for mothers was 7.4 (SD = 4.0). Most parents worked in semiskilled or unskilled occupations, typically in hotels, restaurants, factories, or canneries. All but three of the families had incomes of $40,000 per year or less, and their children were receiving free or reduced-price lunches at school, which is our operationalization of low-income.

Procedure

Parents were interviewed at home in their language of choice, typically Spanish. Interviews were audiotaped and parents' answers were transcribed verbatim and coded in the language of the interview. Interviews usually spanned one-and-a-half to two hours.

Path of Life Interview

The interviewer explained to parents that the researchers had been told about the good and the bad path of life by other parents and showed them a diagrammatic representation of a pathway that forked into two: one path was labeled "*el buen camino*" (the good path) and the other "*el mal camino*" (the bad path). The fork was labeled "*encrucijadas*" (crossroads). The good and the bad branches had connecting paths between them. These branches were designed to capture the dynamic nature of an adolescent's journey: After selecting the good path, one can always stray and even if one strays, one can always recover and return to the good path. Parents were asked the following open-ended questions:

1. *¿Qué significa para usted "el buen camino de la vida"?* (What does "the good path of life" mean to you?)

2. *¿Qué significa para usted "el mal camino de la vida"?*(What does the "bad path of life" mean to you?)

Each of the following questions was then asked separately about the younger and the older sibling:

3. *Pensando en su hijo/a y en esta idea del buen y el mal camino: ¿Podría usted decirme donde pondría a su hijo/a? ¿Por qué escogería usted ese lugar?* (Thinking about your child and this idea of the good and the bad paths, could you point to the place where you would put him/her at this time? [The parent wrote the child's name on the diagram at the identified location]. Why would you choose this place?)

4. *¿Ha habido alguna vez en el pasado que ud. penso que su hijo/a estaba en el mal camino o en las encrucijadas? Si es así, ¿qué edad tenía? ¿Porqué piensa que su hijo/a estaba allí.* (Has there been a time in the past that you thought that your child was on the bad path or at a crossroads? If yes, how old was he or she? Why do you think that he or she was there?)

5. *¿Cuáles piensa usted que son los retos que va a encontrar su hijo/a para que siga el buen camino o sobrepase las encrucijadas?* (What do you think the challenges of staying on or choosing the good path might be for your child?)

6. *¿Está usted haciendo algo para que su hijo/a siga en el buen camino (o escoga el buen camino)?* (Is there anything you are doing to keep your child on the good path or help him/her get through the crossroads? To help your child choose the good path and avoid the bad path?)

Coding of Parent Interviews

A coding system to characterize parents' responses to these questions was derived inductively from the transcripts. This coding system was concerned with parents' discussions of four topics. First were parents' descriptions of the good and the bad paths of life. Second were their explanations for where each of their children stood relative to the good path. Third were the challenges parents anticipated for their children's progress along the good path of life. The final topic was the guidance strategies parents employed to encourage their children to stay on the good path or return to it if they had strayed.

Thematic Categories in Parent's Open-Ended Responses

The Good Path

Four themes were evident in parents' responses to our question asking them to describe what the phrase "the good path of life" meant to them.

1. *Respect for values and morals.* This category, which embodies the components of the concept of *educación* identified by Reese, Balzano, and their colleagues (1995), included a broad range of attitudes and behaviors and encompassed statements addressing showing proper demeanor, living a moral, responsible life, behaving as parents had taught, being responsible to home and family, being a respectful person, and developing oneself spiritually.

   Todo lo bueno que pueda hacer mi hijo cuando no está cerca de mi. (Everything good that my son can do when he isn't near me.)
   El ser una persona responsable, respetuosa de la demas gente, y claro, respetandose uno también a uno mismo. (To be a responsible person, respectful of other people, and, of course, of oneself.)
   El buén camino significa para mi pues, que ellos ya están grandes, y ya saben lo que es bueno y lo que es malo. (The good path means to me that, well, they are older and they already know right from wrong.)

2. *Avoiding bad influences.* These statements referred to avoiding drugs, vices, and bad companions.

   El buen camino es . . . que no se junte con personas malas. (The good path is that [he/she] does not hang out with bad people.)
   Es que no tengan vicios, que no se dejen arrastrar de las otras muchachas. (It is that they don't have vices, that they don't let themselves be influenced by the other girls.

3. *Education and work.* This category included statements referring to education and career, such as the realization of one's goals and performing well in school and work.

   Que sea buen estudiante. (That he is a good student.)
   Que tengan ambiciones en la vida tambien. Y se forgen metas para alcanzar lo que quieran obtener. (That they have ambitions in life. And that they set goals so they can attain what they want to get.)
   Seguir una meta y realizarse. (To follow a goal and be self-actualized.)

4. *Marriage and family.* These statements spoke of the goal of marriage and family, but unlike the first category, there was no mention of family values or obligations.

   Que se casen y tengan una familia. (That they marry and have a family.)

The Bad Path

Parents' descriptions of the "Bad path" included a variety of activities and attitudes. These were:

1. *Alcohol and drug use*

    El mal camino es envolverse en drogas, también que sean adictivos a temprana edad. (The bad path is getting involved in drugs, also that they are addicts at a young age.)

2. *Bad companions*

    Pues, las pandillas, usted sabe, los amigos que no son amigos. (Well, gangs, you know, and friends that aren't true friends.)

3. *Poor character*

    El mal camino para mi es ser una persona egoista y irresponsable y ofensiva hacia las demas personas. (For me, the bad path is being a selfish, irresponsible person who is offensive to other people.)

4. *To be estranged from home*

    Bueno, cuando los muchachos se entregan a la calle . . . no importarles ni si quiera su familia ni sus padres. (Well, when youth hang out in the streets . . . without caring about their families and parents.)

5. *Illegal activities*

    Andar en las calles, quebrando cosas, vandalismo, robando, golpeando, insultando, eso es el mal camino. (Hanging out in the streets, breaking things, vandalism, stealing, hitting, insulting, that is the bad path.)

6. *To abandon goals*

    Pues que el haiga cambiado su vida, que haiga cambiado su opinion de estudiar. (Well, that he has changed his life, that he's changed his opinion about studying.)

Explanation Themes

Up to three themes were coded in the parents' explanation for why they had placed their child in a particular place on the path of life. The categories of explanation themes included:

1. *Peer influence*

    Está conociendo nueva gente. No sabemos que clase de gente es Porque sus amigas la guían mucho. (She is meeting new people. We do not know what type of people they are. Because her friends influence her a lot.)

2. *Developmental stage*

    Ya estan mas grandes; ya andan en el peligro. (They are older; they are already in danger.)
    Ahorita va bien, nada mas tiene 12 años. (Currently she is doing OK. She is only 12 years old.)

3. *Behavior*

   El ahorita esta siguiendo las reglas de la casa. (Right now he is following the rules of the house.)
   No he tenido problemas con el casi nunca. (I have rarely had problems with him.)
   Yo no veo nada malo ahorita en el. (I don't see anything wrong with him right now.)
   (La maestra) tiene muchas quejas de el . . . de que no ponía atención. (The teacher) had a lot of complaints about him . . . he wasn't paying attention.)

4. *Character or attitude*

   Días viene muy rebelde . . . llega (de la escuela) como exaltado . . . Y mas bien, enfadoso. (There are days that he is very rebellious . . . he comes home (from school) wound up . . . its more like in a bad mood.)
   Por que ella es muy buena muchacha. (Because she is a very good girl.)

5. *Other including gender, school transitions, drug use*

   Porque el ya pudo bajar hasta abajo por las drogas . . . un medio hermano de el le dio a probar mariguana. (Because he has reached rock bottom because of the drugs . . . his half brother gave him marijuana so he could try it.)

Challenge Themes

Up to three challenge themes were coded in parents' answers for each child. Several challenge theme categories paralleled the explanations for where children were on the path of life. As anticipated, peers figured prominently in parents' perceptions of challenges in their children's paths.

1. *Peer influence (including boyfriends or girlfriends)*

   Pues, los amigos, porque los amigos influyen, verdad. (Well, friends because friends have influence, right?)
   Cuando se enamoran dejan de estudiar, no se interesan en ni una cosa. (When they fall in love they stop studying, they lose interest in everything.)

2. *School-related (including both academic and social challenges and violence or gang activity at schools).*

   Para mi, la junior high school es una época muy difícil y es algo bien decisivo entre las personas y si pasan esto, es por que han superado una encrucijada. (For me, junior high school is a very difficult time and it's a very crucial time in people [their lives] and if they get through it, its because they have made it through a crossroads.)

3. *Adolescence*

   Tiene once años, cuando tenga trece años, catorce anos, va a encontrar obstaculos. (She is 11. When she is 13, 14, then she is going to find challenges.)

4. *Drugs*

   Pues, ahorita especialmente en la . . . en la actualidad de muchos problemas con drogadicción y todo eso. (Well, right now especially . . . currently there are many problems with drug addiction and all of that.)

5. *Personal character (including mood or attitude)*

Pues si, como un reto, porque cuando tiene problemas, no puede hacer la tarea, dice, "No puedo, no puedo aprendérmelo, no lo entiendo." (Well, it's like a challenge because when he has problems he can't do his homework. He says "I can't do it, I can't learn it. I don't understand.")

6. *No challenges seen.* Several parents could not describe or did not see any particular challenges facing their children.

7. *Other.* This category included discrimination, money, gender, and family stress.

Bueno, la discriminación que haiga en las escuelas. (Well, discrimination at school.)

El es un hombrecito, y yo creo que los hombrecitos tienen mas riesgos, porque se les hace mas facil, los hombres fuman, los hombres esto y lo otro. (He is a young man, and I think that males have more risks because it's easier [to take risks], men smoke, men do this and that.)

Guidance Strategy Themes

Up to three guidance strategy themes were coded for each parent response. Parents advocated five distinct kinds of guidance strategies. These were:

1. Consejos (*advise and teach values*)

Ahorita, lo que hago es darle consejos. (Right now, what I do is give advice.)

Pues, la major parte del tiempo nosotros hablamos de progresar, de alcanzar una meta, de ser alguien positivamente. (Well, most of the time we speak about progress, about reaching a goal, about being someone positive).

Hay ejemplos, platicas que tenemos, porque eso si, ya platico mucho con ellas, del mal camino, de lo que es bueno, de lo que es malo, de lo que les conviene, también. (There are examples, talks that we have. Because that's what I do, I talk a lot with them, about the bad path, about what's good, what's bad, what is good for them also.)

2. *Role model*

Siempre tratamos de darles buen ejemplo sobre todo. (We always try, more than anything, to give them a good example.)

Yo siempre le pongo el ejemplo de su papá, porque mi esposo no sale, es tranquilo, es sensato . . . buen cristiano. Siempre le digo, "El ejemplo a seguir es el papá." (I always give him the example of his father, because my husband doesn't go out, he is peaceful, sensible, a good Christian. I always tell him, "The example to follow is your father.")

3. *Emotional support*

Me gusta mucho convivir con ellos, de estar alli con ellos cuando se estan vistiendo y ellos me tienen confianza tambien. (I like to spend time with them, to be with them when they are getting dressed, and they trust me too.)

Le digo (a su papá), "Mientras tu seas su amigo, mientras tu platiques con el y participes con el en lo que tu tienes que hacer, invítalo, convídalo, ser amigo de el para que no caiga con otros amigos que lo llevan por otro lado." (I tell him [his father] "As long as you are his friend, you talk to him, ask him to join you in what you have to do, invite him, be his friend so that he doesn't fall in with other friends that will take him to another path.")

4. *Monitor or restrict*

Ahora, lo que yo hago es poner mas atención a los niños de repente. (Now, what I do is pay more attention to the children.)

Pues si, este, no dejandolo salir yo, es lo que hago. (No los dejo tanto salir con gentes, asi con los chiquillos que vienen a convidarlo que "vamos p'aca, que vamos p'alla." (Well, yes, what I do is that I don't let them go out. I don't let them go out with people, with the kids that come to invite him, that say "come with us to this or another place.")

Estando mas al tanto de el. Hablando con los maestros, estar mas cerca de el por medio de actividades en la casa. (Being aware of what he is doing. Talking to the teachers, to try to be closer to him through activities at home.)

5. *Involve outside assistance (including school, therapists, church)*

Yo le digo a los maestros y a las maestras, "Si el esta haciendo algo malo, usted dígame, porque el ahorita esta en, pues, esta bien loco." (I tell the teachers: "If he is doing something wrong, tell me. Because right now, well, right now, he is acting crazy.)

Pues, nada mas tratándo de llevarla a que tenga tambien un ejemplo que vaya a la iglesia, que haga buenos sentimientos. (Well, only trying to take her so that she has an example, that she goes to church, that she has good intentions.)

It was like a deep depression that he went into . . . and then he would call me at work and he would tell me that he felt weird. Finally, I took him to a counselor.

6. *Other (including contracts and rewards, involving other family members, prayer)*

I think he'll do it [stay on the good path] because, not just myself, but the rest of the family is not letting up on him, we're not letting him make that choice. They talk to him constantly, reinforce the positive things he does do.

Parental Concern

After coding each transcript, the coder made a global rating of the level of parents' concern about each child's progress on the good path of life. The entire transcript was used to make these judgments; however, particular attention was paid to parents' answers to two questions. The first was where the parent had indicated the child was on the path diagram (see the section entitled "Explanation Themes"). The second was whether the parent believed the child had ever strayed off the good path or been at a crossroads. For each child the coder determined that either the parent had concerns about their progress along the good path of life (of concern) or that the parent was confident that all was well with the child (not of concern).

Reliability

The two coders (the two authors of this paper) who developed the coding system for the path of life interview also coded all of the transcripts and resolved all differences in coding by consensus. Reliability was established by the two coders using transcripts from nine families (33% of the sample). The percent intercoder agreement and modified kappa (Brennan and Prediger, 1991) for each of the categorical codes were as follows: Good Path (.89, .83), Bad Path (.95, .94), Explanation Themes (.94, .93), Challenge Themes (.88, .87), Guidance Strategy Themes (.88, .87), and concern (.95, .90).

RESULTS

The path of life metaphor provides a rich context with which to assess Latino parents' beliefs about adolescence, their children's life pathways, and their guidance strategies. As hypothesized, and consistent with the work of Reese, Balzano, and their colleagues (1995), parents' beliefs about the good path of life emphasized the moral dimension of life. Parents saw peers as the greatest challenge for their children staying on the good path of life, but most indicated that their fears about peers had not yet been realized. Still, for adolescents who were at a crossroads or on the bad path, peers emerged as a major factor in parents' perceptions of what was causing them difficulties or had derailed them. Not surprisingly, parents were more concerned about the older than the younger siblings' progress. We will address age, gender, and time-related variations in their concerns. *Consejos* (advice) emerged as the most frequently used guidance strategy, although parents of adolescents who were experiencing difficulties did not merely rely on *consejos*; they also restricted and monitored their children's activities to help them through a difficult situation or help them return to the good path if they had strayed.

The Good and the Bad Paths of Life

Table 4.1 presents the frequencies by thematic category of parents' responses to the question of what the good and bad path of life meant to them. None of the parents' descriptions of the good or the bad path included more than two thematic categories.

Parents' descriptions of the good path were most frequently concerned with being respectful and maintaining high morals and values. Their observations frequently included descriptions of character traits—"*una persona responsable, respetuosa*" (a responsible and respectful person)—and generalized or abstract descriptions of moral behavior—"*tener buen comportamiento, ser buen miembro de la sociedad*" (be well behaved, be a good member of society). Some parents' comments reflected an awareness that their children were moving on into a world beyond the family and would take with them what they had learned from their parents. For example, one described the good path as "*lo que uno de padre platique con ellos*" (what one, as a parent, talks with them about) and another as "*todo lo bueno que pueda hacer mi hijo cuando no este cerca de mi*" (all the good that my son can do when he is not with me). Respect for morals and values was mentioned first by all of the parents who cited it ($n = 22$, 81%).

Table 4.1
Percent (and Frequency) of Parents' Responses in Each "Good" and "Bad"
Path Thematic Category Following the Transition to Junior High School
(Year 2)

Theme	Percent
"Good" Path Themes	
Respect, morals, and values	81 (22)
Avoiding bad influences	33 (9)
Education and work	33 (9)
Marriage and family	11 (3)
"Bad" Path Themes	
Alcohol and drug use	56 (15)
Bad companions	33 (9)
Poor character	26 (7)
To be estranged from home	15 (4)
Illegal activities	19 (5)
Abandon goals	14 (4)

Note. The sum of percentages exceeds 100 because parents could give more than one thematic category. None of the parents' descriptions included more than two categories.

Morals and values were represented in the second most frequently cited theme as well, avoiding bad influences. Avoiding bad influences was cited by about one-third of parents. As anticipated, chief among bad influences were *malas compañías* (bad company, typically, peers.) The influence of *malas compañías* was included in most parents' descriptions of what to avoid, even when they also spoke of avoiding drugs or alcohol. For example, one parent noted that the way to avoid drugs and alcohol was to hold to one's own standards and not be guided by others. Education and work was a third theme parents used to describe the good path, although this theme always appeared in conjunction with one of the themes associated with morality. Some parents emphasized the activity of studying or working hard—*"Que sea buen estudiante, buen trabajador"* (That he be a good student, a good worker)—while others stressed achievement—*"Que tengan ambiciones y que se forjen metas para alcanzar lo que quieran obtener"* (That they have ambitions and that they set goals so they can attain what they want). Several parents linked education with moral development, as when one explained that without an education one was more likely to follow a bad path—*"Si no esta bien preparado, va a llevar por un mal camino"* (If he is not well schooled, he will end up in the bad path). The fourth good path theme, marriage and family, was referred to by parents of both girls and boys.

While good path descriptions focused principally on abstract notions of successful development or personal character traits, parents' descriptions of the bad path emphasized specific behaviors and activities, with alcohol and drug use the most frequently cited. Parents often listed multiple activities that they associated with the bad path, for example, *"Andar en las calles, quebrando cosas, vandalismo, robando, golpeando, insultando, eso es el mal camino"* (To be in the streets, breaking things, vandalizing, stealing, hitting, insulting, that is the bad path). To *"andar en la calle"* (hang out in the streets) or to associate with *"malas compañías"* (bad company) figured prominently in parents' responses, as did gang activity.

Parents' Explanation Themes, Challenge Themes, and Guidance Strategy Themes: Descriptive Results

Next examined were parents' responses to the following questions: Why did the parent choose to place each child at a particular site on the path of life diagram (explanations); what challenges did they see facing each child; and what guidance strategies did they advocate for each. The frequencies of themes parents used to answer these questions were summed and are presented in Table 4.2. Frequencies are presented separately for parents' responses to questions about the younger and the older sibling and as a total frequency of responses per category. The total number of explanation, challenge, or guidance themes in Table 4.2 exceeds the total number of children in the sample because up to three themes were coded for each response. In addition, for each question, several parents' responses were either missing or not codable. The number of younger and older siblings for whom the questions were coded is included in the note to the table.

Explanation Themes

The most frequent explanation parents gave for where their children were on the path of life was a description of that child's behavior. These included both positive and negative examples and ranged from simple statements that a child's behavior had always been good to examples of bad behavior (e.g., instances of fighting at school). Contrary to our prediction, external influences, specifically "peer influences"—*"Los amigos que tiene"* (The friends that he has)—were no more frequently cited explanations than internal influences, such as the child's character or attitude—*"Esta muy rebelde ahorita"* (Right now, she is very rebellious)—to explain where children were on the path of life.

Challenge Themes

As hypothesized, peer influence did figure prominently when parents were asked what challenges lay ahead for their children. Peer influence was more

Table 4.2
Percent (and Frequency) of Parents' Explanation Themes for Where the Younger and Older Adolescent Siblings Are on the "Path of Life," Challenges to Staying on the "Good Path of Life," and Parents' Guidance Strategies

| Themes | Age of Sibling | | |
	Younger	Older	Total
Explanation Thematic Category			
Behavior	71(15)	44(11)	56(26)
Peer Influence	14(3)	40(10)	28(13)
Personal character or attitude	33(7)	24(6)	28(13)
Developmental Stage	24(5)	12(3)	17(8)
Other	9(2)	16(4)	13(6)
Challenge Thematic Category			
Peer Influence	74(18)	73(19)	74(37)
School-related	17(4)	32(8)	24(12)
Drugs	13(3)	4(1)	8(4)
Personal character or attitude	13(3)	2(1)	8(4)
No challenges	8(2)	4(1)	6(3)
Adolescence	4(1)	0	2(1)
Other	17(4)	15(4)	16(8)
Guidance Strategy Thematic Category			
Consejos	64(16)	73(19)	69(35)
Monitor or restrict	28(7)	23(6)	25(13)
Emotional support	20(5)	19(5)	19(10)
Role model	16(4)	4(1)	10(5)
Outside assistance	9(2)	8(2)	8(4)
Other	4(1)	15(4)	10(5)

Note. The sum of percentages exceeds 100 because parents could give more than one response; up to three responses were coded per parent. Number of parents responding to explanation themes: Younger sibling = 21, older sibling = 25; Challenge themes: Younger sibling = 24, older sibling =26; Guidance strategy themes: Younger sibling =25, older sibling = 26.

than three times as likely to be considered a potential challenge by parents than any other challenge theme. School challenges ranked second and included both academic challenges and discipline issues. While most parents mentioned only one or two challenges, there was some variability in the number of challenges parents saw ahead for their children, ranging from "none" to five distinct challenge themes. The other category included several child- or family-specific challenges, as well as one mother's observation that her children would be challenged by the *la discriminación en la escuela* (discrimination in the school). Finally, while adolescence may have been implicit in parents' descriptions of challenges faced by their children, it was only explicitly mentioned once.

Guidance Strategy Themes

Parents also showed a preference for one particular guidance strategy; they reported using *consejos* about three times as often as the next most frequent strategy cited: to monitor or restrict children's activities. The *consejos* parents gave their children included anticipatory guidance about potential challenges such as drugs, alcohol, or *malas compañías*. They also included advice and conversations parents had with children who had already faced challenges such as the influence of undesirable friends. As one mother explained, *"Es lo único que le queda uno de padre, verdad?"* (It's the only thing that one can do as a parent, right?). Giving children positive emotional support, being the child's friend or confidant(e), was the third most frequently cited theme. Seeking outside assistance was relatively rare, as has been discussed in other studies of Latino families (Keefe, Padilla, & Carlos, 1979), and included both teachers at school and therapists.

Uniformity of Parents' Beliefs

Taken together, the results of the descriptive analysis present a picture of relative uniformity in parents' beliefs, particularly with respect to beliefs about what constitutes the good path, what challenges parents envisioned ahead for their adolescents, and what guidance strategies they advocated. These patterns may reflect the relatively enduring nature of abstract cultural belief systems (D'Andrade & Strauss, 1992). It is important to point out, however, that although some of these beliefs may be specific to Latinos, it is likely that many represent universal concerns of parents of adolescents (e.g., that their children live a moral life, avoid bad peers, etc.). We next assessed the extent to which there was variation in parents' responses for their individual children, an analysis that allowed us to assess within-family variability.

Individual Differences

We examined associations between three different characteristics of the adolescents and the frequency with which their parents reported each thematic category of beliefs. These were: age, gender, and concern about the child's progress on the path of life. In each set of analyses, parents' answers were divided between those made for one group (i.e., younger siblings) versus the other (e.g., older siblings). Then, comparisons were made between the two groups of the number of parents who cited a given theme category in each set of responses (explanations, challenges, and guidance strategies) using McNemar's chi-square test for related samples (see Siegel & Castellan, 1988).

Younger Versus Older Sibling

The first comparisons were made based on the child's age. As mentioned, both the younger and the older sibling were adolescents and in school, and in all cases the older sibling was at least one grade ahead of the younger sibling. These data are presented in Table 4.2 as part of the presentation of overall distribution of theme categories. Parents' explanations for where either the younger or the older sibling was on the path of life revealed only one statistically significant difference: More parents cited peer influence on the older sibling than cited this influence on the younger sibling as an explanation for where this child was on the path of life (40% vs. 14%, $z = -2.83$, $p < .01$). Parents also distinguished between younger and older siblings in only one challenge theme category. More parents cited school as a challenge for the older siblings than they did for the younger ones (32% vs. 17%, $z = -2.98$, $p < .01$). There were no statistically significant differences in the frequency with which parents advocated guidance strategies for either child.

Gender

Next we examined whether parents' responses differed for sons and daughters. Among the siblings there were 32 sons and 22 daughters. There were four categories of responses for which parents' responses were different based on gender. First, parents' responses to the question of why their children were at a given place on the path of life (explanations) differed in the frequency of peer influence responses. As with their older children, more parents generated explanations for daughters that had to do with the influence of peers than they did for sons (37% vs. 22%, $z = 2.64$, $p < .01$). Second, more parents cited the child's developmental stage to explain where sons were on the path of life than they did for daughters (22% vs. 16%, $z = -3.67$, $p < .01$). Third, school was more often cited as a challenge theme for sons than for daughters (29% vs. 16%, $z = 3.80$, $p < .001$). Fourth, parents of daughters more often than of sons said they used monitoring or restricting activities as a *guidance strategy* (35% vs. 19%, $z = -3.18$, $p < .01$).

Concern About Adolescents' Progress on the Path of Life

The final comparisons were made based on whether parents had expressed concern about the child's progress on the path of life. Parent concern, as noted in the method section, referred to parental expression of concern that the child was at a crossroads, had deviated, or was at risk for deviating from the good path of life or had strayed in the past. Five parents expressed concern about the younger sibling's progress and 16 parents expressed concern about the older sibling's progress on the path of life. Thus, parents expressed more concern for their older than their younger children. An examination of their responses indicated that parents of both younger and older siblings saw junior high school as the most challenging age and context their children had encountered thus far.

The only statistically significant difference found among explanations was the number of parents citing peer influence as an explanatory theme. More parents cited peer influence for where the child was on the path of life if they also expressed concern about that child (43% vs. 16%, $z = -2.18, p < .05$).

Categorical comparisons of parents' challenge themes revealed only one statistically significant difference. Parents who were not concerned about a given child were more likely to cite school as a challenge for that child than were parents who expressed a concern about the child's progress on the path of life (27% vs. 20%, $z = 1.96, p < .05$). Finally, categorical comparisons revealed two statistically significant differences in the number of parents who cited a given guidance strategy as a function of whether they were concerned about the child's progress on the path of life. Parents who expressed concern about the child were more likely to use monitoring or restricting strategies for guidance (43% vs. 13%, $z = -2.00, p < .05$), while parents who were not concerned about a given child or sibling's progress were more likely to use *consejos* as a guidance strategy (73% vs. 62%, $z = -2.56, p < .05$).

Changes Over Time in Parents' Beliefs

Data from the 13 parents interviewed at both year 1 and year 2 of this longitudinal study are presented in Table 4.3 (good and bad path themes) and Table 4.4 (explanation themes, challenge themes, and guidance strategy themes). Parents' descriptions of the good and the bad path changed little from year 1 to year 2. In particular, the rank order of the frequency with which each theme was cited did not change from year 1 to year 2. When individual parents' responses at year 1 and year 2 were compared, it was again evident that there was little change in parents' descriptions of the good and bad paths of life over time. All but one parent repeated at year 2 one or both themes they had used to describe the good path at year 1 and all but one parent repeated one or more themes for the bad path across the two time points. Although parents' references to personal character and attitude decreased and their references to behavior and peer influence increased, there were also no statistically significant differences in the rank order of the frequency of themes among parents' explanations for where they saw their children on the path of life at year 1 and year 2 (see Table 4.4).

There was also overall consistency in the challenges these 13 parents saw ahead for their children and the guidance strategies they reported (see Table 4.4). For each of these response groups, one theme dominated parents' responses in both years: peer influence was cited three times as often as the second most frequently cited challenge theme category—drugs. Similarly, *consejos* was advocated as a guidance strategy more than twice as often as to monitor or restrict in both year 1 and year 2. There were also no statistically significant

Table 4.3
**Longitudinal Comparison of the Percent (and Frequency) of Parents'
Descriptions of the "Good" and "Bad" Paths of Life**

Themes	Year 1	Year 2
"Good" Path Themes		
Respect, morals, and values	77(10)	85(11)
Education and work	46(6)	54(7)
Avoiding bad influences	23(3)	31(4)
Other (marriage and family, ecological values)	15(2)	15(2)
"Bad" Path Themes		
Alcohol and drug use	85(11)	54(7)
To be estranged from home	23(3)	0
Illegal activities	31(4)	31(4)
Bad companions	31(4)	23(3)
Abandon goals	38(5)	31(4)
Poor character traits	8(1)	38(5)

Note. Thirteen parents were interviewed on both years. The percentages sum more than 100 because parents could give more than one response. Up to three responses were coded for each parent.

differences in the rank order of the frequency of themes among challenges or guidance strategies at year 1 and year 2. Two individual guidance strategy themes did change over the year: There was an increase in the frequency with which parents said they used emotional support and a decrease in the frequency of citing outside assistance as guidance strategies. Confirmation of these observed trends must await significance testing with larger samples.

DISCUSSION

Immigrant Latino parents' beliefs about their adolescent children's progress along the path of life can provide a rich source of information concerning adolescent development, the role of schooling in parents' concepts of desirable pathways, and the guidance strategies they use to guide their children to adulthood in their new home country. Our results replicated those of Reese and her colleagues (Reese, Balzono et al., 1995; Reese, Gallimore et al., 1995b) in that

Table 4.4
Longitudinal Comparison of Percent (and Frequency) of Parents' Explanations of Where the Younger and Older Sibling Are on the "Path of Life," Challenges to Staying on the "Good Path," and Parents' Guidance Strategies

Themes	Year 1	Year 2
Explanation Thematic Category		
Behavior	35(9)	50(13)
Personal character or attitude	38(10)	27(7)
Developmental stage	19(5)	15(4)
Peer influence	19(5)	27(7)
School related	4(1)	4(1)
Other	0	8(2)
Challenge Thematic Category		
Peer Influence	77(20)	69(18)
Drugs	27(7)	19(5)
School related	15(4)	23(6)
Personal character and attitude	12(3)	12(3)
No challenges	(2)	12(3)
Adolescence	0	0
Other	12(3)	19(5)
Guidance Strategy Thematic Category		
Consejos	77(20)	65(17)
Monitor and restrict	35(8)	31(8)
Emotional support	12(3)	23(6)
Outside assistance	23(6)	4(1)
Role model	12(3)	4(1)
Other	1(4)	12(3)

Note. Thirteen parents were interviewed in both years. Therefore, the total frequency possible in each category was 26. The sum of percentages exceeds 100 because parents could give more than one response; up to three responses were coded for each parent.

parents emphasized the moral dimension of the path of life with school being only one component of what they view as being *bien educado* (well educated).

We also replicated their finding that *malas compañías*, and especially peers, were the challenge parents most worried about concerning their children staying on the good path. However, few adolescents had had negative peer experiences, and, thus, for most parents, peers were only a hypothetical concern given their understanding of adolescent development and the salience of peers during this stage of life. It is worth noting that peers are a concern of all cultures that allow their children more freedom during adolescence, not just Latino immigrants. The European American families who are participating in the longitudinal study from which the present Latino sample was drawn have also expressed a high degree of concern about peer influences. Harris (1995) has argued that as children begin to spend a significant part of their day away from the family, peers may begin to play an even more important role in their socialization than parents, and this was the essence of both Latino and European American parents' concerns. However, while all parents of adolescents may worry about peer influences, immigrant parents, and in this case Latinos, had concerns that European American parents did not express. For example, many feared that their children would lose their culture, language, and religious beliefs or reject their families. Although they wanted their children to learn English and be accepted by and make friends with majority culture peers, parents also worried that their children would adopt their peers' more liberal attitudes and lose respect for their elders.

In support of Goodnow's (1988) and D'Andrade and Strauss's (1992) view that abstract cultural belief systems or schemas are fairly resistant to change, we found little within-group variability in parents' definitions of the good and the bad paths of life and their descriptions of their guidance strategies. Our short-term longitudinal analysis also revealed stability in parents' beliefs. Parents defined the good path of life primarily in terms of having moral values such as being respectful and responsible and avoiding the kinds of things parents associated with the bad path, such as drugs, alcohol, and distancing oneself from one's family. Parents' preferred guidance strategy was *consejos*. As illustrated by the quotes, parents' *consejos* conveyed to their children a rich set of cultural values interwoven with life lessons parents had learned or observed in others.

That *consejos* are a powerful tool of parent involvement in children's schooling and moral development is also illustrated by the work of Delgado-Gaitán (1994a), who carried out extensive ethnographic studies of Mexican-descent parents' socialization strategies. However, while *consejos* was the most favored guidance strategy in our study, it was not the only strategy parents advocated, particularly when they perceived that their children had strayed from the good path or were at a difficult crossroad. In these situations, parents also intervened in their children's lives by restricting and constraining their activities, particularly with peers. The mother of an adolescent daughter who had joined a chola group in high school and had begun to do poorly in school told us, for example, that she and her husband had burned her daughter's chola clothes and asked the teachers to keep an eye on her at school. When the daughter challenged their attempts to help her get back on track, they attended family counseling to understand their daughter's motives better and work toward finding a solution that both the parents and the daughter could abide by. The agency displayed by these parents, which was not atypical in families in which a child had strayed, contradicts the view, often perpetuated by the media, that Latino immigrant parents are not involved in their children's lives or lack the knowledge and personal resources to help them navigate the life challenges that they encounter in the United States. As Grusec et al. (2000) suggested, parents' adaptations to their particular children's needs can reveal within-group variability in the application of abstract cultural belief systems. In our current work, we are focusing on these applications of parental beliefs because they are also likely to reveal the mechanisms through which participation in a new culture may eventually lead to shifts in parents' cultural schemas.

In addition to examining within-culture variability in parents' beliefs and guidance strategies, we also examined within-family variability by asking parents to describe the developmental paths and guidance strategies they used to guide two of their adolescent children. Our results showed that junior high school (early adolescence) is a time of particular concern for parents; parents of the younger adolescent children worried about the potential problems that might occur during their children's transition to junior high school and parents of older siblings who had strayed from the good path often mentioned that their children's problems began in junior high school.

Not surprisingly, parents had more concerns about older than younger siblings. For the older siblings, peer challenges were often a reality, and, especially for boys, school difficulties (doing well, staying in school) were also worries. The finding that boys were doing more poorly in school than girls is consistent with other reports showing that Latino males have the highest rates of school dropout in California (Larson & Rumberger, 1995). Our interviews showed that parents were concerned about their children's school difficulties and wanted to make schoolwork a priority. For example, in other parts of the interview, they spontaneously commented that although helping with chores and child care were important responsibilities that children have to the family, homework took priority. Some parents added, however, that ultimately the arrangements and sacrifices families make for the sake of their children's schooling will not matter if the students themselves do not value school and do the work.

Concerning gender variation in parents' beliefs and strategies, parents were more concerned about negative peer influences for their daughters than their sons. This gender difference may stem from parents' worries that running with a bad crowd sullies the reputation of their daughters more than that of their sons. This speculation was supported by the finding that parents were more likely to constrain or restrict their daughters' than their sons' activities. Still, however, it was not the case that parents were not worried about their sons. In some ways, they saw adolescence as more challenging for boys because as illustrated by the quote offered earlier, boys were more likely to spend time outside the home than girls, be exposed to more bad influences such as alcohol and drugs, and receive more peer pressure to engage in risky behaviors to prove their manhood. In addition, boys were experiencing more school difficulties, a significant area of concern for their parents. Many of the study's parents disclosed that one of their primary motives for coming to the United States was to ensure a better education and future for their children. As their older children progressed through junior high school and high school, they were seeing their dream slip away and were imagining a life of hardship for their children.

Our analyses of the subset of families for whom we had two years of data showed very little change in parents' beliefs and guidance strategies. Possibly, this stability was due to most of these adolescents experiencing few changes in their progress along the path of life from year 1 to year 2. Thus, there was little need for parents to alter their beliefs or guidance strategies (see also Sameroff, 1975). Perhaps with a longer time period between assessments or a larger sample, shifts in parents' beliefs would have been evident.

In any case, the results of this study illustrate Latino parents' rich network of beliefs about their children's lives and their active engagement in their development. While parents expressed much concern about peers, most of these concerns had not materialized at the time of the study. Still, peer influences should not be discounted because parents of adolescents who had strayed often attributed their children's difficulties to hanging out with the wrong crowd. It is important to remember, however, that while peers can exert negative influences, they can also be positive forces in adolescents' lives. Other researchers have documented the important role that peers play in Latino students' development and success at school (Alva, 1991; Gandara, 1995), and in other sections of the interview, the parents who participated in this study indicated that they were generally satisfied with most of their children's friendships because they knew the friends and their families. Thus, while peers can certainly challenge family values, in many cases they support them and contribute to adolescents' progress along the good path of life.

Although this chapter focused on immigrant Latino families, many of the themes that emerged are universal beliefs and concerns of parents of adolescents. We are currently examining the responses of the European American parents in our sample to assess similarities and differences between their beliefs and those expressed by the immigrant families who were the focus of this chapter. Identifying these similarities and differences is essential for developing theories and methodologies that are appropriate for carrying out cross-cultural or cross-ethnic work as well as studies involving more than one income group.

In the past, one group was often used as the "standard" against which others were compared. For example, in many studies middle-class European American families set the standard, and differences in minority or low-income families' practices were seen as deficits that could be eliminated with proper training.

This practice has been criticized widely by researchers (e.g., Delgado-Gaitán & Trueba, 1991; Raffaele & Knoff, 1999; Tharp, 1989) who have demonstrated that these differences reflect communities' adaptations to their ecologies and their developmental goals and, consequently, should not be considered deficits. Some of these scholars have suggested that researchers conduct in-depth investigations of particular communities to understand their practices and map their developmental pathways. Trying to avoid a deficit account by focusing on a single group, however, can be problematic because it can lead to particularistic accounts that obscure universal features of development. In our work, we are attempting to avoid both deficit and particularistic accounts by beginning with an in-depth analysis of each ethnic group and then proceeding to identify similarities and differences between them (see also Sue & Sue, 1987). Once we identify these similarities and differences, we will consider the life circumstances that may have produced them, hoping to eventually construct a theory that is sensitive to the cultural ecologies of our participants' lives. We are also using this approach to identify sources of within-group variability. Assessing within-group variability will be useful toward challenging stereotypes of Latino families and identifying potential causes of changes in beliefs systems.

Although the results of the present study yielded more homogeneity than variance in parents' beliefs, there was some suggestion that these beliefs are influenced, to an extent, by their children's age, gender, and experiences. In the future, we would like to develop more sensitive methods for studying change in parents' beliefs. Longitudinal work that spans a longer time period may be useful toward this goal; Sabogal et al. (1987) and others, for example, have described how Latinos' conception of familism changes across generations. Studying recent immigrants may also be useful toward understanding changes in parents' beliefs because the challenges of adapting to a new culture and raising children who will succeed in their new home may lead parents to reflect on their values and assess which ones to retain and which ones to modify. The participants in this study had generally lived in the United States for a few years and, thus, may have already undergone this process.

We close with some thoughts on how our work can inform school policy and other institutions that serve Latinos. Teachers and schools often assume that Latino parents and adolescents have low educational aspirations or that they are passive in their approach to schooling, failing to act in the face of difficulties or accepting school policies without questioning them. Our findings painted a very different picture. For example, many parents had come to the United States so their children could have a better education that would allow them to obtain a good job that would keep them from experiencing the hardships that they had endured. However, while these parents hoped that their children would succeed in school and work, they did not want this success to come at the expense of living a moral life. Adolescents' pathways through school may benefit from parents and school personnel working together to find ways of integrating morality and schooling in ways that capture Latino parents' concept of *bien educado* and provide continuity between home and school goals and values. Educators should also consider that parents' and students' apparent passivity may result from Latinos' emphasis on respect for elders and other authorities. As Delgado-Gaitán (1994b) showed, community or school programs that inform parents about their rights and school expectations for agency can help parents navigate the system, learn ways to make their needs known, and participate actively in school governance.

Parent and teacher dialogues could also help teachers learn about the different ways in which Latino parents are helping their children in school and through adolescence as well as help parents learn new ways to guide their children along the good path of life. These conversations can also help parents and teachers negotiate mutually acceptable solutions to problems. For example, Latino parents, and especially parents of girls, often prevent their children from participating in academic activities that they fear may derail them from the good path. One such experience is the weeklong overnight science camp attended by sixth graders in our community. Parents prevent their daughters from attending these camps because they fear that they will have unsupervised interactions with boys or discuss topics that they disapprove off (e.g., sex, drugs). Teachers, however, worry that Latino girls' lack of exposure to these engaging science activities will be an obstacle toward their mastery of science knowledge and their consideration of future careers in science. Through discussion, parents and teachers could convey their concerns and develop strategies for helping girls attend the camp while providing a level of supervision that satisfies parents.

Finally, we need to find ways to help Latino immigrant parents become aware of resources in their community. Our interviews showed that parents were often unaware of potential resources, such as after-school homework programs, affordable health care, and counseling services. Awareness of resources is not enough, however. Parents and adolescents must feel comfortable accessing these resources. For example, parents and adolescents may be more likely to initiate a meeting with a school counselor if the counselor was a Latino(a) who understood their background or, at a minimum, a counselor of another ethnicity who spoke Spanish and was knowledgeable of issues unique to Latino families, students, and communities. School counselors can be important assets not only for helping students and their families plan educational and job trajectories and resolving school problems but also for helping immigrant families adjust to the unavoidable challenges of making their way in a new culture.

AUTHORS' NOTES

The research reported in this chapter was supported by grants from the U.S. Department of Education's Office for Educational Research and Improvement to Margarita Azmitia and Catherine R. Cooper through the Center for Research on Education, Diversity, and Excellence and the University of California Linguistic Minority Research Institute to Catherine R. Cooper and Jane R. Brown. Portions of this chapter were presented at the biennial meetings of the Society for Research in Child Development, Albuquerque, NM, 1999. The authors thank the parents and adolescents who participated in the interviews that provided the foundation for this chapter. Catherine R. Cooper and the participants in the Kent State University Forum on Latino Children and Families in the United States provided helpful feedback on an earlier draft. Address correspondence to Margarita Azmitia, Psychology Department, Social Sciences 2, University of California, Santa Cruz, CA 95064 or e-mail to: azmitia@cats.ucsc.edu

REFERENCES

Alva, S. A. (1991). Academic invulnerability among Mexican-American students: The importance of protective resources and appraisals. *Hispanic Journal of Behavioral Sciences, 13*, 18–34.

Arnett, J. J. (1999). Adolescent storm and stress, reconsidered. *American Psychologist, 54*, 317–326.

Azmitia, M., & Cooper, C. R. (1996). *Navigating and negotiating home, school, peer, and community linkages in adolescence.* Grant from the U.S. Department of Education's Office of Educational Research and Improvement through the Center for Research on Education, Diversity, and Excellence, University of California, Santa Cruz.

Brenan, R. L., & Prediger, D. J. (1991). Coefficient kappa: Some uses, misuses, and alternatives. *Educational and Psychological Measurement, 41*, 687–699.

Canto, M. (1998, December 22). Schools woo Latino parents. *Monterrey County Herald,* p. 15.

Chacón, M. A., & Cohen, E. G. (1982). *Chicanas in postsecondary education.* Palo Alto, CA: Stanford University Center for Research on Women.

Cooper, C. R., Azmitia, M., García, E. E., Ittel, A., Lopez, E. M., Rivera, L., & Martinez-Chavez, R. (1994). Aspirations of low-income Mexican American and European American parents for their children and adolescents. In F. A. Villarruel & R. M. Lerner (Eds.), *Community-based programs for socialization and learning: New directions for child development* (pp. 65–81). San Francisco: Jossey-Bass.

Cuellar, I., Arnold, B., & Gonzalez, G. (1995). Cognitive referents of acculturation: Assessment of cultural constructs in Mexican Americans. *Journal of Community Psychology, 23*, 339–356.

D'Andrade, R., & Strauss, C. (1992). *Human motives and cultural models.* Cambridge, England: Cambridge University Press.

Daniels, D., & Plomin, R. (1985). Deferential experience of siblings in the same family. *Developmental Psychology, 21*, 747–760.

Delgado-Gaitán, C. (1992). School matters in the Mexican-American home: Socializing children to education. *American Educational Research Journal, 29*, 495–513.

Delgado-Gaitán, C. (1994a). *Consejos:* The power of cultural narratives. *Anthropology and Education Quarterly, 25*, 298–316.

Delgado-Gaitán, C. (1994b). Socializing young children in Mexican-American families: An intergenerational perspective. In P. M. Greenfield & R. R. Cocking (Eds.), *Cross-cultural roots of minority child development* (pp. 55–86). Hillsdale, NJ: Erlbaum.

Delgado-Gaitán, C., & Trueba, H. (1991). *Crossing cultural borders: Education for immigrant families in America.* London: Falmer Press/Taylor & Francis.

Dunn, J., & Plomin, R. (1990). *Separate lives: Why siblings are so different.* New York: Basic Books.

Gandara, P. (1995). *Over the ivy walls: The educational mobility of low-income Chicanos.* Albany: State University of New York Press.

Goldenberg, C., & Gallimore, R. (1995). Immigrant Latino parents' values and beliefs about their children's education: Continuities and discontinuities across cultures and generations. *Advances in Motivation and Achievement, 9,* 183–228.

Goldenberg, C., Gallimore, R., Reese, L., & Garnier, H. (1998). *Cause or effect? A longitudinal study of immigrant Latino parents' aspirations and expectations and their children's school performance.* Manuscript submitted for publication.

Goodnow, J. J. (1988). Parents' ideas, actions, and feelings: Models and methods from developmental and social psychology. *Child Development, 59,* 286–320.

Grusec, J. E., Goodnow, J. J., & Kuczynski, L. (2000). New directions in analyses of parenting contributions to children's acquisition of values. *Child Development, 71,* 205–211.

Harkness, S., Super, C. M., & Keefer, C. H. (1992). Learning to be an American parent: How cultural models gain directive force. In R. D'Andrade & C. Strauss (Eds.), *Human motives and cultural models* (pp. 163–178). Cambridge, England: Cambridge University Press.

Harris, J. (1995). Where is the child's environment? A group socialization theory of development. *Psychological Review, 102,* 458–489.

Harwood, R. L., Schoelmerich, A., Ventura-Cook, E., Schulze, P. A., & Wilson, S. P. (1996). Culture and class influences on Anglo and Puerto Rican mothers' beliefs regarding long-term socialization goals and child behavior. *Child Development, 67,* 2446–2461.

Henderson, R. W. (1997). Educational and occupational aspirations and expectations among parents of middle school students of Mexican descent: Family resources for academic development and mathematics learning. In R. D. Taylor & M. C. Wang (Eds.), *Social and emotional adjustment and family relations in ethnic minority families* (pp. 99–131). Mahwah, NJ: Erlbaum.

Hill, J. P., & Lynch, M. E. (1983). The intensification of gender-related role expectations during early adolescence. In J. Brooks-Gunn & A. C. Petersen (Eds.), *Girls at puberty: Biological and psychosocial perspectives* (pp. 201–228). New York: Plenum.

Keefe, S. E., Padilla, A. M., & Carlos, M. L., (1979). The Mexican-American extended family as an emotional support system. *Human Organization, 38,* 144–152.

Kroesen, K., Reese, L., & Gallimore, R., (1998). *Navigating multiple worlds: Latino children becoming adolescents in Los Angeles.* Manuscript submitted for publication.

Larson, K., & Rumberger, R. (1995). Doubling school success in highest-risk Latino youth: Results from a middle school intervention study. In R. F. Macias & R. G. García Ramos (Eds.), *Changing schools for changing students: An anthology of research on language minorities, schools, and society* (pp. 157–181). Santa Barbara: University of California Linguistic Minority Research Institute.

Leyendecker, B., & Lamb, M. E. (1999). Latino families. In M. E. Lamb (Ed.), *Parenting and child development in "nontraditional" families* (pp. 247–262). Mahwah, NJ: Erlbaum.

Raffaele, L. M., & Knoff, H. M. (1999). Improving home-school collaboration with disadvantaged families: Organizational principles, perspectives, and approaches. *School Psychology Review, 28,* 448–466.

Reese, L., Balzano, S., Gallimore, R., & Goldenberg, C. (1995). The concept of *educación*: Latino family values and American schooling. *International Journal of Educational Research, 23,* 57–81.

Reese, L., Gallimore, R., Goldenberg, C., & Balzano, S. (1995). Immigrant Latino parents' future orientations for their children. In R. F. Macias & R. G. Garcia Ramos (Eds.), *Changing schools for changing students: An anthology of research on language minorities, schools, and society* (pp. 205–230). Santa Barbara: University of California Linguistic Minority Research Institute.

Romo, H. D., & Falbo, T. (1996). *Latino high school graduation: Defying the odds.* Austin: University of Texas Press.

Rowe, D. C. (1994). The limits of family influence. In *Genes, experience, and behavior.* New York: Guilford.

Sabogal, G., Marín, G., Otero-Sabogal, R., Marín, B.V., & Perez-Stable, E. J. (1987). Hispanic familism and acculturation: What changes and what doesn't? *Hispanic Journal of Behavioral Sciences, 9,* 397–412.

Sameroff, A. (1975). Transactional models of early social relations. *Human Development, 18,* 65–79.

Siegel, S., & Castellan, N. J. (1988). *Nonparametric statistics* (2nd ed.). New York: McGraw-Hill.

Sigel, I. E., & McGillicuddy-Delisi, A. V. (Eds.). (1992). *Parental belief systems: The psychological consequences for families* (2nd ed.). Hillsdale, NJ: Erlbaum.

Suarez-Orozco, C., & Suarez-Orozco, M. (1995). *Transformations: Migration, family life, and achievement motivation among Latino students.* Palo Alto, CA: Stanford University Press.

Sue, D., & Sue, S. (1987). Cultural factors in the clinical assessment of Asian Americans. *Journal of Consulting and Clinical Psychology, 55,* 479–487.

Tharp, R. G. (1989). Psychocultural variables and constants. Effects of teaching and learning in schools. *American Psychologist, 44,* 349–359.

Tharp, R. G., & Gallimore, R. (1988). *Rousing minds to life: Teaching, learning, and schooling in social context.* New York: Cambridge University Press.

Valdés, G. (1996). Con respeto: *Bridging the distances between culturally diverse families and schools: An ethnographic portrait.* New York: Teachers College Press.

Valenzuela, A., & Dornbusch, S. M. (1994). Familism and social capital in the academic achievement of Mexican origin and Anglo adolescents. *Social Science Quarterly, 75,* 18–36.

5

Coparenting in Intact Mexican American Families: Mothers' and Fathers' Perceptions

Yvonne M. Caldera, Jacki Fitzpatrick, and Karen S. Wampler

INTRODUCTION

The parenting role traditionally has been viewed as the responsibility of the mother. The continued increase of middle-class mothers in the labor force during the past 50 years, however, has had major implications for the role of the father in the family. Research on fathers in the past 20 years (see Lamb, 1997a,b) has demonstrated that fathers are becoming more involved in the lives of their children and assuming responsibilities for child care and housework, especially in dual-earner households (Coltrane, 1996; Daniels & Weingarten, 1982; Fitzpatrick, Caldera, Pursley, & Wampler, 1999; Robinson, 1988).

The existing research on fathers is limited, however, in that studies have tended to focus on the division of labor between mothers and fathers or the father–child relationship (for reviews, see Lamb, 1997a; Parke, 1995), rather than on joint parenting within the family, or coparenting. Coparenting refers to the extent to which couples work as a team in managing parenting responsibilities and strategies (Lidz, 1963; McHale, Kuersten-Hogan, Lauretti, & Rasmussen, 2000). Until recently, most of the empirical work on coparenting focused on separated or divorced couples instead of on how cohabiting parents work together to raise their children (Hetherington & Stanley-Hagan, 1995; Maccoby, Depner, & Mnookin, 1990). Studies focusing on two-parent families have tended to focus on parent–child interaction or parenting values/practices, rather than on how parents manage their children's lives (Parke, Burks, Carson, Neville, & Boyum, 1994). Finally, studies have primarily been conducted with non-Hispanic White families, ignoring changes that may be occurring in families of color, in particular, Latino families. The present study, therefore, was designed to overcome some of these limitations. More specifically, we investigated how cohabiting Mexican American mothers and fathers manage parenting responsibilities and strategies as they raise their children.

COPARENTING

According to Margolin, Gordis, and John (2001, p. 3), "Coparenting may be the most daunting yet significant experience that two adults share. It is through this relationship that parents negotiate their respective roles, responsibilities, and contributions to their children." Coparenting is a complex but unique process that is different from marital, parent–child, and whole family dynamics (Schoppe, Magelsdorf & Frosh 2001). Key dimensions of this process include negotiation of expectations, cooperation/coordination of task fulfillment, and the conveyance of unity among parents to children. Positively valenced (supportive) coparenting reflects partners' efforts to endorse or complement each other's parenting efforts (e.g., Gable, Belsky, & Crnic, 1995). In contrast, negatively valenced (unsupportive) actions reflect partners' efforts to sabotage or undermine each other's interactions with the children (e.g., Margolin et al., 2001; McHale, 1995).

In early coparenting research, there was much emphasis on post-divorce relationships. Such studies examined the ways in which divorced parents could effectively work together while in different households (Maccoby et al., 1990). Overall, the research indicated that the negative consequences of divorce could be minimized if parents discussed their children; made child-related decisions together; and refrained from divulging what transpired between parents, criticizing the ex-spouse, or manipulating children (Aydintug, 1995). It has been argued that such cooperative processes could be relevant to parenting in non-divorced families as well.

Thus, a second early trend did focus on the coparenting experiences within intact families. These studies primarily examined spousal discrepancies in parental values, beliefs, or behaviors; a premise of such studies was that greater discrepancies would prompt greater conflict between partners and contribute adversely to child development. Indeed some researchers reported that parenting discrepancies have been negatively associated with ego control in preschoolers (Block, Block, & Morrison, 1981; Vaughn, Block, & Block, 1988) and positively associated with sons' internalizing/externalizing behavioral problems (e.g., Jouriles, Murphy, Farris, Smith, Richters, & Waters, 1991). This line of research made some contributions to the field but has been criticized for methods that do not directly measure coparenting mechanisms, and a disproportionate focus on negatively valenced dynamics (e.g., Belsky, Crnic, & Gable, 1995; Margolin et al., 2001; McHale, 1997).

During the last decade, researchers attempted to advance studies by refining the measurement of, as well as integrating, systemic/developmentalist perspectives. Belsky and colleagues (Belsky et al., 1995; Belsky & Hsieh, 1998; Belsky, Putnam, & Crnic, 1996; Gable, Belsky, & Crnic, 1992, 1995) conducted lengthy, naturalistic, home observations as a means to capture more detailed, coparenting processes. Coparenting was defined as "the extent to which husbands and wives function as partners or adversaries in their parenting role" (Gable et al., 1995, p. 610). More specifically, the observers initially identified triadic (mother, father, and child) interactions, and events were then inductively classified as supportive or unsupportive. Supportive behaviors included such actions as repeating a partner's statements to the child or complementing the partner by adding expanded (but consistent) information to the child. Unsupportive behaviors included criticizing the partner to the child or giving a competing, inconsistent directive to the child.

They found that coparenting incidents occurred approximately 10 times per hour, suggesting it is a highly common familial dynamic. In comparison to unsupportive behaviors, supportive behaviors occurred twice as frequently; the most common supportive behavior was complementary exchanges (Gable et al., 1995). A longitudinal analysis indicated that spouses who experience marital deterioration over time have higher proportions of unsupportive coparenting during the toddler years (Belsky & Hsieh, 1998). In examining child outcomes, they reported that children with the lowest level of self-inhibition resided in families with the highest levels of unsupportive coparenting exchanges (Belsky et al., 1996). They further noted that coparenting has a statistical effect beyond intrapersonal characteristics of the parents, suggesting that this relational process plays a unique role in family dynamics.

During the same time frame, McHale and colleagues (McHale, 1995, 1997; McHale et al., 2000; McHale & Rasmussen, 1998) studied coparenting—defined as "mutual support and commitment to parenting the child" (McHale, 1995; p. 985), with intact families. Initially, McHale (1995) videotaped couples with their infants in a structured play situation in the laboratory to explore the relation between marital satisfaction and coparenting behaviors. The observation methodology generated three codes: hostility–competitiveness, harmony, and parental discrepancy. In examining marriage–coparenting associations, it was found that as marital distress increased, hostility–competitiveness increased, discrepancy increased, and harmony decreased.

McHale (1997) then extended this line of research by developing a self-report measure of coparenting. The questionnaire assessed four dimensions: family integrity, which reflects parents' efforts to promote togetherness; disparagement, which reflects undermining the partners' credibility; conflict, which reflects disagreements about children or in the presence of children; and reprimand/solidarity, which reflects setting limits. A cluster analysis was conducted and identified five types of coparenting families: low integrity and low reprimand characterized disconnected families; high integrity, low disparagement, and low conflict characterized supportive families; moderate scores on coparenting dimensions characterized average families; low integrity, high disparagement, and high conflict characterized distressed–conflicted families; and passionate families had high scores on all four dimensions. This study highlighted that coparenting is not a unidimensional process and reflects a diverse range of interaction patterns (McHale, 1997).

Subsequently, McHale and colleagues investigated longitudinal relations among the coparenting measures and assessments of child development. Families were observed in infancy, and parents completed the self-report measure three years later. There was consistency in the observed/self-report coparenting patterns (McHale et al., 2000; McHale & Rasmussen, 1998). Specifically, fathers in families rated as high in harmony reported high levels of integrity and solidarity; mothers and fathers in families rated low on hostlity–competiveness reported high levels of solidarity and integrity. In addition, there were significant associations between coparenting and child development. They found that greater hostility, less harmony, and greater discrepancy at infancy were associated with more teacher reports of child problem behaviors three years later. Examining the associations between concurrent self-reported coparenting and child problems revealed that problems were negatively associated with father integrity and positively associated with mother disparagement (McHale & Rasmussen, 1998).

Such studies have significantly advanced the study of coparenting. It should be noted, however, that the researchers acknowledged some significant limitations to their studies in general. For example, the majority of participants were non-Hispanic White and the findings might not be generalizable to other cultural groups (e.g., Belsky & Hsieh, 1998). In addition, observations indicated that parents sometimes engage in coparenting inadvertently and do not notice the efforts of the partners to support them; in such cases coparenting is inferred (e.g., Gable et al., 1992). This inference might be accurate, but it does raise questions about the importance of intentionality in parenting dynamics. Indeed, McHale et al. (2000) argued that "little is known about parents' perception of own coparenting behavior. Parents are likely to be aware of the things they do to influence coparenting solidarity and of their family's typical group dynamics" (p. 221). Thus, they have noted that observational methods alone are not sufficient and recommended that future studies include other methodologies, such as questionnaires or interviews (Belsky et al., 1995; McHale et al., 2000).

Two investigators explored coparenting in intact non-Hispanic White families utilizing qualitative methodology (Deutsch, 1999; Ehrensaft, 1990). Both investigators examined how mothers and fathers felt about shared parenting, what factors contributed to their decision to coparent, and the consequences of coparenting on the children and families. Most of the families in Ehrensaft's (1990) study had made a conscious choice to coparent and felt a sense of pride in their decision. When asked about reasons for their choice to share parenting, they described values of fairness, equality, and the amount of work parenting requires. Deutsch's (1999) study included those who had decided to share parenting equally and parents who had other less even arrangements. Families in the latter group reported being pushed into it by changing circumstances and many felt resentful of their situation.

In terms of the consequences of their choice to coparent, families in Ehrensaft's (1990) study focused on the impact their coparenting had on their children. On the positive side, they felt their children had more focused love and attention from two parents, a greater sense of trust, a more integrated sense of gender identity, and the opportunity to observe "democracy in action" (p. 212). These families also acknowledged some drawbacks to coparenting for the children, including the need to adapt to different parenting styles—what they called the "changing of the guard" (p. 193), the danger of overparenting, and the possibility of giving the children a sense of entitlement and egocentrism. Families in Deutsch's (1999) study mostly talked about the consequences of coparenting for the parents. On the positive side, they felt their choice had expanded their identity and helped them relinquish stereotypic parts of themselves. On the downside, they felt coparenting had made fathers forgo career decisions and mothers give up some of their maternal role. Although extensive in scope, neither of these studies examined the process by which mothers and fathers negotiate and manage their parenting responsibilities. In addition, these studies did not include families of color, again limiting the available information about coparenting in diverse families.

To date, the only research on coparenting with families of color is a series of studies conducted with African Americans by Brody and colleagues (Brody & Flor, 1996; Brody, Stoneman, & Flor, 1995; Brody, Stoneman, Flor, & McCrary, 1994a; Brody, Stoneman, Flor, McCrary, Hastings, & Conyers, 1994b). In these studies, coparenting was assessed via behavioral structured observations and a self-report instrument. The observations assessed the quality of the marital relationship, and included four indicators: harmony, engagement, communication, and warmth. The self-report measure consisted of five variables derived from Ahron's (1981) Quality of Coparenting Scales (revised): (a) communication and (b) instrumental support from mother to father, (c) communication and (d) instrumental support from father to mother, and (e) parental conflict. The series of studies examined relations between family income, parental functioning, the coparenting variables, and child outcomes. They found higher income to be related to more optimal parental functioning (Brody et al., 1994b) and less conflict (Brody et al., 1995). More optimal parental functioning was associated with more support, higher marital quality, and less conflict (Brody et al., 1994a). These coparenting indices in turn were positively associated with child self-regulation, which in turn was related to academic achievement (Brody, 1994a; Brody, 1994b; Brody et al., 1995). Coparenting in these studies, thus, served a mediating role between parental characteristics and child functioning and had both direct and indirect links with optimal child outcomes.

In sum, the family and child development literature have revealed a budding interest in the coparental relationship in intact families. Investigators have proposed ways to operationalize and measure it through self-report and observational means. The findings of these studies are revealing coparenting to be an important link between the spousal and parent–child dyads, as well as an impact on children's development. Empirical findings, however, are lacking in this area especially with non-White parents. The present study, therefore, was designed to investigate the process of coparenting in Mexican American families.

LATINOS AND COPARENTING

Latinos are the largest growing minority group in the United States. In 2000, the U.S. Census Bureau reported that 32.8 million Latinos were living in this country. This is an increase of more than 60% from 1990. It is estimated that by the year 2025, this segment of the population will grow to over 40 million. There is great diversity within Latinos in the United States because they come from different Spanish-speaking countries, each with its own political history and unique migration patterns and acculturation rates. In addition, the Latino family has not remained static, making it difficult to discern what a typical Latino family looks like today (Levine & Padilla, 1980; Montiel, 1975; Vega, 1990). Because of this diversity, research must begin to focus on specific groups of Latinos individually instead of assuming homogeneity between groups (Zuniga, 1998). Latinos of Mexican origin compose the largest group, at 66.1% of Latinos (Chapa & Valencia, 1993). The large number of Mexican Americans in this country and their unique history point to a need for research in order to understand the changing structure and function of families with Mexican ancestry.

The Mexican American family has been defined, typically, as adhering to traditional values that include familism, traditional male/female roles, and extended family networks (García Coll, Meyer, & Brillon, 1995; Cauce & Domenech-Rodríguez, Chapter 1, this volume). Even with changes resulting from acculturation and socioeconomic pressures, the importance of family unity continues as a major characteristic among Mexican Americans to this day (Becerra, 1988). Mexican Americans adhere to a collectivistic guiding principle that supports family and community life (Roland, 1988). The traditional Latino family also has been described as subscribing to male supremacy, maternal submissiveness, and strict sex roles giving the father a peripheral role in the life of his children (Mirande, 1988). More current research, however, has demonstrated more egalitarian family patterns in the behaviors of Mexican American families (Chilman, 1993) and presents a picture of Mexican American fathers as more actively engaged with their children in play, more affectionate, and providing more emotional support than previously described (e.g., Davis & Chavez, 1995; Maason, Alaniz, & Caldera, 1999; Mirande,

1988). Subgroups of Latino mothers and fathers have been noted to share decision-making responsibility for major family decisions, contradicting the myth that Latino mothers are the ones responsible for the children (Cooney, Rogler, Hurrell, & Ortiz, 1982; Ybarra, 1982).

A common criticism of research on ethnic minority families is that such studies are based on a comparative perspective. Minority families are compared with non-Hispanic White and middle-class families and any differences are considered deficiencies (García Coll et al., 1995; McKinney, Abrams, Terry, & Lerner, 1994; Tripp-Reimer & Wilson, 1991). A more culturally sensitive approach involves collecting data that captures the unique perspectives and practices of their culture without relying on preconceived ideas of what is appropriate or inappropriate. Consistent with this perspective, researchers have proposed that studies focusing on ethnic minority families be conducted using qualitative methodologies and without comparing them to non-Hispanic Whites (Harrison, Wilson, Pine, Chan, & Buriel, 1990; Lamberty & García Coll, 1994). Focus group studies are one type of qualitative research that has proven ideal for studies attempting to identify new constructs without relying on preexisting concepts (Cabrera, Knaug-Jensen, Pinedo, Burrow, Everett, & DesRosiers, 1997). Thus, in the present study, focus group discussions were conducted with mothers and fathers separately in order to ascertain each partner's view of sharing parenting responsibilities. The main question addressed in this study was: How do Latino parents from intact families, work together to raise their children and manage their children's lives? Specifically, we were interested in how Mexican American mothers and fathers negotiate and manage the roles and responsibilities that each has in raising their children in the United States.

METHOD

Participants

Fourteen (28 individuals) lower- to middle-class Mexican American couples participated in the study. Both partners in each couple participated, and each couple had at least one child younger than 11 years of age (M = 5.5, SD = 3.58). All families except one were married. Eight of the families were dual-earner, four were single-earner (in one only the mother was employed), and in one family, neither parent was employed.

Mothers tended to be younger than fathers (mother average age = 31.6 years; father average age = 35.4 years; t = −2.229, $p < .05$). There was no significant difference in the level of formal education (mother education = 12.4 years; father education = 13.1 years). Twenty-nine percent (n = 8) of the participants were born in Mexico, and the remainder was of Mexican descent, born in the United States. Couples had 1–3 children (mean = 1.8), and the target (youngest) children were aged 2 months to 10 years.

Procedure

A set of questions pertaining to how families managed parenting were generated from a review of the parenting literature and formatted to conform with focus group guidelines (Piercy & Nickerson, 1996). Pilot studies were initially conducted with university students in the form of mock interviews in order to refine the questions. In addition, members of the Mexican American community (who did not participate in the study) reviewed the questions and provided feedback about clarity and ease of understanding. The final list of questions were all framed in reference to the participants' child(dren) younger than 11 years. The questions that pertain to this report were:

1. In general, how do the two of you work together to raise your child?
2. What is it like when all of you (spouses and children) are together?
3. If you and your wife/husband disagree about how to parent, how do you handle those disagreements?
4. What was the most recent disagreement about parenting?

Participants were recruited through open announcements in neighborhood settings and referrals from leaders in local communities. All participants came from a west Texas city of 200,000, whose population is 30% Mexican American. A total of seven focus group discussions were conducted; two were held off-campus in a church's facility building and the rest were conducted on campus at a family therapy clinic. One discussion was a mixed-gender group, but the remaining discussions were conducted separately for mothers and fathers.

To enhance participant comfort (e.g., McLoyd, 1994), a series of steps were taken before, during, and after the discussions. First, the parents were invited to bring their children to the discussion groups. A meal was provided for parents and children, and all family members had the opportunity to meet the researchers, discussion moderators, moderator assistants, and child-care providers (refreshments were available during the discussions as well). Second, parents were given the opportunity to tour all clinic rooms, including the room prepared for child care; a tour was unnecessary at the church building because the families were familiar with the facility. Third, children were accompanied by their parents to the child-care room; parents were informed that they were free to (a) stay with their children until they felt comfortable going to the discussion room and (b) return to this room at any time. When they were ready, parents were accompanied by the moderators to the discussion rooms.

Once in the interview rooms the moderator reviewed the consent form and began the discussion. The fourth step was to match staff and participants. More specifically, we were able to provide a moderator and moderator assistant of the same gender for six of the seven discussion groups. In addition, all moderators and assistants were bilingual and trained in group-interview techniques. Four of the moderators/assistants were Mexican American, and two were non-Hispanic White (one Italian), but both spoke Spanish fluently. Fifth, the moderators demonstrated an "enlightened novice approach" and openness to the participants' comments. This was initiated by stating: "The purpose of this discussion is to learn more about mothers' and fathers' opinions about the role of the father in parenting, and how mothers and fathers work together to parent their children. There are no right or wrong answers, we just want to know what you think." Moderators also requested that the participants "teach" the researchers about Mexican American families from their own experiences. Sixth, the assistant moderators made an effort to be as unobtrusive as possible. Their primary tasks were to make note of major themes and monitor the recording equipment, but they responded in a friendly manner if a participant spoke to them. Seventh, the participants were debriefed after the group discussion. The majority of respondents expressed gratitude for the opportunity to share their experiences and/or comfort with the process. In addition, the second author debriefed all moderators and assistant moderators.

Each group discussion was audiotaped and later transcribed. An English-speaking assistant transcribed the discussions that were conducted primarily in English (the campus groups). Two of the bilingual moderators/assistants listened to the audio recording and translated any Spanish phrases that had been omitted. The discussion that was conducted primarily in Spanish was transcribed in Spanish by a bilingual research assistant and then translated into English by a second bilingual research assistant. Two bilingual assistants then verified the accuracy of all transcripts. All participant names were replaced with code numbers, assigning matching codes to spouses/partners.

Data Analysis

To foster accuracy, data analysis was conducted in accordance with common qualitative research guidelines (e.g., Krueger, 1994; Piercy & Nickerson, 1996). First, each of three investigators independently read all transcripts. Next, the investigators worked jointly to conduct code mapping as a means of generating global codes (e.g., family roles, marital history, coparenting, extended family). For this chapter, only statements that fell under the coparenting global code were further analyzed and subcoded. Third, the first author and a research assistant jointly reviewed all transcripts to identify specific coparenting codes. Fourth, the first and second authors independently reread all transcripts to apply the codes to specific coparenting comments from participants. Finally, the first and second author compared the coparenting coding and reached over 90% agreement; the small proportion of disagreement was resolved through collaborative evaluation.

RESULTS

The results presented in this chapter reflect dimensions that attempt to answer the question of how Mexican American mothers and fathers negotiate and manage parenting issues. Two general themes emerged, one dealing with how parents had decided to manage coparenting and a second reflecting an ongoing process of negotiation. From these, six dimensions resulted: (a) joint decision making, (b) support, (c) coordination, (d) compensation, (e) cooperation, and (f) conflict. All but the sixth dimensions represent positively valenced coparenting. In addition, the first four dimensions reflect how parents had managed to settle parenting issues; the last two reflect processes in flux.

Joint Decision Making

Parents talked about the importance of discussing parenting issues and reaching a joint, rather than a unilateral, decision. Unlike the traditional view of Latino families in which the mother is mainly responsible for the children, these parents demonstrated valuing the involvement and input of both parents when dealing with the children. They expressed the need to present a united front for their children, especially when dealing with a decision in response to a child's request. Parents made it clear that they understood the importance of inter-parental consistency when in front of the children. This process seems to be consistent with Gable, Belsky, and Crnic's (1992) description of parents who presented a "simultaneous common front" (p. 287).

FATHER: Then we get together and discuss it and from there, we try to raise her the way it should be.

MOTHER: But I'll never say anything in front of the girls. We always make sure that it's where we can talk about it, because then they're always going to be either coming to mom or going to dad trying to take sides. And we don't do that.

FATHER: Simply, when we go to a dance, well, we talk to the kids: "Son, we're going to a dance. You're going to stay here with your aunt or your grandpa or your grandma."

MOTHER: We will send the children to their room or something like that and then we decide what's going to happen. So, we have to come to a conclusion together.

Both mothers and fathers also talked about the danger of failing to present a united front to their children. These mothers and fathers recognized that disagreeing in front of their children would have negative consequences. Indeed, the studies by Belsky and colleagues, McHale and colleagues, and Brody and colleagues above all point to the detrimental effects on the children when parents do not present a united front. The open-ended nature of our discussions allowed us the unique opportunity to access parents' reasoning for maintaining that unity.

MOTHER: So, when it comes to arguing about how to correct our children, it's away from the kids. We don't say in front of the kids cause then the kids are gonna say "okay, look, Daddy doesn't like it when Mommy does this. So, when Mama does this to me, I'm gonna run to Daddy, I'm gonna run to Daddy." So, we don't let them know that we're disagreeing on how to punish them or how to treat them.

FATHER: When something is finally resolved, that in front of the kids, they have to know that we're in agreement. Because if not, I don't know how, I can only speak of our experience, my experience, but if the kids know that there is a split, or any type of fracture, any crack, they will find it. They'll work the other one. So mom, you know he's being unfair or this and that. So, when we come to some kind of consensus or whatever, that we're going to be in agreement and let the kids know "Hey, we're together on this."

The most frequently used topic when giving examples of joint decision making was education. Unlike the traditional stereotype of Latinos not valuing education (cf. Solis, 1995), the parents in this study clearly perceived education to be an important area in which parents must demonstrate consistency. This finding supports more current literature to the same effect (Zuniga, 1998). Several fathers stated:

FATHER: We had complications with our daughter in public school. And the fact that she wasn't being taught the way we wanted her to be taught and she was having difficulties. And we, you know, we had problems with that. And we addressed it by transferring her into another school and into a private school.

FATHER: You know, we are having trouble with spelling. But I didn't blame the school system, I blamed myself, me and my wife for not making more time to spend with her in her spelling words. And that's what we've done. That was a correct action that we-we took cause we know that her, teacher is a good teacher, So you know we, on our end, we-we took the blame.

FATHER: One thing for instance is being able to speak Spanish, to be able to speak it correctly. Uh, we make a conscious effort to speak Spanish in the house, I guess there was no cable at one time. Now we put that sucker on, just background noise you know, just leave it like that. So, Daughter can roll her R's.

The commonality across focus groups regarding joint decision making is in line with other studies on Latinos in the United States (e.g. Cooney et al., 1982; Ybarra, 1982). Again, the parents in this report contradict the myth that Latino mothers are the ones solely responsible for the children and that they do not value education.

Supporting One Another

Another dimension that emerged from the interviews was the importance of providing support to each other as parents. Support is found in all the research on coparenting we just presented, but in this chapter we are using the term more specifically. We defined support as one parent providing assistance when the other parent is playing a leading role in parenting. Thus, a supportive coparent is one who, at the moment, is playing a supporting role. Parents were supportive of one another in several ways.

For some parents, the spouse/partner provided relief when things were stressful or the other parent was not available. This event seemed to occur when one parent was experiencing role strain and/or accumulation as found in the marriage literature (Sanders, Nicholson, & Floyd, 1997). This dimension of support was not found in the studies that rely on observations or standardized questionnaires just presented, again pointing to the uniqueness of our study.

MOTHER: I don't know what I would do if I didn't have Father. Because sometimes I get really frustrated and I just go "Father, it's your turn, take the kids." And I leave, I just go to the room, I lie down and I just, you know, if I didn't have him with me I don't know what I'd do. I don't know because it really helps to have someone to say, to tell "okay, it's your turn, you handle this now."

MOTHER: But when he gets home before me, I know when I walk in the house is going to be clean because he'll make the girls, pick up their room, cleaned up the living room if they made a mess.

Consistent with Ehrensaft's (1990) findings, mothers, not fathers, typically reported needing this type of support. This situation seems to occur in families that adhere to traditional gender roles. That is, it is under stress and time constraints that the father takes over to provide relief for tasks that are not traditionally his responsibility. In this sense, the families in our study seemed to adhere to a more traditional Latino family style.

Parents also stated they felt supported when the other parent reinforced what they had said, decided, or wished to happen. This type of support is similar to what Belsky and colleagues called "reiteration," and McHale and colleagues included in family harmony. We chose the term "reinforcement," because as that was the term the parents themselves used.

MOTHER: He always reinforces you know, uh if they ever try to talk back, sometimes they just talk back and that's when Father steps in.

FATHER: A lot of times the kids will test you. They'll say "Mom, can I have some of that ice cream?" and she'll say "no." She'll go over to daddy and say "Dad, can I have some ice cream?" So I said "Have you asked your mother?" And she said "yes." "And?" "She said no." "Well, that means no." So you have to back one another up, you know.

FATHER: When they don't pay attention to Mother, well, you know, that's when I throw my two cents. Okay, so I guess maybe I'm more reinforcement of what Mother does, I guess.

Finally, parents also saw themselves as supporting each other by not interfering when the other parent was engaged in disciplining the children. Appropriately, interfering with each others' parenting is included in definitions of unsupportive coparenting by Belsky and colleagues, hostility by McHale and colleagues, and conflict by Brody and colleagues. We were able to include in our description of support the absence of a negative act as a result of the open-ended nature of our questions.

FATHER: Sometimes she is yelling at them and I don't get involved in what she's telling them. Or when I am speaking to them she doesn't get into it.

MOTHER: I try to get in when he wants to discipline and I've learned not to. Because, you know, that is his part. But it hurts me, cause I say, "God I can't let him do that." So I tell myself "if she has to go through it, she has to go through it."

These parents were clearly aware of the negative consequences of interparental inconsistency and disparagement as discussed in the studies by Belsky and colleagues, McHale and colleagues, and Brody and colleagues. Inconsistency and disparagement were found to be associated with low levels of self-inhibition in toddlers (Belsky et al., 1996), teacher-reported problem behaviors in preschool (McHale & Rasmussen, 1998), and lower academic achievement in adolescence (Brody et al., 1994b; 1995).

Coordinating Parenting Tasks

Another dimension that emerged from the interviews was coordinating parenting tasks, which refers to the process by which parents mutually agree to divide tasks between each other. This dimension is widely found in the literature on father involvement and parental division of labor (Lamb, 1997a; cf. Parke, 1995). Typically, however, studies focus on "who does what" instead of the process by which parents divide parenting tasks. In this study, parents coordinated activities in various ways. One way was by alternating responsibility. Who completed the task depended on who was available at the time, and not on a clear division of labor.

FATHER: Sometimes I go pick them up, or she picks them up.

FATHER: I think it's even because sometimes the father has the time to attend and sometimes the mother is there with them and I think it's even. Sometimes it's the father's turn to be with them and it's his turn to be sharing and sometimes the mother isn't there but she will have her turn.

For other tasks, parents had come to an agreed division of labor in which one parent was in charge of some tasks, while the other was responsible for different tasks. This coordinating strategy is also the same as that found in studies of father's participation in family and work (e.g., Barnett & Baruch, 1987). It seems that this type of coordination is most common in mainstream families, when the father is involved in parenting. The coparenting literature discussed previously, however, does not include division of labor.

FATHER: In my case, my wife is in charge of taking the kids, when they were young they got sick a lot. She was the one who took them to the hospital, to the doctor. She is in charge of taking them to the doctor when it is necessary and I become in charge of the house.

MOTHER: I do the housework but he also helps. I go to work at 6 in the evening, . . . and from there on he's in charge of the house. He feeds the children dinner and he leaves the kitchen clean for me.

Sometimes parents seemed concerned with evenly dividing tasks. The focus was on making sure neither parent did more than the other. Similar coordinating strategies were reported by some of the shared parenting families in Ehrensaft's (1990) and Deutsch's (1999) studies.

FATHER: And now we are doing half-and-half, you know. Which is good. It is less that I have to do and less for her to worry about.

MOTHER: We fifty-fifty. Now when I'm nursing the youngest one he has to bathe the other one. We switch kids sometimes.

Finally, some families coordinated parenting by performing the same tasks, but taking different shifts.

MOTHER: When son was born, he was awake during the whole night and he was willing to take shifts. Like "tonight you go ahead and sleep and I will stay up with him." The next night he would sleep and I would stay up with him.

MOTHER: And it gets stressful sometimes. But, then, you know, the weekend comes along and that's when Father, I mean really Friday, Saturday and Sunday Father spends the whole time with the girls. And just really, Monday through Thursday, it's my job to take care of them.

The split shift commonly is found in the work and family literature. Only one of the families in this study, however, had split-shift work schedules in which one parent works at night and the other during the day. The splitting of shifts, in most of the families in this investigation, occurred in the context of parenting. One parent would be in charge one day, the other on another day.

Compensating

Another way in which parents shared parenting was by compensating for each other's shortcomings. Parents talked about feeling responsible for "filling the gap" when their partner was not able to perform certain tasks. In some cases, the gap entailed a life skill that one parent mastered but the other parent lacked.

FATHER: If they need to go somewhere, I am the one that takes them. My wife doesn't drive, only I drive them wherever.

FATHER: Well, in my case, my job is to take him to school, my older boy, and to drop him off at home when he's sick because my wife doesn't drive either.

Another way parents compensated for one another was by taking charge of a situation when the other parent was not being successful. This strategy seems most similar to a type of support reported by Belsky (see Gable et al., 1995). Supportive episodes in that study included times when one parent asked the other for help and received it. The parent who reported this strategy in our study, however, was always the one responding to the need, not the one asking for help.

MOTHER: It's that see, he plays around with her a lot and its like, she doesn't respect him that much. And when he wants her to listen it's like, she's playing around still and he comes and tells me "Well you know, this and you need to tell her you need to do something."

FATHER: Well, when you tell your daughter to do something "Hey do it and don't question my authority." Where with her mother, you know, she can try her to the end.

The parents in Ehrensaft's (1990) study also reported compensating for each other's success in disciplining the children. In both samples, sometimes mothers compensated for fathers, and sometimes fathers compensated for mothers.

Cooperating

Parents also talked about cooperating, working together as a team on a single task. In cooperating, parents saw each other as equally capable of performing the activity or equally responsible for the task. In cooperating, there was a sense of sharing in the act of parenting. The coparenting literature on intact families includes cooperating as a significant coparenting strategy (e.g.; Gable et al., 1995; McHale, 1995). In addition, this dimension is similar to what the divorce literature considers cooperative parenting. That is, cooperative parenting occurs when divorced parents talk with each other about their children, avoid arguments, and support rather than undermine each other's parenting efforts (Maccoby, Buchanan, Mnookin, & Dornbusch, 1993; Maccoby et al., 1990).

MOTHER: Father is wonderful with her. I mean, whatever I give her, he's a big part of the same thing. I mean it's not, there's not a difference between she's gonna go to mom for this and to dad for this.

FATHER: I would have to say if there's a disagreement, the way the child should be disciplined; I would have the final say. And I think my wife acknowledges that I do. But that, I don't think that's ever happened. I mean, maybe once or twice, where we just really disagree about some kind of discipline or something. Cause we pretty much live on the same page. As far as when something happens, how it should be handled.

Although this father acknowledged that he made the final decision, both parents were in agreement regarding this decision process. In some cases, cooperating took the form of compromising. Compromising occurred when parents had differing views or interests and engaged in a give-and-take process to resolve the conflict.

MOTHER: What we set up so we wouldn't have relative fights when we first got married. I told Father, you deal with your family and I deal with mine. If they have a party, or wedding or whatever, he decides whether he wants to go or not. And then, it's the same for my side.

FATHER: But we both give and take a little bit. Because I sometimes realize, well he's twelve years old, you know, I need to back off a little bit. And then she realizes that I'm doing it for him, for his betterment. So we usually just both give and take a little bit.

Conflicted Coparenting

Although most families talked about actively working toward a parenting alliance, all families said there were instances of conflict. Conflict took several forms and included what other researchers have classified as conflict (e.g., Brody & Flora, 1996; Gable et al., 1995; McHale, 1997). In all cases, parents talked about disagreeing with, contradicting, and interrupting each other. Most instances of disagreement concerned the method of disciplining or parenting.

FATHER: We try to talk together, our problem is that when I scold them she tells me "Don't scold them in such an ugly way," or "Don't hit them."

MOTHER: Oh, we disagree big time. I used to be for spanking, and so is my husband, and now both of us are not, but yet, he tends to be the harsh punishment type. I feel bad.

MOTHER: He's always telling Son 1 to do this, to do that, and Son 1 is watching TV. And I'm telling Father "Let him watch television." You know, it bothers me that he interrupts him to pick up the toys so that Son 2 can't get them.

FATHER: Well, the times she gets upset is because like I'll make them stand there. I'll tell her [daughter] to get up and stand right there until I tell you to go to bed. You know and, uh, Mother says "No, tell her to go to bed." I say "No, no," you know. I'm trying to teach her a lesson, you know.

Conflict also was manifested in contradicting one another. One parent would verbally interrupt the other parent's action or statement, similar to McHale's (1997) disparaging dimension.

MOTHER: Our last disagreement was because we go to a store and the boy wants something, and he's stubborn about wanting that thing. And "No" he tells him "No," I say "Come on, let's get it for you son."

MOTHER: Father will get upset because I'll tell the girls "Just go to your room and put on a movie." Because I'm trying to watch TV, and he says "Quit sending them to their room, they want to be in front too, they want to spend time with us."

Another form of conflict was one parent interfering with the other, especially during disciplining the children. Again, interfering seemed similar to the disparagement dimension reported by McHale and colleagues.

FATHER: Sometimes I don't like it when I want to discipline my daughter and Mother gets mad. That is a bad thing for my daughter because she is watching and growing up seeing that her mother is taking her side.

MOTHER: But when I'm calling her, she needs to come when I call her the first time. And that's what we argue about. Because, you know, the other girls come the first time I call them, but not her. . . . And I don't know if Father tells her not to go but she won't. And that makes me really mad because I tell Father "You need to stop that, she needs to pay attention to me."

The types of conflict reported by the families in our study parallel the descriptions of conflict provided by Belsky and colleagues, McHale and colleagues, and Brody and colleagues. Belsky's observational code included disagreeing in front of the child, disregarding stated desires of the other parent, interrupting, opposing other's views, and actively refusing to provide assistance. McHale's observational code included interference and one-upmanship; and the self-report measure included disparagement, undermining, disputes, and disagreements. Brody's scale also included covert and overt disagreements about child rearing. All of these conflicts seem to fit into Gottman's (1979, 1993) arguing phase of marital conflict. During the arguing phase, couples attempt to find areas of common ground, persuade the other partner and argue in favor of one's point of view. The examples provided by the families in this study go beyond Gottman's description of the arguing phase. These parents were not only disagreeing but also were engaging in strategies that undermined the other parent's authority (McHale, 1997). However, this undermining tactic was rare, and most parents appeared to be trying to solve conflicts more amiably.

DISCUSSION

The present study explored the ways in which Mexican American parents develop and maintain a coparenting relationship. Overall, our findings defied the traditional view of Latino fathers as uninvolved in parenting (Mirande, 1988) and supported a growing empirical trend indicating that, similar to non-Hispanic White parents, Latino fathers are becoming more actively engaged with their children (Chilman, 1993; Davis & Chavez, 1995; Maason et al., 1999). Indeed, our study indicated that both fathers and mothers were highly involved in parenting activities, perhaps reflecting a Latino emphasis on familism.

Utilizing a qualitative methodology allowed us to give these parents a voice, a way to express their views of coparenting processes. We think that this was a valuable research procedure because the parents seemed quite mindful and articulate about their familial experiences. Indeed, the participants in our study exhibited a fairly broad range of coparenting dynamics. The Mexican American parents identified actions such as supporting each other, cooperating, and joint decision making, which have been commonly identified in studies with non-Hispanic White families as well (e.g., Brody et al., 1996; Gable, et al., 1992; McHale, 1995). Both Latino and non-Hispanic parents appear somewhat aware of the importance of presenting a united front to their children as a means of providing consistency to their children and aiding their partner. Given the emphasis on respect within the Latino culture, this might be a means as well of maintaining or enhancing respect for the parental unit.

In addition to these common actions, parents described two additional processes that have received less attention in the previous literature. The first process of coordination focused on the ways in which parents divide parenting tasks. At first glance, this process might seem quite mundane because the parents divide such tasks as taking children to the doctor or bathing children. However, when we consider the large number and diversity of parenting tasks that must be managed in a single day (especially with more than one child), the cumulative effects of this process become quite salient. In addition, some parents in our study indicated an awareness of the importance of doing 50% of the parenting tasks, which can make coordination more complicated. Since coordination implies that parents are sometimes doing separate tasks at the same time (e.g., one parent dresses a child as another parent feeds an infant), it is possible that such a dynamic would not be captured by observational studies that focus on interactions between both parents and a child. Thus, this study might have allowed us to tap into a more global parenting sequence. Finally, we would note that this process is consistent with the family-systems literature on the balance between flexibility and stability that is necessary for effective family functioning (e.g., Zabriskie & McCormick, 2001).

Similarly, the Latino fathers and mothers in this study identified a coparenting process of compensation. This process reflected a parent's awareness that his/her partner was unable to fulfill a certain task and a willingness to take on the task himself/herself. It should be noted that the inability was sometimes considered circumstantial (e.g., work hours, lacks driving skills) and not characterological (e.g., high-strung temperament). This specific process was not associated with the unsupportive or aversive behaviors reported by other researchers (e.g., Belsky et al., 1996; McHale et al., 2000). For example, parents in our study did not report that they criticized their partner in front of their child or belittled the partner. Rather, the participants evidenced a desire to support and help their spouse with the complementary skill, suggesting this was a more prosocial dynamic. Ehrensaft (1990) also reported a compensatory process in which fathers described being better disciplinarians and utilizing their authority to endorse mothers' parenting efforts. This is consistent with the concept of a parenting alliance, a dynamic that has been found to play a significant role in children's development and in a couple's sense of competence as parents (e.g., Floyd & Zmic, 1991; Frank, Hole, Jacobson, Justkowski, & Huyck, 1986).

Across these coparenting processes, we noticed a trend in which both parents commonly perceived that fathers provided relief to mothers, but mothers were rarely reported as providing relief to fathers. Ehrensaft (1990) also reported that in the non-Hispanic White families she studied; more specifically, mothers in families in which shared parenting resulted out of necessity frequently described feeling overwhelmed and demanding their husbands help them cope. Similarly, Belsky (see Gable et al., 1995) reported that fathers supported mothers' parenting twice as often as mothers supported fathers. There was no difference, however, in the frequency of unsupportive acts from either parent. Consistent with these findings, even though most respondents in the present study were in dual-earner families, the mother was perceived as the individual experiencing greater task overload, and thus in need of greater relief. Not all mothers, however, reported having to demand that father help. Some of the fathers in our study seemed aware that they needed to provide relief without being asked. These findings highlight that an awareness of the partner is as important as an awareness of the child in parenting dynamics.

Most of the processes discovered in this investigation can be described as being positively valenced. Parents generally talked about how well they manage their coparenting rather than criticizing each other. Thus, our findings are generally in line with results reported by Belsky and colleagues (Belsky et al., 1996; Gable et al., 1995), McHale and colleagues (McHale, 1995, 1997; McHale & Rasmussen, 1998), and Brody and colleagues (Brody & Flor, 1996; Brody et al., 1995; Brody, 1994a; Brody, 1994b). Indeed, Belsky et al. found that supportive behaviors occurred twice as frequently as unsupportive behaviors. In a critique of his own study, McHale (1995) also noted that "the behavior enacted by parents in front of their children was generally positive and devoid of intense conflict, though subtle signs of conflict and distress did color many family interactions" (p. 992).

We also identified one form of conflict in the coparenting processes. Consistent with the work of Belsky and colleagues and McHale and colleagues, our sample reported that they contradicted each other in front of their children, thus potentially undermining their parental authority. The most common topic of conflict was discipline, and particularly the degree of compliance expected by children. In general, fathers were firmer than mothers in disciplinary expectations. Although it is possible that the Latino respondents' attitudes reflected some dimensions of patriarchy, it should be noted that a similar trend was detected in non-Hispanic White families (Deutsch, 1999; Ehrensaft, 1990). Thus, disciplinary styles of mothers and fathers might reflect more strongly gender differences that transcend culture.

In sum, Mexican American mothers and fathers generally demonstrated a collaborative parenting approach. They discussed their coparenting beliefs, often avoided arguing in front of the children, and worked toward supporting each other's parenting efforts. Such processes are essential to productive parenting (Maccoby et al., 1990, 1993; Sanders et al., 1997). Unlike the stereotypic image of Latino fathers as authoritarian and the mothers as deferential, parents in this study appeared to have more egalitarian views of themselves and to be actively responsible for the care and upbringing of their children.

LIMITATIONS, STRENGTHS, AND FUTURE DIRECTIONS

There are some limitations to this study that should be noted. First, the sample was small and not randomly selected. It is possible that there was a self-selection bias, such that parents who were happy and supportive were more likely to participate. Second, our study relied solely on self-report methods, which have inherent risks of memory lapse or overgeneralization (e.g., Converse & Presser, 1986). It is possible that our participants reported events and/or processes that were highly salient but did not mention other dynamics that might have been evident had we conducted observations. This might explain some of the differences noted in the present study and past research.

Third, it could be argued that a focus group method might have enhanced social desirability effects because parents were aware that they were being audiotaped. In addition, Latinos have been found to "save face" in front of outsiders in order to appear in a positive light (Lynch & Hanson, 1998). We tried to minimize these effects by (a) assuring parents that their responses were anonymous and not reported to their partner, (b) trying to support respondent comfort in the pre-interview procedures, (c) taking a novice approach in the interviews, and (d) providing bilingual moderators. Given that both mothers and fathers shared negative experiences, it is possible that desirability effects were low. A similar argument was made by McHale (1997) in an analysis of his research. More specifically he noted being somewhat surprised by "the relative candor of respondents in replying to questions asking about activities that were clearly both negative and personal" (p. 196).

Finally, our study would have been strengthened if we had collected data on children's adjustment. From our findings, it is not possible to state whether the coparenting techniques used by the families have positive or negative consequences for their children. However, the similarity of our findings with those of other researchers who investigated that association lends support to the possibility that the children in these families would be similarly affected.

In balance, this study also has some notable strengths. First, the study examined the experiences of Mexican American families. With the growth of the Latino population in the United States, this culture deserves more empirical consideration than was received in past decades. Second, this study utilized qualitative research, which approaches participants' beliefs and values from an emic perspective. That is, the research was not guided by a theory or model derived from non-Hispanic White studies, but rather allowed the voice of Latino parents to stand in its own right. Third, the researchers utilized a multilayered coding approach to enhance the accuracy of data analysis. Fourth, the study included the perspectives of both mothers and fathers to provide a more expansive view of the parenting dynamic. Fifth, the parents in this study seemed highly aware and mindful of some important coparenting processes. Although interview techniques might not be as common as observational studies, we would note that the parents' words can be highly illustrative. Indeed, Gable et al. (1992) noted that simple statements between partners can sometimes "reveal whether a couple is working together to accomplish their parenting tasks" (p. 288).

There is much to be accomplished in future research to extend our knowledge of coparenting. First, random sampling might provide more information about both supportive and unsupportive processes. Second, multi-method studies would provide greater capabilities to compare insider (parent) and outsider (researcher) perceptions of parenting dynamics. Third, longitudinal studies would track changes in coparenting processes and outcomes for children, couples, and families over time. Fourth, cross-national studies would identify differences in coparenting as well; it is possible, for example, that parenting dynamics in families in Mexico contrast the dynamics in Mexican American families in ways not previously considered. Finally, adding the perspective of Latino children in studies of parenting will provide a more holistic picture of Latinos in the United States.

REFERENCES

Ahrons, C. (1981). The continuing coparental relationship between divorced spouses. *American Journal of Orthopsychology, 51*, 415–428.

Aydintug, C. D. (1995). Former spouse interaction: Normative guidelines and actual behavior. *Journal of Divorce and Remarriage, 23*, 147–161.

Barnett, R. C., & Baruch, G. K. (1987). Determinants of father participation in family work. *Journal of Marriage and the Family, 49*, 29–40.

Becerra, R. M. (1988). The Mexican American family. In C. H. Mindel, R. W. Habenstein, & R. Wright, Jr. (Eds.). *Ethnic families in America: Patterns and variations* (pp. 141–159). Englewood Cliffs, NJ: Prentice Hall.

Belsky, J., Crnic, K., & Gable, S. (1995). The determinants of coparenting in families with toddler boys: Spousal differences and daily hassles. *Child Development, 66*, 629–642.

Belsky, J., & Hsieh, K. (1998). Patterns of marital change during the early childhood years: Parent personality, coparenting, and division of labor correlates. *Journal of Family Psychology, 12*, 511–528.

Belsky, J., Putnam, S., & Crnic, K. (1996). Coparenting, parenting, and early emotional development. *New Directions for Child Development, 74*, 45–55.

Block, J., Block, J., & Morrison, A. (1981). Parental agreement and disagreement on child-rearing orientation and gender-rearing orientation in children. *Child Development, 52*, 965–974.

Brody, G. H., & Flor, D. (1996). Coparenting, family interactions, and competence among African American youths. *New Directions for Child Development, 74,* 77–91.

Brody, G. H., Stoneman, Z., & Flor, D. (1995). Linking family processes and academic competence among rural African American youths. *Journal of Marriage and the Family, 57,* 567–579.

Brody, G. H., Stoneman, Z., Flor, D., & McCrary, C. (1994a). Religion's role in organizing family relationships: Family process in rural, two-parent African American families. *Journal of Marriage and the Family, 56,* 878–888.

Brody, G. H., Stoneman, Z., Flor, D., McCrary, C., Hastings, L., & Conyers, O. (1994b). Financial resources, parent psychological functioning, parent co-caregiving, and early adolescent competence in rural two-parent African American families. *Child Development, 65,* 590–605.

Cabrera, E., Knaug-Jensen, D., Pinedo, J., Burrow, R., Everett, J., & DesRosiers, F. (1997, April). *A comparison of childrearing methods: Mexican and Mexican-American mothers tell us about raising toddlers.* Poster presented at the Society of Research in Child Development Biennial Meeting, Washington, DC.

Chapa, G., & Valencia, R. R. (1993). Latino population growth, demographic characteristics, and an educational stagnation: An examination of recent trends. *Hispanic Journal of Behavioral Sciences, 15*(2), 165–187.

Chilman, C. S., (1993). Hispanic families in the United States: Research perspectives. In H. McAdoo (Ed.), *Family ethnicity: Strength in diversity* (pp. 141–163) Newbury Park, CA: Sage.

Coltrane, S. (1996). *Family man.* New York: Oxford University Press.

Converse, J., & Presser, S. (1986). *Survey questions: Handcrafting the standardized questionnaire.* Newbury Park, CA: Sage.

Cooney, R. S., Rogler, L. H., Hurrell, R., & Ortiz, V. (1982). Decision making in intergenerational Puerto Rican families. *Journal of Marriage and the Family, 44,* 621–631.

Daniels, P., & Weingarten, K. (1982). *Sooner or later: The timing of parenthood in adult lives.* New York: Norton.

Davis, S., & Chavez, V. (1995). Hispanic househusbands. In A. Padilla (Ed.), *Hispanic psychology: Critical issues in theory and research* (pp. 257–270). Thousand Oaks, CA: Sage.

Deutsch, F. M., (1999). *Having it all: How equally shared parenting works.* Cambridge, MA: Harvard University Press.

Ehrensaft, D. (1990). *Parenting together: Men and women sharing the care of their children.* Chicago: University of Illinois Press.

Fitzpatrick, J., Caldera, Y., Pursley, M., & Wampler, K. (1999). Hispanic mother and father perceptions of fathering: A qualitative analysis. *Family and Consumer Sciences Research Journal, 28,* 133–166.

Floyd, F. J. & Zmich, D. E. (1991). Marriage and the parenting partnership: Perceptions and interactions of parent with mentally retarded and typically developing children. *Child Development, 62,* 1434–1448.

Frank, S. J., Hole, C. B., Jacobson, S., Justkowski, R. & Huyck, M. (1986). Psychological predictors of parents' sense of confidence and control and self versus child-focused gratification. *Developmental Psychology, 22,* 348–355.

Gable, S., Belsky, J., & Crnic, K. (1992). Marriage, parenting, and child development: Progress and prospects. *Journal of Family Psychology, 5,* 276–294.

Gable, S., Belsky, J., & Crnic, K. (1995). Coparenting during the child's second year: A descriptive account. *Journal of Marriage and the Family, 57*, 609–616.

García Coll, C., Meyer, E., & Brillon, L. (1995). Ethnic and minority parenting. In M. Bornstein (Ed.), *Handbook of parenting: Vol. 2. Biology and ecology of parenting* (pp. 189–209). Hillsdale, NJ: Erlbaum.

Gottman, J. M. (1979). *Marital interaction: Experimental investigations.* San Diego, CA: Academic Press.

Gottman, J. M. (1993). The roles of conflict engagement, escalation, and avoidance in marital interaction: A longitudinal view of five types of couples. *Journal of Consulting and Clinical Psychology, 61*, 6–15.

Harrison, A., Wilson, M., Pine, C., Chan, S., & Buriel, R. (1990). Family ecologies of ethnic minority children. *Child Development, 61*, 347–362.

Hetherington, E. M., & Stanley-Hagan, M. M., (1995). Parenting in divorced and remarried families. In M. Bornstein (Ed.), *Handbook of parenting: Vol. 3. Status and social conditions of parenting* (pp. 233–254). Hillsdale, NJ: Erlbaum.

Jouriles, E., Murphy, C., Farris, A., Smith, D., Richters, J., & Waters, E. (1991). Marital adjustment, parental disagreements about child rearing, and behavior problems in boys. *Child Development, 62*, 1424–1433.

Krueger, R. (1994). *Focus groups: A practical guide for applied research.* Thousand Oaks, CA: Sage.

Lamb, M. (1997a). The developing father–infant relationship. In M. Lamb (Ed.), *The role of the father in child development* (pp. 104–120). New York: Wiley.

Lamb, M. (1997b). Fathers and child development: An introductory overview and guide. In M. Lamb (Ed.), *The role of the father in child development* (pp. 1–18). New York: Wiley.

Lamberty, G., & García Coll, C. (1994). Overview. In G. Lamberty & C. García Coll (Eds.), *Puerto Rican women and children: Issues in health and development* (pp. 11–28). New York: Plenum.

Levine, E., & Padilla, A. (1980). *Crossing cultures in therapy: Pluralistic counseling for the Hispanic.* Monterey, CA: Brooks-Cole.

Lidz, T. (1963). *The family and human adaptation.* New York: International University Press.

Lynch, E. W., & Hanson, M. J. (1998). *Developing cross-cultural competence: A guide for working with children and their families.* (2nd ed.). Baltimore: Brookes.

Maason, D., Alaniz, Y., & Caldera, Y. (1999, April). *Mexican American mothers and fathers: Child rearing beliefs and behavioral styles with their toddlers.* Presented at the Society for Research in Child Development Biannual Conference, Albuquerque, NM.

Maccoby, E. E., Buchanan, C. M., Mnookin, R. H., & Dornbusch, S. M. (1993). Postdivorce roles of mothers and fathers in the lives of their children. *Journal of Family Psychology, 7*, 1–15.

Maccoby, E. E., Depner, C. E., & Mnookin, R. H. (1990). Co-parenting in the second year after divorce. *Journal of Marriage and the Family, 52*, 141–155.

Margolin, G., Gordis, E. B., & John, S. R. (2001). Coparenting: A link between marital conflict and parenting in two-parent families. *Journal of Family Psychology, 15*, 3–21.

McHale, J. P. (1995). Coparenting and triadic interactions during infancy: The roles of marital distress and child gender. *Developmental Psychology, 31*, 985–996.

McHale, J. P. (1997). Overt and covert coparenting processes in the family. *Family Process, 36,* 183–210.

McHale, J. P., Kuersten-Hogan, R., Lauretti, A., & Rasmussen, J. L. (2000). Parental reports of coparenting and observed coparenting behavior during the toddler period. *Journal of Family Psychology, 14,* 220–236.

McHale, J. P., & Rasmussen, J. L. (1998). Coparental and family group-level dynamics during infancy: Early family precursors of child and family functioning during preschool. *Development and Psychopathology, 10,* 39–59.

McKinney, M., Abrams, L., Terry, P., & Lerner, R. (1994). Child development research and the poor children of America: A call for the developmental contextual approach to research and outreach. *Family and Consumer Sciences Research Journal, 23,* 26–42.

McLoyd, V. (1994). Research in the services of poor and ethnic/racial minority children: Fomenting change in models of scholarship. *Family and Consumer Sciences Research Journal, 23,* 56–66.

Mirande, A. (1988). Chicano fathers: Traditional perceptions and current realities. In P. Bornstein & C. Cowan (Eds.), *Fatherhood today: Men's changing role in the family* (pp. 93–106). New York: Wiley.

Montiel, M. (1975). The Chicano family: A review of research. *Social Work, 18*(2), 22–31.

Parke, R. D. (1995). Fathers and families. In M. Bornstein (Ed.), *Handbook of parenting: Vol. 3. Status and social conditions of parenting* (pp. 27–64). Hillsdale, NJ: Erlbaum.

Parke, R. D., Burks, V., Carson, J., Neville, B., & Boyum, L. (1994). Family–peer relationships: A tripartite model. In R. D. Parke & S. Kellam (Eds.), *Advances in family research: Vol. 4. Family relationships with other social systems* (pp. 115–145). Hillsdale, NJ: Erlbaum.

Piercy, F., & Nickerson, V. (1996). Focus groups in family therapy research. In D. Sprenkle & S. Moon (Eds.), *Research methods in family therapy* (pp. 173–185). New York: Guilford.

Robinson, J. (1988). Who's doing the housework? *American Demographics, 12,* 24–28.

Roland, A. (1988). *In search of self in India and Japan: Toward a cross-cultural psychology.* Princeton, NJ: Princeton University Press.

Sanders, M. R., Nicholson, J. M., & Floyd, F. J., (1997). Couple's relationship and children. In W. K. Halford & H. J. Markman (Eds.), *Clinical handbook of marriage and couples interventions* (pp. 225–253). New York: Wiley.

Schoppe, S. J., Mangelsdorf, S. C., & Frosch, C. A. (2001). Coparenting, family processes, and family structure: Implications for preschoolers' externalizing behavior problems. *Journal of Family Psychology, 15,* 526–545.

Solis, J. (1995). The status of Latino children and youth: Challenges and prospects. In R. E. Zambrana (Ed.), *Understanding Latino families: Scholarship, policy, and practice* (pp. 62–81). London: Sage.

Tripp-Reimer, T., & Wilson, S. E. (1991). Assessing commitment in personal relationships. *Journal of Marriage and the Family, 54,* 595–608.

U.S. Census Bureau. (2000). *The Hispanic population in the United States: Population characteristics, March 1999.* Washington, DC: U.S. Government Printing Office.

Vaughn, B., Block, J., & Block, J. (1988). Parental agreement on child rearing during early childhood and psychological characteristics of adolescents. *Child Development, 59,* 1020–1033.

Vega, W. A. (1990). Hispanic families in the 1980s: A decade of research. *Journal of Marriage and the Family, 52,* 1015–1024.

Ybarra, L. (1982). When wives work: The impact on the Chicano family. *Journal of Marriage and the Family, 44,* 169–177.

Zabriskie, R., & McCormick, B. (2001). The influence of family leisure patterns on perceptions of family functioning. *Family Relations, 50,* 281–289.

Zuniga, M. (1998). Families with Latino roots. In E. Lynch & M. Hanson (Eds.), *Developing cross-cultural competence: A guide for working with children and their families* (pp. 209–250). Baltimore: Brookes.

6

Child-Rearing Beliefs and Practices During Feeding Among Middle-Class Puerto Rican and Anglo Mother–Infant Pairs

Robin L. Harwood, Amy M. Miller,
Vivian J. Carlson, and Birgit Leyendecker

In the past, psychological research on Latino families has generally employed a comparative framework that conceptualizes differences as deficits; this deficit perspective has been facilitated by the use of populations that have confounded ethnicity with other important predictor variables, such as poverty and teen parenthood. In other words, studies that purport to examine child-rearing beliefs and practices among Latino mothers have in fact tended to examine beliefs and practices among mothers living in poverty in the inner city (García Coll, Meyer, & Brillon, 1995). This research tradition has coexisted with a general tendency within the field of psychology to define parental competence primarily in terms of White, Anglo-Saxon, middle-class standards and ideals. As a result, we know little regarding normative beliefs and practices among Latino mothers, and the ways in which these may differ from those of their Anglo American counterparts. Therefore, several researchers have urged that future studies of Latino families focus on normative beliefs and behaviors among low-risk, middle-class mothers, rather than continue to study primarily high-risk mothers in poverty (García Coll et al., 1995).

CONTRIBUTIONS OF PRESENT INVESTIGATION

The present study addresses the need for research on normative socialization processes among Puerto Rican mother–infant pairs by examining child-rearing beliefs and practices among middle-class Puerto Rican mothers in San Juan, Puerto Rico, and middle-class Anglo American mothers in northeastern Connecticut. The long-term objectives of the project are to contribute to a theoretical understanding of cross-cultural variation in our models of normative development, and acquire knowledge about Puerto Rican culture without the confounds imposed by immigration and poverty; such an awareness is a critical first step to understanding child-rearing beliefs and practices among mainland Puerto Rican mothers, which is a rapidly growing group within the United States.

Individualism–Sociocentrism Debate

Puerto Rican culture is generally considered to emphasize a more sociocentric, and Anglo culture a more individualistic, view of the person and of interpersonal relationships (Harwood, Miller, & Lucca Irizarry, 1995; Lauria, 1982). Briefly, Anglo American culture is often described as "individualistic" in that it conceives of the individual as an "independent, self-contained, autonomous entity who (a) comprises a unique configuration of internal attributes . . . and (b) behaves primarily as a consequence of those internal attributes" (Markus & Kitayama, 1991, p. 224). In contrast, many other cultures are described as "sociocentric" or "interdependent" in that they emphasize the fundamental connectedness of human beings to one another: "Experiencing interdependence entails seeing oneself as part of an encompassing social relationship and recognizing that one's behavior is determined, contingent on, and, to a large extent organized by what the actor perceives to be the thoughts, feelings, and actions of *others* in the relationship" (Markus & Kitayama, 1991, p. 227; emphasis in the original).

Researchers have cautioned against using terms such as "individualism" or "sociocentrism" to create or reinforce a false sense of within-group homogeneity (Killen & Wainryb, 2000; Nucci, 1994; Spiro, 1993). Indeed, diversity among Latino families includes not only country of origin, circumstances for being in the United States, socioeconomic status, and acculturation but also individual variation in beliefs and practices regarding parenting and child rearing (Gonzales, Knight, Morgan-Lopez, Saenz, & Sirolli, Chapter 3, this volume; Roosa, Morgan-Lopez, Cree, & Specter, Chapter 2, this volume). At this point, substantial evidence exists documenting the tendency for Puerto Ricans, when compared to European Americans, to adhere to child-rearing beliefs and values that are consonant with a more sociocentric perspective (Cauce & Domenech-Rodríguez, Chaper 1 this volume); however, statistical tendencies by no means obviate individual variation. Therefore, one challenge for research on parenting among Puerto Ricans is to examine both shared beliefs and sources of heterogeneity. That is, it is important to acknowledge the ways in which Puerto Ricans as a cultural group may adhere to normative models of parenting and child development that differ from those of the European American cultural majority. On the other hand, it is equally important to investigate internal sources of variation that may lead Puerto Rican mothers to differ among themselves with regard to child rearing beliefs and practices.

CHILD-REARING BELIEFS AND VALUES AMONG PUERTO RICANS

In previous research (Harwood et al., 1995), we have referred to a concept we have chosen to call "Proper Demeanor." This construct emerged in the open-ended interviews we did with 60 lower- and middle-class Puerto Rican mothers of 12–18-month-old infants, living both on the island and the mainland, regarding their long-term socialization goals. According to Harwood et al., "Proper Demeanor implicitly assumes appropriate relatedness (both intimate and nonintimate). . . . [It] is intrinsically contextual; it involves, by definition, knowing the level of courtesy and decorum required in a given situation in relation to other people of a particular age, sex, and social status. The cardinal rule governing Proper Demeanor in Puerto Rico is *respeto*, or respect, which will manifest itself differently in different contexts" (p. 98).

Since then, we have attempted to address the long-standing confounds between socioeconomic status and culture in the literature on child-rearing values among Puerto Rican mothers (Harwood, Schoelmerich, Ventura-Cook, Schulze, & Wilson, 1996). In particular, in a study examining 100 middle- and lower-class Puerto Rican and Anglo mothers on both the island and the mainland, findings suggested that culture rather than socioeconomic status made the major contribution to group differences in mothers' beliefs regarding long-term socialization goals, whereas socioeconomic status emerged as the major predictor for descriptions of child behavior. In other research, we have similarly found that Proper Demeanor and a construct we have called "Self-Maximization" (self-confidence, independence, and the development of personal skills and talents) represent important constructs that have served, across socioeconomic status and on both the island and the mainland, to organize Puerto Rican and Anglo mothers' beliefs regarding desirable long-term socialization goals and child behavior (Harwood, 1992; Harwood & Miller, 1991; Harwood, Schoelmerich, Schulze, & Gonzalez, 1999).

We thus find considerable support for a high valuing of *respeto* or Proper Demeanor among Puerto Rican mothers. Moreover, these findings have been obtained across diverse socioeconomic backgrounds on both the island and the mainland. However, within-group heterogeneity on this topic remains under-examined, as does the ways in which a greater emphasis on Proper Demeanor may relate to specific child-rearing practices. In the following study, we examine both group patterning and within-group variation in middle-class Anglo and Puerto Rican mothers' child-rearing beliefs and practices during feeding, a universal everyday setting of childhood.

METHOD

Population

The research was conducted with middle-class Anglo American and middle-class island Puerto Rican mothers of infants aged 4–12 months. The rationale for choosing middle-class Anglo and middle-class island Puerto Rican mothers as the subject population was twofold: (a) Middle-class Anglo mothers were expected to provide an index of the mainstream, dominant U.S. culture that has shaped the articulation of most normative theories of child development, thus providing an appropriate comparison point for the study of other groups; and (b) middle-class island Puerto Rican mothers were expected to represent an educated, professional group in a highly industrialized society. Nonetheless, it was anticipated that these mothers would demonstrate behaviors and perceptions concordant with a cultural-meaning system that is different from that of the middle-class Anglo mothers. The reasons for using middle-class island rather than lower-class or migrant Puerto Rican mothers are that they provide (a) an index of the mainstream Puerto Rican culture, thus providing normative data on this population; and (b) a benchmark of the behaviors and cultural-meaning systems of Puerto Rican mothers before the assimilation process begins—a process that acts as a confounding factor.

Sampling

The sample was comprised of women with at least a baccalaureate degree who were from families in which the household head was employed in a white-collar or professional occupation (Levels I and II on the Hollingshead index [Hollingshead, 1975]). Anglo mothers (n = 32) were born, reared, and educated in the mainland United States and spoke American English as their first language; Puerto Rican mothers (n = 28) were born and reared primarily in Puerto Rico, and spoke Puerto Rican Spanish as their first language. All mothers had a healthy, full-term 4-month-old infant at the time of enrollment in the study. Information was obtained from all subjects on a variety of sociodemographic variables.

Similar subject recruitment procedures were employed in the two cultural settings. Specifically, the mothers were obtained through invitational letters distributed through pediatric practices serving middle-class populations. As can be seen in Table 6.1, the resulting samples of mothers were well matched on 10 of 13 major sociodemographic indices (child's gender and birth order; mother's age, education, and marital status; father's age and education; Hollingshead score; total number children; total household size; percent mothers employed outside the home; number of hours worked per week outside the home; and religious background). The groups differed on just three variables. In particular, compared to the Anglo mothers, Puerto Rican mothers were more likely to be employed outside the home when the infant was 12 months old and, if employed, worked on average more hours per week at each age point; in addition, Puerto Rican mothers were more likely to describe their religious background as Catholic, whereas Anglo mothers were more likely to describe their religious background as "none."

Table 6.1
Demographic Characteristics

	Anglo (n=32)	Puerto Rican (n=28)	p
Mother's age	32.2	30.1	
Mother's education	15.8	15.9	
Total number children	1.5	1.6	
% Firstborn	53.1	46.4	
% Male	46.9	53.6	
% Mothers married	90.6	82.1	
Total household size	3.6	3.8	
Father's education	16.1	16.0	
Father's age	33.6	31.9	
Household Hollingshead	51.4	51.3	
Religious Background (%)			*
None	31.3	7.1	
Protestant	25.0	32.1	
Jewish	6.3	0.0	
Catholic	37.5	60.7	
% Mothers Employed			
4 months	67.6	78.6	
8 months	62.5	78.6	
12 months	62.5	85.7	*
No. Hours Worked Per Week Among Employed Mothers			
4 months	22.5	36.2	**
8 months	27.3	35.5	*
12 months	26.5	36.1	**

* = $p < .05$, ** = $p < .01$.

Among the Puerto Rican mothers, 46.4% identified themselves as bilingual Spanish–English. Seven of the mothers had spent some time in the mainland United States (mean = 2.9 years, range 1–7 years). To gain an index of psychological acculturation to the United States, Puerto Rican mothers completed a standardized instrument developed specifically for Puerto Ricans by García Coll and her colleagues (Tropp, Erkut, Alarcón, García Coll, & Vázquez, 1994). The instrument contains 31 items measuring cultural competence, behaviors, preferences, and identification. In this sample, the alpha for the Psychological Acculturation Scale was .94. The items use a 1–9 Likert scale, with A1" representing high Puerto Rican cultural preference and identity, and "9" representing high Anglo cultural preference and identity. The possible range for the total scale is a low of 31 (high Puerto Rican identity) to a high of 279 (high Anglo identity). As can be seen in Table 6.1, the Puerto Rican mothers in this study fell into the lower half of this scale (mean = 84.4, range 41–142), indicating high Puerto Rican identity.

Procedures to Promote Cross-Cultural Validity

All mothers were interviewed in their native languages (i.e., Puerto Rican Spanish for the Puerto Rican mothers and American English for the Anglo mothers). Several steps were taken to promote the cultural appropriateness of the research materials in the Puerto Rican context. First, all research protocols were examined for cultural suitability by the first author in consultation with two Puerto Rican cultural consultants in the laboratory of Dr. Glorisa Canino at the University of Puerto Rico School of Medicine; the protocols were revised on the basis of their comments. Complete translations were then undertaken by bilingual, bicultural (Puerto Rican) graduate assistants at the University of Connecticut at Storrs, and then checked for preservation of meaning and cultural appropriateness by the cultural consultants. Finally, pilot testing was undertaken to ensure that all materials were readily comprehensible and ethnographically valid.

OVERVIEW OF OUR STUDY

The mothers and infants were observed and interviewed when the target infant was 4, 8, and 12 months of age. These three time points were selected in order to provide information regarding mother–infant interactions at evenly spaced intervals representing significantly different periods of infancy. Procedures were administered in the mothers' homes in single sessions lasting about 90 minutes at each time point. In Connecticut, interviews were conducted by trained graduate assistants in the first author's laboratory at the University of Connecticut; in Puerto Rico, Dr. Glorisa Canino of the University of Puerto Rico School of Medicine made available trained, master's-level personnel from her Behavioral Sciences Research Center for the purposes of subject recruitment and data collection. The first author traveled to Puerto Rico prior to each wave of data collection in order to train interviewers and conduct piloting.

All interviewers were blind to the study hypotheses. The home observations were videotaped, and the oral interviews were audiotaped and then transcribed verbatim in the laboratory of the first author. Following transcription, all Spanish-language interviews were translated by bilingual, bicultural

(Puerto Rican) graduate assistants. Data coding of both the videotaped interactions and the transcribed interviews was performed by trained graduate assistants who were blind to the study hypotheses.

Maternal Beliefs and Practices

In an attempt to understand normative beliefs and practices, mothers (a) responded to questions regarding their socialization goals (8-month visit); (b) completed a checklist concerning their expectations for the age at which a variety of developmental milestones are reached (12-month visit); (c) responded to specific questions about practices and routines for feeding and sleeping (each visit); (d) provided a time diary regarding the target child's activities during a 24-hour time period (each visit); and (e) furnished information concerning the type and frequency of the infant's social contacts (each visit).

Semi-Structured Observations

At each time point, mothers were also videotaped in their homes interacting with their infants for approximately 40 minutes in five different everyday settings: (a) Feeding (8 minutes)—mothers were asked to feed their child as they normally would; (b) Free play (8 minutes)—mothers were provided with age-appropriate toys and asked to play with their infant as they normally would; (c) Social play (5 minutes)—toys were put out of sight and mothers were asked to play with their infant without using toys or books (such activities—e.g., peek-a-boo, pat-a-cake, "horsie"—are common in both cultures); (d) Teaching tasks (2 minutes each)—mothers were asked to "teach" their infants specific object-oriented and social actions (e.g., at 12 months, mothers were asked to teach the infant to draw a line with a crayon, stack two blocks together, use one toy to push another, "give momma a kiss," and clean up the toys that had been used in the free-play session; at the 4-month visit, there were two teaching tasks, at the eight-month visit there were four tasks, and at 12 months there were five tasks); and (e) Bathing/dressing (10 minutes)—mothers were asked to bathe and dress the child as they normally would.

CURRENT STUDY

Because previous research (Harwood, 1992; Harwood et al., 1999) has suggested that Anglo and Puerto Rican mothers' socialization goals and interactions with their infants during feeding are particularly rich arenas for the study of cultural differences in infancy, this study will concentrate on these two domains. In addition, to simplify the presentation of study results, this paper will focus on feeding at 12 months.

Socialization Goals

In order to provide an index regarding cultural belief systems, mothers were administered the Socialization Goals Interview (SGI), a semi-structured interview in which parents are asked to describe the qualities they (a) would and (b) would not like their own children to possess as adults and to describe toddlers they know who possess at least the beginnings of those (c) positive and (d) negative qualities. Specifically, in the SGI, mothers respond in an open-ended fashion to the following questions:

1. What are some of the qualities and/or behaviors that you would like to see your child grow to possess?
2. What are some of the qualities and/or behaviors that you would NOT like to see your child grow to possess?
3. Describe a child you know who possesses at least the beginnings of some of the positive qualities you mentioned.
4. Describe a child you know who possesses at least the beginnings of some of the negative qualities you mentioned.

Together, these four questions have been found to provide a rich picture of Anglo and Puerto Rican mothers' indigenous beliefs regarding long-term socialization goals and perceptions of child behavior (Harwood, 1992; Harwood et al. 1995).

Coding of SGI

Mothers' responses to the SGI were coded at the level of individual word and phrase descriptors. For instance, "that they not pick up vices and they behave well" counted as two phrase descriptors, whereas "honest and decent and treat people with respect" counted as two word descriptors and one phrase descriptor. Each descriptor was coded into one of six mutually exclusive categories identified through previous work as culturally relevant to Anglo and Puerto Rican mothers (Harwood, 1992; Harwood et al., 1995): (a) Self-Maximization, or concern that a child be self-confident, independent, and develop his or her talents and abilities as an individual; (b) Self-Control, or the ability to curb negative impulses toward greed, egocentrism, and aggression; (c) Lovingness, or concern that a child be friendly, emotionally warm, and able to maintain close affective bonds with others; (d) Decency, or the ability to meet basic societal standards for decency, such as being a hard-working, honest person who does not use drugs; (e) Proper Demeanor, or concern that a child be respectful, cooperative, and accepted by the larger community; and (f) Miscellaneous, a sixth category containing all content responses not codable in the above five categories (e.g., "She's not a big television watcher"; "I hope he doesn't eat meat"). Fewer than 5% of mothers' responses were coded as Miscellaneous, attesting to the broadly encompassing character of the five content categories.

Mothers' responses to the SGI were coded by a trained graduate student blind to the study hypotheses as well as to each mother's sociocultural group membership; reliabilities were calculated between the primary coder and one independent (blind) judge on 50% of the sample. Overall agreement reached a level of .84 (Cohen's kappa, range .82–.89).

Observations of Mother–Infant Interactions During Feeding

To examine maternal behavior during feeding across the two groups, culturally relevant categories of maternal behavior were created, based on frequently occurring behaviors within each group regarding (a) frequency of seven maternal physical behaviors (signal attention, position, offer affection, caretaking, place food, playful interaction, restrain infant); (b) frequency of nine maternal verbal behaviors (suggest, comment, signal, command, nonlinguistic vocalization, affection, praise, encourage eating, speak for infant); and (c) duration of eight situation-specific settings and behaviors (bottle-feed, spoon-feed, infant self-feed, other types of feeding, no feeding activity, infant in high chair, infant in lap, infant free to move around room). Two ethnically matched, trained graduate students coded the videotaped mother–infant interactions into these categories, using Interact (Dumas, 1993), a software program that computes frequencies of different behaviors and durations of different settings. Both coders were blind to the study hypotheses. Reliabilities were calculated between the two coders using 20% of the sample. Overall agreement for the 12-month feeding data reached a level of .89 (Cohen's kappa, range .66–1.00).

RESULTS

The specific goals of this study were to (a) examine the ways in which Puerto Ricans as a cultural group may adhere to normative models of parenting and child development that differ from those of the European American cultural majority; and (b) to investigate internal sources of variation that may lead Puerto Ricans to differ among themselves with regard to child-rearing beliefs and practices. To further these goals, both between-group and within-group analyses were performed. Specifically, a stepwise discriminant analysis examined between-group differences in mothers' beliefs and behaviors, whereas cluster analyses investigated both group-patterning and within-group differences.

Between-Group Differences

Preliminary Analyses

To begin to examine group differences in the patterning of maternal beliefs and behaviors, a MANOVA was performed by group on transformed scores representing mothers' responses to the SGI, and on the 24 maternal and feeding behaviors described in the previous section. This analysis yielded a significant main effect for group, $F(29,29) = 7.1$, $p < .01$ (Wilks' lambda). In follow-up univariate ANOVAs, 11 of these 29 variables emerged as significant: position, signal verbally ($p < .05$); and suggest, place food for infant, spoon-feed, self-feed, no feeding activity, time spent in mother's lap, time spent in high chair, proportion of mothers' responses falling into category of Self-Control, and proportion of mothers' responses falling into the category of Proper Demeanor ($p < .01$). Of these variables, six occurred with greater frequency among Puerto Rican mothers (position, signal verbally, spoon-feed, no feeding activity, time spent in mother's lap, and proportion of responses related to Proper Demeanor), whereas five occurred significantly more among Anglo mothers (suggest, place food for infant, self-feed, time spent in high chair, and proportion of responses related to Self-Control). These 11 variables were selected for use in a stepwise discriminant analysis.

Stepwise Discriminant Analysis

A stepwise discriminant analysis was performed using the 11 variables that had emerged as significantly different by group in the MANOVA. This analysis yielded a single discriminant function—chi-square (4df) = 96.2, $p < .01$—containing four predictor variables: duration infant self-feed (.92), frequency mother suggest to infant (.57), duration infant in mother's lap (-.33), and proportion responses pertaining to Proper Demeanor (−.37). Together, these four variables correctly predicted the group membership of 96.9% of Anglo and 100% of Puerto Rican mothers. An examination of group means indicated that, compared to Anglo mothers, Puerto Rican mothers were (a) less likely to have infants who spent time self-feeding at 12 months (respective means = 348.5 and 15.3 seconds, $p < .01$); (b) less likely to phrase their directives as suggestions (respective means = 6.4 and 1.3, $p < .01$); (c) more likely to have infants who spent time in their laps during feeding (respective means = 4.6 and 112.6 seconds, $p < .01$), and (d) more likely to place emphasis on Proper Demeanor as a child-rearing goal (respective means = .14 and .35, $p < .01$).

Group Patterning in Maternal Beliefs

To explore group patterning in mothers' socialization goals, we looked at mothers' responses codable into each of the five content categories across all questions of the SGI (Self-Maximization, Self-Control, Lovingness, Decency, and Proper Demeanor). In order to control for individual differences in the total number of descriptors generated by mothers, analyses related to differences in category use employed percentages rather than frequencies. In addition, arsine transformations appropriate for the use of proportional data were performed on all subsequent analyses.

Cluster Analysis

Transformed proportional scores representing each mother's responses to the SGI were used as variables in a cluster analysis (K-means). Specifically, this analysis was employed to group subjects based on similarity of patterning in the relative frequency of their category usage across all four questions of the SGI. To allow for the emergence of at least two divergent viewpoints regarding socialization goals among mothers within each group, the number of clusters was set to four.

This analysis converged after nine iterations. In particular, as can be seen in Table 6.2, the solution identified the following four clusters: (a) Cluster 1 (13 mothers) was dominated by use of the Self-Maximization category; (b) Cluster 2 (23 mothers) showed relatively strong emphases on Self-Control and Self-Maximization; (c) Cluster 3 (18 mothers) revealed relatively strong emphases on Proper Demeanor and Self-Control; and (d) Cluster 4 (6 mothers) was characterized primarily by use of the Proper Demeanor category, with somewhat less emphasis on Decency.

Cluster x Group Membership

To examine whether mothers were more or less likely to be classified into the different clusters based on their group membership, a 2 × 4 (Group × Cluster) chi-square analysis was performed. This analysis yielded a Pearson Chi-Square (3df) of 15.8, $p < .01$. As can be seen in Table 6.3, 61.5% of the mothers falling into Cluster 1 (characterized predominantly by use of the Self-Maximization category), and 78.3% of those classified into Cluster 2 (characterized by relatively strong emphasis on Self-Control) were Anglo mothers. Among Anglo

Table 6.2
Cluster Analysis (K-Means), Mothers' Socialization Goals

Category	Cluster			
	1	2	3	4
Self-Maximization	.57*	.21	.19	.10
Self-Control	.16	.32*	.21	.05
Lovingness	.08	.19	.12	.05
Decency	.11	.18	.13	.22
Proper Demeanor	.12	.11	.37*	.63*

* = dominant category in each cluster

Table 6.3
Cluster Classification by Group Membership (%)

	Cluster			
Group	1	2	3	4
Anglo	25.0	56.3	18.8	0.0
Puerto Rican	17.9	17.9	42.9	21.4

Cluster 1 = Self-Maximization
Cluster 2 = Self-Control/Self-Maximization
Cluster 3 = Proper Demeanor/Self-Control
Cluster 4 = Proper Demeanor

mothers, 56.3% fell into Cluster 2 and 25% into Cluster 1. Thus, roughly 79% of all Anglo mothers were classified into one of the two clusters placing relatively greater emphasis on Self-Maximization and Self-Control.

By contrast, 66.7% of the mothers falling into Cluster 3 (characterized by relatively strong emphases on Proper Demeanor and Self-Control) and 100% of the mothers classified into Cluster 4 (characterized predominantly by use of the Proper Demeanor category) were Puerto Rican. Among Puerto Rican mothers, 42.9% fell into Cluster 3 and and 21.4% into Cluster 4. Thus, roughly 63% of all Puerto Rican mothers were classified into one of the two clusters placing relatively greater emphasis on Proper Demeanor.

Group Patterns in Beliefs and Behaviors

Transformed proportional scores representing mother's responses codable within the five SGI categories, duration of eight feeding behaviors, and frequency of 16 maternal behaviors were used as variables in a preliminary cluster analysis (K-means) examining group differences in patterns of behaviors during feeding. Beliefs were included with behaviors in this analysis in order to provide some direct measure of the relation between these two sets of variables. As in the group patterning in maternal beliefs, to allow for the emergence of at least two divergent patterns among mothers within each group, the number of clusters was set to four. This analysis indicated that 14 of 24 coded variables were contributing significantly to the cluster results:

position, suggest, signal verbally and nonverbally, place food, bottle-feed, spoon-feed, self-feed, no feeding activity, infant in mother's lap, infant in high chair, infant free to wander, and proportional emphases on Self-Control and Proper Demeanor. These 14 variables were selected for use in the final cluster analysis.

Cluster Analysis

The 14 belief and behavior variables were used in a cluster analysis (K-means, number of clusters set to four). Specifically, this analysis was used to group subjects based on similarity of patterning in the relative frequency of a variety of maternal beliefs and behaviors during feeding.

This analysis converged after three iterations. In particular, as can be seen in Table 6.4, the solution identified the following four clusters: (a) Cluster 1 (24 mothers) was characterized by infants who were primarily self-fed in high chairs and whose mothers were likely to place food in front of them to eat at their own pace, to phrase their directives indirectly as suggestions rather than commands (e.g., "Do you want some juice?" as opposed to, "Here's your juice"), and to emphasize self-control as a child-rearing goal; (b) Cluster 2 (19 mothers) was characterized by mothers who primarily spoon-fed their infants in high chairs, made frequent attempts to signal their infants' attention verbally, and emphasized Proper Demeanor; (c) Cluster 3 (11 mothers) was comprised of mothers who primarily bottle-fed their infants on their laps, engaged in relatively frequent physical positioning, and placed strong emphasis on Proper Demeanor; and (d) Cluster 4 (6 mothers) was characterized by infants who spent the majority of their feeding time wandering about freely and whose mothers frequently signaled their attention and attempted to position them.

Cluster × Group Membership

To examine whether mothers were more or less likely to be classified into the different clusters based on their group membership, a 2 × 4 (Group × Cluster) chi-square analysis was performed. This analysis yielded a Pearson Chi-Square (3 df) of 38.1, $p < .01$. As can be seen in Table 6.5, 75% of Anglo mothers fell into Cluster 1 (characterized predominantly by self-feeding in high chairs, placing food for the infant to eat, the use of suggestions, and an emphasis on Self-Control). An additional 18.8% were classified into Cluster 2 (characterized by spoon-feeding in high chairs, verbal signaling, and an emphasis on Proper Demeanor), and 6.3% fell into Cluster 4 (characterized primarily by the infant wandering about freely during feeding).

By contrast, 46.4% of Puerto Rican mothers fell into Cluster 2, and 39.3% were classified into Cluster 3 (characterized by bottle-feeding in the mother's lap, the use of positioning behaviors, and a strong emphasis on Proper Demeanor). Thus, roughly 86% of all Puerto Rican mothers were classified into either Cluster 2 or 3. An additional 14.3% fell into Cluster 4.

Table 6.4
Cluster Analysis (K-Means), Mothers' Beliefs and Behaviors

	Cluster			
	1	2	3	4
Type of Feeding (Duration in Seconds)				
Bottle-Feed	16.7	8.6	**166.2**	19.8
Spoon-Feed	18.4	**318.1**	37.6	**178.7**
Self-Feed	**421.9**	40.7	8.3	98.3
No Feeding Actvty	18.1	55.8	82.4	**104.2**
Highchair	**480.5**	**437.8**	41.1	0.0
Mother's Lap	0.0	10.1	**244.0**	70.7
Infant Wander	0.0	0.0	19.1	**373.2**
Maternal Behaviors (Frequency)				
Place Food	**5.2**	.53	0.0	2.7
Position	.08	.42	**1.3**	**1.8**
Suggest	**5.6**	3.6	2.2	2.3
Verbal Signal	.75	**3.5**	1.0	**4.0**
Nonverbal Signal	.42	.21	.09	**2.0**
Maternal Beliefs (Proportion)				
Self-Control	**.29**	.21	.11	.20
Proper Demeanor	.16	**.27**	**.36**	.24

Within-Group Differences

To examine the potential influences of specific sociodemographic variables on within-group differences in patterning of beliefs and behaviors, analyses were undertaken within each group for all sociodemographic data collected. Specifically, multivariate analyses of variance were used to examine the potential influence on cluster group membership of eight variables (mother's age and education, father's age and education, household Hollingshead score, total number of children, total household size, and number of hours worked per week by the mother; among Puerto Rican mothers, the analysis also included number of years spent in the United States and psychological acculturation score); and chi-square analyses examined the potential influence of five variables (child's gender and birth-order status, mother's employment and marital status, and mother's religious background; among Puerto Rican mothers, the analysis also included whether or not the mother identified herself as bilingual).

These analyses yielded a few within-group differences. In particular, when considering belief cluster membership among Anglos, mothers who identified

Table 6.5
Cluster Classification by Group Membership (%)

	Cluster			
Group	1	2	3	4
Anglo	75.0	18.8	0.0	6.3
Puerto Rican	0.0	46.4	39.3	14.3

Cluster 1 = Self-feed, Highchair, Place food, Suggest, Self-Control
Cluster 2 = Spoon-feed, Highchair, Verbal signal, Proper Demeanor
Cluster 3 = Bottle-feed, Lap, Position, Proper Demeanor
Cluster 4 = Spoon-feed, No feeding activity, Wander, Place food, Position, Signal

their religious background as Catholic, compared to mothers who identified their religious background as "none," were more likely to be in belief Cluster 2 emphasizing Self-Control (respective percentages = 47.1 and 17.6), and less likely to be in belief Cluster 1 emphasizing Self-Maximization (respective percentages = 0 and 50, Fisher's Exact Test = 10.7, $p < .05$). In terms of belief–behavior patterns, a trend emerged among the Anglo mothers, with mothers who were employed outside the home more likely than unemployed mothers to be in Cluster 1, which emphasized self-feeding (respective percentages = 85 and 58.3, Fisher's Exact Test = 4.0, $p = .10$).

Within the Puerto Rican group, mothers who fell into belief Clusters 1 and 2 (characterized by strong emphases on Self-Maximization and Self-Control) had spent significantly more time in the United States than mothers who fell into Clusters 3 and 4 (characterized by emphasis on Proper Demeanor, mean Clusters 1 and 2 combined = 1.7 years, mean Cluster 3 and 4 combined = .22 years), $F(3,22) = 8.5, p < .05$.

In terms of belief–behavior patterns, trends emerged among Puerto Rican mothers with regard to parental education and religious background. In particular, mothers who were more highly educated—$F(2,24) = 13.4, p < .10$—and who had more highly educated husbands—$F(2,24) = 24.9, p = .05$—were more likely to fall into Cluster 2, characterized by spoon-feeding in high chairs (respective means for father's and mother's education in Cluster 2 = 16.6 and 16.5, in Cluster 3 = 15.7 and 15.8, and in Cluster 4 = 14.0 and 14.5).

In addition, mothers who described their religious background as Catholic were more likely than Protestant mothers to fall into belief–behavior Cluster 3 (characterized by bottle-feeding on mother's lap, respective percentages = 64 and 18.2, Fisher's Exact Test = 6.9, $p < .10$).

DISCUSSION

The results of this study support the hypothesis that child-rearing beliefs and behaviors among middle-class Anglo and Puerto Rican mothers are patterned in group-specific ways. Within each group, variability also occurs, although certain patterns appear to be more typical of each group than other patterns.

First, a cluster analysis examining group patterning in the use of all five categories of the SGI yielded four distinct clusters, two of which represented relatively greater emphasis on more individualistic qualities associated with Self-Maximization and Self-Control, and two of which represented relatively greater emphasis on more sociocentric qualities associated with Proper Demeanor. Significantly, 81% of the Anglo mothers were classified into one of the first two clusters, whereas roughly 63% of the Puerto Rican mothers were classified into one of the two clusters emphasizing Proper Demeanor.

It is important to note in this regard that the category of Self-Control has been, in past research using the SGI (Harwood et al., 1995, 1996), most likely to characterize Anglo mothers' descriptions of qualities they would *not* like their child to possess. Harwood et al. (1995) suggest in particular that the category of Self-Control appears to represent for many Anglo mothers qualities associated with a negative excess of individualism. Thus, they want their child to feel good about himself (Self-Maximization), but not to be egocentric (Self-Control); they want their child to succeed in her career (Self-Maximization), but not to become too greedy or materialistic (Self-Control); they want him to feel that "the world is his oyster" (Self-Maximization), but nonetheless be able to tolerate frustration of his wishes (Self-Control). It is therefore not surprising, given that these analyses collapsed mothers' responses across all questions of the SGI, that separate clusters emerged based on these two categories, both of them particularly likely to be comprised of Anglo mothers.

A second cluster analysis examining maternal behaviors during feeding at 12 months, together with maternal beliefs, also yielded four clusters. One cluster was characterized by greater use of self-feeding in high chairs, placement of food for the infant to eat, maternal suggestions, and a relatively strong emphasis on Self-Control. A second cluster was characterized primarily by spoon-feeding in high chairs, verbal signaling, and an emphasis on Proper Demeanor, whereas a third was characterized by bottle-feeding in the mother's lap, positioning, and an emphasis on Proper Demeanor. A fourth cluster was characterized by infants who spent their feeding time wandering about freely. Significantly, 75% of Anglo mothers were classified into the first cluster emphasizing self-feeding and Self-Control, whereas roughly 86% of Puerto Rican mothers were classified into the two clusters emphasizing spoon-feeding and bottle-feeding and Proper Demeanor. A small number of infants in both groups were classified in the fourth cluster. In addition, a stepwise discriminant analysis indicated that 96.9% of Anglo and 100% of Puerto Rican mothers could be correctly classified on the basis of four variables: a greater tendency to encourage self-feeding and use suggestions to structure infant behavior (Anglo mothers), and a greater tendency to feed on mother's lap and emphasize Proper Demeanor as a child-rearing goal (Puerto Rican mothers).

Thus, these findings are consistent with a greater emphasis among Anglo mothers on qualities and practices associated with individualism (e.g., Self-Maximization, Self-Control, self-feeding, phrasing directives as suggestions, and placing food on the high chair for the infant to eat by herself), and with a greater emphasis among Puerto Rican mothers on qualities and practices associated with sociocentrism (e.g., Proper Demeanor, spoon-feeding, bottle-feeding on the mother's lap, and signaling of infant's attention). In both groups, the majority of mothers expressed beliefs and engaged in behaviors that fall into one or the other of these group-typical patterns.

However, these analyses provide support not only for coherent patterns typical of the majority of mothers within each group but also for within-group variability. Specifically, although 75% of the Anglo mothers fell into the clusters emphasizing self-feeding, suggestions, and Self-Control, 25% did not; similarly, although 86% of Puerto Rican mothers were classified into the two clusters emphasizing spoon-feeding, bottle-feeding, and Proper Demeanor, 14% were not. Thus, support is evident for considerable within-group variation in mothers' beliefs and behaviors, coexisting with what appear to be more typical patterns.

An examination of 13 sociodemographic variables (with an additional 3 variables pertaining to acculturation among Puerto Rican mothers) indicated that sociodemographic variables predicted differently: (a) among Puerto Rican as compared to Anglo mothers and (b) with regard to the belief–behavior clusters as compared to beliefs alone. In particular, among Anglo mothers, religious background and maternal employment status emerged as significant indicators, with mothers who described their religious background as "none" more likely to emphasize Self-Maximization, mothers who described themselves as Catholic more likely to emphasize Self-Control, and mothers who were employed outside the home more likely to have infants who self-fed. Among Puerto Rican mothers, the predictors were different, with mothers who had spent time in the United States more likely to emphasize Self-Maximization and Self-Control, and mothers who were more highly educated, had more highly educated husbands, and described themselves as Protestant more likely to spoon-feed their infants in high chairs.

Several of these findings are consistent with expectations. For example, employed Anglo mothers may place greater emphasis on self-feeding both because they themselves value independence and because it is convenient in a busy household to have more self-sufficient infants; Puerto Rican mothers who spent time on the mainland United States as children may place greater emphasis on Self-Maximization and Self-Control because they have been more intensively exposed to U.S. culture; higher levels of education have often been associated with placing greater value on individual initiative (Kohn, 1977) and may also reflect more intensive exposure to U.S. culture.

It is noteworthy that religious background emerged as a significant predictor among both groups of mothers. In particular, religious background is generally considered to correlate with ethnic identity (e.g., Italian or Irish Catholicism as compared to English or German Protestantism), and as such may represent a significant source of within-group variation. In addition, findings that Anglo mothers who said they lacked a religious background were more likely to emphasize Self-Maximization, and Catholic Puerto Rican mothers were more likely to bottle-feed their infants, may also reflect adherence to traditional versus nontraditional attitudes toward child rearing.

As a cautionary note, it must be emphasized that although within-group differences reached conventional levels of significance ($p < .05$) with regard to the belief clusters, only trends ($p < .10$) were obtained with the belief–behavior clusters. Given the small group sizes (n = 32 Anglo and 28 Puerto Rican mothers), it is not surprising that several of these analyses failed to reach conventional levels of significance. Although it is possible that increased power would yield similar, more robust findings within each group, it is also possible that examining sociodemographic influences among a larger number of middle-class Anglo and Puerto Rican mothers would alter these findings. They must therefore be viewed as only preliminary.

The findings regarding within-group variability must serve as a caution against overgeneralizing observed group patterns based on the individualism–sociocentrism dimension. Researchers have observed that using ethnicity as a variable for examining group differences can create false impressions of internal homogeneity, and thus carries with it the risk of reinforcing stereotypes (Roosa et al., Chapter 2, this volume). As Wolf (1982) states, "By turning names into things we create false models of reality. By endowing nations, societies, or cultures with the qualities of internally homogeneous and externally distinctive and bounded objects, we create a model of the world as a global pool hall in which the entities spin off each other like so many hard and round billiard balls" (p. 6). The challenge is to find a way of conceptualizing culture that recognizes group differences without reifying them.

For our purposes in this chapter, we would like to elaborate briefly on a perspective articulated by Harwood, Handwerker, Schoelmerich, and Leyendecker (2000), which locates culture not in the group but in the contextualized individual: Culture is viewed not as an entity equivalent to group membership labels but as a shifting continuum of shared commonality among individuals. In particular, definitions of culture as "shared discourse," shared "scripts" for the understanding of self and other, or shared "norms" for social interaction imply a relatively fluid definition of what constitutes a cultural community. A person may simultaneously be a member of multiple groups, each with its own particular "morally enforceable conceptual scheme . . . that is exemplified or instantiated in practice" (see Shweder, 1996, p. 20). Conversely, any cultural community is comprised of individuals who also participate in multiple other cultural communities. According to this approach, a cultural community may be viewed not as a bounded, static entity but as a group of individuals who co-construct a shared reality in one or more domains of life, and who involve themselves in discourse and activities appropriate to an agreed upon level of commonality (Harwood, Schoelmerich, & Schulze, 2000).

By definition, this level of commonality represents a shifting continuum: At the broadest, most inclusive level, we are all human beings who must confront the issues inherent in physical survival, procreation, and group life. At the narrowest, most exclusive level, we are each absolutely unique individuals. In between these extremes are differing levels of commonality, each with their concomitant markers and appropriate levels of shared discourse and practice. From this perspective, any cultural community is comprised of individuals who will tend to exhibit both general agreement regarding specific defining constructs and internal variation regarding either certain particulars or non-relevant constructs.

U.S. Latinos, regardless of age, gender, and socioeconomic status, may use a common body of knowledge because they share an ethnic heritage, and this knowledge may differ significantly from understandings shared by Anglo Americans. At the same time, however, education, employment status, years in the United States, and religious background may all serve as markers of commonality or difference among both Latinos and Anglo Americans. Thus, everyone participates in and is influenced by many group memberships reflecting a variety of life-experience markers. From this perspective, what is of primary interest is not the ultimately arbitrary boundary we draw to define the cultural community in question, but instead what we can learn about the extent to which specific types of discourse are indeed shared among those we have chosen to include as members of the same cultural community.

This study has examined child-rearing beliefs and practices during feeding among middle-class Puerto Rican mothers in San Juan. These mothers demonstrate a marked degree of similarity in their beliefs and practices, based on just a few sociodemographic indices (location and socioeconomic status). However, mothers who are less educated, who live in rural areas of Puerto Rico, who have extensive experience with migration to the mainland, or who are considered high risk for any one of a variety of reasons will undoubtedly diverge in specific ways from the patterns obtained here. Further research is needed examining the sources of both commonality and heterogeneity in child-rearing beliefs and practices among Puerto Rican mothers across a diverse range of backgrounds.

AUTHORS' NOTE

This research was made possible through a grant to the first author from the National Institute of Child Health and Human Development (HD32800). We are also grateful to Dr. Glorisa Canino of the University of Puerto Rico School of Medicine for making available the resources of her laboratory for the collection of the Puerto Rican data. We would like to express appreciation to Margaret Adams, Eugenio Ayala, Delia Collazo, Jorge Colon, Olguimar Cruz, Zenaida Gonzalez, Carmen Irizarry, Helena Mendez, Sylvia Meredith, Amy Schubert, Pamela Schulze, and Stephanie Wilson for their assistance with data collection, transcription, and coding.

REFERENCES

Dumas, J. (1993). *Interact Software System, v. 2.0*. West Lafayette, IN: Purdue University.

García Coll, C., Meyer, E. C., & Brillon, L. (1995). Ethnic and minority parenting. In M. H Bornstein (Ed.), *Handbook of parenting: Vol. 2. Biology and ecology of parenting* (pp. 189–209). Hillsdale, NJ: Erlbaum.

Harwood, R. L. (1992). The influence of culturally derived values on Anglo and Puerto Rican mothers' perceptions of attachment behavior. *Child Development, 63*, 822–839.

Harwood, R. L., Handwerker, W. P. Schoelmerich, A., & Leyendecker, B. (2001). Ethnic category labels, parental beliefs, and the contextualized individual: An exploration of the individualism-sociocentrism debate. *Parenting: Science and Practice, 1*, 217–236.

Harwood, R. L., & Miller, J. G. (1991). Perceptions of attachment behavior: A comparison of Anglo and Puerto Rican mothers. *Merrill-Palmer Quarterly, 37*, 583–599.

Harwood, R. L., Miller, J. G., & Lucca Irizarry, N. (1995). *Culture and attachment: Perceptions of the child in context*. New York: Guilford.

Harwood, R. L., Schoelmerich, A., & Schulze, P. A. (2000). Homogeneity and heterogeneity in cultural belief systems. In S. Harkness, C. Raeff, & C. M. Super (Eds.), *Variability in the social construction of the child* (pp. 41–57). San Francisco: Jossey-Bass.

Harwood, R. L., Schoelmerich, A., Schulze, P. A., & Gonzalez, Z. (1999). Cultural differences in maternal beliefs and behaviors: A study of middle-class Anglo and Puerto Rican mother–infant pairs in four everyday situations. *Child Development, 70*, 1005–1016.

Harwood, R. L., Schoelmerich, A., Ventura-Cook, E., Schulze, P. A., & Wilson, S. P. (1996). Culture and class influences on Anglo and Puerto Rican mothers' beliefs regarding longterm socialization goals and child behavior. *Child Development, 67*, 2446–2461.

Hollingshead, A. B. (1975). *Four factor index of social status*. Unpublished manuscript, Yale University, New Haven, CT.

Killen, M., & Wainryb, C. (2000). Independence and interdependence in diverse cultural contexts. In S. Harkness, C. Raeff, & C. M. Super (Eds.), *Variability in the social construction of the child* (pp. 5–20). San Francisco: Jossey-Bass.

Kohn, M. L. (1977). *Class and conformity: A study in values.* Chicago: University of Chicago Press.

Lauria, A. (1982). *Respeto, relajo,* and interpersonal relations in Puerto Rico. In F. Cordasco & E. Bucchioni (Eds.), *The Puerto Rican community and its children on the mainland* (2nd edition, pp. 58–71). Metuchen, NJ: Scarecrow.

Markus, H. R., & Kitayama, S. (1991). Culture and the self: Implications for cognition, emotion, and motivation. *Psychological Review, 98,* 224–253.

Nucci, L. (1994). Mothers beliefs regarding the personal domain of children. In J. G. Smetana (Ed.), *Beliefs about parenting: Origins and developmental implications* (pp. 81–97). San Francisco: Jossey-Bass.

Shweder, R. A. (1996). True ethnography: The lore, the law, and the lure. In R. Jessor, A. Colby, & R. A. Shweder (Eds.), *Ethnography and human development: Context and meaning in social inquiry* (pp. 15–52). Chicago: University of Chicago Press.

Spiro, M. (1993). Is the Western conception of the self peculiar within the context of the world cultures? *Ethos, 21,* 107–153.

Tropp, L. R., Erkut, S., Alarcón, O., García Coll, C., & Vázquez, H. (1994). Toward a theoretical model of psychological acculturation. Working Papers No. 268. Wellesley, MA: Center for Research on Women, Wellesley College.

Wolf, E. R. (1982). *Europe and the people without history.* Berkeley: University of California Press.

7

A Conceptual Model of the Determinants of Parenting Among Latina Adolescent Mothers

Josefina M. Contreras, David Narang,
Madinah Ikhlas, and Jennifer Teichman

Research has documented that, in comparison to adult childbearing, early childbearing is associated with less optimal parenting (Field, Widmayer, Stringer, & Ignatoff, 1980; Osofsky, Hann, & Peebles, 1993) and adverse outcomes both for the young mothers and their children (Baldwin & Cain, 1980; Brooks-Gunn & Furstenberg, 1986). Adolescent mothers have been described as being more affectively negative and restrictive and less responsive to their children than adult mothers. These parenting problems and adverse outcomes are more strongly associated with contextual variables (e.g., socioeconomic status, education) than with chronological age per se (Baldwin & Cain, 1980; García Coll, Hoffman, & Oh, 1987). Adolescent mothers are more likely than their non-parenting peers to come from lower socioeconomic backgrounds, to have lower intellectual ability, and to have poorer school performance (Flick, 1986; Klerman, 1993). They are also more likely than adult mothers to reside in neighborhoods with fewer resources and to be raising their children in poverty (Klerman, 1993). Despite these conditions, considerable variability in the parenting quality of teen mothers (Shapiro & Mangelsdorf, 1994) and their children's developmental outcomes have been noted (Furstenberg, Brooks-Gunn, & Morgan, 1987). Thus, it is important to identify factors that might enable some young mothers to parent more competently in these disadvantaged conditions.

Understanding the factors associated with more optimal parenting among Latina adolescent mothers is particularly important in light of the fact that although recently overall teen birth rates have declined slightly, the decline has been smallest among Latina youth, and the rate for Latino youth (94 per 1,000 births; 15–19 years) is now larger than that for any other group in the United States (79 per 1,000 births for Black teens; 33 per 1,000 births for non-Hispanic White teens; National Center for Health Statistics, 2001). Moreover, Latinos represent the fastest growing segment of the population under the age of 21 (Aponte & Crouch, 1995). Latinos are also overrepresented among the poor, have high unemployment rates, and tend to reside in neighborhoods with few resources (Romero, 2000), suggesting that adolescent parenting among the Latino population will continue to be a serious concern. Further knowledge regarding the social ecology of young Latina mothers and the factors related to their parenting competence is clearly needed in order to develop prevention and intervention programs that can appropriately serve this population.

The goal of this chapter is to propose a conceptual model of the determinants of parenting competence among Latina adolescent mothers. Current models of parenting competence (Abidin, 1992; Belsky, 1984) have been largely developed and tested on adult parents and middle-class populations. Thus, it is unclear whether they apply to minority adolescent parents and their offspring. Although the literature on adolescent parenting is now growing, the preponderance of research to date has focused on White and African American mothers and remarkably little is known about factors related to parenting competence among Latino families. To the extent that young Latina mothers differ from other adolescent parents, factors associated with their parenting competence will also differ. Indeed, research suggests that Latino parenting beliefs and child socialization goals differ from those of Anglo mothers (Harwood, Schoelmerich, Schulze, & Gonzalez, 1999; Harwood, Schoelmerich, Ventura-Cook, Schulze, & Wilson, 1996) and that family structure and social network variables distinguish Latina adolescent mothers from other groups of adolescent parents (Becerra & de Anda, 1984; Brunelli, Wasserman, Rauh, Alvarado, & Caraballo, 1995; Wasserman, Brunelli, Rauh, & Alvarado, 1994). Thus, in addition to the need to develop a parenting model that can adequately explain parenting among adolescent mothers (as opposed to adult mothers), the model needs to also account for the social ecology and cultural context of Latina adolescent mothers living in the United States.

The limited available research on Latina adolescent mothers has been largely based on indirect indices of parenting (e.g., self-report of parenting attitudes) and not on behavioral observations of parenting behaviors. It has also relied primarily on comparative methodology, examining mean differences between adolescent mothers of different ethnic backgrounds or between adolescent and adult mothers, rather than on within-group designs that take into account the cultural and ecological context in which these families are embedded. Oftentimes, researchers have been forced to use measures that have not been validated for this population or that were designed to assess aspects of parenting that are central to parenting in other populations but that may not adequately reflect important aspects of parenting among Latina mothers. A conceptual framework that can guide future research in this area is clearly needed.

The proposed model builds on Belsky's model of parenting (1984). Belsky proposes three major influences on parenting: the psychological characteristics and resources of the parent, the characteristics of the child, and the social context in which the parent–child relationship is embedded, including the parent' social network, marital relationship, and work experiences. These influences are seen as interdependent, and the extent to which the system as a whole supports optimal parenting and child outcomes depends on the degree of stress or support provided by each subsystem. The model assigns a central role to the psychological functioning of the parent in that this factor is seen as a mediator of the sociocultural influences on parenting.

Our model (see Figure 7.1) attempts to account for both the developmental stage (adolescent vs. adult) and the cultural and sociodemographic ecology of Latina adolescent mothers in the United States by (a) examining what constitutes optimal parenting based on culturally derived norms regarding the maternal role and socialization goals for children, and the socioeconomic and political environment to which Latino children need to adapt in the United States; (b) adding parenting factors that are either not considered or not adequately emphasized in Belsky's model (1984); (c) redefining some of the links between the different parenting factors; (d) considering the role of acculturation and enculturation processes in terms of both how optimal parenting is defined and the expected relations among the different parenting factors; and (e) reevaluating the extent to which the different systems actually function toward the same goal, as is assumed in adult models of parenting.

In this chapter, we first discuss the need to arrive at a definition of optimal parenting that appropriately captures both universal and culture-specific aspects of what constitutes "ideal parenting" for Latinos in the United States. We then present the different factors that need to be included in a conceptual model of parenting competence applicable to Latina adolescent mothers. Where available, research supporting the consideration of each of these factors will be presented. Given the paucity of research examining Latina adolescent mothers of any country of origin, research examining adult Latina mothers and adolescent mothers of other ethnic groups will also be included where applicable.

DEFINING OPTIMAL PARENTING

A model of Latina adolescent mothers' parenting competence must be grounded on a definition of optimal parenting quality that is applicable to Latino parents. Unfortunately, longitudinal studies specifying parenting behaviors leading to more optimal child development among Latino families in the United States have not been conducted. Whereas certain parent characteristics and behaviors are integral aspects of competence that cut across cultural boundaries, other behaviors must be defined within specific cultural contexts (García Coll, Lamberty, Jenkins, McAdoo, Crnic, Wasik, & Garcia,

Figure 7.1
Model of the Determinants of Parenting Among Latina Adolescent Mothers

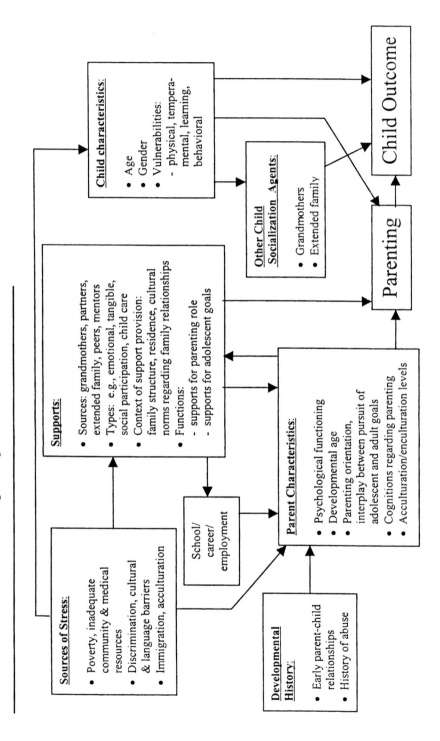

1996) and considering the environment to which children will need to adapt. In fact, there is indication that at least some of the maternal behaviors that are related to more optimal child development in Latino families are different from those of mothers of other ethnic backgrounds. For example, in a study of Latina adult mothers, some of the behaviors that distinguished mothers of securely and insecurely attached infants were different from those found in non-Latino samples (e.g., increased use of physical interventions; Fracasso, Busch, & Fisher, 1994).

In defining optimal parenting, some maternal characteristics and behaviors will be common to parents of different ethnic backgrounds. For example, research with families from different cultural backgrounds, both within and outside of the United States, has demonstrated that maternal sensitivity (the ability to accurately perceive and promptly and appropriately respond to the child's needs and signals; Ainsworth, Blehar, Waters, & Wall, 1978) is significantly associated with more adaptive functioning in young children (Ainsworth et al., 1978; Grossman, Grossman, Spangler, Suess, & Uzner, 1985; Valenzuela, 1997). Thus, maternal sensitivity must be one of the constructs included in a definition of optimal parenting for Latino parents. Importantly, however, because mothers of different ethnic backgrounds achieve sensitivity through different means—a mother can be physically, verbally, or visually responsive to a child's needs (Richman, Miller, & LeVine, 1992)—assessment of sensitivity must be conducted in a culturally congruent manner.

In arriving at a more complete specification of optimal Latino parenting that also includes culture-specific aspects of parenting, a number of factors need to be considered. First, it is crucial to consider Latino cultural values and norms regarding parenting beliefs and strategies and socialization goals for children; some of these are common to all Latino subgroups in the United States, while others vary by nationality (see Cauce & Domenech-Rodríguez, Chapter 1, this volume and Roosa, Morgan-Lopez, Cree, & Specter, Chapter 2, this volume, for a detailed description). As in any culture, parenting behaviors would need to be in line with socialization goals for children. These parenting behaviors would actually predict more optimal child development because they instill characteristics and skills that are valued and needed in the context in which children need to adapt as adults. For immigrant populations, such as Latinos in the United States, however, defining what constitutes optimal parenting behaviors is complicated by the fact that as Latino children develop they must adapt to a context that does not necessarily match the original one. Therefore, parenting that is in line with traditional Latino cultural values does not necessarily lead to optimal child adaptation in the United States, specially if adaptation is defined based on mainstream American values. For example, researchers (Gonzalez-Ramos, Zayas, & Cohen, 1998; Harwood et al., 1996, 1999) have uncovered a set of culturally determined long-term socialization goals shared by Puerto Rican adult mothers of various economic backgrounds that is different from that of Anglo mothers. Puerto Rican mothers emphasize child qualities related to

"Proper Demeanor" such as appropriate interpersonal behavior, the ability to get along with others, and the fulfillment of role obligations, particularly within the family. In contrast, Anglo mothers place relatively greater emphasis on qualities related to "Self-Maximization," such as fulfillment of personal potential, self-confidence, and self-reliance. These child socialization goals, in turn, are in line with the parenting behaviors exhibited by the mothers (Harwood et al., 1999; Harwood, Miller, Carlson, & Leyendecker, Chapter 6, this volume). Although these child characteristics are valued by Puerto Rican parents and presumably lead to better adaptation in the Puerto Rican society, they are not necessarily associated with successful adaptation in mainstream American culture. In fact, some of the academic difficulties young Latino children exhibit in U.S. schools have been attributed to the lack of a match between children's learning experiences at home and at school, with Latino families valuing obedience and conformity and the schools valuing independence, self-direction, and creativity (Laosa, 1982; Moreno, 1991). Thus, the parameters used in defining successful child outcomes are also an important factor in arriving at a specification of optimal parenting among Latinos in the United States.

Further complicating the picture is the fact that Latinos vary in level of both acculturation (extent to which Latinos have taken on important aspects of the dominant culture; Marín, Sabogal, VanOss Marín, Otero-Sabogal, & Perez-Stable, 1987) and enculturation (degree to which Latinos have acquired or maintained the values and traditions of their original culture; Knight, Bernal, Cota, Garza, & Ocampo, 1993), and adhere to Latino and Anglo cultural traditions to different degrees. Thus, the set of cultural values that guide their parenting strategies and behaviors are likely to vary accordingly. Latino parents' goals for their children also vary, with some parents aspiring to instill characteristics and skills that will allow their children to successfully adapt to the mainstream society, and others hoping their children will acquire and maintain their cultural heritage. Indeed there is some empirical evidence suggesting that acculturation level is related to the child-rearing values and types of parenting strategies used by Latina adolescent and adult mothers. Among adult Puerto Rican mothers, those who were more highly acculturated rated the child-rearing values of independence and creativity higher than those who were less acculturated; these values were among the top three ranked by Anglo mothers (Gonzalez-Ramos et al., 1998). Similarly, in an investigation of the teaching strategies used by Latina adolescent mothers, more highly acculturated adolescents were found to rely more heavily on verbal and nondirective teaching strategies than their relatively unacculturated peers (Teichman & Contreras, 2002). These findings for adolescent mothers are consistent with the literature on adult mothers' teaching strategies, which indicates that Latina mothers use more nonverbal (e.g., modeling, visual cues) and fewer verbal (e.g., verbal praise) strategies than White mothers (Laosa, 1980), and that among Latina mothers acculturation level is positively related to the use of verbal inquiry and praise (Planos, Zayas, & Bush-Rossnagel, 1995).

The issues discussed in this section are important in defining what constitutes optimal parenting. Following, we present the different factors that we propose determine individual differences in parenting quality among Latina adolescent mothers. Interrelations among these different factors and the ways in which they function to determine parenting quality are also discussed.

PARENTING FACTORS AND SUBSYSTEMS

Following Belsky's model (1984), we organized the different parenting factors into three subsystems: factors related to the parent, the context in which the parent–child relationship is embedded, and child characteristics.

Factors Related to the Parent

Developmental History of the Parent

Parents' early relationships with their own parents and subsequent thoughts and feelings associated with those relationships influence how they perceive and behave toward their own children (for a meta-analytic review, see van IJzendoorn, 1995). Although the specific form and characteristics of early attachment relationships among Latino families may be somewhat different from that of Anglo families (Harwood, 1992), these early relational experiences of Latina adolescent mothers are nonetheless reflected in aspects of their subsequent close interpersonal relationships (Rhodes, Contreras, & Mangelsdorf, 1994), and likely influence their perceptions and reactions toward their own children.

Given that a substantial percentage of adolescent mothers have histories that include sexual abuse and victimization, and these experiences are associated with difficulties in sustaining stable relationships and with an increased risk for mental health problems (Stevenson-Simon & Reichert, 1994), a history of abuse must be considered as a possible important influence on adolescent mothers' parenting. However, the associations between a history of abuse and parenting difficulties have not been studied among Latina adolescent mothers.

Developmental Stage of the Parent

Age per se is not likely to have a strong direct effect on parenting quality, especially when considering adolescents in the 15–19-year-old age range, the age range in which most Latina adolescent mothers give birth (Latina birth rate for 10–14-year-olds = 2 per 1,000; 15–17 = 60 per 1,000; 18–19 = 143.5 per 1,000; National Center for Health Statistics, 2001). This is because many of the parenting difficulties of adolescent mothers are associated with the context of risk in which they are embedded (e.g., poverty, low educational attainment, single status), and these risk factors mediate the relations to poor parenting and child outcomes (Chase-Landsdale, Brooks-Gunn, & Zamsky,

1994). Similarly, differences between Latina adult and adolescent mothers are likely to be attenuated once socioeconomic and educational status variables are taken into account, as has been found for mothers of other ethnic groups (Baldwin & Cain, 1980; García Coll et al. 1987). In the only study to directly compare the parenting behaviors of adult and adolescent Latina (Puerto Rican and Dominican origin) mothers, Wasserman and collaborators (1994) found no significant differences in the quality of adult and adolescent mothers' interactional style (although the quality of the home environment for adolescent mothers was poorer than that of adult mothers). In their study, the two groups were not different in socioeconomic status.

However, the developmental age of the parent is likely to have an important effect on two aspects of the parenting system. First, age influences the relative importance of the different sources of support available to the parent. For example, availability of support from parents has a greater influence on psychological adjustment and parenting competence among adolescent than adult mothers. Second, and more important, because of their age, adolescent mothers are faced with divergent developmental tasks and goals. The extent to which adolescent mothers attempt to meet adult (e.g., parenting) and/or adolescent (e.g., complete high school) goals has implications for their parenting competence. Moreover, support or resources that enhance or facilitate the adolescent's individual development (e.g., child-care assistance to pursue education, peer involvement to facilitate exploration and identity development) may not facilitate, and might even hinder, her development as a parent, or vice versa.

Therefore, we have expanded our model of parenting competence to account for these divergent goals. Contrary to models of adult parenting that assume that all of the subsystems are functioning toward the same goal, our model allows for the fact that the individual goals of the adolescent mother may be contradictory to her goals as a parent, and does not assume that all subsystems function toward the same goal. In our specification of the support resources available to the parent, we have separated those that function to support the adolescent versus the adult goals of the parent. We have also added the centrality of the parenting role as another important characteristic of the parent that influences parenting directly.

In our own studies of Latina adolescent mothers, we have found some support for these contentions. Adolescent mothers who were enrolled in school displayed less sensitive and affectively positive behaviors during social play with their young children. In fact, this association remained significant even after partialling out the effects of parenting orientation and maternal age. Parenting orientation, or the extent to which the mothers believed parenting was an important and fulfilling aspect of their life, was significantly correlated with the level of sensitivity and expressivity they displayed, whereas maternal age was unrelated to parenting quality. Moreover, those who lived with a partner were less likely to be enrolled in school (even after partialling out maternal age) but displayed more sensitive and affectively positive behaviors during mother–child interaction (Contreras, 2002).

Given the importance of maternal sensitivity in early parent–child interactions for children's social and emotional development (Ainsworth et al., 1978; Grossman et al., 1985; Valenzuela, 1997), these findings are of clear concern. Mastering an important developmental goal of adolescence (completing high school), which can have long-term benefits for the adolescent and her child, may come at the expense of the appropriate development of the parent–child relationship and, in turn, the child's social and emotional functioning. Thus, in understanding parenting among Latina adolescent mothers, the interplay between the young mothers' pursuit of adolescent and adult goals must be considered and examined in the context of both the adolescent and her offspring's short- and long-term adjustment across different domains of functioning.

Psychological Adjustment of the Parent

The direction of the effects of psychological adjustment (e.g., degree of symptomatology, self-esteem) on parenting is likely similar among adolescent and adult mothers as well as among mothers of different ethnic backgrounds. However, cultural factors may influence the expression or symptom presentation of psychological dysfunction. For example, among Latinos, psychological distress appears to be commonly expressed through somatization (Koss, 1990). Therefore, for Latina adolescent mothers, the assessment of psychological functioning must include culturally sensitive indices in order to appropriately examine the way in which various symptoms influence parent–child interaction.

Given that a substantial percentage of adolescent mothers report at least moderate levels of depressive symptoms (Leadbeater & Linares, 1992; Wasserman et al., 1994) and this type of psychopathology has been associated with impaired parenting in adult mothers (Downey & Coyne, 1990), depression must be one of the syndromes included in the assessment of psychological adjustment. However, the empirical relation between depression and parenting difficulties has not been well established for adolescent mothers of any ethnic background and has not been investigated in Latino samples. In the only study that had a representation of Latina adolescent mothers (43% Puerto Rican, 53% African American; Leadbeater, Bishop, & Raver, 1996), depressive symptoms were related to fewer maternal contingent responses displayed during free-play mother–toddler interactions, but were unrelated to mother–toddler conflict in the same interactions (analyses were not reported separately by ethnic background).

Future studies of the relations between psychological adjustment and parenting among Latina adolescent mothers are clearly needed. It would be important for these studies to consider adolescent mothers' parenting orientation in examining the associations between psychological functioning and parenting quality. The individual psychological adjustment (e.g., degree of symptomatology or distress) of adolescent mothers for whom the parenting role is not central may not have as strong an effect on parenting quality as it has among adolescents for whom parenting is central. This is especially the case when the adolescent is embedded in a social network that supports her individual development and provides child-care support.

Cognitions Regarding Parenting

Cognitive characteristics of mothers—specifically, knowledge of child development, parenting style, and parenting attitudes—have been proposed as important determinants of parenting quality among adolescent mothers (O'Callaghan, Borkowski, Whitman, Maxwell, & Keogh, 1999; Whitman, Borkowski, Schellenbach, & Nath, 1987). While these variables have been found to be related to maternal reports of aspects of parenting such as parenting stress among African American and White adolescent mothers, they have not shown consistent relations to observer rating of parent–child interactions, especially when the effects of demographic variables are controlled (Sommer et al., 1993). The strength of the direct relations between these cognitive variables and Latina adolescent mothers' parenting competence still needs to be assessed. In our own samples, measures of knowledge of child development and parenting style have been unrelated to observer ratings of parenting quality (unpublished data).

Acculturation and Enculturation Levels

Within our model, the parents' level of acculturation and enculturation are thought to influence parenting in at least three ways. First, the extent to which a Latina mother has taken on mainstream values and has retained or acquired Latino values will help define both the socialization goals she has for her children and the parenting strategies she considers optimal. Second, these variables affect parenting indirectly through their influence on the psychological adjustment of the parent. For adolescent Latina mothers who depend both on their extended families and mainstream systems (e.g., medical, social service, schools), a bicultural orientation (i.e., relatively high levels of both acculturation and enculturation) may lead to more optimal psychological adjustment and, in turn, greater parenting competence. A greater ability to negotiate their way through both cultures may allow adolescent mothers to maximize the benefits they derive from the support provided by their families as well as facilitate adjustment in the school and work environments. In fact, among mainland Puerto Rican adolescent mothers, biculturality has been found to be a stronger predictor of psychological adjustment than a measure of unidimensional acculturation (López & Contreras, under review).

Finally, levels of acculturation and enculturation influence parenting indirectly through their effects on the mothers' expectations regarding family relationships and the specific roles that the individual members play. These expectations, in turn, influence the types and amount of support that are provided, the relationship context in which the social support process takes place, and the extent to which the mother benefits from the available support. This is especially important among families whose members differ in acculturation and enculturation levels and therefore may have different expectations regarding family relationships. Thus, the third way in which acculturation level influences parenting is through its role as moderator of the associations between family-based support variables and psychological or parenting competence among adolescent Latina mothers.

There is empirical evidence suggesting that the functions of social support provided by Latina adolescent mothers' own mothers differ depending on the cultural and family relationship context in which the support is embedded. Specifically, among Puerto Rican adolescent mothers, acculturation level moderated the associations between grandmother involvement (indexed by the residential, social support, and child-care assistance they provided) and the young mothers' psychological adjustment and parenting stress (Contreras, López, Rivera-Mosquera, Raymond-Smith, & Rothstein, 1999). Among relatively unacculturated Latina adolescent mothers, who are more likely to follow cultural traditions that encourage grandmothers' involvement and interdependence as opposed to independence–individuation during adolescence (Blos, 1967; Grotevant & Cooper, 1986; Roland, 1988), greater grandmother involvement was related to lower levels of symptomatology and of parenting stress. Thus, in this relational context, adolescent mothers were able to benefit from the support provided by their mothers. In contrast, among more highly acculturated Latina adolescent mothers, who may follow American traditions and expect greater independence from their families of origin, greater grandmother involvement tended to be related to greater symptomatology and parenting stress (Contreras, López et al., 1999).

The Context in Which the Parent–Child Relationship Is Embedded

Socioeconomic Background

Given the low socioeconomic status of most Latina adolescent mothers, contextual variables are likely to play a crucial role in their adjustment. Contextual influences such as socioeconomic status and level of education do not appear to be adequately emphasized in current models of parenting but have been found to explain differences between adult and adolescent parents' competence (Baldwin & Cain, 1980; García Coll et al., 1987) as well as the types of teaching strategies used by Latina mothers (Laosa, 1980). Socioeconomic-status variables have also been proposed as major explanatory variables for understanding parenting among minority populations (Ogbu, 1981) and function as a context of risk that affects all aspects of the parenting system (i.e., availability to internal/psychological and external resources for parenting).

Stressors That Tax the Resources of the Parenting System

As in adult models of parenting, levels of stress experienced by adolescent mothers are likely to negatively impact their psychological well-being and ability to parent competently and consistently. In addition to the stress related to the off-time transition to parenting (McLaughlin & Micklin, 1983) and the ongoing demands of parenthood, young mothers often struggle with the various developmental tasks of adolescence (Panzarine, 1986). In fact, research indicates that young mothers experience more parenting stress than adult mothers (Brown, Adams, & Kellan, 1981). Latina mothers face additional stressors related to the immigration and acculturation processes as well as to discrimination, racism, and poverty (Shorris, 1992). This heightened level of stress likely has a negative influence on both their psychological adjustment and parenting competence.

Social Support Resources

Social support has been highlighted as an important positive influence on psychological adjustment and parenting competence, especially for those parenting under conditions of high stress or social risk, such as young minority mothers (Wilcox, 1981). Because the social support networks of Latina mothers differ from that of other mothers in the United States, and these differences have implications for the role of support on adjustment, we first provide descriptive information regarding the social networks of Latina adolescent mothers. We then discuss how we view the role of social support on the young mothers' psychological and parenting competence.

Latino values include a deep sense of familism (feelings of obligation, solidarity, and reciprocity within the family) and family member interdependence (Vega, 1995). Latina mothers tend to turn to family members more during times of stress, are more receptive to their child-rearing advice, and tend to share child-care responsibilities with members of the extended family rather than seek outside services more than other groups of parents (Shorris, 1992). Grandmothers appear to have a prominent and influential role within the extended family and are commonly in charge of child rearing when the mother is employed (Ramos-McKay, Comas-Díaz, & Rivera, 1988). Consistent with these cultural traditions, Latinos tend to establish new households in the same neighborhoods as their family of origin and to reside in close proximity to extended family members, thus facilitating close and frequent contact (Keefe, 1984). Latina adolescent mothers (of Puerto Rican and Dominican origin) report lower levels of overall social support than African American adolescent mothers (Wasserman et al., 1994). However, when considering support from family members as opposed to support from any provider, pregnant and parenting adolescents of Puerto Rican origin report higher levels of family support and closer family ties than African American adolescents (Dore &

Dumois, 1990). Consistently, in comparison to Anglo adolescent mothers, Mexican American adolescent mothers report more daily contact with extended family members and perceive their own mothers as providing more support (Becerra & de Anda, 1984; de Anda & Becerra, 1984).

Young Latina mothers (of Puerto Rican, Cuban, and Dominican origin) are more likely to reside with and be in long-term relationships with partners than are African American (Wasserman et al., 1994) and White (de Anda & Becerra, 1984) adolescent mothers. This is consistent with their cultural background. Early marriages (not prompted by unplanned pregnancies) have been historically common in Latino countries, and in the case of unplanned pregnancies, cultural traditions encourage fathers to assume their parental role and legitimize the offspring through marriage (García Coll & Vazquez García, 1996). In addition, Spanish-speaking Latina adolescent mothers (Mexican origin) identify their partners as their main source of support; their English-speaking peers identify their partners as their second most common source of support, with grandmothers reported as the main source of support in this subgroup (de Anda & Becerra, 1984).

Despite the higher likelihood of being in long-term relationships with partners, however, Latina adolescent mothers report less child-care and emotional support from them than do their African American (Brunelli et al., 1995; Wasserman et al., 1994) and White (de Anda & Becerra, 1984) peers. The lower level of reported child-care (but not emotional) support is also consistent with their cultural background because culturally prescribed gender roles for fathers or partners do not include substantial involvement in child rearing (Shorris, 1992).

Given Latino culture and these family and social network characteristics, several factors need to be considered when attempting to explain the influence of social support on Latina adolescent mothers. First, because of the unique functions of individual network members, it is imperative to consider not only the overall support resources available to the mother but also the unique influences of the different sources of support (e.g., mothers, fathers, partners/spouses, peers, mentors) that are available to the mother. Given the central role of grandmothers within the extended family and the distinct traditional Latino gender roles that emphasize the importance of having a partner/husband for women (Shorris, 1992), the influence of these two support providers must be considered, both in terms of their individual and relative impact on the young mothers' adjustment. Similarly, because the adolescent mother is faced with divergent developmental goals and tasks, it is also crucial to differentiate the sources, types (e.g., emotional, child care, socializing, tangible assistance), and amounts of support that serve to enhance her functioning in different spheres of her life. Whereas some types of support provided by a particular network member (e.g., child-care assistance provided by grandmothers) may have a positive effect on one area of functioning (e.g., completing high school), the effect may be negative in another domain (e.g., developing parenting skills). As discussed in the section "Acculturation and Enculturation Levels," the culturally derived expectations regarding family relationships and goals for normative adolescent development also need to be taken into account when attempting to understand the functions of family support.

With regard to sources of support, the literature, which has focused primarily on African American and White adolescent mothers, has concentrated on the support provided by the adolescents' mothers ("grandmothers"). Consistent with current conceptualizations of the functions of social support, grandmother social support has been found to be positively associated with adolescent mothers' psychological well-being (Leadbeater & Linares, 1992; Spieker & Bensley, 1994; Unger & Wandersman, 1985), short-term educational attainment (Furstenberg et al., 1987), and parenting adjustment (Chase-Lansdale, Brooks-Gunn, & Zamsky, 1994).

However, a number of studies have raised questions regarding a simple, direct, and positive association between social support and higher competence among young mothers (Chase-Lansdale et al., 1994; Shapiro & Mangelsdorf, 1994; Spieker & Bensley, 1994; Unger & Cooley, 1992). In these studies, grandmother support has been related to more parenting difficulties, especially when adjustment beyond the perinatal period was examined. For example, among African American teen mothers, those who relied more on their family for emotional and material support assumed less child-care duties and had more negative feelings about their infants. In a sample of African American and White teen mothers, emotional support from grandmothers was positively related to extent of grandmother involvement in child care and negatively related to the teen's nurturance toward her infant (Oyserman, Radin, & Saltz, 1994). These negative associations are thought to be due to the added conflict that is often present in the mother–adolescent relationships of adolescent mothers (Caldwell & Antonucci, 1997). The adolescent's reliance on her mother for support at the same time that she pursues her independence is thought to increase relationship conflict and parenting stress, and to impact negatively on the adjustment of adolescent mothers who reside with their mothers or rely on them for extensive support. Thus, expectations regarding the development of independence during adolescence and the optimal level of involvement within mother–adolescent relationships appear to influence the extent to which young mothers can benefit from the support provided by their mothers. These expectations, which are culturally determined, differ among Anglo and Latino families; in general, Anglos expect the development of independence—individuation during adolescence—and Latinos expect continued involvement and interdependence (Blos, 1967; Grotevant & Cooper, 1986; Roland, 1988).

As Latinos become more acculturated, their values begin to resemble those of the American culture (although they do not become equal; Sabogal, Marín, Otero-Sabogal, VanOss Marín, & Perez-Stable, 1987). For example, higher acculturation levels are related to lower levels of attitudinal familism (Sabogal et al., 1987). Thus, one would expect that at high levels of acculturation, grandmother social support would show similar associations with measures of competence as it does among other adolescent parents in the United States. We have found some empirical support for this expectation. Among English-speaking, relatively highly acculturated Latina adolescent mothers of Mexican and Puerto Rican origin, consistent with findings for White and African American adolescents, child-care assistance and extensive social support from grandmothers were associated with lower maternal sensitivity during unstructured social play, even after the adolescents' overall support resources (which had positive relations with parenting quality) were considered (Contreras, Mangelsdorf, Rhodes, Diener, & Brunson, 1999). In a sample of English- and Spanish-speaking mainland Puerto Rican adolescent mothers of varying acculturation levels, however, the associations between grandmother support and psychological adjustment and parenting stress were moderated by level of acculturation (Contreras, López et al., 1999). The results for highly acculturated mothers were consistent with the findings for African American and White adolescent mothers we reported earlier, and revealed a negative association between grandmother involvement and psychological adjustment and parenting stress. The results for minimally acculturated adolescents showed a positive association between grandmother involvement and psychological adjustment and parenting stress and were consistent with traditional Latino cultural values that emphasize interdependence and continued direct family involvement even after adolescence (Vega, 1995). Thus, in understanding the role of grandmother support among Latino families it is imperative to consider the cultural context in which the grandmother–adolescent relationship is embedded.

We have also found evidence for the importance of differentiating among the various types of support that are provided by grandmothers. Specifically, among Latina adolescents that coresided with their mothers, extent of grandmother social support and child-care assistance had unique and opposite functions on maternal behaviors during a teaching task. Whereas extent of social support was related to more sensitive and affectively positive behaviors, greater child-care assistance was associated with less sensitive and positive behaviors (Contreras, 2002).

The few studies that have examined the role of partner support in White and African American young mothers have found mixed results. Although some of these studies have documented a positive relation between partner support and psychological well-being among African American adolescent mothers (Leadbeater & Linares, 1992; Thompson & Peebles-Wilkins, 1992), others have failed to show an association (Turner, Grindstaff, & Phillips, 1990). Still another found partner child-care and material support to be related to lower levels of maternal expressivity during mother–child interaction among White adolescent mothers (Shapiro & Mangelsdorf, 1994). Partners are also described as a major source of stress for the young mother (Musick, 1993).

The few studies that have examined partner support and psychological well-being among Latina adolescent mothers found positive associations. In a sample that combined African American and English-speaking Puerto Rican adolescent mothers (analyses were not reported separately for each ethnic group), partner support was related to less depressive symptoms (Leadbeater & Linares, 1992). Consistent with this finding, among Spanish- and English-speaking Latina adolescent mothers of Puerto Rican origin, social support from partners was related to lower levels of symptomatology (Contreras, López et al., 1999). By contrast, studies examining partner support and parenting adjustment have found mixed results. Partner support has been related to lower levels of power-assertive child-rearing attitudes among Puerto Rican and Dominican mothers (Brunelli et al., 1995) but was unrelated to parenting stress among Puerto Rican adolescent mothers in another sample (Contreras, López et al., 1999). Observer ratings of maternal sensitivity during mother–child play interactions were negatively associated with availability of child-care support from partners in our English-speaking sample (Contreras, Mangelsdorf et al., 1999). In contrast in our sample that included both Spanish- and English-speaking adolescent mothers, those who perceived higher levels of social support and child-care assistance from their partners displayed more sensitive and affectively positive behaviors during social play. Social support from partners was also positively related to maternal sensitivity displayed during a teaching task (Contreras, 2002).

Studies examining the relative impact of partner and grandmother support have found that support from these two providers has unique and additive power in explaining both the psychological adjustment (degree of symptomatology) and the parenting behaviors of young Latina mothers. Moreover, partner support accounted for similar and at times greater amounts of variance in the criterion variables (Contreras, 2002; Contreras, López et al., 1999; Contreras, Mangelsdorf et al., 1999. Thus, contrary to the current focus away from examining partners as an important influence on adolescent mothers' adjustment, for Latina adolescent mothers it appears to be crucial to examine the ways in which partners may have both positive and negative influences on different aspects of these young mothers' adjustment. The available data suggests that partner support may be at least as important as that of grandmothers, who have been identified in the literature as the main sources of support for adolescent mothers. Partner support may be especially crucial for Latina adolescent mothers who have recently immigrated and may not have available the support of their extended family network.

Family Structure and Living Arrangements

The residential arrangements (e.g., coresidence with family of origin, with partners, alone) of adolescent mothers of different ethnic backgrounds have been found to be related to their psychological and parenting competence (Chase-Lansdale et al., 1994; Contreras, 2002; Speiker & Bensley, 1994; Unger

& Cooley, 1992). Although this relation is not likely to be a causal one—characteristics of the adolescent and of her family likely influence both her parenting adjustment and whether she remains at her parents' home—family structure and residential arrangements should nonetheless be included in a model of adolescent parenting. This is because living arrangements function as a context variable that can affect both the types of support that are offered to and/or expected by the adolescent mother and the extent to which she benefits from the support provided by coresiding and non-coresiding support providers (i.e., coresidence moderates the relations between support and adjustment). Understanding which residential arrangements are related to more optimal maternal and child functioning for which subgroups of adolescents is also important in light of recent welfare policies requiring nonmarried adolescent mothers to reside with a parent or guardian to receive benefits (Leven-Epstein, 1996).

Among adolescent mothers of Cuban origin (English speaking only), those who resided with their partners displayed a greater frequency of positive behaviors (e.g., looking, smiling, talking, reading) during mother–infant play interactions than those who resided with their families of origin or lived alone (Field, Widmayer, Adler, & de Cubas, 1990). In our sample of Puerto Rican adolescent mothers, those who coresided with their partners displayed more sensitive and affectively positive behaviors during social play than those who resided with their mothers and those in other living arrangements (Contreras, 2002). These findings are consistent with those for African American and White young mothers that indicate a negative association between coresidence with grandmothers and parenting quality (Chase-Lansdale et al., 1994; Speiker & Bensley, 1994; Unger & Cooley, 1992), especially for older adolescents. However, the negative association between grandmother coresidence and parenting found in our study was no longer significant when maternal characteristics related to a grandmother coresidence were controlled (i.e., those that coresided with a grandmother were younger and reported a weaker orientation toward parenting), suggesting that it is not coresidence per se that drives the negative association between grandmother coresidence and parenting (Contreras, 2002).

There is also evidence that coresidence is related to the levels of support provided by grandmothers and partners. Adolescents who reside with their mothers report more child-care assistance (although not social support) from them than those in other living arrangements; coresidence with partners is related to more extensive social support and child-care assistance by partners (Brunelli et al., 1995; Contreras, 2002).

Empirical evidence has also been found for the moderating role of coresidence on the relations between support and adjustment among adolescent mothers of different ethnic backgrounds. In a predominantly White sample, high support from grandmothers was related to more secure infant attachments only for adolescents living with their partners and not for those residing with their parents (Spieker & Bensley, 1994). Similarly, in our Puerto Rican sample, grandmother social support and child-care assistance were more strongly related to the adolescents' parenting behaviors among coresiding mothers than among non-coresiding mothers, with social support showing a positive association with parenting and child-care assistance a negative one (Contreras, 2002). Partner coresidence was related to greater symptomatology mainly when mothers perceived their coresiding partners as providing low levels of social support and child-care assistance (Contreras, López et al., 1999). These results emphasize the need to consider the moderating role of coresidence and the importance of assessing partner support among Latina adolescent mothers who, although more likely to reside with a partner, appear to derive lower levels of support from them than other adolescent mothers (Brunelli et al., 1995; de Anda & Becerra, 1984; Wasserman et al., 1994). Perceptions of low availability of support in a context in which support is expected (marital/romantic relationships, coresidence) may have an especially detrimental effect.

Other Child Socialization Agents

In adult models of parenting, sources of support are thought to influence the child primarily through their effects on the psychological characteristics of the parent and the quality of his or her parenting. For adolescent mothers who share the parenting responsibilities with other family members, these sources of support may also have direct effects on the child. This is especially important for understanding parenting and child development in Latino families because of their tendency to live in extended family households and rely on family members and friends for the daily care of the child (Shorris, 1992). In fact, the daily routine of infants of adult immigrant parents from Central America has been shown to include significantly more time interacting with several people (extended family and family friends) than infants of White middle-class parents, who engage primarily in dyadic interactions within the nuclear family (Leyendecker, Lamb, Schoelmerich, & Fracasso, 1995). Thus, the social network of the adolescent mother may influence child characteristics and outcomes directly in addition to having an indirect effect through their influence on the young mother.

Child Characteristics

As members of an ethnic minority group that is overrepresented among the poor, children of Latina adolescent mothers are exposed to a number of risk factors associated with socioeconomic disadvantage (e.g., inadequate access to medical care, substandard housing, neighborhoods with inadequate resources, exposure to environmental hazards such as lead) that negatively influence their mental and physical health. Moreover, Latinos in the United States also tend to underutilize preventive medical services including prenatal care, and this may further compromise the health status of children of adolescent mothers. These mental and physical health problems, in turn, lead to behavioral and learning difficulties that can make parenting even more challenging for

Latina adolescent mothers. These child difficulties are likely also compounded by the adolescent mothers' parenting difficulties, creating a cycle of negative reciprocal influences that may further exacerbate behavioral and learning difficulties in these children. Unfortunately, the reciprocal influences between child characteristics and maternal behavior among Latina adolescent mothers have not been addressed in the literature.

CONCLUSIONS

As we start the 21st century, the birth rate for Latina adolescents is the highest of all adolescents in the United States. Given the sustained growth of the Latino population in the United States, the numbers of Latina adolescents becoming parents is likely to continue to grow. In order to successfully address the needs of these families, further research aimed at understanding the social, economic, and cultural ecology of Latina adolescent mothers and the factors associated with more optimal parenting in this population is clearly needed. We hope that the conceptual model that we have presented will provide a useful framework that can guide this future research.

AUTHORS' NOTE

The preparation of this chapter was supported by grants awarded to the first author by the Kent State University Applied Psychology Center, Kent, OH. The authors would like to thank all of the families who have participated in our studies and the community leaders and agency staff who have facilitated recruitment and data collection. Address correspondence to Josefina M. Contreras, Department of Psychology, Kent State University, Kent, OH 44242-0001. Electronic mail may be sent to jcontrer@kent.edu.

REFERENCES

Abidin, R. (1992). The determinants of parenting behavior. *Journal of Clinical Child Psychology, 21*, 407–412.

Ainsworth, M. D. S., Blehar, M. C., Waters, E., & Wall, S. (1978). *Patterns of attachment: A psychological study of the strange situation.* Hillsdale, NJ: Erlbaum.

Aponte, J., & Crouch, R. (1995). The changing ethnic profile of the United States. In J. Aponte, R. Y. Rivers, & J. Wohl (Eds.), *Psychological interventions and cultural diversity* (pp. 1–18). Needham Heights, MA: Allyn & Bacon.

Baldwin, W., & Cain, V. S. (1980). The children of teenage parents. *Family Planning Perspective, 12*, 34–43.

Becerra, R. M., & de Anda, D. (1984). Pregnancy and motherhood among Mexican-American adolescents. *Health and Social Work, 9*, 106–123.

Belsky, J. (1984). The determinants of parenting: A process model. *Child Development, 55*, 83–96.

Blos, P. (1967). The second individuation process of adolescence. *Psychoanalytic Study of the Child, 22*, 162–186.

Brooks-Gunn, J., & Furstenberg, F. (1986). The children of adolescent mothers: Physical, academic, and psychological outcomes. *Developmental Review, 6,* 224–251.

Brown, H., Adams, T., & Kellan, S. (1981). *The longitudinal study of teenage motherhood and symptoms of distress: Research and community mental health.* Greenwich, CT: JAI.

Brunelli, S., Wasserman, G., Rauh, V., Alvarado, L., & Caraballo, L. (1995). Mothers' responses to paternal support: Associations with maternal child-rearing attitudes. *Merrill-Palmer Quarterly, 47,* 152–171.

Caldwell, C. H., & Antonucci, T. (1997). Childbearing during adolescence: Mental health risks and opportunities. In J. Schulenberg, J. Maggs, & K. Hurrelmann (Eds.), *Health risks and developmental transitions during adolescence* (pp. 220–245). New York: Cambridge University Press.

Chase-Lansdale, P. L., Brooks-Gunn, J., & Zamsky, E. (1994). Young African-American multigenerational families in poverty: Quality of mothering and grandmothering. *Child Development, 65,* 373–393.

Contreras, J. (2002). *Parent–child interactions among Puerto Rican adolescent mothers: Associations with partner and grandmother involvement.* Manuscript in preparation.

Contreras, J., López, I., Rivera-Mosquera, E., Raymond-Smith, L., & Rothstein, K. (1999). Social support among Puerto Rican adolescent mothers: The moderating effect of acculturation. *Journal of Family Psychology, 13,* 228–243.

Contreras, J., Mangelsdorf, S., Rhodes, J., Diener, M., & Brunson, L. (1999). Parent–child interaction among Latina adolescent mothers: The role of family and social support. *Journal of Research on Adolescence, 9,* 417–439.

de Anda, D., & Becerra, R. (1984). Social networks for adolescent mothers. *Social Casework, 65,* 172–181.

Dore, M., & Dumois, A. (1990). Cultural differences in the meaning of adolescent pregnancy. *Families in Society, 71,* 93–101.

Downey, G., & Coyne, J. (1990). Children of depressed parents: An integrative review. *Psychological Bulletin, 108,* 50–76.

Field, T., Widmayer, S., Adler, S., & de Cubas, M. (1990). Teenage parenting in different cultures, family constellations, and caregiving environments: Effects on infant development. *Infant Mental Health Journal, 11,* 158–174.

Field, T. M., Widmayer, S. M., Stringer, S., & Ignatoff, E. (1980). Teenage, lower class, black mothers and their preterm infants: An intervention and developmental follow-up. *Child Development, 51,* 426–436.

Flick, L. H. (1986). Paths to adolescent parenthood: Implications for intervention. *Public Health Reports, 51,* 132–147.

Fracasso, M., Busch, N., & Fisher, C. (1994). The relationship of maternal behavior and acculturation to the quality of attachment in Hispanic infants living in New York City. *Hispanic Journal of Behavioral Sciences, 16,* 143–154.

Furstenberg, F., Brooks-Gunn, J., & Morgan, S. (1987). *Adolescent mothers in later life.* Cambridge, England: Cambridge University Press.

García Coll, C., Hoffman, J., & Oh, W. (1987). The social ecology and early parenting of Caucasian adolescent mothers. *Child Development, 58,* 955–963.

García Coll, C., Lamberty, G., Jenkins, R., McAdoo, H. P., Crnic, K., Wasik, B. H., & Garcia, H. V. (1996). An integrative model for the study of developmental competencies in minority children. *Child Development, 67,* 1891–1914.

García Coll, C., & Vazquez García, H. (1996). Definitions of competence during adolescence: Lessons from Puerto Rican adolescent mothers. In D. Cicchetti &

S. Toth (Eds.), *Rochester Symposium on Developmental Psychology: Vol. 7. Adolescence: Opportunities and challenges.* (pp. 283–308). Rochester, NY: University of Rochester Press.

Gonzalez-Ramos, G., Zayas, L., & Cohen, E. (1998). Child-rearing values of low-income, urban Puerto Rican mothers of preschool children. *Professional Psychology: Research and Practice, 29,* 377–382.

Grossman, K., Grossman, K. E., Spangler, G., Suess, G., & Unzner, J. (1985). Maternal sensitivity and newborns' orientation responses as related to quality of attachment in northern Germany. In I. Bretherton & E. Waters (Eds.), *Growing points in attachment theory and research* (pp. 233–256). *Monographs of the Society for Research in Child Development, 50* (1–2, Serial No. 209).

Grotevant, H., & Cooper, C. (1986). Individuation in family relationships. *Human Development, 29,* 82–100.

Harwood, R. L. (1992). The influence of culturally derived values on Anglo and Puerto Rican mothers' perceptions of attachment behavior. *Child Development, 63,* 822–839.

Harwood, R. L., Schoelmerich, A., Schulze, P. A., & Gonzalez, Z. (1999). Cultural differences in maternal beliefs and behaviors: A study of middle-class Anglo and Puerto Rican mother–infant pairs in four everyday situations. *Child Development, 70,* 1005–1116.

Harwood, R. L., Schoelmerich, A., Ventura-Cook, E., Schulze, P., & Wilson, S. (1996). Culture and class influences on Anglo and Puerto Rican mothers' beliefs regarding long-term socialization goals and child behavior. *Child Development, 67,* 2446–2461.

Keefe, S. E. (1984). Real and ideal extended families among Mexican Americans and Anglo Americans: On the meaning of close family ties. *Human Organization, 43,* 65–70.

Klerman, L. V. (1993). Adolescent pregnancy and parenting: Controversies of the past and lessons for the future. *Journal of Adolescent Health, 14,* 553–561.

Knight, G., Bernal, M., Cota, M., Garza, C., & Ocampo, K. (1993). Family socialization and Mexican American identity and behavior. In M. Bernal & G. Knight (Eds.), *Ethnic identity* (pp.105–129). Albany: State University of New York Press.

Koss, J. (1990). Somatization and somatic complaint syndromes among Hispanics: Overview and ethnopsychological perspectives. *Transcultural Psychiatric Research Review, 27,* 5–29.

Laosa, L. (1982). School, occupation, culture, and family: The impact of parental schooling on the parent–child relationship. *Journal of Educational Psychology, 74,* 791–827.

Laosa, L. M. (1980). Maternal teaching strategies in Chicano and Anglo-American families: The influence of culture and education on maternal behavior. *Child Development, 51,* 759–765.

Leadbeater, B., Bishop, S., & Raver, C. (1996). Quality of mother–toddler interactions, maternal depressive symptoms, and behavior problems in preschoolers of adolescent mothers. *Developmental Psychology, 32,* 280–288.

Leadbeater, B., & Linares, I. (1992). Depressive symptoms in Black and Puerto Rican adolescent mothers in the first three years postpartum. *Development and Psychopathology, 4,* 451–468.

Leven-Epstein, J. (1996). *Teen parent provisions in the new law.* Washington, DC: Center for Law and Social Policy.

Leyendecker, B., Lamb, M., Schoelmerich, A. & Fracasso, M. (1995). The social worlds of 8- and 12-month-old infants: Early experiences in two subcultural contexts. *Social Development, 4,* 195–208.

López, I., & Contreras, J. (under review). *The best of both worlds? Biculturality, acculturation, and psychological adjustment among mainland Puerto Rican adolescent mothers.*

Marín, G., Saboqal, F., VanOss Marín, B., Otero-Sabogal, R., & Perez-Stable, E. J. (1987). Development of a short acculturation scale for Hispanics. *Hispanic Journal of Behavioral Sciences, 9,* 183–205.

McLaughlin, S., & Micklin, M. (1983). The timing of the first birth and changes in personal efficacy. *Journal of Marriage and the Family, 45,* 47–55.

Moreno, R. (1991). Maternal teaching of preschool children in minority and low-status families: A critical review. *Early Childhood Research Quarterly, 6,* 395–410.

Musick, J. (1993). *Young, poor, and pregnant: The psychology of teenage motherhood.* New Haven, CT: Yale University Press.

National Center for Health Statistics. (2001, July 24). *National Vital Statistics Report, 49* (5). Retrieved November 1, 2001, from http://www.cdc.gov/nchs/births

O'Callaghan, M. F., Borkowski, J. G., Whitman, T. L., Maxwell, S. E., & Keogh, D. (1999). A model of adolescent parenting: The role of cognitive readiness to parent. *Journal of Research on Adolescence, 9,* 203–225.

Ogbu, J. (1981). Origins of human competence: A cultural ecological perspective. *Child Development, 52,* 413–429.

Osofsky, J., Hann, D., & Peebles, C. (1993). Adolescent parenthood: Risks and opportunities for mothers and infants. In C. Zeanah, Jr. (Ed.), *Handbook of infant mental health* (pp.106–119). New York: Guilford.

Oyserman, D., Radin, N. & Saltz, E. (1994). Predictors of nurturant parenting in teen mothers living in three generational families. *Child Psychiatry and Human Development, 24,* 215–230.

Panzarine, S. (1986). Stressors, coping, and social supports of adolescent mothers. *Journal of Adolescent Health, 7,* 153–161.

Planos, R., Zayas, L., & Bush-Rossnagel, N. (1995). Acculturation and teaching behaviors of Dominican and Puerto Rican mothers. *Hispanic Journal of Behavioral Sciences, 17,* 225–236.

Ramos-McKay, J. M., Comas-Díaz, L., & Rivera, L. (1988). Puerto Ricans. In L. Comas-Díaz & E. E. H. Griffith (Eds.), *Clinical guidelines in cross-cultural mental health* (pp. 204–232). New York: Wiley.

Rhodes, J., Contreras, J., & Mangelsdorf, S. (1994). Natural mentor relationships among Latina adolescent mothers: Psychological adjustment, moderating processes, and the role of early parental acceptance. *American Journal of Community Psychology, 22,* 211–227.

Richman, A., Miller, P., & LeVine, R. (1992). Cultural and educational variations in maternal responsiveness. *Developmental Psychology, 28,* 614–621.

Roland, A. (1988). *In search of self in India and Japan: Towards a cross cultural psychology.* Princeton, NJ: Princeton University Press.

Romero, A. J. (2000). Assessing and treating Latinos: Overview of research. In I. Cuéllar, & F. Paniagua (Eds.), *Handbook of multicultural mental health: Assessment and treatment of diverse populations* (pp. 209–223). San Diego, CA: Academic Press.

Sabogal, F., Marín, G., Otero-Sabogal, R., VanOss Marín, B., & Perez-Stable, E. (1987). Hispanic familism and acculturation: What changes and what doesn't? *Hispanic Journal of Behavioral Sciences, 9*, 397–412.

Shapiro, M., & Mangelsdorf, S. (1994). The determinants of parenting competence in adolescent mothers. *Journal of Youth and Adolescence, 23*, 621–641.

Shorris, E. (1992). *Latinos: A biography of the people.* New York: W.W. Norton.

Sommer, K., Whitman, T., Borkowski, J., Schellenbach, C., Maxwell, S., & Keogh, D. (1993). Cognitive readiness and adolescent parenting. *Developmental Psychology, 29*, 389–398.

Spieker, S., & Bensley, L. (1994). Roles of living arrangements and grandmother social support in adolescent mothering and infant attachment. *Developmental Psychology, 30*, 102–111.

Stevenson-Simon, C., & Reichert, S. (1994). Sexual abuse, adolescent pregnancy, and child abuse: A developmental approach to an intergenerational cycle. *Archives of Pediatric and Adolescent Medicine, 148*, 23–27.

Teichman, J., & Contreras, J. (2002). *Acculturation level and the teaching strategies of Latina adolescent mothers.* Manuscript in preparation.

Thompson, M. & Peebles-Wilkins, W. (1992). The impact of formal, informal, and societal support networks on the psychological well-being of Black adolescent mothers. *Social Work, 37*, 322–328.

Turner, R., Grindstaff, C., & Phillips, N. (1990). Social support and outcome in teenage pregnancy. *Journal of Health and Behavior, 31*, 43–57.

Unger, D., & Cooley, M. (1992). Partner and grandmother contact in Black and White teen parent families. *Journal of Adolescent Health, 13*, 546–552.

Unger, D., & Wandersman, L. (1985). Social support and adolescent mothers: Action research contributions to theory and application. *Journal of Social Issues, 41*, 147–156.

Valenzuela, M. (1997). Maternal sensitivity in a developing society: The context of urban poverty and infant chronic undernutrition. *Developmental Psychology, 33* (5), 845–855.

van IJzendoorn, M. (1995). Adult attachment representations, parental responsiveness, and infant attachment: A meta-analysis on the predictive validity of the adult attachment interview. *Psychological Bulletin, 117*, 387–403.

Vega, W. A. (1995). The study of Latino families: A point of departure. In R. E. Zambrana (Ed.), *Understanding Latino families: Scholarship, policy, and practice* (pp. 3–17). Thousand Oaks, CA: Sage.

Wasserman, G., Brunelli, S., Rauh, V., & Alvarado, L. (1994). The cultural context of adolescent childrearing in three groups of urban minority mothers. In G. Lamberty & C. García Coll (Eds.). *Puerto Rican women and children: Issues in health, growth, and development* (pp. 137–160). New York: Plenum.

Whitman, T., Borkowski, J., Schellenbach, C., & Nath, P. (1987). Predicting and understanding developmental delay of children of adolescent mothers: A multidimensional approach. *American Journal of Mental Deficiency, 92*, 40–56.

Wilcox, B. (1981). Social support, life stress, and psychological adjustment: A test of the buffering hypothesis. *American Journal of Community Psychology, 9*, 371–386.

Part III

Research Methods and Interventions with Latino Families

8

Measurement Equivalence and Research on Latino Children and Families: The Importance of Culturally Informed Theory

George P. Knight, Jenn-Yun Tein, Justin H. Prost, and Nancy A. Gonzales

The size of Latino populations in the United States has been growing at a substantial pace for many years. Between 1990 and 1997, the growth rate for the Latino populations was nearly five times that of the White population (U.S. Census Bureau, 1998). This greater growth rate in these ethnic populations is a function of relatively higher birth rates, compared to the White population, and a substantial immigration rate. Forty percent of the growth in the Latino population, between 1990 and 1997, was the result of immigration (U.S. Census Bureau, 1998). Furthermore, the size of Latino populations is projected to grow as a percentage of the total population between 2000 and 2025 (U.S. Census Bureau, 1998). Latino populations are projected to grow from an estimated 11.4% of the total population to 17.6% of the total population between the year 2000 and 2025 (U.S. Census Bureau, 1998). One result of this growth is the enhanced focus on understanding Latino individuals and families in those social science disciplines that support research on children and families. That is, with the growth of the Latino population in the United States, there has been elevated research on Latino children and families. Furthermore, there is good reason to expect that there will continue to be an expansion of the research literature on Latino children and families over the next few decades.

This chapter is designed to discuss how issues of measurement equivalence are relevant to those studying Latino children and families and to provide a perspective on how to evaluate the equivalence of a measure for use in diverse populations. This perspective will include a description of basic measurement theory and the application of measurement theory to the study of diverse populations. There have been significant advances in the methodologies that can be used to address the equivalence of measures across groups; however, the purpose of this chapter is to discuss a number of important conceptual issues regarding measurement equivalence. Although a brief overview of these methods is included, readers interested in a more detailed description of these methodologies are directed to Camilli and Shepard (1994), Hines (1993), Knight and Hill (1998), Labouvie and Ruetsch (1995), Malpass and Poortinga (1986), McDonald (1995), Reise, Widaman, and Pugh (1993), Rudner, Getson, and Knight (1980), and Widaman (1995). Finally, this chapter will address several practical issues that researchers must often consider when studying diverse populations.

The first question of relevance here is, Why is it important to consider issues of measurement equivalence when studying Latino children and families? If the researcher is going to make cross-ethnic comparisons, either statistically or descriptively, measurement equivalence is necessary. Scalar equivalence—the degree to which any particular score on a measure reflects the same magnitude of the construct across ethnicities—is essential if the comparison of two scores from individuals of different ethnicities, or two sets of scores from different ethnic groups, is to reflect any meaningful real difference between individuals or groups. For example, if researchers were interested in determining whether Latino individuals are more family oriented (i.e., higher in familism) than Anglo American individuals, it is necessary to administer a measure of familism to members of each of these two ethnic groups that is scalar equivalent. In other words, for the comparison of the familism scores of these two ethnic groups to be meaningful it is necessary for any given score to indicate the same degree, intensity, or magnitude of familism in each ethnic group.

Measurement equivalence is an important consideration even if one does not wish to make cross-ethnic comparisons. Let us consider the case in which the researcher is not interested in making cross-ethnic comparisons but is administering measures to a sample that is diverse. This sample may be diverse in that it contains individuals from multiple ethnic or racial groups, or it may be diverse in that it contains individuals from one ethnic or racial group but who differ in their degree of ethnic identity and acculturative status. If the researcher is examining the relations among scores on several measures in that diverse population, the absence of measurement equivalence can bias the observed relations. Thus, if the population sampled is ethnically diverse, the biasing effect of the nonequivalence of the measures may produce inaccurate findings. There are at least two ways in which a sample of Latino children or families themselves can be diverse. First, the Latino label refers to a variety of ethnic groups with roots in quite different cultures of origin. Most notably, the largest Latino groups in the United States have origins in Cuba, Mexico, and Puerto Rico. If one is studying a sample of individuals that contains some representation of each of these cultures (as well as the numerous other cultures of origin that are represented in the United States), then measurement equivalence across these groups is critical. Second, even if one is studying

Latino individuals from the same culture of origin, these individuals are likely to differ in their levels of acculturation and enculturation into the host and ethnic cultures, or their language use. These types of diversity, even within the Latino populations, also necessitate the consideration of measurement equivalence.

Another case in which the consideration of measurement equivalence is necessary occurs when a researcher wishes to administer a measure developed in some other cultural group to investigate social science phenomena in Latino populations (or any other groups). That is, even if the researcher is studying a very homogeneous Latino sample, if one wishes to use a measure of some underlying construct developed in a different population, the researcher would want to know that this measure is assessing the same underlying construct in this particular Latino population. Perhaps the only research context in which measurement equivalence may not be directly relevant is when the researcher is investigating some phenomena in a homogeneous population of Latino children and families, and the researcher is specifically developing each measure for use in that population.

BASIC MEASUREMENT THEORY

The creation of a reliable and valid measure of any underlying construct requires a set of methodological procedures that are relatively well-known (cf.: Cronbach, 1970; McDonald, 1999; Nunnally, 1967). Ideally, this process starts with a theory that specifies critical features of the underlying construct. This theory about the nature of the underlying construct of interest is instrumental in two fundamental ways. This theory defines the nature of, or the elements of, the underlying construct. The theory must specify the basic nature of, or the elements of, the underlying construct in the population of persons of interest because this provides the basis for the generation of items or observations that reflect that construct. Theory also describes how the underlying construct of interest relates to other constructs, or fits into the nomological net of underlying constructs. Furthermore, it is essential that the theory be informed by an understanding of the ethnic/racial groups in which the measure is to be administered. The theory must specify the basic nature of, or the elements of, the underlying construct in the population because this provides the basis for the generation of items or observations that reflect that construct in that respective population. The first step in the measurement development process is to identify a set of items to be used as the measure of the underlying construct of interest. To obtain an unbiased assessment of this underlying construct, it is necessary to select a sample of items that is representative of the population of items defining the construct. As the set of items becomes less representative (i.e., a select subset) of the population of items in the ethnic or racial population of persons of interest, it becomes less likely that the set of items accurately assesses the underlying construct in that ethnic or racial group.

The traditional psychometric conceptualization of the measurement process is based on several premises that have important implications for our understanding of the issues of cultural bias and measurement equivalence associated with the use of measures in diverse populations. One important premise is that any measurement system involves error. Measures in social science hardly produce numerical values that perfectly represent the degree to which the underlying construct of interest is present in the individual. In the ideal case, errors in measurement are random. Symbolically, this is represented by a linear model:

$$X_i = UC_i + E_i$$

where X_i represents the individual's score of the measure of interest, UC_i represents the individual's level of the underlying construct, and E_i represents the random measurement error associated with the individual's score on the measures of specific underlying construct. These random errors represent inaccuracies in the degree to which scores produced by a measure describe the level of the underlying construct in the individual. In addition, since these errors (in the ideal case) are random, they cannot be correlated with any other variable. Therefore, these random errors limit the degree to which the scores produced by a measure can be correlated with scores produced by another measure, including the same measure administered at another time. Thus, this measurement error (i.e., the degree of unreliability associated with a measure) influences the correlations of the scores produced by the measure with the scores produced by other measures (i.e., the validity coefficients associated with a measure). Random measurement error results in the validity coefficients being attenuated by reducing the proportion of systematic variance. The reliability of the scores generated by a measure creates an upper limit to the degree to which these scores can be related to the scores produced by another measure. Therefore, if this measure includes substantial random measurement error (i.e., the scores are not highly reliable), the validity coefficients (i.e., the correlations with other scores) will be a substantial underestimate of the degree of covariation between the true scores of the two constructs in the population.

This discussion is based largely on the ideal case in which the variance in a set of scores produced by a measure is influenced by the underlying construct of interest and random errors. Unfortunately, often this ideal case does not exist. Indeed, often the variance in a set of scores produced by a measure is influenced by more than one underlying construct as well as random measurement errors. Symbolically, this is represented by a linear model:

$$X_i = UC1_i + UC2_i + E_i$$

where X_i represents the individual's score on the measure of interest, $UC1_i$ represents the individual's level of the primary or focal underlying construct,

$UC2_i$ represents the individual's level of a secondary underlying construct, and E_i represents the random measurement errors associated with the individual's score on the underlying construct of interest.

This secondary underlying construct ($UC2_i$) represents systematic variance in the measure attributable to some construct other than the target construct. Often these secondary underlying constructs are response biases or other methodological artifacts that are undesirable but often unavoidable. For example, there is evidence that Latinos more frequently endorse extreme responses compared to non-Latino Whites (Hui & Triandis, 1989; Marín, Gamba, & Marín, 1992) and that less acculturated Latinos more often endorse extreme responses than more acculturated Latinos (Marín et al., 1992). The impact of these secondary constructs may be quite important. Unfortunately, the systematic variance contributed by a secondary underlying construct increases the variance in the scores derived from a measure and can lead the validity coefficients associated with a measure to be either upwardly or downwardly biased. If the measure of interest and the measure being used to establish the validity of the measure of interest both introduce variance from the same (or very related) secondary underlying construct, then the correlation between the two sets of scores will overestimate the degree of covariation between the true scores of the key constructs in the population. That is, since the squared validity coefficient (i.e., squared correlation) is an estimate of the proportion of shared variance between the two sets of scores, increasing the variance of each set of scores with similar (i.e., highly correlated) systematic influences, increases the correlation between the two sets of scores. For example, if children's reports of their parents' disciplinary practices and their own aggressive behaviors are each influenced by individual differences in a self-presentation bias (e.g., the desire to represent oneself in a positive manner), then the correlation between the two sets of scores will likely overestimate the correlation of the parental discipline practices and children's aggression constructs in the population. If the measure of interest and the measure being used to establish the validity of the measure of interest introduce very different systematic secondary underlying constructs, the correlation between the two sets of scores will underestimate the degree of covariation between the true scores of the key constructs in the population. That is, the systematic measurement bias will be increasing the variance of the scores, but this increased variance in each set of scores, will not be shared variance, and the correlation between the two sets of scores will be downwardly biased.

MEASUREMENT EQUIVALENCE AND MEASUREMENT THEORY

As noted earlier, it is imperative in the construction of a measure that the sample used to examine and refine the items or observations in that measure are representative of the population of persons in which the measure is to be used. In addition, it is imperative that the items or observations included in the measure are a representative set of the population of items or observations that define that construct. The implication is that conducting assessments in ethnic or racial minority populations that are designed to be comparable with assessments in other populations necessitates that these assessments be equivalently representative in each population. It is important that this population of items or observations is defined by the theory about the construct that is informed by the nature of the population of individuals in which the items or observations are to be used.

Another of the challenges in conducting assessments in ethnic minority populations is the possibility that measures developed for a given construct or attribute in majority populations may not be assessing the same construct or attribute in the ethnic minority population (Hughes, Seidman, & Williams, 1993; Kleinman & Good, 1985; Malpass & Poortinga, 1986; Vega & Rumbaut, 1991). Since we presume that our understanding of the attribute being assessed with a measure is largely a function of the nature of the relations of the scores generated by that measure to scores produced by other measures, it is clear that measurement equivalence is largely a question of the degree of similarity of the reliability and validity of the measure across ethnic/racial populations. This is to say that the scores generated by a measure must be related to scores produced by other measures in a manner consistent with the theory that specifies the nature of the construct in each population of interest, and that the compatibility of these interrelations with the theory is approximately equivalent across ethnic or racial groups. This does not necessarily suggest that these interrelations must be similar across ethnic and racial groups. Indeed, if the culturally informed theory indicates that the construct is differentially related to some other constructs, then measurement equivalence would be indicated by somewhat different but theoretically consistent interrelations with other constructs. For example, Gonzales, Cauce, and Mason (1996) found that African American parental behaviors that non-Latino White observers thought were hostile and harsh were interpreted as warm and loving by African American observers. If these interpretational differences represent cultural specificity in the meaning of these behaviors, then a measure of these specific behaviors should be differentially related to other positive and negative parental behavior patterns.

In the ideal measurement case, described earlier, in which the scores on a measure for each ethnic group are influenced only by one underlying construct and random measurement error, there are two ways in which empirical nonequivalence can occur. First, the proportion of variance in the scores, at either the level of individual items or at the level of the scale scores, owing to random errors may be different across groups. If so, then the scores generated by this measure should produce group differences in both reliability and validity coefficients. However, even if the difference in the proportion of variance in the scores attributable to random errors was very large there are statistical and/or methodological adjustments that may allow one to conduct meaningful group comparisons in this case. Second, the underlying construct being assessed by the measure may be totally different across groups. If so, then the scores produced by this measure should produce group differences in validity coefficients. That is, if a measure is actually assessing a different construct in the majority group and the minority group, then the scores produced by this measure should be differentially correlated with scores produced by other measures in the majority and minority groups. This type of measurement nonequivalence is quite possible but may be fairly rare when considering individuals in relatively similar environments such as when examining majority and minority group members within one country. In contrast, when trying to compare individuals from radically different cultures (e.g., a modern Westernized culture vs. a remote tribal culture), this type of culture bias may occur very frequently. When this type of nonequivalence of measures does occur, group difference comparisons are really very meaningless.

If the situation is less than the desirable measurement case and the variance in the scores produced by a measure is influenced by the underlying construct of interest and one or more secondary underlying constructs, and assuming that the underlying construct of interest is the same across groups, there are several ways in which cultural bias (or measurement bias) can occur. First, as earlier, the proportion of variance in the scores owing to random errors may be different across groups. However, if the secondary underlying construct contributing to the variance of the scores is the same in the majority and minority group, and if this measurement bias is relatively comparable across groups, then this bias may not necessarily invalidate group comparisons given that one recognizes and cautiously accounts for this bias. Second, there may be a common secondary underlying construct contributing to the scores across groups, but there may be a systematic difference between groups in the proportion of the variance in the scores attributable to that secondary underlying construct. If so, then this difference may represent a cultural difference in the measure, there will be notable group differences in the reliability and validity coefficients, and group comparisons on the scores produced by the measure will be relatively meaningless. Third, there may be group differences in either the nature of the secondary underlying construct or the mere existence of a secondary underlying construct. Once again, in this situation the difference represents a cultural difference in the measure, there may be notable group differences in the reliability and validity coefficients, and group comparisons on the scores produced by the measure will be relatively meaningless.

METHODS FOR EXAMINING MEASUREMENT EQUIVALENCE

Many authors have written about various types of measurement equivalence (e.g., Hines, 1993; Hughes et al., 1993; Hui & Triandis, 1985; Knight & Hill,

1998; Malpass & Poortinga, 1986). Fundamentally, the most important type of equivalence is scalar equivalence. Scalar equivalence exists when a given score on a measure refers to the same degree, intensity, or magnitude of the underlying construct in each group in which the measure is used. There have been significant advances in the methodologies that can be used to address the equivalence of measures across groups (e.g., Camilli & Shepard, 1994; Hines, 1993; Knight & Hill, 1998; Knight, Virdin, & Roosa, 1994; Labouvie & Ruetsch, 1995; Malpass & Poortinga, 1986; McDonald, 1995; Reise et al., 1993; Rudner et al., 1980; Widaman, 1995). These relatively newer methodologies are quite sophisticated, therefore a description of these is beyond the scope of this chapter. It is clear, however, that it is necessary for researchers to apply these newer statistical methodologies to their data as a part of their ongoing substantive research if that research utilizes diverse samples.

There has also been some debate regarding what the appropriate evidence of measurement equivalence is and this debate has focused on the relative importance of item-level and scale-level equivalence (Drasgow, 1995; Labouvie & Ruetsch, 1995; McDonald, 1995; Meredith, 1995; Nesselroade, 1995; O'Dell & Cudeck, 1995; Widaman, 1995). Labouvie and Ruetsch (1995) argued that evidence of invariance in the relationships between constructs across groups is sufficient for inferring measurement equivalence even if the individual items function differently across groups. Thus, Labouvie and Ruetsch allow for variation across groups in the relative importance of individual items in defining a construct. Other authors (Drasgow, 1995; McDonald, 1995; Meredith, 1995; Nesselroade, 1995; O'Dell & Cudeck, 1995; Widaman, 1995) argued that the variation in factor loadings allowed by Labouvie and Ruetsch may well lead to variation in the definition of the construct across groups. For example, Drasgow (1995) argues that scale-level equivalence alone is sufficient evidence of measurement equivalence only when the researcher is certain that the set of items truly reflects the breadth of the construct for all groups.

Our position is that it is important to examine evidence of equivalence at both the item and scale level in the context of expected similarities and differences based on culturally informed theory. That is, theory informed by an understanding of the culture in which the measure is to be used should specify the basic nature of the underlying construct and the manner in which that underlying construct should relate to other constructs. Item-level analyses are necessary to confirm that the items on the measure reflect the basic nature of the underlying construct in the culture. Scale-level analyses are necessary to confirm that the scores produced by the measure relate to scores produced by measures of other constructs in the manner proscribed by the theory informed by an understanding of that culture.

Item-level approaches to the assessment of measurement equivalence involve comparing the relationship between the item score and the total scale score for each item, or the inter-item relations. This strategy allows for the systematic identification of specific items that are, as well as items that are not, similarly related to the scale score across ethnic or racial groups. There are two data analysis strategies that are useful for this purpose: (a) an item-response-theory analysis of a differential item functioning through item-response-theory analyses and (b) confirmatory factor analysis (Camilli & Shepard, 1994; Hambleton, Swaminathan, & Rogers, 1991; Lord, 1980; Rudner et al., 1980). In item-response-theory analyses, the relationship between the responses on a given item and the underlying construct measured by the item can be described by a monotonically increasing function called an Item Characteristic Curve (ICC). In essence these ICCs are curves indicating the probability of a particular response on an item as a function of the total score of the measure that includes that item. Lord (1980) claims that an item is biased only when individuals from different groups who have the same ability or level of the measured trait do not have the same probability of responding correctly or appropriately to that item.

Confirmatory factor analysis is a structural modeling procedure in which each item is represented by a linear function of one or more factors (see Bollen, 1989). That is, the researcher specifies a theoretical model that identifies what factors or underlying constructs are represented in each item from a measure. Furthermore, the linear functions can be constrained such that the factor loading must be equal across groups for each item or for specifically selected items. If the fit indices indicate that the data fit the model, this provides evidence that the item–total relations are similar across ethnic or racial groups (for a brief description of this comparison procedure, see Reise et al., 1993). If the pattern of similarities and differences in item–total relations or item–item relations, examined in either item-response-theory analyses or confirmatory-factor analyses, are consistent with the expectations created by the culturally informed theory, it begins to appear as though these measures are equivalent across the ethnic or racial groups investigated.

Scale-level approaches to examining the cross-group equivalence of a measure involve the examination of the validity coefficients associated with that measure across ethnic and racial groups. These validity coefficients should identify the relationship between the score produced by the measure of interest and either scores produced by other measures of the same construct (empirical validity) or scores produced by measures of theoretically related constructs (construct validity). There are at least a couple of procedures that one can use to examine the validity coefficients for a measure across ethnic and racial groups.

One approach to examining the ethnic or racial differences or similarities in the validity coefficients associated with measures is to examine the comparability of these relations across groups with structural modeling analyses (or Box's M in Multivariate Analysis of Variance) in which the covariances can be selectively constrained to be equal across groups (see Bollen, 1989). Another very useful approach to examining ethnic and racial differences and similarities in validity coefficients is to test the moderating effects of ethnicity or race on the regression coefficients (slopes) and intercepts describing the relationships between constructs. If the regression equation for such an analysis produced homogeneous slopes and intercepts across ethnic or racial groups, and if similarity in these coefficients is theoretically proscribed, then it is likely that the measures involved have scalar equivalence. For example, if a given score on any particular socialization or family interaction subscale leads to the same expected score on a mental health indicator for Latino and Anglo American children and adolescents, and if the culturally informed theory regarding the nature of these constructs in these two groups indicates that these relations should be similar, then it is most likely that comparable scores on the socialization/family interaction and mental health measures refer to the same degree, intensity, or magnitude of the respective constructs across ethnic or racial groups. This analysis would proceed by entering a theoretically appropriate predictor (e.g., a vector of scores on a socialization or family interaction measure) and vector or vectors defining the ethnic or racial diversity in the sample, followed by entering cross-product (i.e., interaction) vectors into the regression analysis. If the cross-product vector(s) accounts for a significant proportion of the variance in the criterion, then the regression coefficients are different across groups. If the cross-product vectors do not account for a significant proportion of the variance in the criterion, one can then test whether the intercepts are significantly different across ethnic and racial groups. If the pattern of similarities and differences in slopes and intercepts, examined in either structural modeling analyses or regression analyses, describing the empirical relationship between the theoretically interrelated constructs are consistent with the expectations created by the culturally informed theory, it begins to appear as though these measures are equivalent across the ethnic or racial groups investigated.

Qualitative research may also be useful in addressing the equivalence of measures. In the initial stages of instrument development, qualitative research methods can be used to determine the breadth of the construct across populations and the accuracy of the operational definition of the construct. For example, qualitative methods may be instrumental in allowing one to determine whether there are variants of the construct or whether there are culturally specific forms of the underlying construct. Thus, if a researcher wanted to develop an instrument to assess nonpunitive discipline in Latino families, the researcher could begin by conducting a series of focus groups with Latino parents (for detailed methods, see Berg, 1995). The essence of a focus group is to elicit discussion from participants. A focus group facilitator should be prepared with a few open-ended discussion questions and use them to assist the discussion and direct it so that it remains on topic. These should include, but not be limited to, defining the construct (nonpunitive discipline), discussing what kinds of nonpunitive discipline practices are used in their families, and the effectiveness of these practices.

The data are examined for themes and important issues raised by the participants, and these themes can be compared and contrasted across ethnic groups. Feldman (1995) and Bryman and Burgess (1994) describe detailed methods for analyzing focus group data. Often focus groups provide enough information to develop a measure that is equivalent across various groups; however, issues may be raised in focus groups that require a more detailed investigation in order to understand how the issue relates to discipline in different families. The researcher may want to conduct individual qualitative interviews with parents to obtain clarification or more information about a theme raised in the focus group (for an introductory explanation of conducting qualitative interviews and ethnographic research in general, see Fetterman, 1989). Information gained from the focus groups and/or interviews can be used to develop items for a quantitative instrument assessing the target construct—for example, the amount of nonpunitive discipline in a particular family.

Gonzalez-Ramos, Zayas, and Cohen (1998) provide a good example of the use of these types of techniques to examine child-rearing goals in Puerto Rican mothers. These authors also describe an example in which the meaning of a construct—autonomy or independence—may be quite different in different cultural groups. For example, when Puerto Rican mothers, in contrast to European American mothers, assert that they want their children to be more autonomous or independent they likely do not mean that they want to encourage the type of physical separations associated with attending summer camps and sleepovers. Similarly, Puerto Rican children who display limited eye contact and a deferring style in school may be displaying complacent, obedient, and respectful behavior rather than inhibited, shy, and withdrawn behavior.

In addition to its use for instrument development, qualitative research methods can be used to explore the degree of measurement equivalence of existing measures. For example, if nonequivalence was suspected for a series of parenting measures based on the quantitative methods described earlier, qualitative methods can be used to have parents, from each target ethnic or racial group, evaluate the items and operational definition of the construct to assist in determining where the measures may not be equivalent and how they may be modified to obtain equivalence. Similar to the focus group method, a small group of individuals may be asked to examine the operational definition of a construct such as nonpunitive discipline, and determine if the operational definition effectively defines nonpunitive discipline as it occurs in their families. The purpose of such panels or focus groups is to determine if the items make sense to the members of the target ethnic or racial group and whether important behaviors have been omitted from the measure.

Qualitative and quantitative methodologies may provide unique perspectives on measurement equivalence. However, the complementary use of qualitative and quantitative methodologies may lead to an understanding of the reason a measure is not equivalent across groups and provide guidance for making revisions to a measure in order to achieve equivalence. When developing new measures, qualitative methodologies may be used to determine which types of behaviors or items should be included to enhance the likelihood of achieving cross-group equivalent measures. Quantitative methodologies are useful for evaluating the degree of statistical success in creating new measures that are cross-group equivalent. For established measures, quantitative and qualitative methodologies may be used in conjunction to ferret out sources of nonequivalence. Quantitative methodologies may be useful in identifying which measures or parts of measures are nonequivalent, while qualitative methodologies may be useful in the confirmation of nonequivalences and modifying the measure, particularly when the nonequivalence is the result of the omission of relevant behaviors or items.

IMPLICATIONS FOR RESEARCH PRACTICES

The overall perspective developed throughout this chapter provides a basis for researchers to consider in resolving important issues that occur in the process of studying Latino children and families. The particular issues that we are concerned with are those that are likely to occur in either (a) the development of new measures that will be administered in diverse Latino samples or diverse Latino and Non-Latino samples or (b) the administration of a measure in Latino samples that has been developed in some non-Latino population. Although each researcher must consider how this perspective would lead toward the resolution of their specific research problems, following we address some types of conceptual questions that often arise in this research context. These are designed to be illustrative rather than exhaustive.

1. *How can researchers obtain the information needed to inform their theories by an understanding of the ethnic or racial groups in which a measure is to be used?*
As noted earlier, the theory describing the nature of the construct must be specific to the populations being sampled. This information can only come from those with considerable knowledge of the cultures associated with those populations. Perhaps the best source of this knowledge is from those persons who live within each culture. For example, Gonzales and colleages (Gonzales, Gunnoe, Samaniego, & Jackson, 1995; Gonzales, Tein, Sandler, & Friedman, 2001) developed a stressful life events scale for adolescents living in multicultural urban environments. Separate focus groups were conducted with Mexican American, African American, and Anglo adolescents to generate items for the scale. Many similar items were identified across groups in the school, peer, family, and community domains. However, events related to limited English-speaking abilities emerged specifically for the Mexican American adolescents, particularly in focus groups conducted in Spanish. Though these events are not relevant to most Anglo and African American adolescents, they represent an important dimension of daily stress for many Mexican Americans and other youths with a recent history of immigration.

There has been substantial development of the methods available to generate this type of information (e.g., Bryman & Burgess, 1994; Feldman, 1995; Hines, 1993; Hughes et al., 1993) and these methods are often quite qualitative in nature. Individuals who have a history of studying these cultures, but who may not actually live within the culture, may also provide some useful information about how the underlying construct is represented in each population. However, these individuals may be of limited utility because it is often the case that the development of a measure for use in a particular ethnic or racial group is the first opportunity these individuals may have to study this construct in this group. In this case, individuals who have a history of studying the respective populations may be better able to specify how the construct of interest should relate to other constructs but less able to adequately specify the nature of, or elements of, the construct of interest.

Informing our theories about the nature of constructs in Latino populations is no small task. Although we may begin with relatively qualitative or more subjective data, this must lead to methodologies that are more standardized and objective. That is, the process of science often begins with relatively informal observation, much the way a member of a cultural group might observe the culture in their daily lives. However, subsequent scientific observations must move toward meeting the more rigorous demands associated with being scientifically verifiable, much the way a social scientist might survey or conduct structured observations of members of the culture. As this process of science proceeds, we must continually reevaluate and revise the theory about the nature of the underlying construct of interest as it applies to the ethnic or racial population of interest. In turn, this changing understanding of the target ethnic or racial population may lead to revisions in the measurement of the construct of interest and the need to again evaluate the equivalence of that measure.

   2. *How does empirical evidence direct decision making in the process of evaluating the equivalence of measures across ethnic and racial groups? More specifically: Should items be discarded automatically if these items do not demonstrate the same psychometric properties (i.e., demonstrate differential item functioning or different factor loadings) in each group? When assessing measurement equivalence, is it necessary to administer identical items in each ethnic or racial group in which the underlying construct is being measured? Does differential item functioning or differences in factor loading across ethnic or racial groups necessarily indicate that a measure is not equivalent across these groups?*

The answer to these types of questions depends on the theory that specifies the nature of the underlying construct as it applies to each target population. If one has sufficient theory, backed by the necessary culture-specific knowledge, to suggest that the underlying construct has the same indicators in each culture, then a common set of items is appropriate. In this case, differences across groups in the psychometric properties for some individual items must be examined to determine whether these differences are chance occurrences or indicative of failure of the initial theory about the nature of the underlying construct within each group. In contrast, if the culturally specific theory suggests that there are some subtly different features of the underlying construct, then it may be necessary to administer sets of items that are somewhat different across groups. In this latter case, a particular pattern of differences in item-level psychometric properties would be expected, based on the culturally specific theory about the nature of the underlying construct, and the occurrence of this expected pattern of findings would be indicative of measurement equivalence. Indeed, the strategy of dropping items from the measure simply because they do not have similar psychometric characteristics across groups may be misguided. For example, an item assessing the frequency of suicidal thought may be quite appropriate on a scale measuring depression. However, it is possible that this item may be a good indicator of depression in each of two groups, but there may be less variability in the responses to this item in one ethnic or racial group because of the prohibition of such behavior, and corresponding thought, because of a religion associated with that culture. In this case, this item may have a differently factor loading or function somewhat different across ethnic or racial groups just because of the difference in variance of the responses. Dropping such an item because it either appears not to be an indicator or to function differently in a second group (i.e., solely for empirical reasons) may produce a nonrandom and nonrepresentative selection of the population of items in either one or both ethnic or racial groups. Furthermore, once the measure contains a nonrandom selection of items from the population of items defining the underlying construct, it becomes possible that the measure may not be a representative assessment, or may not be an equally representative assessment, of the construct of interest. Of course, retaining such an item may produce differences in the variance in the scale scores that must then be considered when conducting scale-level analyses of equivalence. Exactly this problem has arisen in Michaels, Barr, Roosa, and Knight (2000), who found that all but one item on the Behavioral Conduct scale of Harter's Self-Perception Profile for Children (Harter, 1985) had similar confirmatory factor loadings in samples of low-income Mexican American and Anglo American youths. Indeed, the expected factor did load on this item (I usually act the way I know I am supposed to) within each ethnicity, but the magnitude of the factor loading was different across ethnic groups. Many researchers would relatively automatically drop this item from the computation of the scale score. However, the significant factor loadings for this item in the within-ethnicity analyses suggests that this may well be an adequate indicator of behavioral conduct in each ethnic group. Furthermore, if there were some culturally related phenomena that explains the ethnic difference in the magnitude of the factor loading on this item, eliminating this item from the scale would threaten the representativeness of the sample of items within each ethnic group.

Similarly, the items defining a target construct may produce evidence of differential item functioning or differences in confirmatory factor loadings because of the existence of a secondary construct such as the response bias noted earlier (Hui & Triandis, 1989; Marín et al., 1992). Such a response bias could impact the variance of the responses to each item sufficiently to, in turn, produce ethnic differences in item–total relations. Of course, knowledge that such a response bias is associated with the Latino culture would allow the researcher to address this issue and to conduct an appropriately fair test of the similarity of the item–total and inter-item relations. One possibility is to use a broader response format. Hui and Triandis (1989) found that Latinos endorsed more extreme responses on 5-point response scales but not on 10-point response scales. Alternatively, the analysis strategy, and perhaps the scoring strategy, for a scale could fix the item variances to be constant across groups before examining the similarity of item–total or inter-item relations.

Dropping whole scales or subscales simply because the factor structure of those scales are not consistent across ethnic and racial groups may also be misguided. For example, Prelow, Tein, Roosa, and Wood (2000) found that coping styles such as restraint, acceptance, denial, focus on venting of emotion, and humor have similar indicators across Mexican American and Anglo American groups of mothers. However, for the Mexican American mothers, the relations between denial and acceptance and between restraint and venting of emotions were positive, while these relations were negative for the Anglo mothers. These findings suggest that these coping strategies do not function in the same manner in low-income Mexican American mothers as they do in middle-class Anglo mothers. One potential explanation for these differences revolves around the cultural script *simpatia*. That is, low-income Mexican American mothers may use more coping strategies that would avoid conflict such as denial, acceptance, and restraint; and thereby account for the positive relations between these coping strategies. Another possibility is that low-income Mexican American mothers may initially use strategies such as denial and venting of emotions to reduce negative emotions associated with stressors; this, in turn, may later facilitate the use of other coping strategies such as restraint and acceptance strategies (Lazarus & Folkman, 1984). To the degree to which these differences in the interrelations among coping factors are consistent with expectations one might generate from any theory regarding the nature of coping strategies and how these strategies are utilized in these specific cultures, these subscales may well be equivalent.

3. Does similarity of item functioning or factor loading across ethnic or racial group necessarily indicate that the measure is equivalent across these groups?
Once again the answer to this type of question depends on the nature of the theory regarding the underlying construct as it applies to each target population of persons. If theory suggests that the indicators of an underlying construct are the same in several ethnic or racial groups, then similarity of item

functioning or factor loadings would be expected and is a good beginning to the assessment of equivalence. However, we should also expect, as a part of the validation of the measure, the scores produced by a measure of the underlying construct of interest to be related to scores produced by measures of other underlying constructs in a manner consistent with theory. That is, ultimately the meaning of scores produced by a measure of an underlying construct of interest are understandable only in terms of the relations of those scores to scores that are produced by measures of other underlying constructs in a manner prescribed by theory.

Similarity of item functioning or factor loading would not be indicative of complete measurement equivalence if the culturally informed theory specifies that the underlying construct has some differences in indicators across the target ethnic or racial groups. For example, the focus group work of Gonzales et al. (1995), clearly suggests that a stressful life-events scale should have different indicators among Mexican American adolescents, particularly those who prefer to speak Spanish, than Anglo American and African American adolescents. In this case, items related to limited English capabilities would be part of the population of items defining stressful life events among Mexican American adolescents but not Anglo American or African American adolescents. A measure of stressful life events that included only items regarding school, peer, family, and community stressors might well indicate a highly similar factor structure across these groups. However, because this measure is not equally representative of the population of items defining stressful life events in these three ethnic/racial groups, such similarity of factor structure would not be indicative of measurement equivalence.

4. *Do differential construct validity coefficients across ethnic or racial groups indicate nonequivalence of measures or, conversely, does similarity of construct validity coefficients across these groups indicate measurement equivalence?*

Here again the theory about the nature of the underlying construct as it exists in the respective ethnic or racial groups is critical. If the culturally informed theory regarding the function of the construct suggests that the construct functions in the same way in each group, then the relations of that construct to other constructs should be the same across groups. If, however, the theory and understanding of the underlying construct suggest that the underlying construct functions differently, at least to some extent, in different cultures, then full similarity of construct validity coefficients should not be expected. Indeed, in this latter case, differences in construct validity coefficients that precisely mirror the theoretically prescribed differences in functioning would be indicative of measurement equivalence. For example, there is emerging evidence that harsh parenting and restrictive control, rather than representing an overcontrolling quality of parental behavior, may be an adaptive parenting strategy in ethnic and racial minority children who live in a community with high rates of violent behaviors (Baldwin et al., 1993; Coulton & Pandey, 1992; Gonzales,

Cauce, Friedman, & Mason, 1996; Lamborn, Dornbusch, & Steinberg, 1996; Mayer & Jencks, 1989; Tolan, Gorman-Smith, Huesmann, & Zelli, 1997). Thus, this parental control may make the lives of children in these communities more predictable and safe and, in turn, have relatively positive, rather than negative, mental health outcomes. Indeed, it is argued that parents in these environments must rely on harsh, restrictive control strategies because the consequences of children's behavioral risk taking are so severe (McLoyd, 1998). If so, then one would expect parental control to relate differently to mental health outcomes in samples of children from relatively risky environments compared with safer middle-class environments. This differential expectation regarding the relationship between parental control and mental health would lead to an expectation of different slopes in the structural modeling or regression analyses examining the relations between these constructs, if the measures of these constructs are indeed equivalent across these groups of persons. Of course, parental control might be similarly related or differentially related to a myriad of other constructs across groups depending on the breadth of the culturally informed theory. Similarly, ethnic or racial group differences in response biases (Hui & Triandis, 1989; Marín et al., 1992) could lead to ethnic differences in the variance of a scale score, which in turn could differentially attenuate construct validity coefficients describing the relation of the target construct to other constructs. The knowledge that there is a specific response bias associated with an ethnic or racial group allows the researcher to make adjustments that can address this type of empirical problem and ultimately to make for more educated inferences regarding the equivalence of the measure of the target construct.

5. *If the indicators of a construct, and hence the items used to measure that construct, are different across ethnic or racial groups, how can one investigate the equivalence of that measure across groups?*
If it is necessary to have different items across groups because the nature of the construct is somewhat different across groups, it is most likely that only a subset of the population of items is different across ethnic or racial groups. If so, then a representative set of items for each group would contain some, probably many, common items. In this case, one can conduct differential-item-functioning analyses or confirmatory-factor analyses and adjust one's analyses and expectations in a manner consistent with the culturally informed theory that led to the inclusion of some different items. For example, one could conduct confirmatory-factor analyses in which the factor loadings on a common item are constrained to be equal across ethnic or racial groups, and the factor loadings on the noncommon items are constrained to be zero in one group and free to vary in the other. In addition, one could compare construct validity coefficients across groups using the scale scores that are the composite of the culturally appropriate items for each ethnic or racial group. These construct validity coefficients should be compatible with the relations among

constructs specified by the culturally informed theory about the nature of the construct, even if the individual items that are used to assess the target construct are somewhat different across groups. Of course, in any of these analyses, researchers need to be cautious and may need to make statistical adjustments for such things as different variances in the scale scores as a function of either different items or different numbers of items across ethnic or racial groups.

CONCLUSION

In conclusion, issues of measurement equivalence are important in any research on Latino children and families that (a) compares these children and families to those in other ethnic or racial groups, (b) includes Latino children and families in diverse samples with children and families from other ethnic or racial groups, or (c) includes diverse samples of Latino children or families that are either heterogeneous with regard to the specific Latino population sampled or that are heterogeneous with regard to their degree of ethnic identity and acculturative status. Although there has been considerable development in the statistical methods that can be used to investigate the cross-ethnic or cross-race equivalence of measures, our understanding of the importance of theory regarding the nature of the target-underlying construct in examining the equivalence of measures has not kept pace. It is essential that the theory that specifies the nature of the indicators of the target-underlying construct, as well as the relations of the target construct to other constructs, must be informed by an understanding of the nature of the culture in which the measure is to be used. Finally, it is this culturally informed theory that provides the necessary expectations regarding the outcomes of the statistical analyses of item–total relations and construct validity relations to allow researchers to make credible judgments of the equivalence or nonequivalence of measures for use in diverse populations of persons.

REFERENCES

Baldwin, A. L., Baldwin, C. P., Kasser, T., Zax, M., Sameroff, A., & Seifer, R. (1993). Contextual risk and resiliency during late adolescence. *Development and Psychopathology, 5*, 741–761.

Berg, B. L. (1995). *Qualitative research methods for the social sciences* (2nd ed.). Boston: Allyn & Bacon.

Bollen, K. A. (1989). *Structural equations with latent variables.* New York: Wiley.

Bryman, A. & Burgess, R. (Eds.). (1994). *Analyzing qualitative data.* New York: Routledge.

Camilli, G., & Shepard, L. A. (1994). *Methods for identifying biased test items.* Measurement Methods for the Social Sciences Series. Thousand Oaks, CA: Sage.

Coulton, C. J., & Pandey, S. (1992). Geographic concentration of poverty and risk to children in urban neighborhoods. *American Behavioral Scientist, 35*, 238–257.

Cronbach, L. J. (1970). *Essentials of psychological testing* (3rd ed.). New York: Harper & Row.

Drasgow, F. (1995). Some comments on Labouvie and Ruetsch. *Multivariate Behavioral Research, 30,* 83–85.

Feldman, M. S. (1995). *Strategies for interpreting qualitative data.* Thousand Oaks, CA: Sage.

Fetterman, D. M. (1989). *Ethnography: Step by step.* Newbury Park, CA: Sage.

Gonzales, N. A., Cauce, A. M., Friedman, R., & Mason, C.A. (1996). Family, peer, and neighborhood influences on academic achievement among African-American adolescents. *American Journal of Community Psychology, 24,* 365–387.

Gonzales, N. A., Cauce, A. M., & Mason, C. A. (1996). Interobserver agreement in the assessment of parental behavior and parent–adolescent conflict: African American mothers, daughters, and independent observers. *Child Development, 67,* 1483–1498.

Gonzales, N. A., Gunnoe, M. L., Samaniego, R., & Jackson, K. (1995). *Validation of a multicultural event schedule for adolescents.* Paper presented at the Biennial Conference of the Society for Community Research and Action, Chicago, IL, June.

Gonzales, N. A., Tein, J., Sandler, I. N., & Friedman, R. J. (2001). On the limits of coping: Interactions between stress and coping for inner-city adolescents. *Journal of Adolescent Research, 16,* 372–395.

Gonzalez-Ramos, G., Zayas, L. H., & Cohen, E. V. (1998). Child-rearing values of low-income, urban Puerto Rican mothers of preschool children. *Professional Psychology: Research and Practice, 29,* 377–382.

Hambleton, R. K., Swaminathan, H., & Rogers, H. J. (1991). *Fundamentals of Item Response Theory.* Measurement Methods for the Social Sciences Series. Newbury Park, CA: Sage.

Harter, S. (1985). *Manual for the Self-Perception Profile fr Children.* Unpublished manuscript, University of Denver, CO.

Hines, A. M. (1993). Linking qualitative and quantitative methods in cross-cultural survey research: Techniques from cognitive science. *American Journal of Community Psychology, 21,* 729–746.

Hughes, D., Seidman, E., & Williams, N. (1993). Cultural phenomena and the research enterprise: Toward a culturally anchored methodology. *American Journal of Community Psychology, 21,* 687–704.

Hui, C. H., & Triandis, H. C. (1985). Measurement in cross-cultural psychology: A review and comparison of strategies. *Journal of Cross-Cultural Psychology, 16,* 131–152.

Hui, C. H., & Triandis, H. C. (1989). Effects of culture and response format on extreme response style. *Journal of Cross-Cultural Psychology, 20,* 296–309.

Kleinman, A., & Good, B. (1985). Introduction: Culture and depression. In A. Kleinman and B. Good (Eds.), *Culture and Depression* (pp. 1–33). Berkeley: University of California Press.

Knight, G. P., & Hill, N. E. (1998). Measurement equivalence in research involving minority adolescents. In V. C. McLoyd and L. Steinberg (Eds.), *Studying minority adolescents: conceptual, methodological, and theoretical issues* (pp. 183–210). Mahwah, NJ: Erlbaum.

Knight, G. P., Virdin, L. M., & Roosa, M. (1994). Socialization and family correlates of mental health outcomes among Hispanic and Anglo American children:

Consideration of cross-ethnic scalar equivalence. *Child Development, 65,* 212–224.

Labouvie, E., & Ruetsch, C. (1995). Testing the equivalence of measurement scales: Simple structure and metric invariance reconsidered. *Multivariate Behavioral Research, 30,* 63–70.

Lamborn, S. D., Dornbusch, S. M., & Steinberg, L. (1996). Ethnicity and community context as moderators of the relations between family decision making and adolescent adjustment. *Child Development, 67,* 283–301.

Lazarus, R. S., & Folkman, S. (1984). Stress, appraisal, and coping. New York: Springer.

Lord, F. M. (1980). *Applications of item response theory to practical testing problems.* Hillsdale, NJ: Erlbaum.

Malpass, R. S., & Poortinga, Y. H. (1986). Strategies for design and analysis. In W. J. Lonner & J. W. Berry (Eds.), *Field methods in cross-cultural research* (pp. 47–84). Newbury Park, CA: Sage.

Marín, G., Gamba, R. J., & Marin, B.V. (1992). Extreme response style and acquiescence among Hispanics: The role of acculturation and education. *Journal of Cross-Cultural Psychology, 23,* 498–509.

Mayer, S. E., & Jencks, C. (1989). Growing up in poor neighborhoods: How much does it matter? *Science, 243,* 1441–1445.

McDonald, R. P. (1995). Testing for approximate dimensionality. In D. Laveault, B. D. Sumbo, M. E. Gessaroli, & M. W. Boss (Eds.), *Modern theories of measurement: Problems and issues* (pp. 63–86). Ottawa, Ontario, Canada: Edumetric Research Group, University of Ottawa.

McDonald, R. P. (1999). *Test theory: A unified treatment.* Mahwah, NJ: Erlbaum.

McLoyd, V. C. (1998). Socioeconomic disadvantage and child development. *American Psychologist, 53,* 185–204.

Meredith, W. (1995). Two wrongs may not make a right. *Multivariate Behavioral Research, 30,* 89–94.

Michaels, M. L., Barr, A., Roosa, M. W., & Knight, G. P. (2000). *Harter's Self-Perception Profile for Children: A test of measurement equivalence in a low income, ethnically diverse sample.* Unpublished manuscript, Arizona State University.

Nesselroade, J. R. (1995). ". . . and expectations fainted, longing for what it had not." Comments on Labouvie and Ruetsch's "Testing for equivalence . . ." *Multivariate Behavioral Research, 30,* 95–99.

Nunnally, J. C. (1967). *Psychometric theory.* New York: McGraw-Hill.

O'Dell, L., & Cudeck, R. (1995). Relationships among measurement models for dichotomous variables and associated composites. *Multivariate Behavioral Research, 30,* 77–81.

Prelow, M. P., Tein, J.-Y., Roosa, M. W., & Wood, J. (2000). Do coping styles differ across sociocultural groups? The role of measurement equivalence in making this judgment. *American Journal of Community Psychology, 28,* 225–244.

Reise, S. P., Widaman, K. F., & Pugh, R. H. (1993). Confirmatory factor analysis and item response theory: Two approaches for exploring measurement invariance. *Psychological Bulletin, 114,* 552–566.

Rudner, L. M., Getson, P. R., & Knight, D. L. (1980). Biased item detection techniques. *Journal of Educational Statistics, 5,* 213–233.

Tolan, P. H., Gorman-Smith, D., Huesmann, L. R., & Zelli, A. (1997). Assessing family processes to explain risk for antisocial behavior and depression among urban youth. *Psychological Assessment, 9,* 212–223.

U.S. Census Bureau. (1998). *Resident populations of the United States: Estimates, by sex, race, and Hispanic origin, with median age* [On-line]. Available: www.census.gov/population/estimates/nation/infile3-1.txt

Vega, W. A., & Rumbaut, R. G. (1991). Ethnic minorities and mental health. *Annual Review of Sociology, 17,* 351–383.

Widaman, K. F. (1995). On methods for comparing apples and oranges. *Multivariate Behavioral Research, 30,* 101–106.

9

Parenting Interventions Adapted for Latino Families: Progress and Prospects

Larry E. Dumka, Vera A. Lopez, and Sara Jacobs Carter

The goals of intervention research are to identify factors that contribute to problematic outcomes and then to find ways to modify these factors in order to alter negative developmental trajectories into positive ones. The family and household represent primary socialization contexts for children. These proximal networks of repetitive interactions provide a means for transmitting family and cultural norms as well as teaching children how to cope with life's stresses. Research has linked the child, family, and household management skills of parents to children's adjustment (Feldman & Kazdin, 1995; Rogers-Weise, 1992; Sanders, 1992). Consequently, various interventions have been developed to strengthen parenting skills in order to prevent and treat mental and behavioral health problems in children (e.g., depression, delinquency, drug use). Moreover, research has demonstrated that parenting interventions have been effective in modifying parenting characteristics and enhancing children's adjustment (Office of Juvenile Justice and Delinquency Prevention [OJJDP] & University of Utah, 1998). However, to date, much of the research guiding the development of parenting interventions and evaluating intervention effects has been conducted on English-language interventions with largely European American origin majority culture families (Hayes, 1995). In this chapter, for the sake of parsimonious expression, we will use the general term "Anglo" to refer to these English-language interventions and the families for which they were developed. We will use the general term "Latino" to refer to the heterogeneous groups living in the United States who have ancestral origins in Spanish-speaking countries and regions in the Western Hemisphere.

More recently, there have been attempts to adapt parenting interventions for Latino populations and to evaluate these interventions. There are a number of reasons for this. The Latino population in the United States is the fastest growing of the country's ethnic groups. Most of the increase has come from immigration, with the largest proportion from Mexico (U.S. Census Bureau, 1996). Latino immigrants encounter substantial acculturation challenges that may represent incremental risk factors for children's adjustment (e.g., English literacy, documentation status, financial viability, strange new neighborhoods that may have high levels of violence, obtaining schooling and health care). Thus, taking an acculturative stress and coping perspective, a number of parenting interventions have been adapted to make them accessible to Spanish speakers and to help orient immigrants to American majority culture (e.g., by including information on child protection laws and public school expectations).

Another factor contributing to the development of Latino adapted parenting interventions is that Latinos are overrepresented in low-income and low-education groups (Aponte & Crouch, 1995). Economic stress on parents has been linked to lower parenting efficacy (Elder, Eccles, Ardelt, & Lord, 1995) and children's adjustment problems (Dumka, Roosa, & Jackson, 1997). Consequently, interventions for Latino parents have been seen as a means to increase protective factors for children at elevated risk because of poverty.

Another motivation for adapting programs is that recruitment and retention rates for parenting interventions have been low overall (Braver, 1989), but these rates seem to have been particularly low for Latino and other ethnic minority groups (Alvy, 1994; Myers et al., 1992). Culturally adapted interventions have been seen as a means for increasing attractiveness of these services and thus enhancing the participation of Latino parents in these programs. Also, more recently, there has been growing advocacy for the proposition that elements of Anglo parenting interventions (e.g., the promotion of democratic vs. hierarchical family structures) may be discordant with the values of Latino parents, particularly those of low-income status (Forehand & Kotchick, 1996). Accordingly, these advocates have encouraged the development of culturally competent interventions (Bernal, Bonilla, & Bellido, 1995).

We view cultural competence as having both knowledge (or content) and skill (or process) dimensions. The knowledge dimension of cultural competence includes at least two key components. First, there is general knowledge of a cultural group's values, beliefs, and practices. This general knowledge typically can be deduced from descriptive literature and an awareness of the group's history. The widely acknowledged Latino value of *familisimo* and the nature of gender relations in immigrant families from rural central Mexico are examples of this component of cultural knowledge (see Cauce & Domenech-Rodríguez, Chapter 1, this volume). Second, there is particular knowledge of the dynamics of a cultural group currently living in a certain location (e.g., whether the location is urban or rural, high or low-income, has high or low levels of violent crime, whether the cultural group forms a majority or minority in the neighborhood, the politics of the neighborhood). Gaining this type of locationally contextualized knowledge usually requires more proximal contact with members of the cultural group in the community of interest. Locationally contextualized knowledge is critical to increasing ecological validity, which Bronfenbrenner (1977) defined as the degree of congruence between the environment as experienced by the targeted cultural group member and the qualities of the environment the investigator assumes it has. Ecological validity is critical to designing and implementing culturally competent parenting interventions. In addition to knowledge, culturally competent parenting interventions need to employ and advocate skills and processes that accommodate the cultural group's values, beliefs, and practices. For example, advocating that Latino parents organize family fun times might be seen as more culturally competent than insisting that Latino parents arrange one-on-one times with a target child.

Besides making interventions accessible to Spanish speakers, the reasons for adapting parenting interventions converge toward a central proposition: Culturally competent interventions will be more effective in influencing parenting behavior that is linked to children's healthy development than interventions that are not culturally competent. In this study, our purpose was to identify parenting interventions purported to be adapted for Latino families, to describe the adaptations developers made, to analyze and categorize these adaptations, to identify the strengths and limitations of these adaptations, and, finally, to make recommendations for future Latino adapted parenting intervention development and research.

METHOD

Sampling

Parenting interventions were identified from searches of the scientific literature databases (PsycINFO, ERIC), reviews of parenting and family strengthening interventions (e.g., OJJDP & University of Utah, 1998), and consulting people knowledgeable about the parenting intervention field. With regard to searching electronic databases, the keywords that were used to refer to the target group were parents, parenting, and family. Keyword alternatives for intervention were program, training, education, counseling, intervention, and therapy. The keywords Latinos, Hispanics, Mexican American, Mexican, Chicanos, Cuban American, and Puerto Rican served as alternatives for ethnicity. All possible combinations of these categories were used to conduct a search of the literature spanning the years 1977 to 1999. This search resulted in an assortment of clinicians' reports of Latino values, beliefs, customs, societal contexts, and implications for treatment (e.g., Comas-Díaz, 1995); descriptions of the development and implementation of parenting interventions, intervention manuals, and reports of intervention evaluations.

The main criteria for selection of materials was that the materials had to be published (as a journal article, book chapter, or intervention manual; dissertation abstracts were not selected) and describe or refer to an intervention with

Latino parents, with one of the goals of the intervention being to enhance parenting behavior to improve children's adjustment. Materials dealing with multiple component interventions (e.g., family strengthening interventions or interventions that tried to influence child, parent, school, neighborhood subsystems) were selected as long as the interventions included a component specifically aimed at improving parenting behavior.

At the outset, we acknowledge that, even with our best efforts, the materials we identified and selected are not exhaustive of the field. We believe, however, that the materials we selected adequately represent the range of adaptation efforts to date. Also, we had to rely on written descriptions of interventions that varied greatly in terms of amount of detail provided. We are aware that many more elements go into the development, implementation, and evaluation of a parenting intervention than are included in written reports. Therefore, it is likely that there are instances in which we coded a characteristic of an intervention as "Not Specified" or absent based on the materials we had, when in fact this characteristic may have been specified by the developers in other places.

Data Reduction

The coding schemes we present in this chapter were determined in stages. We first developed a list of codes based on our first review of the intervention reports. Through discussion and several iterations, we revised and expanded this list of codes in order to capture the various distinctions among the interventions. Next, we compared our codes to others' dimensions for culturally competent psychosocial interventions (e.g., Bernal et al., 1995) and integrated our codes with these dimensions. Finally, we reduced the list of codes, through the constant comparison method. We then proceeded to code the selected interventions according to these codes. The codes are presented in Table 9.1 as are two examples of coded interventions. After coding the interventions, we examined the coded data and discerned the types of adaptations that were made. Table 9.2 contains a summary of pertinent data from all the interventions we reviewed.

In the text, we have referred to interventions by their name or title. The interventions are arranged alphabetically in Table 9.2; citations for these interventions are found just below the intervention name.

RESULTS

Overview of the Interventions

A number of interventions met what we termed the "language-translation-only" level of adaptation, which consisted of translating of English intervention manuals, recruitment, instructional, evaluation, and videotape stimulus

Table 9.1
Examples of Coding of Interventions and Adaptations

Intervention Citation	Targeted Population	Cultural Knowledge Sources	Adapted Change Objectives	Adapted Symbols and Concepts	Adapted Intervention Methods
Format, Session and Intervention Duration Locations program developed / presented Evaluation Data for Latino Adaptation	**Selectiveness** National origin Child age Educ/Income status **Acculturation status** Neighborhood locatn	Latino values, customs (pan Latino or national origin specific)			**Recruitment** Para intervention services Who, what, where, when Intervention methods used
Los Niños Bien Educados (Alvy, 1994) **Parents meet in groups for 3 hr. sessions over the course of 12 weeks.** Southern California **Some pre-test / post-test data only High attrition rate**	**Universal/ selected** Latino NS **3-10 years old** Low/low Low NS	Conducted Qual/quant study of low and middle income Mex Ams; revealed low-income, low-accult Mex Ams value themes of learn/teach, obedience/ respect; From research literature, one study derived predominant themes of targets, accommodated valuing traditional sex and family roles. Hired 2 experts on Latino parenting to review intervention	Derived from behavioral parent training (Confident Parenting) Explicitly addresses ways immigrants adjust; Information about US child abuse laws; more active involve with schools	Bien Educados theme; use of respectful and disrespectful to refer to appropriate/ inappropriate behavior; use of term "family expectations" to refer to family rules; Used Dichos (sayings) to identify behavioral change methods; Use of terms cafecita breaks and platicas; Goals framed in terms of parents role to teach children to be bien educados	**Spanish flyers** NS **Initial exercises reveal level of participants' acculturation** Leaders self-disclose (personalismo);parents get to decide what are bien and mal educados behaviors; opportunities for personalization and mutual support at end of each session as leaders recede and participants direct their own platicas. Unstructured cafecita breaks to permit socializing and connection to other parents.

(continued)

Table 9.1
(Continued)

Intervention Citation	Targeted Population	Cultural Knowledge Sources	Adapted Change Objectives	Adapted Symbols and Concepts	Adapted Intervention Methods
Format, Session and Intervention Duration Locations program developed / presented Evaluation Data for Latino Adaptation	Selectiveness National origin Child age Educ/Income status Acculturation status Neighborhood locatn				Recruitment Para intervention services Who, what, where, when Intervention methods used
Preparing for the Drug-Free Years (Hawkins & Catalano, 2001; Harachi, Catalano, & Hawkins, 1997)	Universal Mostly Mexican and Cuban American	Dependent upon the bicultural staff members recruited to be leaders			Bilingual individuals recruited family members through personal networks and face-to-face contact at church services conducted in Spanish, at the public elementary school, and at the recreation center. Additionally, recruitment took place at "naturally occurring events" such as tupperware and birthday parties in the community. Incentives included transportation, child care, and snacks
Parents meet in groups for 5-2 hour sessions	8-14 years old				NS
NS	NS				NS
Recruitment rates and attrition. No outcome data for adapted program	NS				From Anglo Program

NS = Not Specified

208

Table 9.2
Latino Adapted Parenting Intervention Summary Table

Program Name (Citation) Sorted Alphabetically	Length (a): Long Term	Length (a): Short Term	Format: In Home	Format: Group	Format: Individual (b)	Of Children Aged (c)	Low Education/ Income Level	Accult-uration: Low	Accult-uration: Mid-Range	Selectiveness: Universal	Selectiveness: Selective	Selectiveness: Indicated	Sources: Other Literature	Sources: Own Resrch	Sources: Expert	Sources: Programmatic Revision	Change Objectives Adapted	Symbols & Concepts Adapted	Eval (d): Pre-Test	Eval (d): Post-Test	Eval (d): Comparison Group
Active Parenting Today (Padres Activos de Hoy)(Popkin, 1999)(f)		✓		✓		2-12 yrs.	NS (e)	NS	NS	✓			✓					✓			
AVANCE Parent Child Education Program (Walker, Rodriguez, Johnson, & Cortez, 1995)(f)	✓			✓		<2 yrs.	✓		✓		✓		✓			✓	✓	✓	✓	✓	✓
CEDEN's Parent-Child Program (Arocena, Adams, & Davis, 1992)	✓		✓		✓	<3 yrs.	✓	✓			✓	✓	✓				✓	✓	✓	✓	✓
Cuento Therapy with Children (Costantino, Malgady, & Rogler, 1986)	✓			✓	✓	M age 7	✓	✓			✓		✓		✓		✓	✓	✓	✓	✓
Detroit AIDS Education Program (De Carpio, Carpio-Cedraro, & Anderson, 1990)		✓	✓	✓		NS	✓	NS	NS	✓			✓				✓	✓			

(continued)

209

Table 9.2
(Continued)

Program				Age										
Fair Start for Children (Winters-Smith, & Larner, 1992)	√	√	√	<1 yrs.	√	√		√		√			√	√
Family Based Cardiovascular Risk Reduction Program (Nader, et al., 1992)	√			5th & 6th graders	N S	N S	NS	√					√	√
Family Effectiveness Training (Szapocznik, Rio, Pérez-Vidal, Kurtines, & Santisteban, 1985)	√	√		Pre-teens, teens	N S	N S		√					√	
Hispanic Foster Parents Program (Delgado, 1978)	√	√	√	NS	N S	N S	NS	√	√			√	√	√
Houston Parent Education Program (Johnson, 1990)		√	√	1-3 yrs.	√	N S	NS	√	√	√		√	√	√
Los Niños Bien Educados (Alvy, 1994)	√	√	√	3-10 yrs.	√	√	√	√	√		√	√	√	√
MADRE Parent Education Program (Herrerías, 1988)		√	√	<7 yrs.	N S	√	√	√	√			√	√	√
Nueva Familia (MELD, 1994) (f)	√	√	√	1-3 yrs.	√	√	√	√	√	√	√	√	√	√
Nurturing Program for Parents and Children (0 to 5 Yrs; 4-10 Yrs) (f) (Bavolek, 1985)	√	√	√	<5yrs; 4-12 yrs.				NS		√		√	NS	√
Parents as Teachers (program for parents of retarded children) (Prieto Bayard, & Baker, 1986)	√		√	3.5-16 yrs.	√	√	√		√					

(continued)

210

Program				Age										
Preparing for the Drug Free Years (Hawkins & Catalano, 2001; Harachi et al, 1997)	√		√	8-14 yrs.	NS	√	√		√					√
Project P.I.A.G.E.T. (Sung, Kim, & Yawkey, 1997).		√	√	M age 5	√	√	√		√				√	√
Project Profile Ninos Especiales Program (Bruder, Anderson, Schutz, & Caldera, 1991)		√	√	Infants	NS	√		√	√	NS		√	√	
Raising Successful Children (El Programa Criando Ninos Trimfantes) (Dumka, 1994)		√		8-10 yrs.	√	√ √	√ √		√					
STEP(PECES;Early Childhood STEP, American Guidance Service, 1991, 1993) (f)	√		√	0-5 yrs.; NS	NS	√	√	√		√				
Strengthening Families: A Curriculum for Hispanic Parents (COSSMHO, 1990)	√		√	Teens	NS	√	√	√	√	√	N S	N S	N S	N S

(a) – Programs were coded short-term they met for fewer than 15 sessions or weeks, programs were long-term if they met for longer than 15 weeks or sessions.

(b) – Individual formats were those that met with an individual family, an individual parent-child dyad, or individual parent

(c) – "M age" indicates participants' children were described as a mean age

(d) – of interventions adapted for Latinos

(e) – NS indicates the idea was mentioned but no specifics were reported; blanks spaces indicate nothing was mentioned

(f) – These interventions have separate versions that have been adapted to some degree for parents of different age/stage children

211

materials (if used) into Spanish. Some of these interventions included "Latino-looking" persons in the illustrative and videotape materials. However, in the language-translation-only adaptations, there were minimal or no attempts to modify the objectives, content, or methods of these basically Anglo interventions for Latino parents. Some of the most widely disseminated parenting interventions belonged to this language-translation-only category (e.g., Active Parenting, STEP, Nurturing Program, Preparing for the Drug Free Years). Other interventions went further than language translation only and included modifications to change objectives, intervention symbols, concepts, and methods.

Aside from these categories, we acknowledge that the recruiting, training, and monitoring of bilingual intervention personnel represent considerable and laudable expenditures of effort and expense. Moreover, bilingual group leaders can function in the role of informal cultural translators of interventions. For example, a group of Latino parents might be shown a videotape segment (from a language-translation-only intervention) depicting a disciplinary sequence. The group leader in commenting on the videotaped interaction might elicit discussion about the ways parents of that cultural group can accomplish the same disciplinary goal in a more culturally syntonic manner. This discussion might be critical to parents' understanding of the disciplinary concept and to motivating them to implement it. At the same time, this informal cultural translation was not a documented part of the intervention and was probably idiosyncratic to the group leader. It seems that leaders' informal adaptations, while quite variable, represent a potentially significant source of influence on intervention outcomes.

The adapted interventions we reviewed (both language translation only and more than language translation) varied greatly in length or dosage. Interestingly, a number of the interventions aimed at parents of infants and toddlers were highly represented in the long-term category (e.g., AVANCE, Houston Parent Education Program, Nueva Familia/MELD). The adapted interventions also varied in format. The most prevalent format was one in which small groups of parents (often 6 to 12) met together on a regular basis for a specified number of sessions at a non-home location (e.g., a room in a public school). In contrast, some therapy interventions (e.g., Family Effectiveness Training) met with individual family members (e.g., a parent) or combinations of family members (parents and children) at a family guidance center–type setting for varying numbers of sessions. A third type of format, used often in the long-term interventions with parents of infants and toddlers, was in-home visits with individual parent–child units.

Targeted Parents

This code refers to ways in which the target population of parents for the intervention was specified in the materials. Greater specification of the target group has the advantage of permitting increased adaptation of the intervention to accommodate particular characteristics. Parenting interventions adapted for Latino families can be specified along several dimensions. One of these dimensions is selectiveness (Gordon, 1987; Mrazek & Haggerty, 1994). Using terminology from prevention science, interventions can be "universal" and directed at all members of a population without regard to risk level for negative outcomes (e.g., all Latino parents of a certain age group of children). Other interventions are termed "selective" and are directed at families that are identified in some way to be at greater risk for experiencing a negative child development outcome (e.g., Latino families who have a mentally handicapped child or a child with some conduct problems). Still other interventions are "indicated" interventions and are directed at families that are already experiencing significant signs of negative outcomes (e.g., school truancy, disruptive school behavior, delinquency). We categorized therapy interventions as indicated.

The highest proportion of the parenting interventions adapted for Latino families we reviewed appeared to be universal. That is, the authors implied that the interventions were appropriate for all Latino families and thus were not limited to families at greater risk due to some factor. At the same time, many of these universal interventions also could have been classified as selective because they were designed for low-income families likely experiencing economic hardship (e.g., Raising Successful Children, Houston Parent Education Program). Economic hardship is a risk factor for children's maladjustment because of the accumulation of accompanying stresses (Brooks-Gunn & Duncan, 1997). Consequently, we coded quite a number of the interventions as both universal and selective to reflect this linked status. A few of the interventions were clearly selective in that parents' and/or children's risk levels were assessed and used as criteria for participation (e.g., Parents as Teachers, Fair Start, CEDEN). Finally, Family Effectiveness Training is an example of an indicated intervention adapted for Latino families with adolescents already exhibiting signs of substance abuse and/or delinquency.

Another way of specifying target parents was by the age and developmental stage of the children. Although some parenting competencies span developmental stages (e.g., the ability to communicate love and limits), there are differences in how these competencies are optimally expressed depending on the developmental stage of the child. Also, there are some parenting competencies that become important when a child reaches a certain age or stage (e.g., interacting with children's teachers when children become school age, knowing the signs of drug use when children reach middle school age). As is evident from Table 9.2, most of the Latino-adapted interventions have been directed at parents with children who are younger than teenagers. The interventions for Latino parents of teenagers tended to be of the language-translation-only type (Active Parenting, Preparing for the Drug Free Years) or therapy interventions for families of teenagers already exhibiting significant problems (e.g., Family Effectiveness Training).

Two related ways of specifying targeted parents were acculturation level and education level. Acculturation level refers to immigrants' orientation to the dominant culture's language, values, rules, and laws, whereas education level contributes to participants' ability to understand intervention information. Castro, Cota, and Vega (1999) have asserted that the high-acculturated, high-education parents (typically the most advantaged) would be most likely to respond positively to a parenting intervention designed for middle-class Anglos, whereas the low-acculturated, low-education parents (typically the least advantaged) would be least likely to benefit from such an intervention. Thus, interventions aimed at low-acculturated, low-education Latino groups (often recent immigrants) would require more deliberate and wide-ranging adaptations to be effective than interventions for high-acculturated, high-education groups.

A number of parenting interventions have been adapted to better fit Latino parents who have low levels of formal education and thus low literacy skills (in Spanish or English). These adaptations typically have included using the simplest and clearest language in presentations and reducing reliance on materials requiring high degrees of literacy (e.g., Raising Successful Children, Los Niños Bien Educados). However, the most prevalent adaptation for parents with low acculturation levels was having the program conducted in Spanish.

The national or regional origin of Latino participants (e.g., Mexico, Puerto Rico, Cuba, other Central or South American countries) is yet another way of specifying targeted parents. Various authors have described and explained differences among Latinos with different national origins (e.g., Cauce & Domenech-Rodríguez, Chapter 1, this volume; Falicov, 1998). Although a number of the interventions have been conducted primarily with participants from one national origin, most developers have implied that the adaptations they made were appropriate for all Latino groups.

One notable exception was Cuento Therapy with Children (Costantino, Malgady, & Rogler, 1986). We decided to include Cuento Therapy with Children in our review, even though it is technically not a parenting intervention because it represents a unique model for developing culturally competent interventions. In Cuento Therapy, the presentation and discussion of folktales (*cuentos*) native to Puerto Rico were used to highlight and teach adaptive coping behavior to children. Clearly, Cuento Therapy would be more relevant to Puerto Rican children than to Latino children of other backgrounds.

Sources of Cultural Knowledge

This code refers to sources of information about a specific culture's values, customs, and beliefs. A premise underlying Latino-adapted parenting interventions is that the interventions account for important characteristics of Latino culture. Thus, knowing with confidence what these important characteristics are is key. We were interested in reviewing the sources of cultural knowledge intervention developers used to substantiate their adaptations. Developers of a number of interventions identified one or more of the often cited pan-Latino values of *simpatia, personalismo, familismo, respeto,* and *machismo* as the basis for an adaptation (for definitions of these values, see Cauce & Domenech-Rodríguez, Chapter 1, this volume). Frequently, however, no citations were provided to substantiate the validity of these values. When developers did cite literature, it tended to be impressionistic rather than empirical in nature. In some cases the source of cultural knowledge was identified as "experts," variously defined as either members of a Latino subgroup or people who had studied Latino culture. We also questioned the degree to which pan-Latino characteristics might be descriptive of particular Latinos living in specific contexts.

Obtaining particular cultural knowledge requires the collection of data from particular groups. Developers of several interventions did this (e.g., Los Niños Bien Educados, Family Effectiveness Training). For example, the developers of Los Niños Bien Educados (Alvy, 1994) conducted a preliminary study, integrating qualitative and quantitative data, to determine the salient parenting themes of two Latino population segments in southern California (a middle-income, high-acculturated Mexican American group and a low-income, low-acculturated Mexican immigrant group). Based on their results, the developers decided to accommodate the themes that were salient for the low-income, low-acculturated Mexican immigrant group (i.e., showing respect, having children who were *bien educados*). Similarly, Szapocznik, Scopetta, Aranalde, and Kurtines (1978) at the University of Miami (Coral Gables, FL) conducted a survey to identify pertinent characteristics of Cuban parents that included hierarchical family relations and preference for a pragmatic problem-solving approach to intervention. These authors then used these results to choose a therapeutic approach suited to these characteristics (i.e., Structural Family Therapy; Aponte & VanDeusen, 1981).

Another important source of cultural knowledge is feedback obtained from repeated implementation and evaluation of the intervention (using both quantitative and qualitative data). One example of this type of programmatic revision is the Fair Start for Children Program in which the family health workers decided to do away with evening visits because they discovered this was considered family time by many of the migrant farmworker families targeted by the intervention. Growing awareness of the isolated and impoverished nature of migrant life stimulated the family health workers to adapt the program further by helping mothers obtain food stamps, health clinic cards, and job training.

A scientifically rigorous process of gaining particular cultural knowledge in the service of intervention development is illustrated by two exemplary programs of research: the Hispanic Research Center at Fordham University (New York, NY; Cuento Therapy with Children) and the Center for Family Studies at the University of Miami (Family Effectiveness Training). An overview of these two programs of research (see Coatsworth, Szapocznik, Kurtines, & Santisteban, 1997) reveals admirable long-term strategies of conducting randomized controlled tests of adapted interventions and then using the results of these tests to revise the interventions to increase efficacy. The cultural knowledge gained is rich because the studies have analyzed the effects of a range of variables on outcome. For example, one study of Cuento Therapy found that its effectiveness was moderated by the gender of the child and the presence of the child's father in the household. In a controlled study of an intervention engagement process, the University of Miami group found that the process was effective with Latino parents from Central America but not with more acculturated Cuban parents (Santisteban et al., 1996).

An additional source of cultural knowledge that can be used to develop parenting interventions is assessing the values, needs, and beliefs of the actual recipients. When the results are used to immediately modify the intervention, this fosters a more collaborative relationship between providers and recipients as compared to the more typical complementary relationship. An even bigger step toward collaborative provider/recipient relationships would be for providers to involve future recipients of the intervention in all stages of intervention design. This kind of collaboration creates new channels of two-way communication that permit deeper knowledge of the local culture. We did not encounter an example of intervention developers using either of these more collaborative processes to gain cultural knowledge.

Change Objectives

This code refers to what the parenting intervention is attempting to change. The change objectives of parenting interventions typically focus on modifying parenting behaviors that mediate the effects of risk factors (e.g., poverty) on children's adjustment (e.g., depression, conduct problems). The challenge facing researchers is to find answers to the specificity question: What parenting behaviors, defined and implemented by what type of parent or person (e.g., Latino parents), used with what type of child, in what circumstances, have what kinds of child adjustment outcomes, according to whose report?

Understandably, the main change objectives of many of the universal/selective interventions we reviewed have been derived from Anglo parenting interventions. Most of the interventions (e.g., Raising Successful Children, Los Niños Bien Educados, Preparing for the Drug Free Years) appeared to have change objectives related to the major parenting dimensions that research with Anglos has shown are linked to positive child adjustment—that is, warmth, control, and involvement (Baumrind, 1995). A number of the interventions, particularly those aimed at parents of infants and toddlers (e.g., AVANCE, Houston Parent Education Program, Nueva Familia), sought to increase parents' knowledge of normal child development in order to encourage realistic expectations. Others tried to expand parents' understanding of factors contributing to misbehavior (e.g., Los Niños Bien Educados, Raising

Successful Children). Along similar lines, one of the change objectives of the Strengthening Families intervention was to increase parents' awareness of their teens' sexuality. Moreover, a number of parenting interventions had change objectives that addressed nonparenting variables such as parents' ability to calm themselves (e.g., Raising Successful Children), parents' social support (e.g., Nueva Familia), and parents' educational attainment (e.g., AVANCE). Finally, a few interventions had change objectives related to the specific goals of the interventions (e.g., Family Based Cardio Vascular Risk Reduction Education, Detroit AIDS Education Program).

There were, however, a number of ways in which the change objectives of universal/selective parenting interventions had been adapted for Latino families. One was to adapt change objectives to the conditions of recent immigrants. Several interventions addressed the various ways immigrants go about adjusting to living in the United States (Los Niños Bien Educados, Family Effectiveness Training). These interventions encouraged parents to consider taking a bicultural position in which they retained important aspects of their culture of origin (e.g., Spanish-language facility) and at the same time adopted aspects of their new host culture that would aid in their adjustment (e.g., English literacy). Some interventions provided information on child protection laws in the United States (e.g., Los Niños Bien Educados, Raising Successful Children). Others encouraged parents to explore their neighborhoods and locate sources of help, and presented good ways to approach these sources (e.g., Nuevo Familia).

Two notable interventions—Cuento Therapy with Children (a selective intervention) and Family Effectiveness training (an indicated intervention)—identified the resolution of culture-related conflict as a change objective. The idea underlying Cuento Therapy is that internal cultural conflict is the basis for symptomatic behavior in Puerto Rican children and adolescents (Malgady, Rogler, & Costantino, 1990). Accordingly, in later revisions of Cuento Therapy, developers used biographical stories of prominent Puerto Ricans in order to expose adolescents to role models of achievement. The change objectives were intended to increase adolescents' ethnic pride, strengthen positive ethnic identity, and develop adaptive ways of coping with the stresses of poverty, discrimination, and urban life. Another intervention—Family Effectiveness Training—was designed specifically for Latino families (primarily of Cuban origin) with acting-out adolescents in which the effects of immigration and acculturation were exacerbating family conflict (Szapocznik, Rio, Pérez-Vidal, Kurtines, & Santisteban, 1986). Generative research had found that parents and adolescents often acculturated at different rates and that this increased intergenerational conflict and adolescent conduct problems (Szapocznik & Kurtines, 1979). Therefore, the change objectives of Family Effectiveness Training were to restore intergenerational communication, reconstruct appropriate hierarchical structures in the family, and have parents and adolescents forge functional bicultural identities. Family Effectiveness Training and

Cuento Therapy highlight the issue of directly addressing culture-related conflict in parenting interventions for Latinos.

Finally, we noted that some of the interventions aimed at Latino parents may have contained change objectives that were potentially countercultural. Several of the language-translation-only adaptations of interventions (i.e., Active Parenting, STEP) were based on the Adlerian parenting ideas of Rudolf Dreikers (1964). Two prominent change objectives of these interventions were increasing parents' promotion of children's autonomous decision making and the use of democratic processes in family management. These change objectives appear to run counter to the widely acknowledged Latino family values of interdependency and respect for generational hierarchies. To the degree this is true, the fit between these interventions and many Latino parents might not be optimal and, thus, the efficacy of the interventions might be compromised. Research comparing the processes and outcomes of these interventions with more extensively adapted interventions would be needed to resolve this question.

Intervention Symbols and Concepts

This code refers to interventions' use of symbols, concepts, linguistic phrases, metaphors, and images that are part of the cultural background of the Latino parents participating in the intervention. The use of shared symbols and concepts have several important functions that can increase the effectiveness of interventions. First, use of shared symbols and concepts signals similarity between the interveners and the participants. Perceptions of similarity tend to reduce participants' anxiety, increase comfort, and facilitate the development of rapport and positive collaboration. Second, the use of shared symbols and concepts increases the accuracy and efficiency of communication between the parties. Third, in group-format interventions, shared symbols and concepts can assist in the growth of group cohesiveness.

At the most basic level, the use of Spanish as the language of the intervention provides a degree of shared symbols and concepts. However, the degree of shared meaning is influenced by the extent to which the intervener's dialect and use of Spanish is similar to that of the participants. Degree of shared meaning also is influenced by the amount of perceived similarity between the interveners' and participants' life experiences. For example, an intervener who had grown up in a migrant farmworker family would potentially be able to demonstrate a higher degree of shared meaning with parents who were migrant farmworkers than interveners who had not experienced this lifestyle. This sense of shared meaning might be accomplished by the interveners' use of special words and descriptions of experiences unique to this lifestyle.

There were several examples of the intentional use of language to avoid potential alienation of participants. For example, the Strengthening Families manual recommended that leaders use the more formal *usted* rather than the familiar *tu* until rapport had been established. Also, the MADRE intervention deliberately used the term "parent home educators" to refer to their home visitors rather than *consejeras* (counselors) in order to avoid the possible implication that the participants were deficient in some way.

Another type of adaptation of symbols was what we termed "appearance elements." These were adaptations such as including Latino-looking actors in videotape demonstrations of interactions, using pictures or illustrations of Latino-looking family members in intervention materials, and referring to foods commonly eaten by the particular Latino group and to customs and celebrations characteristic of that group when illustrating family interactions.

There were also interventions that demonstrated a deeper level of adaptation of concepts to fit Latino families. For example, the Raising Successful Children program intentionally highlighted the importance of parents (of fourth graders), maintaining their hierarchical leadership role in the family. The Los Niños Bien Educados' intervention featured the concepts of *respeto* and raising children to be *bien educados*. In addition, this intervention framed the parents' role as "teaching" their child to be *bien educados*, used the term "family expectations" to refer to parents' rules, and employed *dichos* (sayings) to encapsulate important parenting concepts.

Although not a parenting intervention, Cuento Therapy for Puerto Rican children and adolescents illustrates an unusually comprehensive use of culturally adapted symbols. The developers provided children and adolescents with stories featuring role models of adaptive emotional and behavioral functioning within American and Puerto Rican cultures. In order to make the characters more appealing, and thus more likely to be emulated, fictional characters were chosen that represented indigenous Puerto Rican folk heroes (Costantino & Malgady, 1996). Thus, in Cuento Therapy, the intervention change objectives (i.e., increasing adaptive coping) have been fully integrated with culturally relevant symbols (i.e., Puerto Rican folk heroes) and learning methods (i.e., the use of teaching stories).

Intervention Methods and Processes

This code refers to the methods, processes, or activities used to accomplish the intervention's change objectives. One category of adapted methods pertained to the processes used to recruit and retain participants. Even though successful recruitment and retention are critical components of intervention effectiveness (Mrazek & Haggerty, 1994), most of the interventions we reviewed did not report methods or rates. Recruitment, especially for universal and selective parenting interventions, is challenging for a number of reasons. First, the targeted populations are usually not experiencing the problem for which they are at risk. Thus, program developers have to provide sufficient incentives for parents in order to offset the perceived costs of participating (e.g., time, effort, self-consciousness). Also, group-format parent meetings in which strangers share family information may be alien to many recent immigrants. In addition, meetings held at schools might make some parents feel uncomfortable as a result of their own negative school experiences.

To counteract these barriers, a number of interventions used outreach recruitment strategies in which intervention representatives (sometimes people living in the targeted neighborhoods) visited homes or special events to make personal contact with targeted parents, explain the intervention, invite participation, and inquire about friends and family members who might also be interested (e.g., AVANCE, Houston Parent Education Program, Preparing for the Drug Free Years). One intervention (Raising Successful Children) directed recruiters to ask to speak to the male head of the household (if there was one) during these visits as a way of adapting to the possible *machismo* value orientation of the families.

In the Raising Successful Children intervention, the staff's personal contact with parents' during the completion of a somewhat lengthy pre-intervention assessment battery was linked to comparatively high participation rates (Dumka, Garza, Roosa, & Stoerzinger, 1997). The encouraging results indicated a possible advantage of using research procedures that include increased personal contact and contracting as part of the intervention recruitment strategy.

Szapocznik and his colleagues appear to have conducted the only controlled study of the effectiveness of different intervention recruitment and retention methods (Szapocznik et al., 1988). In Strategic Structural Systems Engagement (SSSE), recruiters endeavored to engage families by changing the family interactions supporting resistance to participating in treatment. To accomplish this, recruiters affirmed parents' expertise about their family and that the therapy could not be successful without them. Recruiters used the culturally prevalent theme of mothers' self-sacrifice for the family to motivate mothers to convince other family members to attend treatment. Recruiters also supported parents' need to view themselves as leading their family into new patterns (rather than normalizing adolescent rebellion) and emphasized that therapy would be a no-nonsense problem-solving activity (as contrasted to a growth-enhancing process). Additionally, recruiters assessed family interactions and various family members' willingness to participate in the intervention. Recruiters also provided advice about how to persuade reluctant family members to attend, spoke directly with reluctant family members, and, if necessary, made home visits and convened influential family members for discussions. Results have shown that SSSE was significantly more effective in engaging Latino substance-abusing youth and their families in treatment than engagement as usual (Szapocznik et al., 1988). In a more recent study (Santisteban et al., 1996), SSSE was not found to be effective with more acculturated Cuban parents exhibiting resistance, perhaps because these Cuban parents held to the more individualistic orientation of the mainstream culture (i.e., preferring hospitalization or individual treatment for the drug-abusing youth rather than family therapy) and were more skillful in manipulating the mental health system to accommodate their orientation. This finding highlights the importance of accounting for acculturation status when designing recruitment methods.

Another category of adapted intervention methods involved providing auxiliary services to remove barriers to participation and, at the same time, honor the needs and preferences of many Latino families. For example, providing child care removes a barrier to participation and at the same time permits the whole family to come to the site of the intervention together (e.g., Raising Successful Children program). Providing a meal for the whole family addresses the barrier of parents needing to stay home to prepare a meal for other family members and, at the same time, provides an opportunity for parents to socialize in a relaxed atmosphere. Using an in-home format or combining group and in-home elements (e.g., Houston Parent Education Program, MADRE Parent Education Program) reduces the need for transportation and is preferred by some segments of Latino parents (Powell, Zambrana, & Silva-Palacios, 1990). Facilitating access to English classes, housing, job training, and employment can increase the engagement of low-income immigrants (e.g., MADRE Parent Education Program).

Some interventions adapted intervention activities. For example, Los Niños Bien Educados begins with an exercise that provides information about parents' levels of acculturation. Parents also are invited to decide what comprises *bien* and *mal educados* behaviors and are given an opportunity to increase the personal application of the material and show mutual support at the end of each session as participants direct their own *platicas* (friendly discussions). Unstructured socializing is encouraged during a *cafecito* (coffee) break in each session.

Family Effectiveness Training (Szapocznik, Río, Pérez-Vidal, Kurtines, & Santisteban, 1986) illustrates one of the most comprehensive adaptations of intervention methods to fit Cuban American families. The developers had previously conducted generative research that found that Cuban Americans (as compared to Anglo Americans) had a more present-oriented as compared to future-oriented time orientation, related to others more in terms of hierarchical position, and had a more interdependent family orientation as compared to an individualistic orientation (Szapocznik, Scopetta, & King, 1978). To accommodate these characteristics, the developers chose a structural-family-therapy approach (Aponte & VanDeusen, 1981). In the structural-family-therapy approach, the therapist sees the family as a whole, gains entry to and joins with the family system, temporarily assumes the leadership role in the family hierarchy, takes responsibility for change, and actively directs the family to communicate in ways that clarify roles, boundaries, and hierarchies. Thus, the careful matching of the intervention methods with the cultural characteristics of particular Cuban American participants was seen to be instrumental in the efficacy of Family Effectiveness Training (Szapocznik et al., 1986).

Intervention Evaluation

Although a comprehensive analysis of the quality of the evaluations of the parenting interventions is beyond the scope of this chapter, we did code for the main evaluation methods. It is important to note, however, that our coding in Table 9.2 is based on whether the adapted Spanish-language version had been evaluated using the particular evaluation design. In some interventions (e.g., Preparing for the Drug Free Years), the Anglo version of the intervention had been subjected to evaluation, whereas the Spanish-language adaptation had not.

The majority of interventions we examined reported conducting some form of evaluation of program effects. However, the strengths of the evaluation designs varied greatly, with the average level of rigor being on the low side. The most rudimentary level of evaluation consisted of collecting participants' reactions to and satisfaction with the intervention. The next level of rigor consisted of assessing the achievement of intervention objectives using pretest and/or posttest data from the intervention group (e.g., Project Profile Niños Especiales). At the highest level of rigor, there were several evaluations that used random assignment, comparison groups, and pretest and posttest data, and measured child adjustment outcomes (e.g., Houston Parent Education Program, CEDEN, Family Effectiveness Training). There were only a few interventions that collected data on participant recruitment and retention rates (e.g., Family Effectiveness Training, Raising Successful Children).

Although there were results that supported the efficacy of Latino-adapted parenting interventions, we identified a number of additional threats to the reliability of these intervention results. For example, little attention seems to have been paid to establishing that the Spanish versions of the English measures of change objectives were equivalent. The small sample sizes used in many of the evaluations reduced the power to discern statistical differences. The critical research question pertaining to Latino-adapted parenting interventions is: Are adapted interventions superior to nonadapted interventions? We found only two evaluations that compared the effects of a culturally adapted intervention to a roughly equivalent one that was not culturally adapted (Cuento Therapy with Children, Family Based Cardiovascular Risk Reduction Education). The results of these studies were mixed and thus are inconclusive regarding the superiority of the culturally adapted version.

SUMMARY AND DISCUSSION

Overall, the extent of the efforts that have gone into developing parenting interventions to make them suitable and accessible to Latino families, particularly low-acculturated immigrant families, is impressive. These interventions offer an opportunity for participants to be exposed to novel (sometimes empirically supported) parenting beliefs and practices related to American majority culture, to demonstrate and share their concerns for their children's successful adjustment, and to receive emotional support in coping with stress related to parenting or other demands. What follows is a summary of our conclusions regarding progress that has been made.

Progress and Conclusions

1. The degree to which parenting interventions adapted for Latino families were directly connected to knowledge of the culture of origin or to local cultural conditions (i.e., were culturally competent) spanned a broad range, with most interventions appearing to demonstrate fairly rudimentary connections. The cultural knowledge cited as a basis for many intervention adaptations has been borrowed predominantly from literature purporting to describe Latino culture in general or from a few consultants considered to be knowledgeable about Latino culture in general. This knowledge is de-contextualized because it is separated from the environments (i.e., locations and interactional contexts) that influence its expression. De-contextualized knowledge represents a relatively ambiguous and potentially misleading base on which to design culturally competent interventions for particular Latinos living in a particular place. Thus the cultural competence of the majority of interventions reviewed for this study is constrained by the apparent lack of attention and adaptation to local cultural conditions.

2. At the same time, translating the intervention materials into Spanish and using fluently bilingual personnel to implement the intervention (i.e., what we termed "language-translation-only adaptations") represent worthwhile means of making parenting interventions accessible to monolingual Spanish-speaking Latinos.

3. Increased specification of the targeted parent group usually reduces the fit of the intervention for other groups. For example, including an emphasis on acculturation stress or cultural conflict for recent Latino immigrants might be irrelevant to or possibly even alienate other Latinos who do not acknowledge these tensions.

4. There has been relatively less attention devoted to developing universal/selective interventions for Latino parents of teenagers compared to interventions for parents of pre-teenagers.

5. When studies to gain knowledge of the cultural group were conducted, these studies were most likely not conducted with people who would actually be participating in the intervention in a certain location. We did not encounter any reports of interventions that conducted needs assessments with actual participants and actually altered the intervention to accommodate those needs. Further, we did not find any reports of potential participants collaborating with developers in designing an intervention.

6. Programmatic revision over multiple implementations permitted developers to adapt the intervention to the changing demographic characteristics of Latinos in particular locations.

7. Adapting the look and feel of the intervention to be inclusive of Latino-oriented symbols and concepts represents a worthwhile and efficient means of communicating inclusiveness and avoiding potential alienation.

8. Social learning–based cognitive-behavioral skills acquisition seemed to be the predominant change methodology employed by the majority of interventions reviewed. Two of the most substantially adapted interventions, however, relied on narrative (Cuento Therapy with Children) and experiential (Family Effectiveness Training) change methods rather than skills acquisition methods.

9. When the targeted Latino group is low-income, the value of the intervention to the participants is increased when the intervention includes auxiliary services or connections to auxiliary services that address practical and urgent needs.

10. Based on participation, it would be more accurate to call the great majority of the interventions we reviewed mothering interventions rather than parenting interventions. With rare exceptions (e.g., AVANCE Fatherhood, Nueva Familia for fathers) interventions have not addressed the unique contributions of fathers to parenting in Latino families or even studied the parenting beliefs or intervention preferences of Latino fathers (for examples of studies of fathers, see Dumka, Gonzales, Wood, & Formosa, 1998; Powell, 1995).

11. Most parenting interventions focus on changes in the interactions within the family. Relatively few (e.g., AVANCE, Nueva Familia, Los Niños Bien Educados) attend to changing interactions between members of the family subsystem and other subsystems in the family's environment (e.g., school system, employment systems, health-care systems).

12. There are relatively few scientifically rigorous evaluations of Latino-adapted parenting interventions. For the most part, this research has been outcome oriented as compared to process oriented. Little research attention has been given to recruitment and retention of targeted participants in parenting interventions. Most important, there have also been very few studies comparing culturally adapted and nonadapted versions of parenting interventions.

Prospects and Recommendations

Given the current lack of evidence for the superiority of culturally adapted parenting interventions compared to nonculturally adapted interventions, it is not known which kinds of adaptations contribute most to intervention efficacy and efficiency. For example, we do not know whether comprehensive cultural adaptations are necessary or whether more modest adaptations (e.g., adequate language translation, incorporation of some symbols that communicate respect and inclusion, avoidance of signs of disrespect or exclusion, use of group leaders capable of making cultural translations) achieve sufficiently enhanced outcomes. In light of this lack of knowledge, we venture the following recommendations aimed at enhancing parenting interventions for Latino families.

1. Culturally competent interventions are those that are adapted to accommodate valid knowledge of both the culture of origin and local cultural conditions. The most important area of improvement for Latino-adapted parenting interventions is adaptation to local contexts and conditions. This requires that intervention developers pay more attention to assessing local needs and contexts.

2. One way to accomplish this would be for developers to incorporate more opportunities for collaborating with participants in the actual design of interventions.

3. Moreover, systematic revision of interventions in the same location represents an effective process for adapting interventions to the local cultural ecology. However, systematic revision requires that agencies are capable of sustaining the availability of interventions over time. Sustainability, again, is dependent on intervention costs.

4. Researchers need to conduct cost–benefit analyses in order to begin determining the efficiency of various degrees of intervention for different categories of risk (i.e., universal, selective, indicated). Intervention costs (in terms of money and expertise) affect the disseminability of an intervention and the ability of sponsoring agencies to sustain the intervention over time; the lower the cost, the higher the disseminability and sustainability. For example, the video-based Active Parenting intervention reduces local expertise costs because less training is necessary for fewer group leaders compared to the situation of live leaders presenting the material contained on the videotapes.

5. More attention needs to be given to highly disseminable, empirically based parenting intervention formats adapted for Latino families, particularly for in-home personal use (e.g., videotape, videodisk). Such formats can reduce delivery and expertise costs as well as increase access by reducing participant opportunity costs (e.g., having to leave work early to attend a regularly scheduled parent meeting).

6. Designing Latino-adapted parenting interventions so that certain elements are considered core components (i.e., elements considered important and applicable to nearly all Latino families) and modifiable or optional components (e.g., elements that address particular local needs) represents a viable option for addressing the specificity/generalizability issue.

7. Intervention researchers need to pay more attention to the participation of Latino fathers. Fathers and male partners typically are influential members of family systems. They influence child development directly through their interactions with children and indirectly through their interactions with mothers and through their contributions to household maintenance. Powell (1995) recommends ensuring that program staff are committed to recruiting Latino fathers, being sensitive to the interdependency of husband and wife engagement in an intervention—including unique and respectful ways for fathers to participate in intervention activities—and covering content of particular interest to Latino fathers.

8. Parenting interventions for Latino families need to address inter-parental conflict, particularly as the conflict relates to parenting. Inter-parental conflict over parenting or other issues has been shown to have a negative impact on children's adjustment, whereas parental agreement over child rearing (including parental role expectations) appears to contribute to consistency in discipline and consequently children's mental health (Dadds & Powell, 1991; Jouriles, Farris, & McDonald, 1991). When only one partner of a parenting couple participates in a parenting intervention, the potential influence of the intervention is necessarily limited compared to when both partners participate. Moreover, interventions in which only one partner participates can potentially increase differences and thus conflicts between partners. This potential is even higher when interventions focus on changing parenting behaviors related to acculturation to the majority culture and sex roles. In two-parent households in which both parents participate in a parenting intervention, they are exposed to a common experience and material. This common experience provides an opportunity for increasing inter-parental agreement and consistency in approach. If intervention material precipitates disagreement between partners, these disagreements can be addressed rather than function to oppose intervention goals in ways unknown to the interveners.

9. Conducting research on recruitment and retention of Latino participants is essential for determining intervention efficacy and cost–benefit ratios. Recruitment and retention should be approached as an integral part of the intervention rather than a separate component and included as elements of evaluations of intervention costs and benefits

10. More research attention should be given to interventions targeting parents of teenagers in Latino families (of varying acculturation, income, and education levels). Adolescence is a time when intergenerational and cultural tensions can exacerbate each other to escalate risk for problems.

11. Intervention developers should explore alternatives to skills acquisition–oriented change methods (e.g., experiential, narrative, imagistic).

12. Interventions conducted with low-income parents should include the availability of information about resources that address participants' pressing practical needs

13. Parenting interventions aimed at enhancing children's success need to include methods for helping parents increase their ability to manage interactions among parent, child, peer, and especially school subsystems.

14. More attention needs to be given to parenting intervention process research. Outcome research evaluates the outcome of the intervention as a whole (the big "O" outcome), either immediately at post-intervention and/or at some follow-up date. Process research evaluates the immediate effects of within-session intervention activities through the assessment of little "o" outcomes either within the session or immediately after the session. Research on the contributions of common factors to psychotherapy outcome suggest that the quality of the relationship between interveners and participants' and hope

and expectancy might be good candidates for little "o" outcome variables in parenting intervention research (Asay & Lambert, 1999). This type of process research could address a question such as: Does the use of a participatory role-play exercise result in higher parental confidence in implementing a parenting skill than a videotape demonstration of a successful implementation? Another area for process research is the investigation of incremental effects of including parent–child interaction activities as a component of parenting interventions (i.e., immediate practice opportunities).

15. Research is needed on the contribution of intervener characteristics (e.g., warmth, structuring skills) and intervener training (e.g., for cultural sensitivity, group leadership) to intervention outcome.

16. Earlier, we referred to the role group leaders can play as informal cultural translators of the intervention. This implies that the cultural competence of interventions adapted for Latinos would be enhanced by training group leaders to fulfill the role of cultural translator more effectively.

17. Recently, evidence has been accumulating for what has been termed the "acculturation paradox," that is, the more acculturated some immigrant children become, the worse they seem to perform on some indices of adjustment (e.g., school achievement; Rumbaut, 1999a). This could be because many Latino immigrant children live in poor neighborhoods and thus may be acculturating to the American culture of poverty rather than to American middle-class culture. However, an implication of this acculturation paradox is that children's retention of a positive ethnic identity and adaptive cultural practices may function as protective factors in their development (Rumbaut, 1999b). These findings imply that parenting interventions for immigrant families might be strengthened by promoting particular dimensions of bicultural competency. This intriguing angle merits the serious efforts of researchers to specify resiliency factors and formulate interventions to strengthen them.

Parenting interventions represent a potential source of support and guidance for Latino parents coping with the daunting task of raising children in a world changing at a dizzying rate. This is particularly so for low-income Latino parents experiencing the incremental stressors of poverty, dangerous neighborhoods, and adapting to a foreign culture. Addressing the recommendations just presented will help ensure that Latino families have fair access to the benefits of interventions that can increase the resiliency of future generations.

AUTHORS' NOTE

Work on this chapter was supported, in part, by grants 5-P30-MH39246 to support a Preventive Intervention Research Center and 5-T32-MH18387 to support training in prevention research, and the Cowden Fellowship program of the Department of Family and Human Development at Arizona State

University. The authors gratefully acknowledge Mark Roosa for comments on the draft of this chapter.

REFERENCES

Alvy, K. (1994). *Parent training today: A social necessity.* Studio City, CA: Center for the Improvement of Childcaring.

American Guidance Service (1991). *Systematic training for effective parenting.* Circle Pines, MN: Author.

Aponte, J. F., & Crouch, R. T. (1995). The changing ethnic profile of the United States. In J. F. Aponte, R. Y. Rivers, & J. Wohl (Eds.), *Psychological interventions and cultural diversity* (pp. 1–18). Boston: Allyn & Bacon.

Aponte, H. J., & VanDeusen, J. M. (1981). Structural family therapy. In A. S. Gurman & D. P. Kniskern (Eds.), *Handbook of family therapy* (pp. 310–360). New York: Brunner/Mazel.

Arocena, M., Adams, E., & Davis, P. (1992). CEDEN's Parent–Child Program: A fair start for Mexican-origin children in Texas. In M. Larner, R. Halpern, & O. Harkavy (Eds.), *Fair Start for Children: Lessons learned from seven demonstration projects* (pp. 68–90). New Haven, CT: Yale University Press.

Asay, T. P., & Lambert, M. J. (1999). The empirical case for the common factors in therapy: Quantitative findings. In M. L. Hubble, B. L. Duncan, & S. D. Miller (Eds.), *The heart and soul of change: What works in therapy* (pp. 10–55). Washington, DC: American Psychological Association.

Baumrind, D. (1995). *Child maltreatment and optimal caregiving in social contexts.* New York: Garland.

Bavolek, S. J. (1985). [*Activity manual for parents*]. Park City, UT: Family Development Research.

Bavolek, S. J. (1995). *Crianza con carino: Programma para padres e hijos. Manual de actividades para los padres.* Park City, UT: Family Development Resources, Inc.

Bernal, G., Bonilla, J., & Bellido, C. (1995). Ecological validity and cultural sensitivity for outcome research: Issues for the cultural adaptation and development of psychosocial treatments with Hispanics. *Journal of Abnormal Child Psychology, 23,* 67–83.

Braver, S. L. (1989). Selection issues in children of divorce interventions. IN I. N. Sandler, M. W. Roosa, S. A. Wolchick, S. G. West, & S. L. Braver (Eds.), *Center for the prevention of child and family stress* (pp. 112–129). NIMH Grant Proposal No. MH39246. Washington, DC: National Institute of Mental Health.

Bronfenbrenner, U. (1977). Toward an experimental ecology of human development. *American Psychologist, 32,* 513–531.

Brooks-Gunn, J., & Duncan, G. J. (1997). The effects of poverty on children. *The Future of Children, 7,* 56–71.

Bruder, M., Anderson, R., Schutz, C., & Caldera, M. (1991). Project Profile Niños Especiales Program: A culturally sensitive program. *Journal of Early Intervention, 15,* 268–277.

Castro, F. G., Cota, M. K., & Vega, S. C. (1999). Health promotion in Latino populations: A sociocultural model for program planning, development, and evaluation. In R. M. Huff & Kline, M. V. (Eds.), *Promoting health in multicultural populations: A handbook for practitioners.* Thousand Oaks, CA: Sage.

Coatsworth, J. D., Szapocznik, J., Kurtines, W., & Santisteban, D. A. (1997). Culturally competent psychosocial interventions with antisocial problem behavior in Hispanic youths. In D. M. Stoff & J. Breiling (Eds.), *Handbook of antisocial behavior* (pp. 395–404). New York: Wiley.

Comas-Díaz, L. (1995). Puerto Ricans and sexual child abuse. In L. Fontes (Ed.), *Sexual abuse in nine North American cultures*. Thousand Oaks, CA: Sage.

Costantino, G., & Malgady, R. (1996). Culturally sensitive treatment: Cuento and hero/heroine modeling therapies for Hispanic children and adolescents. In E. Hibbs & P. Jensen (Eds.), *Psychosocial treatments for child and adolescent disorders: Empirically based strategies for clinical practice* (pp. 639–669). Washington, DC: American Psychological Association.

COSSMHO (1990). *Strengthening familes: A curriculum for Hispanic familes*. Washington, DC: COSSMHO—The National Coalition of Hispanic Health and Human Services Organizations.

Costantino, G., Malgady, R., & Rogler, L. (1986). Cuento Therapy: A culturally sensitive modality for Puerto Rican children. *Journal of Consulting and Clinical Psychology, 54*, 639–645.

Dadds, M. R., & Powell, M. B. (1991). The relationship of interparental conflict and global marital adjustment to aggression, anxiety, and immaturity in aggressive and nonclinic children. *Journal of Abnormal Child Psychology, 19*, 553–567.

De Carpio, A., Carpio-Cedraro, F., & Anderson, L. (1990). Hispanic families: Learning and teaching about AIDS: A participatory approach at the community level. *Hispanic Journal of Behavioral Sciences, 12*, 165–176.

Delgado, M. (1978). Program development: A Hispanic foster parents program. *Child Welfare, 7*, 427–431.

Dreikers, R. (1964). *Children: the challenge*. New York: Hawthorn Books.

Dumka, L. E. (1994). *Raising Successful Children Program: Group leader manual*. Tempe: Program for Prevention Research, Arizona State University.

Dumka, L. E., Garza, C. A., Roosa, M. W., & Stoerzinger, H. D. (1997). Recruitment and retention of high-risk families into a preventive parent training intervention. *Journal of Primary Prevention, 18*, 25–39.

Dumka, L. E., Gonzales, N. A., Wood, J. L., & Formoso, D. (1998). Using qualitative methods to develop contextually relevant measures and preventive interventions: An illustration. *American Journal of Community Psychology, 26*, 605–637.

Dumka, L. E., Roosa, M. W., & Jackson, K. M. (1997). Risk, conflict, mothers' parenting, and children's adjustment in low-income, Mexican immigrant and Mexican American families. *Journal of Marriage and the Family, 59*, 309–323.

Elder, G. H., Eccles, J. S., Ardelt, M., & Lord, S. (1995). Inner-city parents under economic pressure: Perspective on the strategies of parenting. *Journal of Marriage and the Family, 57*, 771–784.

Falicov, C. J. (1998). *Latino families in therapy*. NY: Guilford.

Feldman, J. M., & Kazdin, A. E. (1995). Parent management training for oppositional and conduct problem children. *Clinical Psychologist, 48*, 3–4.

Forehand, R., & Kotchick, B. A. (1996). Cultural diversity: A wake-up call for parent training. *Behavior Therapy, 27*, 187–206.

Gordon, R. (1987). An operational classification of disease prevention. In J. A. Steinberg & M. M. Silverman (Eds.), *Preventing mental disorders: A research perspective* (pp. 20–26). DHHS Publication No. ADM-87-1492). Washington, DC: U.S. Government Printing Office.

Harachi, T. W., Catalano, R. F., & Hawkins, J. D. (1997). Effective recruitment for parenting programs within ethnic minority communities. *Child and Adolescent Social Work Journal, 14*, 23–39.

Hawkins, J. D., & Catalano, R. F. (2001). *Preparing for the drug free years.* South Deerfield, MA: Channing Bete Company.

Hayes, P. A. (1995). Multicultural applications of cognitive–behavioral therapy. *Professional Psychology: Research and Practice, 26*, 309–315.

Herrerias, C. (1988). Prevention of child abuse and neglect in the Hispanic community: The MADRE education program. *Journal of Primary Prevention, 9*, 104–117.

Johnson, D. L. (1990). The Houston Parent–Child Development Center project: Disseminating a viable program for enhancing at-risk families. *Preventive in Human Services, 7*, 89–108.

Jouriles, E. N., Farris, A. M., & McDonald, R. (1991). Marital functioning and child behavior: Measuring the specific aspects of the marital relationship. *Advances in Family Intervention, Assessment, and Theory, 5*, 25–46.

Malgady, R., Rogler, L., & Costantino, G. (1990). Culturally sensitive psychotherapy for Puerto Rican children and adolescents: A program of treatment outcome research. *Journal of Consulting and Clinical Psychology, 58*, 704–712.

MELD. (1994). *Nueva familia.* Minneapolis, MN: Author.

Mrazek, P. J., & Haggerty, R. J. (1994). *Reducing risks for mental disorders: Frontiers for preventive intervention research.* Washington, DC: National Academy Press.

Myers, H. F., Alvy, K. T., Arrington, A., Richardson, M. A., Marigna, M., Main, M., & Newcomb, M. (1992). The impact of a parent training program on inner-city African-American families. *Journal of Community Psychology, 10*, 132–147.

Nader, P., Sallis, J., Abramson, I., Broyles, S., Patterson, T., Senn, K., Rupp, J., & Nelson, J. (1992). Family-based cardiovascular risk reduction education among Mexican and Anglo Americans. *Family Community Health, 15*, 57–74.

Office of Juvenile Justice and Delinquency Prevention & University of Utah. (1998). *Strengthening America's families: Model programs for delinquency prevention.* Salt Lake City: University of Utah.

Popkin, M. H. (1999). *Padres Activos de Hoy.* Atlanta, GA: Active Parenting.

Powell, D. R. (1995). Including Latino fathers in parent education and support programs. In R. E. Zambrana (Ed.), *Understanding Latino families* (pp. 85–196). Thousand Oaks, CA: Sage.

Powell, D., Zambrana, R., & Silva-Palacios, V. (1990). Designing culturally responsive parent programs: A comparison of low-income Mexican and Mexican-American mothers' preferences. *Family Relations, 39*, 298–304.

Prieto Bayard, M., & Baker, B. L. (1986). Parent training for Spanish-speaking families with a retarded child. *Journal of Community Psychology, 14*, 134–143.

Rogers-Weise, M. R. (1992). A critical review of parent training research. *Psychology in Schools, 29*, 229–236.

Rumbaut, R. G. (1999a). Assimilation and its discontents: Ironies and paradoxes. In J. DeWind, C. Hirschman, & P. Kasinitz (Eds.), *The Handbook of International Migration: The American experience* (pp. 172–195). New York: Russell Sage Foundation.

Rumbaut, R. G. (1999b). Profiles in resilience: Educational achievement and ambition among children of immigrants in southern California. In R. Taylor (Ed.),

Resilience across contexts: Family, work, culture, and community (pp. 257–294). Mahwah, NJ: Erlbaum.

Sanders, M. R. (1992). New directions in behavioral family interventions with children: From clinical management to prevention. *New Zealand Journal of Psychology, 21,* 25–36.

Santisteban, J., Szapocznik, J., Pérez-Vidal, A., Kurtines, W. M., Murray, E. J., & LaPierre, A. (1996). Efficacy of intervention for engaging youth and families into treatment and some variables that may contribute to differential effectiveness. *Journal of Family Psychology, 10,* 35–44.

Sung, K., Kim, J., & Yawkey, T. (1997). Puerto Rican parents' understanding of their young children's development: P.I.A.G.E.T. program impacts on family involvement in culturally and linguistically diverse populations. *Psychology in the Schools, 34,* 347–353.

Szapocznik, J., & Kutines, W. (1979). Acculturation, biocultralism and adjustment among Cuban Americans. In A. Padilla (Ed.), *Psychological dimensions on the acculturation process: Theory, models, and some new findings.* (pp. 139–159). Boulder, CO: Westview Press.

Szapocznik, J., Pérez-Vidal, A., Brickman, A. L., Foote, F. H., Santisteban, D., Hervis, O., & Kurtines, W. (1988). Engaging adolescent drug abusers and their families in treatment: A strategic structural systems approach. *Journal of Consulting and Clinical Psychology, 56,* 552–557.

Szapocznik, J., Río, A., Pérez-Vidal, A., Kurtines, W., & Santisteban, D. (1986). Family effectiveness training for Hispanic families. In H. P. Lefley, & P. B. Pendersen. (Eds.), *Cross cultural training for mental health professionals.* Springfield, IL: Charles C. Thomas.

Szapocznik, J., Scopetta, M. A., Aranalde, A. M., & Kurtines, W. M. (1978). Cuban value structure: Treatment implications. *Journal of Consulting and Psychology, 46,* 961–970.

Szapocznik, J., Scopetta, M. A., & King, O. E. (1978). Theory and practice in matching treatment to the special characteristics and problems of Cuban immigrants. *Journal of Community Psychology, 6,* 112–122.

U.S. Census Bureau. (1996, May). Resident population of the United States: Middle series projections, 1996–2000, by sex, race, and Hispanic origin, with median age. *Current Population Reports,* Series P25–1130. Washington, DC: Government Printing Office.

Walker, T. B., Rodriguez, G. G., Johnson, D. L., & Cortez, C. P. (1995). AVANCE parent–child program. In S. Smith (Ed.), *Two generation programs for families in poverty: A new intervention strategy; Vol. 9. Advances in developmental psychology* (pp. 67–90). Norwood, NJ: Ablex.

Winters-Smith, C., & Larner, M. (1992). The Fair Start Program: Outreach to migrant farmworker families. In M. Larner, R. Halpern, & O. Harkavy (Eds.), *Fair Start for Children: Lessons learned from seven demonstration projects* (pp. 46–67). New Haven, CT: Yale University Press.

10

Learning from Latino Parents: Combining Etic and Emic Approaches to Designing Interventions

Luis H. Zayas and Lisseth Rojas-Flores

INTRODUCTION

With the recent growth of the U.S. Latino population has also come greater Latino diversity than ever before. This growth raises many important questions for behavioral science researchers and providers of psychological, developmental, and social services. Some of the basic questions deal with matters of understanding and describing the child socialization patterns of Latino parents. What do we know about the socio-emotional and cognitive development of the children of Latino immigrants? How do the different Latino groups raise their children? What are the unique patterns of child-rearing beliefs, values, and behaviors that distinguish them from one another? What commonalities do they share in how they raise their children?

For those of us interested in service provision and service research, applied questions emerge. How do we organize our knowledge about interventions for parents and children in a manner that brings the best that we have to offer to meet the unique needs of Latino families? What adjustments do we have to make to interventions that exist in order to meet the needs of these diverse groups while providing them in a culturally sensitive manner? When creating specific interventions to help Latino parents and their children, we must also be responsive to the cultural characteristics of the groups.

In this chapter, we consider conceptual factors that can be taken into account in designing research and developmental interventions for Latino families. In particular, we propose that using emic approaches to inform our research and service systems leads us to learn from Latino parents and to design culturally congruent and effective interventions. Developmental researchers and children and family services providers can merge emic approaches with extant empirical and theoretical knowledge of child socialization and effective parenting interventions—etic experiences—in order to develop applications for Latino parents in the United States. For definitional clarity, the emic–etic distinction refers to culture-specific (emic) or culture-general (etic) perspectives (López, 1997; Tanaka-Matsumi & Draguns, 1997). The chapter begins with some theoretical issues on culture and child rearing and examines past approaches in the development of treatment services for children and adolescents that reached into families' cultures to inform the design of the interventions. The chapter concludes with examples drawn from the authors' experiences of how emic and etic approaches can be used together in research and in the modification of existing interventions.

STUDYING THE ROLE OF LATINO CULTURES ON CHILD REARING

A discussion of Latino families and children in the United States poses great opportunities to consider the varied ways that culture influences such issues as family structure; child rearing; parental, gender, and generational roles in families; and other characteristics of family functioning. We can focus on cultural influences on how recently immigrated or later-generation Latino parents socialize their children. In this chapter, we define culture in the manner proposed by Herkovits (1948) and Rohner (1984), which emphasizes the influence of groups of people who create a system of meanings about their experience. Groups then share these meanings. From the meanings ascribed to particular behaviors emerge other specific behaviors that embody these meanings and that link persons to their groups. When it comes to parenting young children, parents form their assumptions about child care and development from "cultural models that set the prevailing standards of 'common sense' in their local communities" (LeVine, Miller, Richman, & LeVine, 1996, p. 254). These assumptions, which include values, beliefs, and parenting practices, have often endured for many generations and are considered vital elements of what parents must transmit to children so that their children's accommodation within the family and survival within society are ensured (Harrison, Wilson, Pine, Chan, & Buriel, 1990).

Culture, Child Rearing, and Psychological Science

When it comes to psychologically relevant variables that constitute culture, Triandis et al. (1980) focus on "subjective culture," which, in the case of Latino parents and children, regards family roles, affective styles between parents and children, social and family communication patterns, the communication of emotions, and other culturally specific issues. In this subjective culture, developmentalists are interested in how Latinos parent their children, the degrees of personal control parents wish to see their children display, how much individual autonomy children may have at certain ages, and how individualism can be most "appropriately" demonstrated. The influence of this subjective culture is evident in nearly every activity parents engage in with their children.

While race, ethnicity, and social class play important roles in psychological and social phenomena, we emphasize culture in this chapter because of its "local" implications. By local, we mean those beliefs and behaviors that persons of a particular group subscribe to. Social class has profound implications, as we know, but for this discussion we are holding it constant. We call culture "local" because it may play a more salient role than race in some places than in others. Whereas race plays a preeminent role in the individual's psychology especially when the social context is considered, local culture influences behavioral repertoires and their meanings. For example, being Black is genetically determined, and physiological features may be similar across cultural groups. Therefore, Black persons of Honduran, Cuban, or American background may have similar physiology. However, local culture—Honduran, Cuban, or American—will determine the behavioral aspects we exhibit more than race itself. The culture in which persons were reared will have a distinct impact on how they raise their children, how they instruct girls versus boys, how they demonstrate affection toward children, and other expectations they have of their children. However, the children's and parents' race and the societal reaction toward their race affects child rearing because parents want to equip their children with behaviors that will guarantee the children's survival (Harrison et al., 1990).

Culture is, therefore, a key issue in our discussion of child socialization. By focusing on culture, rather than race or ethnicity, we may be better able to respond to Betancourt and López's (1993) concern that a major problem with American psychology has been its placement of culture in "at best a secondary place" (p. 629) in research and theories. Too often psychology and developmental sciences have relied on universal theories of human behavior created largely from observations of mainstream cultural groups. These theories are then applied to groups that were not observed in the course of developing the theory. Theory-driven research is then conducted using conceptual assumptions that did not include the groups now being observed or employing instruments that were not tested on some ethnic and cultural groups. This practice is a serious matter because using universal models not built from knowledge of other than mainstream groups who hold economic, social, legal, and scientific power places other groups as outsiders or, worse, as deviants. Sue (1999) points out that the emphasis on internal validity in psychological science frequently results in a lack of emphasis on external validity, and that this emphasis harms psychology by discouraging ethnic minority research.

Yet, those of us who are interested in ethnic and cultural minority populations also make a common error, that of failing "to identify the specific aspects of culture and related variables that are thought to influence behavior"

(Betancourt & López, 1993, p. 629). While the study of culture has been taken up by cross-cultural researchers and less so by mainstream researchers, we frequently do not attend to what is "cultural" about the research we do, or, for that matter, to what is "cultural" about culturally competent treatment or services. Often, our research examines two or more cultural, ethnic, or racial groups on some psychological dimension or parenting behavior. Then, when we discover differences among these groups, we attribute the differences to their cultures. Although we learn that culture may be related to psychological or parenting phenomena, we are still not yet at the point of articulating with precision what the specific cultural elements are that account for the relationship between a culture and a particular parenting behavior (Betancourt & López, 1993).

Latino Cultures and Latino Parenting

The advantage of looking at child socialization in U.S. Latino families, it seems to us, is that we can observe specific parental behaviors and link them to cultural meanings associated with the behaviors. We can not only infer what the link is through naturalistic observations but we can also ask the parents directly about the factors that motivate their parenting, such as the values that guide their thinking and attitudes, how they think their local culture (of origin or of adoption) influences them to rear their children in this manner (Harrison et al., 1990) or what the difference is in their behavior toward a child based on the child's age or gender. As the observed children develop and demonstrate the capacity for responding accurately to questions posed at age-appropriate levels (e.g., adolescents), we can also ask children what they think about their parents' behavior. A natural approach is to have Latino parents inform us about the "what" and "why" of parenting behaviors and techniques, leading us back to the specific cultural variables that influence a given behavior. When we operationalize culture by looking at the behaviors and linking them to the relevant psychological elements, we can make them more open to measurement (Betancourt & López, 1993; Triandis et al., 1980).

An interesting illustration of differences between Latino and other children comes from an infant attachment study published by Fracasso, Busch-Rossnagel, and Fisher (1994). This team examined infant attachment using the Strange Situation with 100 Dominican and Puerto Rican mother–infant pairs in New York City and found no significant differences between the two groups. The proportion of securely and insecurely attached infants reflected generally the findings from other research using both White, non-Latino, and African American samples as well as samples from other countries including Germany, Israel, and Japan. An interesting finding, however, in the Fracasso et al. study was that, unlike most samples studied in the past, gender differences appeared: boy infants' behavior tended to be classified as more securely attached than girl infants. We must, however, exercise caution in looking at this finding since it was not a representative sample and the validity of attachment classifications of Latino infants has not been established. However, if gender differences were to hold in replication studies, we would then need to explore why Latino male infants are more likely to be classified as more securely attached than their female counterparts. With replication, we can move away from inferences about, say, the value of the male child in Latino cultures toward a more accurate understanding about parenting attitudes and behavior toward boys. One way we can do this is to ask mothers and fathers themselves about their approaches with male and female children, using structured and semi-structured interviews, narrative material, and employing existing or creating instruments that might tap attitudes toward infant gender in the parents' offspring.

Another finding of the Fracasso et al. (1994) study was that some maternal behaviors associated with security of attachment differed from those in other studies of non-Latino mother–infant pairs. In previous research with non-Latino samples, maternal sensitivity was correlated with secure attachment, while routine holding was associated with insecure attachment. In the sample of Puerto Rican and Dominican mothers, increased maternal intervention in the children's activities was associated with secure attachment, while it correlated with insecure attachment in non-Latino samples. It may be evident, then, that sensitive mothering is defined by the local culture rather than by a universal factor. Mothers' behaviors are based on what they consider is the correct way to interact with their infants based on the meanings these have for their cultural reference group.

In the context of our discussion of Latino families and parenting behaviors, the concept of a cultural ideal is useful because it informs some of the logic by which we are governed psychologically as parents. The psychoanalytic concept of the "ego ideal," or what Erikson (1963) has called the "cultural ideal," is applicable to parenting. The ego or cultural ideal encompasses those human behavioral qualities that individuals in a cultural group are taught to aspire to through their words and deeds. A culture promotes these ideals as the manifestation of the best of its belief system and, in some ways, they act as guidelines for human behavior. There are no universal cultural ideals; rather, ideals are determined by individual or local cultures. Furthermore, ideals are not always good insofar as they may give freedom to some individuals and stifle the voices of others; this is often seen in differences in gender roles. Similarly, cultural or ego ideals differ by gender, context, and role so that there are definitions of what it means to be a "good" person, a "good" parent, a "good" spouse, and so on. With adaptation to a new cultural system, this logic may change, although it commonly takes some acculturation to the new system.

Theoretically, the closer the individual feels he or she is to the ideal, the greater the self-esteem, whereas the further away from the ideal a person feels (or is made to feel), the lower the self-esteem. This is an especially important point when we consider the assessment of and intervention with Latino parents on matters of parenting. If the ideal that is set up is different from the one that has cultural meaning to Latino parents, the likelier the loss of self-esteem or of self-efficacy as parents. There is the possibility also that Latino parents will refuse participation in interventions that are intended to help them when cultural ideals of the mainstream are incongruent with their own. Therefore, we must look at the child-rearing literature that is syntonic with Latino parents' own cultures or learn from the parents' directly. If the literature that informs an intervention is based on cultural and social-class assumptions relevant to non-Latino populations, we run the risk of causing harm. Drawing on the cultural ideals of the Latino parents' own reference group through emic approaches will add much to engaging them in treatment and reducing the possibility of iatrogenic effects of interventions.

EMIC AND ETIC PERSPECTIVES ON RESEARCH AND SERVICES

Emic approaches in parenting research and interventions operate from the culture of the parents and children being studied. Emic research with parents examines cultural constructs (i.e., parenting behaviors, perceptions of children's behaviors, child-rearing beliefs and values, experience) from within a family's culture of origin. Then, the methods of research and intervention are based on their appropriateness to the culture of the family. Discoveries from this approach are considered only in relation to that one culture. Betancourt and López (1993) call this a "bottom-up" approach, in which the investigator begins with an observation of a given culture and moves toward its implications for psychological theory by applying it cross-culturally. Recently in mental health literature, we have seen some advances made in the development of culturally relevant, emically oriented approaches in the development of culturally reliable and valid psychometric instruments (Canino & Bravo, 1994; Manson, Shore, & Bloom, 1985). Other emic approaches in mental health research have moved toward combining subjective and objective measures (Mildred, Alegria, Freeman, Robles, & Pescosolido, 1998) and qualitative and quantitative methods to enhance the knowledge of cross-ethic variations in the experience of mental illness and responses to rehabilitative services and their use. We propose that similar movements be made within the developmental field to inform research on ethnic and cultural minority parenting and on how best to intervene with parents and children.

Within an etic approach, the investigator begins with a theory and applies the framework on the culture under scrutiny (Betancourt & Lopez, 1993). The investigator notes the role of culture in each and searches for some universals, thereby elaborating general psychological theory—a "top-down" approach according to Betancourt and López. This approach studies parenting constructs in one or more cultures from the outside, that is, using methods that reflect the theoretical framework of the researcher. Optimally, this approach yields some generalizations to other cultures (Lonner, 1979). In parenting programs and developmental interventions that include families, this top-down approach, with modifications, has value for working with Latino parents. But it is our position that it cannot be used exclusively. Instead, it is best to combine etic approaches with emic ones.

Within the field of mental health services, Higginbotham (1979, 1984) proposed an emically derived cultural assessment model to address the cultural gap between Western mental health delivery models and non-Western settings. Although the model was conceptualized for mental health programs implemented in developing countries, it holds some promise for exploring the cultural relevancy of parenting research and interventions in U.S. ethnic minority communities. Taking a cross-cultural perspective, this model incorporates an emic approach in the assessment of sociocultural characteristics of clients and then shapes the delivery of mental health services to the culture (Higginbotham, 1979, 1980, 1987), something that has been discussed by Rogler, Malgady Costantino, and Blumenthal (1987).

Higginbotham's model (1979, 1984) has four domains that must be considered in the adaptation of services to match the specific group under consideration. We have adapted them for the purposes of exploring ways of studying and helping Latino parents. The four domains required for implementing the model with a targeted ethnic group or community are (a) assessing parents' cultural perceptions of what they must do as parents in rearing their children, (b) specifying the values and expectations parents have for their children's behavior and children's adjustment, (c) describing natural supports that help parents in a given culture whether these are in the form of family and informal networks or formal networks, and (d) appraising the expected community relationships with the system devised for enhancing parenting. Culture-specific data on parenting behaviors and problems in child rearing are derived and then used to maximize the sensitivity of the psychosocial treatment program and guide services to fit the needs and characteristics of the local ethnic group. In theory, interventionists using this model can assess the degree of congruity between the ethnic group's needs and the services provided.

Higginbotham's work (1984) is preliminary and has not been extended. But since the literature on both clinical and developmental services research lack an understanding of cultural relevancy, Higginbotham's qualitative approach may provide a framework for building knowledge and informing the cultural relevance of community-based psychosocial interventions for parents of different ethnocultural groups. Higginbotham's emic method for assessing cultural domains from multiple perspectives permits the use of data to assess and guide the cultural relevancy of services (Higginbotham & Connor, 1990; Higginbotham, West, & Forsyth, 1988).

EMIC AND ETIC APPROACHES TO RESEARCH WITH LATINO CHILDREN AND PARENTS

Several experiences in the development of clinical interventions for specific Latino groups provide some insight on how emic and etic approaches can be combined.

CUENTO THERAPY

Based on developing culturally sensitive psychotherapeutic interventions for Latino youth in New York City, rather than on child development or parenting skills enhancement, the work of Costantino, Malgady, and Rogler (1985) represents an approach that combines emic and etic approaches. They began their work with a concern about the lack of available modalities of treatment for the predominantly Puerto Rican population that came to a community mental health center in Brooklyn. Costantino, Malgady, and Rogler (1988) also wanted to be responsive to the characteristics of the group. Many children from young, single-parent mother-headed, father-absent households were referred for behavioral and emotional problems. The clinicians saw that at the core of the situation was the absence of appropriate parental role models with whom the children could identify, particularly during adolescence. To find the most effective ways to treat these children, Costantino and his associates (1985, 1988) drew on several traditions from psychology and culture. They examined folk-healing practices in Puerto Rico reported in the literature from sociology and anthropology. Costantino et al. also looked at the function of folktales in different cultures and the role of storytelling—the oldest method by which societal rules and customs, and standards of morality, are transferred from one generation to the next. Folktales, in effect, are enduring repositories of cultural heritage and modes of transmission of values (Costantino et al., 1985).

In an effort to integrate social learning theory and folklore traditions, Costantino and his collaborators first developed Cuento Therapy, a storytelling technique based on cultural folktales to promote adaptive personality development in Puerto Rican children coming to the clinic (Costantino, Malgady, and Rogler, 1986). Aware of the abundance of folktales in Puerto Rican culture and the population of Puerto Ricans in New York City, the researchers first identified through an emic approach (using Puerto Rican folklore specialists, mothers, and grandmothers) 105 *cuentos* that remained part of an oral tradition among transplanted Puerto Ricans in New York City. Thus, the research clinicians could move forward on their hypothesis that *cuentos* were indeed part of this population's tradition.

A follow-up study was conducted to find the most popular *cuentos* and to select 40 that would be used in the Cuento Therapy protocol, continuing their emic approach. Another group of Puerto Rican mothers and grandmothers identified 100 *cuentos* that were then subjected to an analysis of themes of human values. Each *cuento* symbolically represented thoughts, feelings, beliefs, and behaviors of Puerto Rican people directly verbalized or represented through the actions of the characters in the folktales. Forty *cuentos* were selected from the 100 and translated into English, with adaptations made to reflect the settings and cultural values of Puerto Rican children in American society. Each *cuento* had to reflect two or more of the nine personality functions the clinicians had identified as important for the children for whom the treatment modality was being developed, thus including an etic perspective. The nine personality functions were (a) interpersonal relations with parental authority figures, (b) control of aggression and disruptive behavior, (c) control of anxiety and depression, (d) delay of gratification, (e) achievement motivation, (f) self-concept of competence, (g) sexual identity, (h) moral judgment, and (i) social judgment and reality testing. The *cuentos* were adapted to reflect the environment of Puerto Rican children in an urban setting in the United States mainland (Costantino et al., 1985). The adapted *cuentos* thus retained the flavor of the Puerto Rican culture through the characters, their names, and the plots but reflected the children's ecological reality.

After using an emic approach combined with etic approach (i.e., ego psychology), the *cuentos* were tested with a group of children and adolescents. Evaluation of the Cuento Therapy modality showed that younger children readily identified with the Puerto Rican characters in the folktales. By role-playing the stories, children's adaptive behaviors were enhanced by reducing anxiety and aggression and increasing their social judgment in comparison to a traditional treatment approach (i.e., psychodynamically oriented play therapy) or no treatment. However, with adolescents the modality was less effective. Adolescents complained that the *cuentos* were too juvenile (Costantino et al., 1988), they were less interested in the stories, identified less with the characters and plots, and were more resistant to therapeutic change. (For substantive methodological details and specific results, we refer the reader to the published works of these investigators).

Hero/Heroine Therapy

Having developed a culturally proximal modality that was effective with young Latino children, Costantino et al. (1988) now faced the challenge of addressing the absence of efficacy with adolescents. From an etic perspective that took into account the cognitive and social development and needs of adolescents, Costantino and his collaborators used the notion of "cultural heroes" to develop a treatment modality more appealing to adolescents.

A panel of Puerto Rican psychologists, sociologists, and literature specialists were asked to select heroic figures to serve as role models in therapy. The panel selected 10 male and 10 female heroes from Puerto Rican history who embodied important principles of ego psychology: a sense of reality, interpersonal strength, social judgment, self-identity, and autonomous functioning.

Defined as persons who had outstanding abilities in completing tasks under great pressure in a morally, socially, intellectually, and emotionally acceptable manner, the heroes in this therapy would serve as effective means for improving the Latino adolescents' sense of identity and help them negotiate the intergenerational and intercultural conflicts they faced in an urban setting. The investigators felt that talks about heroes would capture the imagination of adolescents more so than the *cuentos* used in their previous research.

The panel of experts used the definition of heroes to compile a large sample of biographies and anecdotes of Puerto Rican persons who possessed the qualities set forth, drawn from and diverse fields (e.g., sports, arts, education, politics, medicine) and different points in history (from the 16th century to the present). The biographies of the heroes highlighted the adversities they had faced, such as discrimination and poverty, and how each hero had coped and effectively overcome adversity, emphasizing ego strengths and community support. The therapy approach used small groups in which the therapist read the biography of a Puerto Rican hero and led the group in an analysis of the hero's personal experience and ability to overcome adversity (Costantino et al., 1988).

Results of the study showed that the adolescents exposed to the hero therapy had significantly improved in their ethnic identity and self-concepts and had lower anxiety levels than adolescents in traditional psychotherapy. In summary, this program of treatment research focused on the needs of a specific Latino cultural group by drawing important means for communication and therapy from the culture (emic approach) and combining this with knowledge of adolescent development that was found in the general literature on adolescents (etic approach).

Child-Rearing Values of Mainland U.S. Puerto Rican Mothers

Gonzalez-Ramos, Zayas, and Cohen (1998) conducted a study to identify the values that guide Puerto Rican mothers' child-rearing beliefs and practices. The emic approach used began with the convening of four focus groups comprised of 20 Puerto Rican mothers recruited from Head Start and daycare programs in New York City. One group was interviewed in Spanish and the other three used both Spanish and English. The focus groups consisted of discussions that would identify and describe values that the mothers felt were important to instill in their preschool children. Probes were included to have the mothers define the values they mentioned and how each value would be evident in children's behaviors. When two values were mentioned that seemed to overlap, focus group participants were asked to explain the differences between them. For example, mothers mentioned "respect" and "obedience" frequently. When asked to distinguish between the two, mothers defined them similarly, leading to the use of the value "respect" to encompass obedience as well. Nineteen broad values were thus derived.

Subsequently, the investigators pilot tested the 19 values with 10 mothers who had not participated in the focus groups, asking them to rank order the values and explain their reasons for the rankings. Definitions and adequacy of their translations were further pilot tested with a sample of 12 Puerto Rican professionals (e.g., pediatricians, educators, psychologists, social workers) and Puerto Rican nonprofessionals (e.g., secretaries, waiters, doormen). Each was asked how they understood each value, how each value would manifest itself in children, and whether the definitions developed accurately portrayed that value. Analysis of the data from the mothers, professionals, and nonprofessionals helped to yield the final 10 values considered important in raising Puerto Rican children, the definitions of each value, and child examples for each. To test differences in values preferred, three values associated with Anglo child rearing, which had been repeatedly mentioned in the child development literature (namely, assertiveness, independence, creativity) were included in the inventory. A translation from Spanish to English was done by a professional translator, and back-translated by another professional translator.

Eighty Puerto Rican mothers in New York City were then interviewed individually in Spanish or English, depending on their preferences. Mothers were asked to read the definition and illustration of each of the 13 values. After completing the review and assuring the researchers that they understood the values and their definitions, each mother then rank ordered the values she believed were most important and least important to teach her preschool-age child.

The results showed that Puerto Rican mothers ranked honesty, respectfulness, and responsibility most highly in raising their preschool children. The mothers then ranked loyalty to family, affectionateness, and sharing with others as next in order of priority to them. Rearing children with the value of independence was ranked seventh, at the midpoint of the rankings of values. Its location in the rank order was contrary to the researchers' expectations based on clinical experience and research reports. These values were followed by getting along with others, dignity, valuing elders, and humility. Mothers ranked two values associated with Anglo culture—assertiveness and creativity—as being of least importance in the ranking of child-rearing values. Table 10.1 presents the ranking of the 13 values.

Through an emic approach, the investigators were able to specify the child-rearing values of one Latino group and then to assess their relative importance. In this manner, the findings could be said to be, with some high degree of confidence, a reflection of that group's values for raising their children.

Adapting Evidence-Based Parent Training Interventions

Empirically tested parent training interventions developed with non-Latino populations can be examined and adapted to the needs and characteristics of Latino parents and families. Rojas-Flores, Miller, and Rodriguez (1999) have

Table 10.1
Ranking of Thirteen Child-Rearing Values by Puerto Rican Mothers (N = 80)

Rank Order	Child-Rearing Value
1	Honesty
2	Respectfulness
3	Responsibility
4	Loyalty to family
5	Affectionate
6	Share with others
7	Independence
8	Get along with others
9	Dignity
10	Value older persons
11	Humility
12	Assertiveness
13	Creativity

begun this process by combining theoretically based interventions with empirically supported ones that lend themselves to adaptation to different Latino groups. These investigators' goal was to develop a parenting program with Latino parents of Head Start–age children that would be developmentally appropriate, build on families' strengths, and preserve their linguistic and cultural integrity.

To advance their work with inner-city Latino preschoolers and their families, Miller and Rojas-Flores (1999) chose the Parent and Children Series (*Series Para Padres e Hijos;* Webster-Stratton, 1992a, 1992b), which has been extensively tested with Euro-American children. The key strategies used in the therapeutic-group process emphasize cultural sensitivity and strategies such as collaboration, empowerment, reframing, and the building of support systems within and outside the group (Webster-Stratton & Herbert, 1993, 1994). Rojas-Flores et al. (1999) set out to test the acceptability and feasibility of Webster-Stratton's program (1993, 1994) with Spanish-speaking, Latino parents of 3- and 4-year-old Head Start children.

Twenty-two parents were randomly assigned to participate in the Webster-Stratton parenting intervention (1993, 1994), and 21 were randomly assigned to a comparison condition. Eighty-one percent of the parents were Dominican,

14% were of other Latino nationalities (Costa Rican, Ecuadorean, El Salvadorean), and 5% were Puerto Ricans. Both linguistic and cultural adaptations were required to make the program effective and relevant to a group of parents from diverse Latin American backgrounds.

The intervention consists of 10 one-and-one-half-hour parent sessions provided over three months. All of the group materials, including videotaped vignettes, written materials, and group discussions are delivered in Spanish. A native Spanish speaker with previous formal training in the Parent and Children Series groups (Miller & Rojas-Flores, 1999) led the intervention groups. The comparison group received the usual Head Start instruction for parents, focusing on topics such as nutrition, children's health, "English as a Second Language," and some computer skills classes. These groups were led by a paraprofessional who was a member of the Head Start staff.

Conducting the intervention groups with a primarily immigrant, inner-city population solely in Spanish demanded that the group leader serve as a "cultural translator" of behavioral principles relatively foreign to most of the immigrant parents. Teaching and interpreting behavioral, cognitive, and developmental concepts in a language in which the parents could understand and come to own and appreciate required that the group leader be familiar with the cultural beliefs, expectations, and child-rearing practices of the Latino cultures represented by the parents. Some language adjustments were made when viewing the videotapes because the vignettes were dubbed in Mexican Spanish and the group participants were primarily of Dominican origin. For instance, when a parent in the vignette told his children to pick up the *popotes* (Mexican word for straws), the group leader had to translate this term into Dominican and Puerto Rican Spanish, that is, *calimete* and *sorbetos*, respectively. Linguistic adjustments were made and cultural examples provided for the Latino cultures represented in the group, thus acknowledging and respecting each culture.

Other cultural adjustments were needed. For example, during the group discussion on handling misbehavior, the pros and cons of using physical punishment were posed. The use of *la chancleta* (the slipper) or *la correa* (the belt) to strike children or having children kneel on uncooked rice as punishment were discussed as corporal punishment thought to be common, if not accepted, in their countries of origin but which differed among the Latino groups. The group reached consensus that these strategies were not effective and might be emotionally harmful to their children, in light of their recollection of their own early experiences with corporal punishment. This frank conversation also led the group to discuss their difficulties in adjusting to the American culture, specifically when related to issues of discipline and child-rearing practices. Many parents voiced their sense of helplessness in disciplining their children, fearing that they would be reported to child protective services for physical abuse. This type of discussion tapped specific cultural perceptions about punishing children without discrediting the parent's own experience (an emic approach). The group leader as cultural consultant and translator introduced parenting concepts to modify children's behavior, such as time-out (an etic approach), which the parents were less familiar with.

The use of Webster-Stratton's (1992b) videotape modeling as a therapeutic method is an effective way to demonstrate behavioral principles and serve as the stimulus for focused discussion, problem-solving, and sharing of ideas and reactions. The videotaped vignettes consist of parents modeling some behaviors correctly but also making mistakes. Role playing also allowed group members to troubleshoot together and figure out how they might have handled interactions more effectively. Through role play and rehearsal, parents showed the group leader what was working and not working at home. This approach not only enabled parents to anticipate problem situations more clearly but it also demystified the notion that there is "perfect parenting" and illustrated how parents can learn from their own mistakes.

Congruent with Webster-Stratton's original program (1992a), building support systems in and outside the group was another emphasis of this pilot intervention with Latino parents. The parent groups provided a model for parents to develop informal support networks. One of the strategies used to encourage parents to build networks among themselves was the "Buddy System," in which a parent was paired up with another member of the group and encouraged to call that parent to discuss group-related issues or any parenting concerns. Parents were also encouraged to have spouses, partners, close friends, or family members attend the program with them to provide mutual support. Several fathers and grandmothers were regular participants of the groups.

Parents were empowered beyond the group sessions through weekly home assignments. These assignments typically asked parents to do some observing and recording of behaviors or thoughts at home and/or experimenting with a particular strategy. The assignments were designed to encourage the parents to continue monitoring and practicing their parenting skills at home. Feedback from the parents in the pilot intervention is very promising. Parents' satisfaction with the program was very high: All the parents indicated that the material covered in the program was "very" to "extremely useful." Another indicator of parents' acceptance of the program was based on the parents' completion and feedback on their weekly home assignments. These assignments were reviewed by the group leader who provided individualized written feedback; they were also discussed at the beginning of each group meeting. During the course of the intervention, 95% of the parents reported that the home activities were "useful" to "very useful."

Preliminary analyses of the outcome data suggest that the intervention program led to significant improvements in parenting practices and child outcomes. Parents in the intervention group displayed more positive parenting strategies and were also rated as significantly more effective, responsive, and attentive during parent–child interactions than parents in the comparison group. Children of parents in the intervention group were also more socially competent and were rated to have fewer conduct problems than controls.

CONCLUSION

In this chapter, we have discussed how developmental researchers and practitioners can combine emic approaches that are drawn from the unique experiences of Latino parents with etic approaches based on empirical reports and universal theories of child development and parenting. The idea behind combining these two methods is to create or adapt interventions that will have the most beneficial outcomes for Latino families. The illustrations that have been provided are intended as departure points for future research and intervention development. More work is needed in developing parenting interventions that draw from the culture of the Latino parents that are being targeted through specific programs. We find that the best sources for the information about culture, parenting and child rearing, and children's behavior are parents themselves, as shown by the illustrations of Cuento Therapy. From parents, too, we can learn what aspects of already existing programs make sense to them and what alterations are needed to make it congruent with their experiences and needs, as shown by the work of Rojas-Flores et al. (1999). Evaluations of the success of these parenting interventions must be undertaken, including consideration for how effective interventions can be sustained by agencies and programs within the community.

AUTHORS' NOTE

Support for work on this chapter was provided, in part, to Luis H. Zayas by NIMH grant R24 MH 60002-01 and to Lisseth Rojas-Flores by a minority supplement through NIMH grant R01 MH 55188-05 (Laurie Miller, Ph.D., principal investigator).
Correspondence should be sent to Luis H. Zayas, Ph.D., Center for Hispanic Mental Health Research, Graduate School of Social Service, Fordham University, 113 West 60th Street, New York, NY 10023 or e-mail: zayas@fordham.edu

REFERENCES

Betancourt, H., & Lopez, S. R. (1993). The study of culture, ethnicity, and race in American psychology. *American Psychologist, 48*(6), 629–637.

Canino, G., & Bravo, M. (1994). The adaptation and testing of diagnostic and outcome measures for cross-cultural research. Inter Review of Psychiatry, 6, 281–286.

Costantino, G., Malgady, R. G., & Rogler, L. H. (1985). *Cuento therapy: Folktales as a culturally sensitive psychotherapy for Puerto Rican children.* Hispanic Research Center Monograph 12. Maplewood, NJ: Waterfront.

Costantino, G., Malgady, R. G., & Rogler, L. H. (1986). Cuento Therapy: A culturally sensitive modality for Puerto Rican children. *Journal of Consulting and Clinical Psychology, 54,* 639–645.

Costantino, G., Malgady, R. G., & Rogler, L. H. (1988). Folk hero modeling therapy for Puerto Rican adolescents. *Journal of Adolescence, 11*, 155–165.

Erikson, E. H. (1963). *Childhood and society*. New York: Norton.

Fracasso, M. P., Busch-Rossnagel, N. A., & Fisher, C. B. (1994). The relationship of maternal behavior and acculturation to the quality of infant attachment in Hispanic infants living in New York City. *Hispanic Journal of Behavioral Sciences, 16*, 143–154.

Gonzalez-Ramos, G., Zayas, L. H., & Cohen, E. V. (1998). Child-rearing values of low-income, urban Puerto Rican mothers of preschool children. *Professional Psychology: Research and Practice, 29*, 377–382.

Harrison, A. O., Wilson, M. N., Pine, C. J., Chan, S. Q., & Buriel, R. (1990). Family ecologies of ethnic minority children. *Child Development, 61*, 347–362.

Herkovits, M. (1948). *Man and his works*. New York: Knopf.

Higginbotham, H. N. (1979). Culture and mental health services. In A. J. Marsella, R. G. Tharp, & T. J. Ciborowski (Eds.), *Perspectives on cross-cultural psychology* (pp. 307–332). New York: Academic.

Higginbotham, H. N. (1980). Culture and the role of client expectancy in psychotherapy. In M. P. Hammet & R. W. Brislin (Eds.), *Research in culture learning* (pp. 35–52). Honolulu, HI: East-West Center.

Higginbotham, H. N. (1984). *Third World challenge to psychiatry: Culture accommodation and mental health care*. Honolulu: University of Hawaii Press.

Higginbotham, H. N. (1987). The culture accommodation of mental health services for Native Hawaiians. In A. B. Robillard & A. J. Marsella (Eds.), *Contemporary issues in mental health research in the Pacific Islands* (pp. 94–126). Honolulu, HI: Social Science Research Institute.

Higginbotham, H. N., & Connor, L. (1990). Culture accommodation of primary health care: A framework for assessing the contribution of patient–provider fit to health transitions. In J. Caldwell et al. (Eds.), *What we know about health transition: The cultural, social, and behavioral determinants of health* (pp. 742–755). Australian National University Printing Service for the Health Transition Center.

Higginbotham, H. N., West, S. G., & Forsyth, D. R. (1988). *Psychotherapy and behavior change: Social, cultural, and methodological perspectives* (Chap. 6). Elmsford, NY: Pergamon.

LeVine, R. A., Miller, P. M., Richman, A. L., & LeVine, S. (1996). Education and mother–infant interaction: A Mexican case study. In S. Harkness & C. M. Super (Eds.), *Parents' cultural belief systems* (pp. 254–269). New York: Guilford.

Lonner, W. J. (1979). Issues in cross-cultural psychology. In A. J. Marsella, R. G. Tharp, & T. J. Ciborowski (Eds.), *Perspectives on cross-cultural psychology* (pp. 37–45). New York: Academic.

López, S. R. (1997). Cultural competence in psychotherapy: A guide for clinicians and their supervisors. In C. E. Walks, Jr. (Ed.), *Handbook of psychotherapy supervision* (pp. 570–588). New York: Wiley.

Manson, S. M., Shore, J. H., & Bloom, J. D. (1985). The depressive experience of American Indian communities: A challenge for psychiatric theory and diagnosis. In A. Kleinman & B. Goode (Eds.), *Culture and depression* (pp. 331–368). Berkeley: University of California Press.

Mildred, V., Alegria, M., Freeman, D., Robles, R., & Pescosolido, B. (1998). Help seeking for mental health care among poor Puerto Ricans: Problem recognition, service use, and type of provider. *Medical Care, 36,* 1047–1056.

Miller, L., & Rojas-Flores, L. (1999, August). *Preventing conduct problems in urban Latino Head Start children.* Paper presented at the Meeting of the Life History Research Society, Kauai, Hawaii.

Rogler, L. H., Malgady, R. G., Costantino, G., & Blumenthal, T. (1987). What do culturally sensitive mental health services mean? The case of Hispanics. *American Psychologist, 42,* 565–570.

Rohner, R. P. (1984). Toward a conception of culture for cross-cultural psychology. *Journal of Cross-Cultural Psychology, 15,* 111–138.

Rojas-Flores, L., Miller, L., & Rodriguez, C. (1999, June). *Preventing conduct problems in Latino Head Start children: A pilot study.* Paper presented at the Ninth Scientific Meeting of the International Society for Research in Child and Adolescent Psychopathology, Barcelona, Spain.

Sue, S. (1999). Science, ethnicity, and bias: Where have we gone wrong? *American Psychologist, 54,* 1070–1077.

Tanaka-Matsumi, J., & Draguns, J. (1997). Culture and psychopathology. In J. Berry, Y. Poortinga, J. Pandy, P. Dasen, T. Saraswathi, M. Segall, & C. Kagitcibasi (Eds.), *Handbook of cross-cultural psychology* (Vol. 3, pp. 449–479). Boston: Allyn & Bacon.

Triandis, H., Lambert, W., Berry, J., Lonner, W., Heron, A., Brislin, R., & Draguns, J. (1980). (Eds.), *Handbook of cross-cultural psychology* (Vol. 1–6). Boston: Allyn & Bacon.

Webster-Stratton, C. (1992a). *The incredible years: A trouble-shooting guide for parents of children aged 3–8.* Toronto, Ontario, Canada: Umbrella.

Webster-Stratton, C. (1992b). *The parents and children videotape series: Programs 1–10.* Seattle, WA: Seth Enterprises.

Webster-Stratton, C., & Herbert, M. (1993). What really happens in parent training? *Behavior Modification, 17,* 407–456.

Webster-Stratton, C., & Herbert, M. (1994). *Troubled families, problem children: Working with parents: A collaborative process.* New York: Wiley.

Part IV

Conclusions and Recommendations for the Future of the Field

11

The Challenges and Rewards of Conducting Ethnic Minority Research

*Angel G. Lugo Steidel, Madinah Ikhlas,
Irene Lopez, Reece O. Rahman,
and Jennifer Teichman*

The authors of this chapter are clinical psychology graduate students at Kent State University, Kent, OH, who participated in the 2000 Kent Psychology Forum. The views presented in this chapter developed out of discussion sessions with researchers and community representatives doing research and clinical or community work with Latino families and children.

Methodological issues regarding research with ethnic minorities, particularly Latinos, were addressed by many of the presenters during the forum. For example, investigators discussed the use of behavioral observations over traditional paper-and-pencil measures to better capture mother–infant interactions; the use of qualitative designs and methods, such as focus groups, to better assess culturally specific phenomena and behaviors; and the importance of measurement equivalency in research with ethnic minorities. Discussion by those in attendance also emphasized the dissatisfaction with the current state of research on Latinos. There was some agreement among participants that some ethnic minority research is assumed to be of poorer quality than studies on "mainstream" populations. Although irritation with these blanket statements was expressed, there was also acknowledgment of the legitimate criticism of some of the work that is poorly conducted. It was discussed that some of the available research is inadequately designed and executed so that the obtained results may be difficult to interpret. It was acknowledged that although conducting meaningful research with Latino populations is difficult, taking the time to plan and execute a study adequately would ultimately aid in answering the research questions and make a more useful contribution to the literature. Because of the challenges involved in conducting ethnic minority

research, the goal of this chapter is to provide comments and recommendations to other graduate students who, like us, are initiating a career in ethnic
minority research. We hope that these comments and recommendations will
also prove useful to established researchers who are considering expanding
their research programs to include ethnic minority populations.

IMPORTANCE OF ETHNIC MINORITY RESEARCH

The number of ethnic minorities in the United States is significantly aug-
menting with each passing year (U.S. Census Bureau, 2000). For this reason,
it is becoming increasingly imperative to make efforts to study non-White
segments of the U.S. population. A way to understand specific minority
groups is to conduct research to uncover normal developmental processes
among specific cultural groups. Ethnic minority populations face unique psychological issues that need to be addressed and better understood. Examples
of such issues include acculturation and bilingualism, parenting strategies that
are based on the culture's specific values and socialization goals, a culture's
view of therapy and mental health, varying incidence rates of some types of
psychopathology including developmental delays, and culturally specific presentation of psychopathology.

Some researchers think that, for the most part, they do not have to be both-
ered with issues that concern ethnic minority individuals. Some state that they
do not plan on working with minority populations so there is no need for them
to learn about such individuals and cultures. Others may shy away from working with these populations because of the difficulties involved. Although it is
unfair and unrealistic to expect any researcher to become an expert in working
with every minority population in the United States, it is also true that researchers will likely need to include participants from ethnic minority populations in their research sample. To address this issue, one idea that circulated at
the forum was that of developing cultural competence. Generally, cultural
competence refers to a general attitude or approach in which every individual
is viewed within his/her cultural context (American Psychological Association,
1993; Arredondo et al., 1996) The importance of cultural competence in psychology has been further highlighted by the creation of the National Institute
of Health Strategic Research Plan to Reduce and Ultimately Eliminate Health
Disparities among minority populations (U.S. Department of Health and
Human Services, 2000). This plan is designed to address differences in factors
such as progression of diseases and incidence of mental health problems among
ethnic minority populations as compared to the White population.

Another reason why research with ethnic minority populations is so vital is
that many of the variables that have been of interest to psychology historically can be influenced by cultural factors. For example, in a study of Puerto
Rican versus Anglo mothers, Harwood, Schoelmerich, Schultz, & Gonzalez
(1999) discovered that child-rearing strategies corresponded to specific cul-

tural constructs. Whereas Anglo mothers were more likely to provide children with opportunities that allow them to learn for themselves, Puerto Rican mothers were more likely to teach children through direct exercise of parental authority. These strategies corresponded to the parent's respective individualistic or collectivistic cultural orientation. This study demonstrates that we can gain more understanding of the psychological construct if we study its cultural variation. It is only by studying individuals of various cultural backgrounds that we can truly begin to discover culturally invariant and culturally specific effects.

Ethnic minority research is invaluable not only because it lends to a better understanding of the populations involved but also because it contributes to a better understanding of research methodology in other areas as well. Other researchers may experience some of the same challenges experienced when conducting ethnic minority research. Therefore, the techniques and methodologies that are developed for the study of ethnic minority populations can be successfully applied to other research areas.

A recommendation made at the forum was to use qualitative research techniques to increase our understanding of the cultural issues that affect psychological phenomena. Sometimes the importance of qualitative design is overshadowed by quantitative methodology, as shown by the smaller number of qualitative research publications. However, when working with ethnic minority populations, relying on purely quantitative designs might not be enough because cultural effects on psychological constructs may still be misunderstood. For example, in test construction one must understand the construct as it is manifested in a particular population before an instrument can be developed to measure the construct. Qualitative techniques could prove useful in exploring such under-researched constructs.

Many of the qualitative methods discussed at the forum are not taught in psychology graduate programs. Because of their importance in minority research, we have decided to include an overview of some of these methods here in order to provide a starting point for those considering using them. Specifically, we present a summary of Morgan's guidelines (1997) for focus group research and a description of translation methodology. These two methods were described on various occasions throughout the forum owing to their relevance to the issues we have just described. Focus group methodology is useful in exploring under-researched areas. Translation methodology is important because ethnic minority populations may not speak English.

FOCUS GROUPS

A focus group is a structured, moderated interview that relies on interaction and sharing among group members to generate data in the form of ideas, insight, and perceptions about the topic supplied by the researcher (Morgan, 1997). Such data would be less accessible in an individual setting. An easier way to understand the purpose of focus groups is to think of them as lying between naturalistic observation and individual interview techniques. In general, focus groups serve several purposes. They can be used to elicit information about new topics, explain unexpected results, generate new hypotheses, evaluate instruments or programs, develop survey items, or explain, in-depth, the attitudes and beliefs of a specific population (Asbury, 1995; Dawson, Manderson, & Tallo, 1993; Morgan, 1997). Thus, the focus group methodology is invaluable when researching cultural issues in psychology, especially if these have been under studied.

The Function of a Focus Group

There are three basic uses for a focus group. First, it can be a self-contained method that has the ability to generate data as a sufficient body of knowledge. In this capacity, the focus group serves as the principal source of data similar to an individual interview. Second, focus groups can be used as supplementary sources of data in studies using primarily quantitative methodology. For example, the focus group data may help to generate instrument items or assist in outcome evaluation. Finally, focus groups can be used as part of a multimethod qualitative study in which there are no primary methods of gathering data. In this capacity, focus groups add to the data that have been gathered via other qualitative techniques such as participant observation or individual interviews. All of these were acknowledged in different conversations at the Kent Forum.

The strength of the focus group, as compared to quantitative methods, is the reliance on group interaction to produce concentrated amounts of data. Focus groups allow for an unbiased presentation of participants' points of view without the investigator leading them or imposing his or her own point of view. The group interaction offers insight into complex behaviors and interactions in a more time-efficient manner as compared to, for example, individual interviews (Morgan, 1997). Other strengths of the focus group technique include the ability to stimulate group communication and the flexibility to explore new attitudes that emerge during the group process that were not anticipated by the researcher (Dawson et al., 1993). Focus group research may be indispensable when attempting to understand relatively unstudied populations. Such research allows investigators to explore constructs that may be culture specific or to clarify any preconceived ideas regarding a particular ethnic group. Furthermore, a focus group's "flexibility" makes it central to increasing the quality and interest of ethnic minority research.

Although it may appear that focus groups could be the research tool of preference in ethnic minority research, researchers need to be aware that the use of focus groups is not without its problems. Some weaknesses of this method include the likelihood that socially desirable responses are elicited, the inability to explore private attitudes that may be socially stigmatized, and the possible controlling influence a person or persons in the group might have on other participants' abilities to discuss issues freely (Dawson et al., 1993; Morgan, 1997).

Although there is discussion of focus groups in the literature, there seems to be limited sources of how to plan, conduct, and analyze focus groups. The following sections will discuss these.

Planning a Focus Group

Researchers who have discussed this stage of the method (Côté-Arsenault & Morrison-Beedy, 1999; Morgan, 1997; Seal, Bogart, & Ehrhardt, 1998) state that to plan for a focus group there has to be a clear statement of the study goals. These will determine the questions or topics to be discussed in the group. Ethical concerns, such as the confidentiality of recorded data, and logistical and budget preparations also need to be considered at this stage. Of particular importance at this stage is the discussion of recruitment strategies. These issues range from recommendations for over recruitment, to control for cancellations and no-shows to reminders to participants.

Conducting a Focus Group

Several rules of thumb have been proposed for conducting focus groups (Morgan, 1997). First, groups should be composed of strangers who share characteristics of importance to the research. Strangers are chosen over acquaintances because of possible confounding effects that might be present in groups composed of friends. Groups should then be segmented or divided in regard to different demographic variables (e.g. sex, age, ethnicity) in order to allow relevant between-group analyses. The language used in the interview is also of importance, especially with a Latino group. The researcher should divide groups based on language abilities and preferences to account for differences in bilingualism. Spanish-speaking moderators should be available to conduct groups when the participants are not fluent in English. Spanish-speaking groups should always be presented as an option in order to ensure that participants feel open to communicate and feel as comfortable as possible.

Second, the group moderator should be highly involved and flexible while also providing a relatively structured interview. There are times when less structure is appropriate, especially if the goal of the focus group is one of topic exploration. Third, groups should be composed of 6 to 10 participants. Discussions may be difficult to sustain if groups have less than six participants. Groups of more than 10 participants may be difficult to control. Finally, it is recommended that there be a total of three to five focus groups per project to allow for between-group analyses.

The interview content should be organized into a guide prior to the group (Morgan, 1997). One common approach is to base this guide directly on the questions that will be discussed. It is recommended that two broad questions or topics be used in more unstructured groups. Four or five topics or questions with preplanned probes are recommended for use in more structured groups. As previously mentioned, even though adherence to the guide is recommended, the moderator should be flexible enough to probe into areas as needed. The total duration of a focus group should be set at 90 minutes, but two hours should be allowed in case the discussion lasts longer.

Several steps should be taken at the initial phase of each focus group (Morgan, 1997): The group should begin with an introduction by the moderator that includes a general overview of the focus group goals and a description of the ground rules (e.g., one person speaks at a time; no side conversations). Icebreakers should be used after the introduction in order for everyone to feel at ease, get to know each other, and set the mood of the group. Discussion starters should be used next. These are questions that everyone should be able to easily respond to that present the basic topic of the focus group and open the discussion for the group as a whole. Discussion starters give each participant the chance to provide some short, meaningful response or opening statement. After all participants have given their responses, the first substantive question or topic should be presented.

Coding the Data

After the focus group is completed, the moderator should take field notes of the interview. These will be used in addition to transcripts of the session as the source of data that will be coded. Morgan (1997) stated that it is important to understand that the unit of analysis in focus group coding is composed of an interplay between what individuals do in the group and the group as a whole. He explains that the three most common ways of coding the data are (a) coding all mentions of a given variable (b) whether each individual participant mentioned a given variable, and (c) whether each group's discussion contained a given variable.

Knodel (1993) recommended four steps in the development of codes once the transcripts are ready for review. The first step is to develop an initial set of codes that correspond to the focus group guide. Secondly, the researcher should develop codes for topics that arise and are of special interest but were not mentioned in the guide. Third, a list of non-substantive codes that will be of particular help in the analysis and a write-up should be developed. Examples of these are codes that mark a reaction to the moderator that appear to bias participants in later discussions. Finally, after the first three steps are performed, another detailed and more specific set of codes should be developed. This set will consist of shorter text segments that became more relevant to the analysis during the first code mapping. Once the codes are constructed, the data can be analyzed qualitatively by exploring the themes that emerged or quantitatively by counting the codes.

TRANSLATIONS

Another important issue in conducting research with ethnic minorities is language translation. Paying closer attention to the language that we use in our test constructions/translations is vital because inaccurate language translations can misconvey information and lead to erroneous conclusions. Thus, accurate language translations are part of the eternal quest for good science. In addition, among Latinos, accurate language translation is needed because this helps ensure that individuals who represent the range of acculturation levels in the United States will be recruited. That is, if a measure is only administered in English, the variability of the Latino sample that is recruited is reduced and generalizability of the results to other Latinos, who may be Spanish dominant, is limited. Furthermore, in the absence of reliable translations, obtained differences may be erroneously attributed to cultural variations, instead of dissimilarities in the translation (Erkut, Alarcón, García Coll, Tropp, & Vázquez García, 1999). Thus bias, defined as an unwanted source of variance, can be introduced and subsequently cannot be disregarded as random error (Malpass & Poortinga, 1973).

Given these grave ramifications, what steps can we take to ensure an accurate translation? The first step is to collaborate with a competent translator(s) who is bilingual and bicultural. That is, a native background ipso facto cannot be assumed to be indicative of bilingualism and biculturality. Thus, efforts are needed to identify truly bilingual and bicultural translators. For example, specific questions should be asked about the number of years of language instruction and previous translation experience. In addition, a sample of previous work should be obtained, as well as a list of references. To assess biculturality, the researcher may choose to administer one of a number of new scales that have been developed to assess level of acculturation (Cortés, Rogler, & Malgady, 1994; Cuéllar, Arnold, & Maldonado, 1995).

However, because of the time and cost involved in these ventures, many will be tempted to avail themselves of a friend, family member, or another graduate student to perform the translation in lieu of a professional translator. Yet, remember that the quality of the translation will only be as good as the quality of the translator, and that at the very least, the person's translation skills, level of vocabulary, and grammatical skills should be informally assessed. In addition, given these requirements, it is also recommended that the investigator not serve as her/his own translator because this may introduce bias. However, if this is the only option available, the investigator should forward the translated work to be checked for the reliability of the translation, grammatical errors, and ease of understanding.

Once a translator has been identified, the investigator should explain to the translator the purposes of the study, clarify the hypotheses, and discuss with the translator the constructs that he/she is trying to assess. This is because a number of decisions will be made regarding the translation, and, thus, it is essential that the translator understands the rationale of the study (Brislin, 1973). The translator, in conjunction with the investigator, may then opt for a direct or concept-driven translation.

Direct and Concept-Driven Translations

In a direct translation there is a literal transcription of the text. Although on face value, this would appear to be the most accurate translation, and indeed it is the most frequently used translation method (Sperber, DeVellis, & Boehlecke, 1994), this method has a number of problems. For example, although a word might be directly translated from one language to another, there is no guarantee that the two words convey the same meaning or that the desired construct is assessed (Erkut et al., 1999). Therefore, although direct translations can be technically accurate they can inadvertently introduce bias (Brislin, 1973).

Instead, translated words should be chosen because they are comparable in meaning, affect, and familiarity (Erkut et al., 1999). This, however, may be difficult to achieve. Translators may be reluctant to use everyday language in their translations because they wish to produce a flawless, and technically accurate, document. As a result, more refined forms of speech may be chosen that may inadvertently introduce an education bias (Erkut et al., 1999). For example, although welfare benefits may be translated in Spanish as *beneficios del gobierno* (government benefits), it is more readily recognizable, at least among low-income participants who receive this service, as *welfea*. This is particularly true among urban Puerto Ricans. This word should then be chosen over the more grammatically correct *beneficios del gobierno*, or at the very least should be placed in parentheses and used as a clarifier in the text (for other examples, see Erkut et al., 1999). That is, efforts should be made to translate materials into everyday language with the knowledge that regional and ethnic differences will affect what constitutes such language. For example, although among Mexicans the word *horita* means "now," it means "later" among Puerto Ricans.

Because of the stated problems associated with direct translation, concept-driven translations have grown in popularity. In concept-driven translations, the emphasis is on creating a translation that conveys the constructs assessed. Yet, because concept-driven translations are not as precise as direct translations, some investigators are reluctant to choose this method. Once the investigator has chosen the type of translation that will be done, direct or concept driven, the following two methods may be used to perform the actual translation.

Back-Translation

By far the most popular method employed has been back-translation (Brislin, 1970, 1973; Werner & Campbell, 1970). With this strategy, one person, or a team, translates the measures from the source language (usually English) into the target language. During this process, meticulous notes are made regarding the translation process. For example, Brislin (1973) recommended that translators identify which items were difficult to translate, which were modified to obtain cultural rather than linguistic equivalence, which required grammatical modification, and which contained idioms. Once this initial translation is completed, a different person or team translates this version back into the source language. Discrepancies between the two language versions are resolved through decentering.

Decentering is a process whereby the source and target versions are modified to ensure a reliable translation such that no vernacular language is the center of the translation (Brislin, 1970). Pilot data may also be gathered to ensure the validity of the translations. Back-translation with decentering is thought to be better than direct translation (Erkut et al., 1999). Brislin (1970, 1973) presented suggestions for a successful translation when choosing or creating a measure in the source (English) language that will be translated into a target language. Some of these include the use of short simple sentences that are no more than 16 words long, the use of the active voice and avoidance of the passive tense, and the repetition of nouns instead of pronouns since pronouns may be difficult to translate.

Despite the popularity of back-translation, a number of criticisms have been leveled against this method (Bontempo, 1993, Olmedo, 1981). Specifically, because the concepts and wording of the scale are principally developed in the source (English) language, measurement equivalence—the extent to which the language versions assess the same underlying construct—cannot be assumed. In addition, this method can be cumbersome with multilingual studies (Sechrest, Fay, & Hafeez Zaidi, 1972). Furthermore, although the semantic structure of Indo-European languages (e.g., Danish, French, German, Italian, Spanish) may be similar to English, this is not true with other languages (e.g., Hebrew, Japanese) (Hulin, 1987), and thus back-translation may be difficult with these languages.

Dual-Focus Approach

Because of these problems, a new method has recently been developed (Erkut et al., 1999). The dual-focus approach draws from Triandis' (1976) distinction between etic (universal) and emic (culture-bound) constructs and suggests that in constructing a translation, etic concepts are operationalized in each culture using emic concepts whose validity may be culture bound (Erkut et al., 1999). The steps for this type of translation are (a) the collaboration of research teams (ethnic and nonethnic members) to jointly define the problem for investigation; (b) an investigation, from an etic and emic perspective, of the concepts to be studied; (c) the creation of specific items to measure these concepts; and (d) the initiation of focus groups, both bilingual and monolingual, to finalize the translations. Once such steps are completed, the measure is evaluated for psychometric proprieties. With this method, English and Spanish become the target languages, and the translators and community members in the focus groups are an inherent part of the study.

This procedure, however, is much more labor intensive and more concept driven than back-translation.

Whichever method is chosen, measurement equivalence must be demonstrated once the data has been collected. For a description of how to evaluate the equivalency of measures for use in diverse populations, the reader is referred to Chapter 8 of this volume. In summary, it is no longer sufficient to have a simple direct translation performed by a close associate and expect this translation to serve as an official translation. As researchers, we must make sure the proper steps are followed when asked to translate scales and when we begin to devise our own measures.

RECOMMENDATIONS FOR GRADUATE STUDENTS

Researchers could take several steps to gain the skills to conduct culturally competent research. The following are some recommendations we have based on discussions at the forum and our own experiences.

One recommendation is additional education and training in areas that could increase our understanding of different cultures. For example, given that Latinos will soon become the largest minority population in the United States (U.S. Census Bureau, 2000) and that many of them are not fluent in the English language, it might be prudent for researchers to take Spanish lessons. Furthermore, researchers might take cross-cultural anthropology courses or history courses to educate themselves on these particular cultures. This kind of knowledge is useful not only to conceptually ground study hypotheses but also to establish relationships with ethnic minority populations. Education on particular cultures might prove useful in the rapport-building process any psychologist studying or treating ethnic minority populations needs in order to work effectively with those minority populations. Researchers may also learn more about qualitative research techniques that could prove useful in ethnic minority research. If these are not available in their own academic department, it might be prudent to go outside the department to learn these techniques. In addition, researchers might benefit a great deal from establishing a network of professional associations not only with psychologists who study cultural issues but also with other types of professionals who are interested in the topic, such as sociologists, anthropologists, statisticians, or physicians.

Graduate student and researcher concerns about publishing were discussed at the forum. Specifically, can we get our work published if we conduct ethnic minority research? Publishing could be easier if one was not working with an ethnic minority population. Difficulties encountered while conducting minority research, such as inaccessibility to minority community samples and the need for adaptation and translation of research instruments before studies can be conducted, might delay submissions for publication. In addition, because some journal editors and reviewers are less familiar with ethnic minority research, the review process may be lengthened. Because of these factors, publication of research of this nature may require greater perseverance, time, and effort. Ethnic minority researchers might benefit from making community contacts and nurturing these so as to have availability to participant pools. Another option is to have discussions with department heads about research challenges so that the faculty become more aware of the particular needs of students doing minority research and make the needed resources more readily available. One should also put great effort in attempting to get some publications in mainstream journals. This will increase the visibility of the ethnic minority research program. In addition, it is important that researchers highlight the psychological phenomenon that is being studied and how culture plays a role in the manifestations of the phenomenon. First and foremost we are psychology researchers, not just ethnic minority researchers. Our research might prove to be more attractive for publication if we think of it in this manner.

This chapter has highlighted some of the issues and challenges that face professionals who are interested in the study of culture and its effects on psychological issues. Yet, despite these challenges, conducting research with Latinos and other ethnic minorities that is simultaneously informative and of sound quality is feasible. Such research is not only beneficial to the studied population but it also can be a rewarding experience for the researcher, including the graduate student investigator.

REFERENCES

American Psychological Association. (1993). Guidelines for providers of psychological services to ethnic, linguistic, and culturally diverse populations. *American Psychologist, 48*(1), 45–48.

Arredondo, P., Toporek, R., Pack Brown, S., Jones, J., Locke, D. C., Sanchez, J., & Stadler, H. (1996). Operationalization of the multicultural counseling competencies. *Journal of Multicultural Counseling and Development, 24*, 42–78.

Asbury, J. (1995). Overview of focus group research. *Qualitative Health Research, 5*, 414–420.

Bontempo, R. (1993). Testing linguistic minorities. *Journal of Cross-Cultural Psychology, 24*, 149–166.

Brislin, R. W. (1970). Back-translation for cross-cultural research. *Journal of Cross-Cultural Psychology, 1*(3), 185–216.

Brislin, R. W. (1973). The wording and translation of research instruments. In W. J. Lonner & R.W. Brislin (Eds.), *Cross-cultural research methods* (pp.137–165) New York: Wiley.

Cortés, D. E., Rogler, L. H., & Malgady, R. G. (1994). Biculturality among Puerto Rican adults in the United States. *American Journal of Community Psychology, 5*, 707–721.

Côté-Arsenault, D., & Morrison-Beedy, D. (1999). Practical advice for planning and conducting focus groups. *Nursing Research, 48*(5), 280–283.

Cuéllar, I., Arnold, B., & Maldonado, R. (1995). Acculturation rating scale for Mexican Americans–II: A revision of the original ARSMA scale. *Hispanic Journal of Behavioral Sciences, 17*(3), 275–304.

Dawson, S., Manderson, L., & Tallo, V. L. (1993). *A manual for the use of focus groups*. Boston: International Nutrition Foundation for Developing Countries.

Erkut, S., Alarcón, O., García Coll, C., Tropp, L. R., & Vázquez, García, H. A. (1999). The dual-focus approach to creating bilingual measures. *Journal of Cross-Cultural Psychology, 30*(2), 206–218.

Harwood, R. L., Schoelmerich, A., Schultz, P. A., & Gonzalez, Z. (1999). Cultural differences in maternal beliefs and behaviors: A study of middle-class Anglo and Puerto Rican mother–infant pairs in four everyday situations. *Child Development, 70*(4), 1005–1016.

Hulin, C. L. (1987). A psychometric theory of evaluations of item and scale translations. *Journal of Cross-Cultural Psychology, 18*(2), 115–142.

Knodel, J. (1993). The design and analysis of focus group studies: a practical approach. In D. L. Morgan (Ed.), *Successful focus groups: Advancing the state of the art* (pp. 35–50). Newbury Park, CA: Sage.

Malpass, R. S., & Poortinga, Y.H. (1973). Strategies for design and analysis. In W. J. Lonner & R.W. Brislin (Eds.), *Cross-cultural research methods* (pp.47–83). New York; Wiley.

Morgan, D. L. (1997). *Focus groups as qualitative research* (2nd ed.). Thousand Oaks, CA: Sage.

Olmedo, E. L. (1981). Testing linguistic minorities. *American Psychologist, 36*, 1078–1085.

Seal, D. W., Bogart, L. M., & Ehrhardt, A. A. (1998). Small group dynamics: The utility of focus group discussions as a research method. *Group Dynamics: Theory, Research, and Practice, 2*(4), 253–266.

Sechrest, L., Fay, T. L., & Hafeez Zaidi, S. M. (1972). Problems of translation in cross-cultural research. *Journal of Cross-Cultural Psychology 3*, 41–56.

Sperber, A. D., DeVellis, R. F., & Boehlecke, B. (1994). Cross-cultural translation: Methodology and validation. *Journal of Cross-Cultural Psychology, 25*(4), 501–524.

Triandis, H. (1976). Approaches toward minimizing translation. In R. Brislin (Ed.), *Translation: Applications and research* (pp. 229–243). New York: Wiley/Halstead.

U.S. Census Bureau. (2000). *Census 2000*. Retrieved October 30, 2001, from http://www.census.gov/

U.S. Department of Health and Human Services. (2000). *National Institutes of Health Strategic Research Plan to Reduce and Ultimately Eliminate Health Disparities Among Minority Populations: Fiscal Years 2002–2006*. Retrieved October 30, 2001, from http://healthdisparities.nih.gov/

Werner, O., & Campbell, D. (1970). Translating, working through interpreters, and the problem of decentering. In I. R. Naroll & R. Cohen (Eds.), *A handbook of method in cultural anthropology* (pp. 398–420). New York: Natural History Press.

12

A Research Agenda on Latino Children and Families: Recommendations from the 2000 Kent Psychology Forum

Josefina M. Contreras

The Latino parenting field is a relatively new area of study. Although some progress has been made in understanding the cultural and contextual factors influencing parenting processes and child developmental outcomes among Latino families, much work still remains to be done. In addition, as with any relatively new area of study, the Latino parenting field is in need of further structure and direction. Thus, one of the main goals of the 2000 Kent Psychology Forum on Latino Children and Families was to address this need by developing frameworks that can provide further integration and direction to the field. To this end, presentations and discussions throughout the forum focused on developing a set of recommendations for a research agenda for the field. In this concluding chapter, I summarize these recommendations. First, I list the content areas that need to be studied in order to better understand parenting and child development processes among Latino families. Although some progress has already been made in each of these general content areas, further research in each is clearly needed. Within each of these, I present the specific subareas or research questions that especially need to be addressed in future research. I then present the characteristics of research programs that are most likely to help advance our understanding of Latino parenting and child development processes, followed by the methodological approaches that are likely to be most fruitful in these research endeavors.

CONTENT AREAS REQUIRING STUDY

1. *Cultural values that guide behavior across different domains, especially those related to parenting and family relationships.* In addition to arriving at a clear

definition of these values, it is important to understand better how and which of these values are affected by exposure to U.S. society and which remain unchanged. Similarly, differentiating which ones are common to all groups of Latinos in the United States and which ones vary by nationality (country of origin) is also important.

2. *Acculturation and enculturation processes.* Although attention has been paid to understanding acculturation processes and their relations to adjustment across different domains of functioning, much less research has been conducted to understand enculturation processes. Future research should focus on understanding both how Latinos take on aspects of the mainstream culture and how they develop and maintain Latino cultural values and traditions. In addition, how these two processes may differ depending on the immigration patterns of the different Latino subgroups (i.e., groups that tend to go back and forth to their native land, those that cannot go back) also needs to be studied. The influences of these processes must be studied at different levels. For example, it is important to study how they affect individuals' adaptation across domains; how they influence parenting values, socialization goals for children, and parenting practices; and how they influence the norms and expectations regarding family relationships and roles within the family. Similarly, acculturation and enculturation levels may influence the type and functions of predictors of adjustment. Thus, research must focus on understanding not only the direct effects of acculturation/enculturation levels on outcomes, but also the moderating effects of acculturation/enculturation levels on the associations between predictors of adjustment and adjustment outcomes.

3. *Normative parenting practices and their relations to child development.* The literature has focused primarily on low-income and at-risk Latino families, and although this research is important and must continue, future research must also focus on normative parenting processes. In addition to arriving at a definition of what constitutes optimal parent–child relationships among Latino families, research should focus on understanding parenting more broadly (i.e., beyond dyadic relationships) and examine how shared parenting, family structure, and the extended family influence parenting processes and child socialization.

4. *Child outcomes.* Outcomes must be studied and understood in terms of both the socialization goals of the specific Latino group being studied and the mainstream U.S. indicators of adjustment. These two criteria for successful outcomes may not always correspond, and their interplay and implications for child development must be studied. Differences due to child gender and developmental stage should also be studied.

5. *How variations based on socioeconomic status, geographical region in the United States, and country of origin influence culture and adaptation among Latinos.* This knowledge would facilitate our understanding of the interplay between cultural and structural (e.g., socioeconomic, political) influences on the functioning and adaptation of Latino families, which have been historically confounded in the literature.

6. Interventions that address the needs of Latino parents. Interventions should be theory driven, and the knowledge gained through the evaluation of these interventions should, in turn, be used to inform the theory and understanding of Latino parenting.

RESEARCH PROGRAMS SHOULD:

1. *Be theoretically driven.*
2. *Informed by an understanding of the values of the Latino group being studied.*
3. *Have the prospect of leading to revision and improvement of both theories specific to Latino populations and those that are currently used in the broader social research.* This is crucial in order to increase our understanding of the culture-specific and culture-invariant aspects of psychological phenomena.

RESEARCH METHODS SHOULD:

1. *Build on meaning systems that are indigenous to the group being studied.*
2. *Use measurement instruments that are reliable and valid for the group under examination.* Given the paucity of such instruments, considerable measurement development work needs to be done. To this end, both quantitative and qualitative research methods should be used. Qualitative methods are crucial to finding out the constructs (e.g., values) that are relevant for a particular group, how these constructs are manifested in the specific group, and how these constructs can be best measured. Quantitative methods are then needed to assess the psychometric properties of the measures. Attention should be paid to the equivalence of measures, not only across ethnic groups but also across different Latino groups and Latino individuals of different acculturation and enculturation levels.
3. *Use the expertise and methods of research from a variety of fields.* Designs should use multi-method and multidisciplinary approaches.
4. *Rely on longitudinal and intergenerational designs in order to examine the life trajectories of both individuals and families.*
5. *Pay attention to representation and selection issues.* The literature must account for variations among Latinos in the United States, including those due to socioeconomic background, acculturation and enculturation levels, geographical region in the United States, and Latino subgroup (nationality).

Index

shared symbols and concepts in,
218–19
Culturally informed theory, 188, 198,
235
Cultural relativity
measurement constructs and, 191, 255
psychological constructs and,
254–55
Cultural stereotypes, and culturally
competent service programs,
37–38
Cultural values, 29, 234
child socialization and, 12, 29–30, 159,
234, 235, 236
peer groups and, 80
definition of, 38–39
Culture, 234
cultural ideal in, 237
local, 235
subjective, 234–35

Delinquency, and acculturation, 53
Depressive symptomatology
acculturation and, 54, 60
adolescent parenting and, 163–64
partner support and, 170
Dominican mothers (*see also* Adolescent
mothers)
infant attachment and, 236–37
social support and, 170
Drug use. *See* Substance use

Eating disorders, 55
Ecological validity, 205
Education
Latino parents and, 77, 100, 101–2
Latino youth and, 9, 16
moral development in, 77–78, 90–91,
96–97, 101–2
Educational outcome
language proficiency and, 62–63, 64
parental residency and, 58
parental socialization goals and, 102,
160
Emic approach intervention, 233–47 (*see
also* Intervention)
theoretical generalizations and,
238–39

Enculturation, 51
child behavior and, 54
parenting and, 31, 160, 164–65
perceived competence and, 54–55
process change and, 66
research recommendations for, 67–69,
266
self-esteem and, 55
Ethnic identity, 29, 56–57, 60, 235
parenting and, 31–32
socialization and, 31, 235
substance use and, 56–57, 60

Familism (*familismo*), 12–14, 166, 182
acculturation and, 79–80, 168–69
generational change and, 101
Family, 5
extended, 32–33, 166
social network and, 172
middle-class, 33, 136–37
social environment and, 18, 172
Family Effectiveness Training
intervention, 210, 215–16,
217–18, 221
behavioral objectives in, 224
evaluation techniques for, 222
targeted family member interactions
in, 212
Focus groups, 255–58
limitations of, 256–57
in measurement equivalence research,
190–91
methodology of, 257–58

Health care, and Latino family, 10–11,
172
Hero/Heroine Therapy, 241–42
Hispanic, 4

ICC (Item Characteristic Curve), 189
Immigrant parents (*see also* Children's
path of life)
child-rearing and, 36, 77–81
child-rearing resources for, 102
children's path of life and, 77–78,
93
Immigration, 18–19
Individualism, 134

About the Editors and Contributors

MARGARITA AZMITIA is a professor of psychology at the University of California at Santa Cruz. Her research focuses on the social and cultural context of development. Most of her work has investigated the role of family, peers, and schools in Latino- and European-descent children's cognitive and socio-emotional development. She is especially interested in mapping positive and problematic developmental pathways in the transition from childhood to adolescence.

JANE R. BROWN received her Ph.D. in human development and family studies at the Pennsylvania State University. Her research has focused on children's family relationships and the development of social understanding. Currently she works as an evaluation consultant to social services and educational organizations with programs that serve children and families in Monterey County, CA.

YVONNE M. CALDERA is an associate professor of human development at Texas Tech University. She received her Ph.D. in developmental and child psychology from the University of Kansas. Her research interest is Latino children and families with focus on child care, the role of the father in children's development, ethnic identity, and parenting.

VIVIAN J. CARLSON received her Ph.D. from the University of Connecticut in 1999. She is currently an assistant professor of child study at St. Joseph College in West Hartford, CT. Her research interests include the cultural construction of infancy and the provision of family-centered early intervention services.

ANA MARI CAUCE earned her Ph.D. in psychology from Yale University with a concentration in child clinical and community psychology. She is currently at the University of Washington where she holds The Earl R. Carlson Professorship in psychology and holds a joint appointment in the Department of American Ethnic Studies. She is presently the director of the University of Washington Honors Program. Dr. Cauce is particularly interested in normative and nonnormative development in ethnic minority youth and in at-risk youth more generally. She has published more than 50 articles and chapters and has been the recipient of grants from the W. T. Grant Foundation, the National Institute of Mental Health, the National Institute of Child Health and Human Development, and the National Institute of Alcoholism and Alcohol Abuse. She is the recipient of numerous awards, including recognition from the American Psychological Association for Excellence in Research on Minority Issues and the University of Washington's Distinguished Teaching Award.

JOSEFINA M. CONTRERAS is currently an assistant professor at Kent State University. She received her Ph.D. in clinical and developmental psychology from the University of Illinois at Chicago. Her research interests include the study of parenting and its relations to social and emotional development in children, with special interest on the role culture and context plays on these processes. Her research focuses on normative aspects of parent–child relationships as well as on factors influencing parenting among Latina adolescent mothers.

WILLA K. CREE is a graduate student, working toward her Ph.D. in family and human development, at Arizona State University.

MELANIE DOMENECH-RODRÍGUEZ is an assistant professor at Utah State University. She earned her Ph.D. in psychology from Colorado State University in 1999. Immediately following her clinical internship at the University of Washington, she was a postdoctoral fellow with the Family Research Consortium III, which emphasized the impact of race, ethnicity, and culture in family processes and mental health. Her research career has focused on ethnic minorities and has included the study of substance use among adolescents, educational issues, media impact on behaviors, and acculturation. Her current research is focused on the development and delivery of parenting interventions to Spanish-speaking Latino families.

LARRY E. DUMKA, PH.D., is associate professor and director of the Marriage and Family Therapy Program in the Department of Family and Human Development at Arizona State University. Dr. Dumka's research focuses on developing and evaluating family-focused interventions to prevent mental health problems in children from ethnically diverse low-income families. He has developed and validated measures related to parenting and is currently codirecting a multiyear study testing the efficacy of a family-based intervention to prevent school disengagement for adolescents making the transition to junior high school.

JACKI FITZPATRICK is an associate professor of family studies at Texas Tech University. She received her Ph.D. from Auburn University. Dr. Fitzpatrick is a recipient of the Texas Tech University New Faculty Award. Her research interests are premarital/marital relationships, social networks, and community services.

NANCY A. GONZALES is an associate professor in the Department of Psychology and coprincipal investigator at the Prevention Research Center at Arizona State University. She received her Ph.D. in clinical psychology at the University of Washington in 1992. Her research interests include ethnic minority mental health, contextual influences on adolescent development, acculturation and enculturation processes and their impact on adolescent development, and development of culturally competent preventive interventions. She is currently principal investigator of a National Institute of Mental Health–sponsored grant to test the efficacy of an intervention to prevent school dropout and mental health disorders for Mexican American adolescents. She also is active as a member of the committee on ethnicity and culture for the Society for Research in Child Development and the Risk, Prevention, and Health Behavior Study Section, Center for Scientific Review, for the National Institutes of Health.

ROBIN L. HARWOOD received her Ph.D. from Yale University in 1991. Currently, she is an associate professor in the School of Family Studies at the University of Connecticut. Her research focuses on culture and parenting in diverse populations. Her most recent project, funded by the National Institute of Child Health and Human Development, examines changes in child-rearing beliefs and practices following migration among Puerto Rican mothers who have migrated to Connecticut, and Turkish mothers who have migrated to Germany.

MADINAH IKHLAS is a doctoral student at Kent State University. She is completing her internship at Lincoln Medical and Mental Health Center in New York City. Her research interests are in the area of racial identity and social support.

SARA JACOBS CARTER, B.S., is currently completing the M.S. specialization in marriage and family therapy in the Department of Family and Human Development at Arizona State University.

KATHRYN A. KERNS is a developmental psychologist with research interests in the area of parent–child and peer relationships. She has investigated how parent–child attachment is related to the quality of children's peer relationships. In addition, she has developed and tested measures of parent–child attachment for preadolescents. Dr. Kerns received her Ph.D. from the State University of New York at Stony Brook and is currently an associate professor at Kent State University.

GEORGE P. KNIGHT received his Ph.D. in social psychology, with specialization in social development, from the University of California at Riverside. He is currently a professor in the Department of Psychology at Arizona State University. He is also a coinvestigator on the Raising Successful Children research team at the Arizona State University Preventive Intervention Research Center funded by the National Institutes of Health, and a principal investigator on the Research on Pathways to Desistence project funded by the National Institute of Justice, Office of Juvenile Justice and Delinquency Prevention, William T. Grant, and the state of Arizona. His research interests include the acculturation and enculturation of Mexican American children and families, cross-ethnic/race measurement equivalence, and prosocial development.

BIRGIT LEYENDECKER received her Ph.D. from the University of Osnabrueck, Germany, and was a Fogarty Fellow at the National Institute of Child Health and Human Development from 1990 to 1996. Her main interests are sociocultural issues and migration. Currently, she is a research fellow at the Ruhr-University in Bochum, Germany, where she is coinvestigator for a major project that examines child-rearing beliefs and practices among Turkish mothers who have migrated to Germany and Puerto Rican mothers who have migrated to Connecticut.

IRENE LOPEZ is a doctoral student in clinical psychology at Kent State University. Currently, she is completing her clinical internship at the Counseling Center at the University of Michigan. Her research interests include the impact of acculturation on adjustment, the intersection of anthropology and psychology, and skin color issues in the Latino community. She recently received a dissertation fellowship from the American Psychological Association to investigate these topics in her dissertation.

VERA A. LOPEZ, PH.D., is an assistant professor in the School of Justice Studies at Arizona State University.

AMY M. MILLER received her Ph.D. from the University of Connecticut in 2000. Currently, she is a postdoctoral research fellow in the Section on Child and Family Research at the National Institute of Child Health and Human Development. Her research interests focus on parenting and culture.

ANTONIO A. MORGAN-LOPEZ is a doctoral student in the quantitative research methods program in psychology at Arizona State University. He has received the Arizona State University Graduate Diversity Fellowship Award and a National Research Service Award from the National Institute of Mental Health as a predoctoral fellow of the Arizona State University Preventive Intervention Research Center. His substantive interests include acculturation/enculturation and resilience among ethnic minority children and families and substance use etiology and prevention. His methodological interests include the evaluation of advanced methods to assess mediated effects.

DAVID NARANG received his Ph.D. in clinical psychology from Kent State University. His research interests focus on child abuse and the transmission of abusive behavior across generations. He is presently employed as a child and family psychologist by ENKI Health and Research Systems of Covina, CA.

ANGELA M. NEAL-BARNETT is an award-winning psychologist and nationally recognized expert in the area of anxiety disorders among African American women and children. She is the author of numerous journal articles and book chapters on African Americans and anxiety. She has been a member of Kent State's psychology faculty since 1989. Along with Drs. Kerns and Contreras, Dr. Neal-Barnett is the editor of *Families and Peers: Linking Two Worlds* (Praeger) and *Forging Links: African American Children Clinical-Developmental Perspectives* (Praeger). Her interactive CD and workbook *Believe and Succeed: Applying and Getting into Graduate School for Psychology Majors of Color* was released Spring 2002 (Rise Sally Rise, Inc. Tallmadge, OH). Dr. Neal-Barnett received her B.A. from Mount Union College (Alliance, OH) and both her M.A. and Ph.D. from DePaul University. She completed a prestigious postdoctoral fellowship in clinical research at the University of Pittsburgh School of Medicine Western Psychiatric Institute and Clinic. Dr. Neal-Barnett is listed in *Who's Who in the 21st Century, Who's Who in American Women, Who's Who,* and *Outstanding Americans.*

JUSTIN H. PROST received his Ph.D. in developmental psychology from Arizona State University specializing in spatial development and with extensive training in quantitative methods. For several years he has been a member of the methodology team at the Arizona State University Preventive Intervention Research Center. For the last year and a half he has been a faculty research associate on the National Institute on Drug Abuse–funded Adult and Family Development Project at Arizona State University. His research interests include developmental spatial cognition and the application of sophisticated research and quantitative methods to psychological issues.

REECE O. RAHMAN is a fifth-year doctoral student in the clinical psychology program at Kent State University. He is currently participating in his clinical internship at the Veterans' Administration Hospital in Ann Arbor, MI. Areas of research interest include ethnic minority issues with a focus on the South Asian population.

LISSETH ROJAS-FLORES is currently a research scientist at New York University School of Medicine Child Study Center. Dr. Rojas-Flores received her M.A. and Ph.D. in clinical psychology from Derner Institute for Advanced Psychological Studies, Adelphi University. She is a recipient of a National Institute of Mental Health Minority Supplement, which supports her research training as a minority investigator. Dr. Rojas-Flores' special interests include family-based interventions with minorities, cultural variables in parental psychopathology and child development, and the treatment of Latino children and families. She is particularly concerned about the needs of children and families at risk and has worked with issues such as child behavior and academic problems and parenting difficulties. Dr. Rojas-Flores is a licensed psychologist specializing in parenting issues and child and family therapy.

MARK W. ROOSA received his M.S. and Ph.D. degrees from Michigan State University. He is a professor in the Department of Family and Human Development at Arizona State University and coprincipal investigator of the Program for Prevention Research. Dr. Roosa is part of a multidisciplinary team of researchers which focuses on risk and resilience of children in poverty, with an emphasis on the roles of culture and context in these children's adaptation.

DELIA SAENZ is an associate professor of psychology and associate research professor in the Hispanic Research Center at Arizona State University. She received her Ph.D. in social psychology from Princeton University. Her central areas of research include the study of tokenism, ethnic identity, intergroup relations, and acculturation/enculturation. Her research, conducted in both the laboratory and the field, has been supported by the National Science Foundation and the National Institute of Mental Health. Currently, Saenz serves as the director of the Social Psychology Program in the Department of Psychology at Arizona State University.

AMALIA SIROLLI is a graduate student in the clinical psychology program at Arizona State University. Her interests include prevention of mental health problems for minority children and families with a specific focus on the role of immigration and acculturation for Latino populations. Her dissertation uses qualitative and quantitative methods to examine the link between acculturation and familism for Mexican American adolescents and parents.

MICHELE M. SPECTER is a child development doctoral student in family and human development at Arizona State University. She works as a research assistant in the Arizona State University Program for Prevention Research. Specter's primary research interests are in the parental influences on and gender differences in the manifestation of delinquent behavior. She is also interested in social policy as it relates to minorities.

ANGEL G. LUGO STEIDEL is currently a clinical psychology graduate student at Kent State University. He received a master's degree in developmental psychology from Fordham University. His current research interests include the study of familism and its effects on psychological variables.

JENNIFER TEICHMAN is currently a doctoral student in the clinical psychology program at Kent State University. Her clinical and research interests include child/family functioning with a focus on parenting skills and styles. She also enjoys teaching undergraduate courses on topics such as child psychology and statistics.

JENN-YUN TEIN received her Ph.D. in quantitative psychology at the Ohio State University and is currently a coprincipal investigator of the National Institutes of Health–funded Prevention Research Center at Arizona State University and the codirector of the Methodology and Data Management Core. Her research interests are analyses of mediation and moderation of preventive interventions and applications of methodology and statistics in prevention research.

KAREN S. WAMPLER is a professor of marriage and family therapy at Texas Tech University and is editor of the *Journal of Marital and Family Therapy*. She received her Ph.D. from Purdue University. Her research interests include attachment processes in couple relationships and therapy and development of observational measures of couple and family interaction.

LUIS H. ZAYAS, PH.D., is a professor at the Graduate School of Social Service of Fordham University, and director of the Center for Hispanic Mental Health Research. He is also a visiting associate professor of Family Medicine at the Albert Einstein College of Medicine and Montefiore Medical Center. Dr. Zayas's research is in the areas of Latino adolescent mental health, parent–child relations, child socialization, family functioning, and parenthood as developmental process. Dr. Zayas is the recipient of the Economic and Cultural Diversity Award given by the American Family Therapy Academy (for work with AIDS orphans and their families) and the Rafael Tavares Award given by the Association of Hispanic Mental Health Professionals (for research and clinical practice with Hispanics).